Hans Jürgen Tertel

Text and Transmission

W DE G

Beihefte zur Zeitschrift für die alttestamentliche Wissenschaft

Herausgegeben von
Otto Kaiser

Band 221

Walter de Gruyter · Berlin · New York
1994

Hans Jürgen Tertel

Text and Transmission

An Empirical Model for the Literary Development of Old Testament Narratives

Walter de Gruyter · Berlin · New York
1994

⊗ Printed on acid-free paper which falls within the guidelines of the ANSI
to ensure permanence and durability

Library of Congress Cataloging-in-Publication Data

Tertel, Hans Jürgen, 1962–
Text and transmission ; an empirical model for the literary development of Old Testament narratives / Hans Jürgen Tertel.
p. cm. – (Beihefte zur Zeitschrift für die alttestamentliche Wissenschaft ; Bd. 221)
Originally published as the author's thesis (doctoral) – University of Liverpool, 1991
Includes bibliographical references.
ISBN 3-11-013921-9 (alk. paper) : $98.00 (approx.)
1. Bible. O. T. Samuel – Criticism, Textual, 2. Bible. O. T. Kings – Criticism, Textual. 3. Bible. O. T. Chronicles – Criticism, Textual. 4. Assyro-Babylonian literature – Relation to the Old Testament. I. Title. II. Series.
BS1325.2.T47 1994
221.6'6–dc20 94-12755
CIP

Die Deutsche Bibliothek – Cataloging-in-Publication Data

[Zeitschrift für die alttestamentliche Wissenschaft / Beihefte]
Beihefte zur Zeitschrift für die alttestamentliche Wissenschaft.
– Berlin ; New York : de Gruyter.
Früher Schriftenreihe
Fortlaufende Beil. zu: Zeitschrift für die alttestamentliche Wissenschaft
NE: HST
Bd. 221. Tertel, Hans Jürgen: Text and transmission. – 1994
Tertel, Hans Jürgen:
Text and transmission : an empirical model for the literary development of old testament narratives / Hans Jürgen Tertel. – Berlin ; New York : de Gruyter, 1994
(Zeitschrift für die alttestamentliche Wissenschaft : Beihefte ; Bd. 221)
Zugl.: Liverpool, Univ., Diss., 1991
ISBN 3-11-013921-9

ISSN 0934-2575

Printed in Germany
Printing: Werner Hildebrand, Berlin
Binding: Lüderitz & Bauer-GmbH, Berlin

Dedicated to my wife Elisabeth
and to our children Jakob, Anne, Kathrin, and Philipp

Preface

The immense religious importance of the Old Testament imposes a great responsibility on the exegete. Since his results are inseparably bound to his presuppositions, a thorough and continuous examination of the latter is essential. The need for a discussion of appropriate methodology is illustrated by the variety of results provided by source-critical studies of the same narratives. The present work, a slightly revised version of my Ph.D. thesis submitted to the University of Liverpool March 1991, aims to contribute to this discussion by suggesting a possible analogy to the transmission of Old Testament narratives.

Two basic assumptions are made: 1. analogies between the transmission of Ancient Near Eastern texts and Old Testament narratives are possible and 2. if the evidence is inconclusive, a hypothesis based on a valid empirical model is to be preferred.

Since *general* tendencies of development have to be isolated, many passages of Ancient Near Eastern texts had to be referred to, which because of space limitations could not all be quoted verbatim. The reader is thus referred to the publications of these texts noted in the relevant passages. I have not aimed to present a complete list of works on the texts discussed, but only referred to books and articles relevant for the present line of investigation. In footnotes only short titles of books and articles are mentioned. The full title with further information is given in the bibliography. I have not aimed to present a complete list of works on the texts studied, but rather concentrated on references to books and articles relevant for the present line of investigation.

I would like to record my gratitude to my supervisor Prof. A.R.Millard for his well-reflected comments, questions, and steady encouragement. My thanks are also due to the Tyndale House Fellowship and the Arbeitskreis zur Förderung evangelikaler Theologie for their generous grants. I would further like to thank my first teacher of the Hebrew language, Prof. R.Laird Harris. I am grateful to Prof. Dr. O.Kaiser for accepting this work for publication in BZAW.

Many friends and relatives have provided financial or other support. Only a few can be mentioned: my fellow-students Dr.E.C.Lucas, Dr. J.Collins, and Dr.Y.Muchiki; Mr.P.Groß (†), Fam.R.Gross, Fam.R.Tertel and Mr.F.Tertel, Fam.G.Denker, Fam.Th.Wusterack, Mr. & Mrs. B.Burk, the members of

Belvidere Road Church in Liverpool of which Mr. & Mrs. E.Walsh and Mr. & Mrs. M.Evans may be specially mentioned. I would also like to thank my parents and my brothers for their sacrificial support. Finally, I wish to express my deep gratitude to my wife and my children for enduring hardships and giving many joyful moments.

J.T.

Table of Contents

Preface VII

I. Methodological Considerations 1
- A. The Necessity of an Analogy 1
- B. The Nature of a Valid Analogy 10
- C. The Investigation of Analogies 15
- D. The Aims of the Present Study 18

II. Previously Proposed Analogies 20
- A. Akkadian Epics 20
  - 1. The Anzu Epic 22
  - 2. The Atraḫasīs Epic 27
  - 3. The Etana Epic 39
  - 4. The Gilgameš Epic 42
- B. The Biblical Books of Samuel-Kings and Chronicles 56

III. A New Analogy: Assyrian Royal *Annals* 67
- A. The Macrostructural Development of Assyrian Royal *Annals* 68
  - 1. Sennacherib's First Campaign 71
    - a) The Structure of the Earliest Extant Version 75
    - b) The Structural Development 85
  - 2. Aššurbanipal's Campaign Accounts 96
    - a) Aššurbanipal's First Campaign in Egypt 101
      - (1) The Structure of the Earliest Extant Version 101
      - (2) The Structural Development 116
    - b) Aššurbanipal's Second Campaign in Egypt 127
      - (1) The Structure of the Earliest Extant Version 127
      - (2) The Structural Development 131
    - c) The Gyges Affair 137
    - d) The Mugallu Affair, the Iakinlu Affair, and Aššurbanipal's Campaign against Ba'alu of Tyre 145
- B. An Example of the Chronicler's Editorial Methods: The Account of Sennacherib's Siege of Jerusalem 156
- C. The Microstructural Development of Assyrian Royal *Annals* 171
  - 1. Omission 172
    - a) Omission of Main Clauses 172
      - (1) Omission of the First Part of a Series of Actions 172
      - (2) Omission of Sentences Without Relevance for the Main Course of Events 173
      - (3) Omission of Descriptive Sentences 174
    - b) Omission of Descriptive Sentence Constituents 175
  - 2. Contraction 178
    - a) Subordination 178
    - b) Replacement of Lists by Common Denominators 181

IV. Application of Results 182
- A. 1 Kgs.22_{1-38} 182
  - 1. E.Würthwein's Analysis 187
  - 2. H.Seebaß' Analysis 195
  - 3. H.Schweizer's Analysis 195
  - 4. O.H.Steck's Analysis 201
  - 5. H.Weippert's Analysis 205
  - 6. S.J.DeVries' Analysis 217

B. 1 Kgs.20 221
1. J.Wellhausen's Analysis 222
2. H.-C.Schmitt's Analysis 224
V. Conclusions 231
Appendix I - The Chronicler's *Vorlage* 237
Table 1: Text Types 237
Table 2: References to *Sources* 245
Appendix II - Discourse Profiles 247
1. Aššurbanipal's Campaign against Aḫšeri 247
2. Aššurbanipal's Campaign against Teummān 252
Appendix III - Participant Orientation Patterns 257
1. Sennacherib's Second Campaign 257
2. Sennacherib's Third Campaign, Part 1 260
3. Sennacherib's Third Campaign, Part 2 261
4. Sennacherib's Third Campaign, Part 3 261
5. Sennacherib's Third Campaign, Part 4 263
6. Aššurbanipal's Campaign against Kirbit 264
7. Aššurbanipal's Campaign against Aḫšeri 266
8. Aššurbanipal's Campaign against Teummān 270
9. Aššurbanipal's First Campaign against Ummanaldasi 274
10. Aššurbanipal's Second Campaign against Ummanaldasi 276
11. Aššurbanipal's Campaign against Dunanu 281
12. Aššurbanipal's Campaigns against Arabs 287
Appendix IV - Ahab in 1 Kgs.22 292
Abbreviations 298
Bibliography 300

I. Methodological Considerations

A. The Necessity of an Analogy

For the understanding of Old Testament narratives[1] as they were intended by their narrators source-critical and redaction-critical analysis to reconstruct their transmission history is of crucial importance. The authors' intentions can only be deduced from passages which may safely be attributed to them and not to later redactors[2] and *vice versa*. Attempting to avoid redaction criticism for dogmatic[3] or pragmatic[4] reasons means to merely ignore the problem but not to solve it.

---

1 Of course, there are substantial differences in form and content between narratives in the Old Testament which must not be ignored. However, unless it is apparent that such differences are due to or prompted different modes of transmission methodological principles and working hypotheses may be regarded as generally valid, but have to be constantly re-examined.
It is important to note that the present investigation is concerned with the literary-critical analysis of narratives only. Texts of other literary genres may be expected to have been treated with different redactorial techniques.

2 At this stage of the investigation the term *redactor* may not be associated with any *redactorial* method. A disctinction between redactors and editors, for example, has to be left to the results of the present analysis. Until it should become apparent that such a disctinction is appropriate, the terms are used interchangeably.

3 Cf. e.g. E.H.Merrill's introductory remarks in *Kingdom of Priests*, pp.13-19.

4 Cf. e.g. R.Alter's literary approach to Old Testament texts. Criticizing scholars who "tend to write about biblical narrative as though it were a unitary production just like a modern novel that is entirely conceived and executed by a single independent writer who supervises his original work from first draft to page proofs" (*Art of Biblical Narrative*, p.19), he takes up a suggestion by Joel Rosenberg, "It may actually improve our understanding of the Torah to remember that it is *quoting* documents, that there is, in other words, a purposeful documentary *montage* that must be perceived as a unity, regardless of the number and types of smaller units that form the building blocks of its composition. Here, the weight of literary interest falls upon the activity of the *final* redactor, whose artistry requires far more careful attention than it has hitherto been accorded" (*Art of Biblical Narrative*, p.19f). Thus Alter can accept the results of historical-critical research and still treat even texts of composite origin as literary unities ("But even if the text [sc. Gen.38] is really composite in origin, I think we have seen ample evidence of how brilliantly it has been woven into a complex artistic whole"). However, the intentions of a redactor, and this includes the final redactor, can only be properly understood if his work is distinguished from his *Vorlage(n)*. Thus redaction critical research remains indispensable. A second difficulty with this approach lies in the presupposition of the redactor's "artistry". What may appear as the discovery of an "artistic" structure is in fact the ordering of literary phenomena by the reader. The choice of phenomena determines the presence or absence of literary structures. It

However, it is impossible to *prove* whether a passage stems from the author himself, or from a later redactor. Since we know that someone wrote an *original*[5] version of the narrative preserved in the Old Testament, but we do not know *a priori* whether it was altered during its transmission, the unity of a text and single authorship have to be assumed until the opposite can be demonstrated. However, from the fact that the assumption of literary unity is to be preferred methodologically it does not follow that *a priori* it carries greater probability than that of literary compositeness. The question whether a given narrative in the Old Testament is the result of various redactions or whether, apart from accidental alterations, it exhibits the *original* version[6] remains to be answered by redaction criticism.

Various criteria have been developed by literary critics to identify diverse author-/redactorship of Old Testament texts. Most prominent among these are the identification of internal inconsistencies, in form or content, or the presence of *doublets*.[7] Methodologically, however, there are some fundamental problems with

---

remains to be shown whether the "discovered" structures conform with the narrator's intentions or whether they are artificially imposed on the narrative by the reader. For a telling example of how subjective such a methodology may be cf. J.P.Fokkelman's studies on narratives in the Books of Samuel (*Narrative Art* I.II).

5 The notion of an *original* is, of course, problematic, since there is no clear-cut distinction between an author and a redactor. We use the term *original* for the earliest identifiable version of a given narrative.

6 Various examples from Ancient Near Eastern literature demonstrate that texts could be transmitted accurately over long periods of time (cf. e.g. R.D.Biggs, "An Archaic Version", p.196: "Although the Abū Ṣalābīkh copies are approximately eight centuries earlier than copies known before, there is a suprisingly small amount of deviation (except in orthography) between them ..."); cf. also J.Læssøe, "Fragments"; J.S.Cooper, *The Return of Ninurta*. For the Late Assyrian fragments of the Atraḫasīs epic, all coming from Aššurbanipal's library, which have well preserved passages of Ku-Aya's edition cf. below, pp.27f.

7 Cf. H.Barth and O.H.Steck, *Exegese*, 32f: "Diese Fragestellung (sc. nach der literarischen Integrität eines Textes) beherrscht traditionell die lk.e (sc. literarkritische) Forschung". J.Stoebe, writing even on the limitations of literary criticism in the Old Testament ("Grenzen der Literarkritik") considers this methodology as "indisputably justified": "Die alttestamentliche Wissenschaft hat für die Beurteilung von Textzusammenhängen, ihrer Entstehung und ihrer Zusammensetzung eine feste *Methode* entwickelt. a) Eine besondere Bedeutung hat in dieser einmal die Beobachtung von *Doppelberichten* über denselben Gegenstand, von sogenannten *Dubletten* ... b) An zweiter Stelle steht die Feststellung von *Sprüngen* und *Spannungen* in der Darstellung, sofern diese zu Widersprüchen und Unvereinbarkeiten führen. ... Die Folgerung, die aus diesen Beobachtungen gezogen wird, ist die, daß sich von hier aus die Entstehung eines

the presuppositions involved. Is it justified to assume that the number and extent of redactions were so limited that we are able to reconstruct even different stages of redactorial activity? Only if we can presuppose that after a certain inconsistency crept into our text the latter was transmitted with some faithfulness, does detailed study make sense. If not, those parts of our narrative now regarded as being consistent with each other could be the result of secondary harmonization. In this case passages which actually had been inconsistent with each other cannot be used to identify a story nucleus. Even if we assume that the consistent portions of a given narrative containing inconsistencies were consistent with each other in the original, we do not know how the (supposed) inconsistency came about, by addition, omission, or alteration, deliberate or accidental. Literary criticism with those underlying presuppositions has to assume such a fundamental change from alteration to preservation for every redaction. The assumption of such a mixture of the initially faithful transmission of the *Vorlage*, unfaithful transmission (that allowed the inconsistency to arise), and, again, faithful transmission that allows us to identify it and explain its origins, needs to be empirically substantiated and may not be *a priori* accepted as a working hypothesis.[8] Detailed research into the literary prehistory of a given narrative of which earlier versions are not extant has to deal with this problem.

Textgefüges, sei es größerer oder kleinerer Art, als literarischer Wachstumsprozeß begreifen läßt. Die Richtigkeit der so entwickelten methodischen Grundsätze ist ebenso unbestreitbar wie die Berechtigung ihrer Anwendung." (p.385). We have to disregard here the question whether our notion of inconsistency was shared by the authors of Old Testament texts, since this could only be answered from the texts themselves. In principle there is not a single word that can or cannot be ascribed with absolute certainty to the author (if we assume that there was an *author* in the first place). Nevertheless, we can only proceed with our investigation if we accept J.Barton's axiom, that "all literary study must assume that even quite remote cultures have *some* affinities with our own" (*Reading the Old Testament*, pp.28f; italics by Barton). The problem lies with the word *some*. We agree that a narrative in its first version can be expected to be internally consistent. Consistency, however, has also to be assumed for the redactor's work. In the Assyrian annals it is nevertheless apparent that even the earliest extant versions did contain inconsistencies (cf. below, pp.106f, n.142).

8 It may be argued that the very concept of canonicity serves as an indication fur such a fundamental change in redactorial activity. However, the question of how the narratives were treated before canonization remains. Entirely faithful transmission from the first version onwards or a gradual development towards the former are just as conceivable as its sudden introduction. Canonization denotes the terminus of redactorial intervention, but does not tell us anything about the latter.

However, there still remains the possibility that the inconsistency was already present in the first version.[9] But even if it is accepted that the inconsistency is secondary, the problem of having to separate the first version from later redactions remains untackled. The designation of a passage as inconsistent denotes the effect, but neither its cause nor its mode of origin. Inconsistency as a redaction-critical criterion is thus necessarily ambiguous. Since the notion of inconsistency is dependent on the phenomena considered it is also subjective. The same is true for the identification of doublets - unless two passages are identical. Again, it has to be emphasized that this does not mean that

---

[9] Thus, for example, J.H.Tigay (*Evolution of the Gilgamesh Epic*, pp.232-234) has referred to formal discrepancies in the Gilgameš epic between the non-flood portions of N(eo-) A(ssyrian version) XI and the flood account, which was taken over into the Gilgameš epic from the Atraḫasīs epic, as indications for different sources. In his account of the flood Utnapištim refers to his wife as *sinništu* ("woman, spouse" - ll.191.194), whereas in the non-flood portions she is termed *marḫītu* ("spouse" - ll.202.105. 209.258); within the flood portions in NA XI *A pâšu īpušamma iqabbi izakkara ana B* ("A opened his mouth to speak, saying to B") is used as speech introduction, whereas outside the flood account in NA Xiv-vi.XI the formula *A ana šâšu / šâšima izakkar*(*a*) *ana B* ("A said to him / her, to B) is used. However, passages mentioning Atraḫasīs's wife have not been preserved in the Atraḫasīs epic, and thus we do not know whether *sinništu* and *marḫītu* indicate different sources or were used because of a slight difference in meaning. "sinništu" also occurs in $IXii_{13.15}$ outside the Flood account. As for the speech introduction formulae, both occur in the Gilgameš-hunter episode:
NA $Iiii_1$: *ṣayyād*[*u pâšu*] *īpušma iqabbi izakkara* [*ana abīšu*
"the hunter opened his [mouth] to speak, saying to [his father")
NA $Iiii_{14}$: [*abīšu pâšu īpušma iqabbi*] *izakkara ana ṣayyād*[*u*]
"[his father opened his mouth to speak,] saying to the hunter"
NA $Iiii_{40}$: *Gilgameš ana šâšuma izakkara* [*ana*] *ṣayyādi* (K4465; cf. R.Campbell Thompson, *Gilgamish*, pll.III and IV)
"Gilgameš said to him, [to] the hunter".
In this scene we cannot automatically relate the different formulae to different sources. A further case, the mention of one messenger as *rakbû* and *mār šipri* in ed. A of Aššurbanipal's annals, will be discussed below (cf. pp.137ff).
An interesting example of literary unevenness in spite of single authorship is found in Xenophon's *Hellenica*. As has been shown by M.MacLaren ("Composition" - reference courtesy Dr. C.Tuplin), the work can be divided into at least two parts on linguistic grounds with the major break in II,3,10. From this MacLaren deduced that Xenophon wrote the second part considerably later than the first part, by which the differences in style and vocabulary could be adequately explained. It is noteworthy that MacLaren was able to substantiate his claim with a great amount of statistical data and that he reckoned with coherent blocks of literature and the use of different styles by one author.

inconsistencies and doublets could not indeed be the result of redactorial intervention. It does mean, however, that we have to be aware of the fundamental uncertainty in the attempt to establish cause and mode of generation of a given effect. A reconstructed redaction history of a given narrative in the Old Testament is dependent not only on the phenomena considered but also on a general picture of how narratives were altered during their transmission. It is important to be aware of this fact. According to the second of the two assumptions basic to the line of argument presented here,[10] we prefer a general picture that is based on an empirical model. The presupposition referred to applies only if the case is undecided and it may be objected that from internal evidence alone the literary history of a narrative may be established with sufficient certainty. It may further be argued that even if the latter cannot be reconstructed from internal evidence alone the mere fact that narratives outside the Old Testament or elsewhere within the Old Testament were treated by redactors in a certain manner does not invalidate such conclusions. If redaction-critical considerations based on features of the text alone only reflect the choice of the phenomena considered and underlying assumptions on the literary development of Old Testament narratives, conclusions drawn from the reference to a suggested analogy can be said to only reflect the choice of an analogy - and thus are not superior. However, preconceptions regarding the general course of literary development of narratives in(to) the Old Testament and observations on the text supplement each other and should not be played off against one another. Without such preconceptions narrative features remain ambiguous and without confirmation from observations on the narrative itself, preconceptions remain arbitrary. Since it is not possible to draw conclusions from features of a given narrative without preconceptions which are not based on the observation of features of that particular narrative, such presuppositions need to be continuously examined.

Such preconceptions cannot be derived from the texts themselves, since they determine our conclusions. However, they can be cross-checked by observations on the texts. The agreement between general conceptions and narrative features is a necessary condition for any reconstruction of the literary pre-history of a given narrative. But as soon as it can be demonstrated that there are further con-

---

[10]Cf. above, p.VII.

ceptions conforming to the evidence provided by the narrative it does not constitute a sufficient condition. Therefore such preconceptions need to be continually examined and, if possible, based on empirical models. Redaction-critical observations are as necessary as considerations regarding general conceptions, but both have to be restricted to their proper function. Carefully reflected preconceptions, ideally based on empirical models, may serve as working hypotheses and, in uncertain cases, tip the balance, while it is a necessary condition for any presupposed general view that it has to be confirmed by observations on individual narratives. This sets limits to the line of argument presented here. Whatever may be suggested as empirical model is only a *possible* analogy and cannot replace observations on the individual narratives. However, the empirical model may influence the choice of phenomena to which attention is paid and the conclusions drawn therefrom, therefore its importance must not be underestimated.

Only if the relationship between redactorial intervention and its effects can be established as unequivocal and only if the effect can still be traced in a given narrative, redaction criticism can claim certainty for its results. If thus redactors mainly altered or omitted material from their *Vorlage* it might be possible to identify where alterations or omissions took place but it would be impossible to reconstruct the *Vorlage*. Only if redactorial activity consisted mainly in additions and expansions, that is to say: only if the earlier version is still hidden in the present one, may it be reconstructed with the help of redaction criticism. The presupposition that literary development of Old Testament narratives essentially means growth is crucial. This basic assumption also lies behind the so-called *Lückenprobe*. This method attempts to isolate or at least to vindicate an identification of a story nucleus, which is imagined as having been expanded later. This procedure is methodologically dubious since it requires not only the assumption that substantially more was added than omitted[11] but also that original versions only give a minimum of information. Both presuppositions need to be substantiated.

---

[11] Cf. H.Barth and O.H.Steck, *Exegese*: "... daß an vielen alttestamentlichen Texten über Jahrhunderte hin gearbeitet worden ist - durch Umformulierung, Erweiterung und Ergänzung, aber auch durch die Einfügung in größere Zusammenhänge" (p.31), "üg. (sc. überlieferungsgeschichtliches) Wachstum" (p.33). Here, possible omissions or abbreviations are completely ignored. Key words are "expansion" or "growth" (cf. also

It thus becomes apparent that *some* presuppositions *have* to be made which *cannot* be derived from the investigated text itself. And it is the aim of the present thesis to investigate such basic assumptions, which have far-reaching consequences for the study of the literary pre-history of Old Testament narratives. Since the text itself cannot lead us any further, an empirical model becomes indispensable.[12] To be sure, it can only serve as a starting point, a working

---

the citation from Stoebe's essay, above, pp.2f, n.7). This assumption would lead to the conclusion that earlier stages of literary development are obtainable. In a brief outline of his methodology applied in a literary critical study of 1 Kgs.22 ("Bewahrheitungen") O.H.Steck argued that any literary critical analysis based on the assumption of lost material or unmotivated addition loses plausibility ("Analysen, die auf der Annahme von Überlieferungstorsi, verlorenen älteren Überlieferungsbestandteilen und unmotivierten Zusätzen beruhen, büßen eo ipso an Plausibilität ein", p.96). However, this by no means affects the veracity of such an analysis. That *detailed* redaction criticism can only deal with expansions, does not necessarily imply the correctness of the assumption that there were no abbreviations. The possibility has to be examined whether such detailed research is possible in the first place.

12 The weaknesses of developmental hypotheses and the need for empirical evidence have been amply described by A.Ungnad, "Gilgamesch-Epos und Odyssee", p.106f: "Die Literarkritik ist nicht zu entbehren, wollen wir nicht auf den Versuch verzichten, zu erkennen, wie der Künstler den Kranz gebunden hat. Nur soll man von solcher doch recht untergeordneten Arbeit nicht soviel Aufhebens machen, wie dies namentlich von der alttestamentlichen Textkritik geschieht ... Wir müssen uns auch über den hypothetischen Charakter solcher Textkritik vollkommen klar sein, und hier könnten klassische Philologen und Alttestamentler manches von der Assyriologie lernen. Altes Testament und Homer liegen uns in einem fertigen Guß vor, und es ist wenig wahrscheinlich, daß uns ein gütiges Geschick einmal Texte beschert, die im Alter wesentlich über die bekannten Rezensionen hinausgehen, also etwa den Jahwisten in seiner reinen Gestalt oder eine noch nicht in dem Sagenkranz verarbeitete Erzählung von Odysseus' Seefahrten und Abenteuern. Deswegen ist gerade hier zügelloser Kritiklosigkeit Tür und Tor geöffnet, und mancher würde mit seinen wilden Hypothesen zurückhalten, wenn er nicht ganz genau wüßte, daß eine Kontrolle seiner Ansichten niemals möglich ist. Ganz anders liegen die Verhältnisse für den Assyriologen. Er muß jederzeit gewärtig sein, daß neue Funde seine Ergänzungen, Vermutungen und Hypothesen einer scharfen Kritik aussetzen können ... Gerade das Gilgamesch-Epos zeigt uns durch seine Geschichte, wie wenig sich voraussagen und vermuten läßt, wenn man sich über den Boden der Überlieferung erhebt ..."

It is interesting to note that in 1899 M.Jastrow published an article ("Adam and Eve"), in which he attempted to demonstrate that in the Gilgameš epic the Enkidu-prostitute episode constitutes a Babylonian counterpart of the Biblical story of Adam and Eve. In order to show the composite nature of the Gilgameš epic Jastrow applied literary-critical methods similar to those mentioned above. Even though J.H.Tigay (*Literary-Critical Studies*, pp.147-150) claimed that Jastrow's analysis was vindicated by later text finds, a closer look at the evidence reveals in fact that Jastrow was proved wrong in his main conclusions.

Jastrow's line of argument can be summarized as follows:

hypothesis, that has to be constantly re-examined during the process of investigation, but nevertheless it is necessary. There is yet another reason for the need for

---

- 1. The name "Ea-bani" (Enkidu) indicates that the person was created by Ea, which would contrast with the epic, where Eabani/Enkidu is described as having been created by Aruru (p.199).
- 2. There is a great cultural difference between Gilgameš and Ea-bani/Enkidu (p.200).
- 3. The course of the narrative is not affected by Ea-bani's (Enkidu's) career (p.200).
- 4. The presence of mediatory characters (e.g. the hunter) shows the independence of Ea-bani's/Enkidu's story (the hero would have proceeded directly against Ea-bani/Enkidu) (p.200).
- 5. Gilgameš is described as the friend of Ea-bani/Enkidu, but that title originally belongs to the prostitute (p.202).
- 6. The narrator gives no reason for the prostitute's disappearance (p.202).
- 7. Enkidu and Gilgameš fight against Ḫumbaba, but only Gilgameš is celebrated after the victory (p.203).
- 8. Ea-bani/Enkidu is punished for the killing of the Bull of Heaven, although it was Gilgameš, who killed it (p.203).

From that Jastrow concluded that the Enkidu-prostitute episode was secondarily attached to the career of Gilgameš. There are, however, objections to be raised:

1. Since Jastrow's study the reading of the name of Gilgameš' friend has been recognized as being ^{d}EN.KI.DU rather than Ea-bani. Although the etymology of ^{d}EN.KI.DU is still obscure (cf. K.Oberhuber, "Gilgamesch", pp.2-3), the better reading proves Jastrow's conclusions to be wrong.
2. The very presence of this feature in the Gilgameš epic shows that at least for a redactor it was possible to have protagonists from different cultural backgrounds in one story. If it was possible for a redactor, why not for an author? Surely, Gilgameš and Ḫuwawa can be said to come from different cultural backgrounds, but nevertheless they appear in the same Sumerian tale ("Gilgameš and the Land of the Living" {cf. S.N.Kramer, "Gilgameš and the Land of the Living"}). In four of the five known Sumerian Gilgameš tales Enkidu, too, is mentioned. The fifth, "The Death of Gilgameš" (cf. S.N.Kramer, "The Death of Gilgamesh"), is not well preserved and thus mentions of Enkidu may have been present in the lost portions. Furthermore, no independent Enkidu tales are known. Thus in this case Jastrow's conclusions were proved to be wrong by later finds.
3. There are many and extensive references to Enkidu in the latter part of the epic (NA VIII-IX$_5$; Xi$_a$-ii$_{14}$ par). His death shortly after the moment of his friend's greatest triumph, the victory over the Bull of Heaven, constitutes the turning-point in the course of events. Gilgameš realizes that eternal life cannot be gained by heroic exploits and decides to visit Utnapištim (cf. NA IX$_{1-7}$; Xii$_{14-17}$ par.).
4. This statement, too, is shown by one of the Sumerian Gilgameš tales to be erroneous. "Gilgameš and Agga of Kiš" (cf. S.N.Kramer, "Gilgamesh and Agga") narrates the siege of Uruk by king Agga. Gilgameš did not proceed directly against Agga, but sent a certain Birḫurturri, and, after the latter is beaten up twice, Enkidu.
5. As has been mentioned under 2., the Sumerian Gilgameš tales show that Jastrow's claim is without foundation.
6. The end of NA IIv and the beginning of IIvi are lost. The prostitute's disappearance might have been explained there. Furthermore, it is of no significance for the further course of events.

an analogy. The redaction of a narrative is, or at least may be, a very complex action. General tendencies may be mixed with the redactor's personal preferences. Only by comparison with the transmission history of other narratives is there the possibility of distinguishing one from the other.[13] By viewing the redaction of a particular narrative against the background of an empirical model the redactor's intentions may become clearer.

Now it still might be objected that the Old Testament and thus the modes of its transmission, too, are unique and that consequently any analogy must fail. However, only if it can be demonstrated that those unique aspects of Old Testament narratives determined the modes of redactorial treatment, so that these differed from those of the suggested analogy, is the objection valid. Yet this is only possible with the help of further analogies. Before the nature of a valid analogy is investigated some limitations of analogies have to be remarked. Any suggested analogy can only be a *possible* analogy, since *actual* analogies could only be established if earlier versions of Old Testament narratives were indeed extant. A second limitation of analogies lies in the fact that even in the case of *actual* analogies these would only refer to and indeed be determined by a set of criteria chosen by the observer. An empirical model remains necessary, but it is important to be aware of the restrictions to its applicability.

---

7. It is difficult to see where Jastrow could find the celebration of Gilgameš for the killing of Ḫumbaba. The concluding part of Tablet V is not extant. Furthermore, already in the Sumerian story of "Gilgameš and the Land of the Living" Enkidu is mentioned as a member of the expedition against Ḫumbaba; there, however, as Gilgameš' servant, rather than the latter's friend.

8. It was Enkidu who insulted Ištar by throwing the thigh of the bull in her face (NA $VI_{158-165}$).

13 The difficulty of separating deliberate alterations from semi- or sub-conscious ones has lead to such contrasting studies as, for the development of the Anzu-epic, by J.S.Cooper, "Symmetry and Repetition", and M.E.Vogelzang, "Kill Anzu!", and, for the Chronicler's treatment of his Vorlage, by A.-M.Brunet, "Le Chroniste I.II" or Th.Willi, *Chronik als Auslegung*, on the one side and W.E.Lemke, "Synoptic Problem", on the other.

B. The Nature of a Valid Analogy

From the early days of Pentateuchal criticism scholars have searched for empirical models to support their theories. Recent times have seen strong efforts by J.H.Tigay and others to revive the quest.[14] Behind these efforts lies the basic thought that once an empirical model is found which shows that texts could indeed have been transmitted in ways similar or identical to those commonly assumed for the development of narratives in the Old Testament, these theories are proven to be right or at least made probable.[15] The question of proof by analogy cannot, however, be answered that easily. The number of *possible* analogies is infinite. These can range from the development of Ancient Near Eastern texts[16] over the Chronicler's work[17] or Tatian's Diatessaron[18] right through to modern times to Reader's Digest editions of novels.[19] The choice of an *appropriate* analogy is decisive. But even then, all that has been obtained is an *analogy* and no more. We shall nevertheless attempt to define criteria for *proper* analogies and their applicability for Old Testament research to obtain a working hypothesis.

In principle no proposed analogy can be ruled out *a priori*, unless it can be shown that it was indeed confined to a particular culture or time. Since there is a strong possibility of cultural influence on redactorial techniques, analogies from a cultural environment and / or time comparable to that of the creation of Old Testament narratives are preferable.

In the Old Testament we generally have narratives in only one stage of literary development.[20] Possible analogies can provide us with texts in different stages of literary development. By investigating the differences between them it

14 Cf. e.g. the collection of essays in J.H.Tigay (ed.), *Empirical Models*.

15 A good example of such a methodology is a recent article by W. Johnstone, "Reactivating the Chronicles Analogy".

16 Cf. e.g. J.H.Tigay (ed.), *Empirical Models*.

17 Cf. e.g. W.Johnstone, "Reactivating the Chronicles Analogy".

18 Cf. G.F.Moore, "Tatian's *Diatessaron*".

19 Cf. e.g. the great range of possible analogies to differences between the synoptic gospels discussed by R.M.Frye, "Synoptic Problems".

20 The most notable exceptions are, of course, found in the Chronicler's work, which will be discussed below. Of further parallel texts within the Old Testament the literary history is not sufficiently clear to permit detailed analysis. Even if the chronological order can be established with some certainty, direct textual dependency may not be *a priori* be assumed. Thus an empirical model may be applied to but not derived from them.

may be possible to deduce editorial methods. Pairs of versions, which we may call *early*, resp. *late*, will be compared.

The analogy should cover as many aspects of transmission as possible. The *late stage* of the empirical model needs to be *comparable* to the Old Testament narrative. This also implies that the Old Testament narrative can be imagined as being the result of a developmental process observable in the empirical model. It should be evident that the transmitters of Old Testament narratives could have carried out alterations *comparable* to those by which the *late stage* of the analogy was achieved. And, finally, the *early stage* of the proposed analogy and that of the Old Testament narrative for which the analogy is proposed have to be *comparable*.

For the possibility of applying the analogy to Old Testament narratives a fixed relationship between the editorial process and the *late stage* needs to be established. This means that there must be certain features in the *late stage* of the analogy that mirror the process by which it was achieved. If these features are also found in certain Old Testament texts then these texts may be regarded as *comparable* to the analogy. Similarly, the hypothetical *early stages* of Old Testament narratives and those of the proposed analogy need to be *comparable*. If it can be shown that the literary development of the proposed analogy was prompted by certain characteristics of its early stages, these are to be assumed to have been shared by the supposed early versions of Old Testament narratives. The *comparibility* of the proposed analogy and the hypothetical literary development of Old Testament narratives is, of course, determined by and valid only for the considered criteria. Different sets of criteria will lead to different results and, possibly, different empirical models. These, however, again apply only to the chosen literary phenomena.

The *comparability* of the processes involved implies that the basic principles of textual development are identical in the transmissions of the two texts. Thus one has to distinguish between alterations carried out because of general tendencies and those made because of certain individual features of texts or the personal preferences of editors or mere scribal errors. It should, however, always be kept in mind that a *general tendency* has no existence on its own, as some kind of force prompting a certain kind of alteration or preservation, but rather is dependent on our grouping of the differences between narrative versions, ascribing common kinds of differences to *tendencies*. Only these may be used as empirical model.

For the investigation of possible analogies this means that first of all analogies must be explorable. Since we are not able to follow up every intention of the editor we have to be content with the investigation of basic tendencies or principles of editorial work. This implies that a sufficient amount of evidence should be available. We need, therefore, as many, ideally successive, versions of a given text as possible. With, for instance, only two versions it is not possible to demonstrate that the differences between the two texts conform to *general tendencies* or that there were general tendencies at all. Or else the different versions of as many texts as possible must be referred to as analogy. The differences between two versions of a given narrative could be atypical for the general course of its literary development. There should be enough evidence to allow distinction between alterations because of the structure and alterations because of the contents of a *Vorlage* in order to isolate alterations due to general tendencies rather than the personal preferences of the individual redactor. To be sure, changes because of contents, too, could be due to general tendencies but, unless this can be shown, the opposite has to be assumed.

Not all kinds of evidence are equally suited for investigation. This means that the differences between the various versions suggested as empirical model should not be too great. The greater the differences are the less exact are statements that can be made about editorial principles and hypothetical earlier versions. If great differences between the text of the versions coincide with great differences in the time and place of the production of the manuscripts, this obstacle becomes even greater. Then it is reasonable to assume that we do not have successive versions and that the text of the actual *Vorlage* of the later version could have been quite different from that of the earlier version. But even a comparison of successive versions can lead to wrong conclusions if not all of them are preserved. *Late* versions might be dependent on very early non-extant versions rather than on their immediate forerunners.[21]

---

21 Cf., for example, the literary development of the accounts of Aššurbanipal's first Egyp-

An illustration may be helpful. We assume that we have an early version, which is comparatively short and a late version which is comparatively long.

early version (short)	1	2	3	. . .
	abbreviation		abbreviation	
	abbreviation		abbreviation	
redactorial activity	expansion	expansion		
	expansion	expansion		
	expansion	expansion	expansion	
late version (long)				

The late version may be the result of progressive expansion (2) or of just one expansion, whereas generally redactors abbreviated (3), or of a mixture of both (1). All permutations of abbreviations and expansions, omissions and additions, and changes could be listed here. We know neither the number nor the extent of the redactorial interventions that caused the differences between the different versions. Thus the differences do not permit the simple deduction of corresponding alterations, but may be due to several changes. Any investigation of redactorial methods has to reckon with these possible sources of error.

For several reasons the present investigation concentrates solely on the transmission of written texts and ignores oral tradition. Firstly, we know that Old Testament narratives were transmitted in writing, but we do not *know* whether this was preceded by a period of oral tradition or not. So far no valid criteria have been developed that would allow us to judge from Old Testament narratives themselves.[22] Secondly, even if they were transmitted orally, our results would still be

---

tian campaign (cf. below, pp.99.124). Without the presence of editions E and HT the investigation of the redactorial treatment of these narratives would have led to completely different results.

22 An attempt to trace such criteria was made by E.Nielsen (*Oral Tradition*) following the ideas of H.S.Nyberg. Nielsen lists the following marks of orally transmitted accounts: "The formal characteristics here are: a monotonous style, recurrent expressions, a fluent, paratactic style, a certain rhythm and euphony which are especially noticeable when one hears the account, and finally anacolutha which a literary writer would hardly have let pass, but which may have been accompanied by a gesture in oral delivery or even have come into existence by the incorporation of a 'stage direction' in the text" (p.36). Nielsen's suggestion was repeated by R.C.Culley ("An Approach to the

valid for the period of written transmission. Anyway, it would have to be demonstrated that orally transmitted narratives developed differently from those transmitted in writing. A corresponding study of oral tradition would be very difficult, if not impossible, since exact dependencies of narrative versions could hardly be established.

Problem of Oral Tradition"), who referred to the results of Milman Parry's and A.B.Lord's research into the characteristics of *oral literature* (cf. A.B.Lord, *Singer of Tales*). Parry and Lord established certain characteristics, especially the re-occurrence of various formulae in orally composed and improvised songs, and applied their results to the study of Homeric epics. Old Testament texts exhibiting such characteristics could be regarded as having been orally composed (for an application of these criteria to the transmission of a Sumerian myth cf. B.Alster, *Dumuzi's Dream*). Formulaic language, however, is not necessarily an indicator for oral composition, as is evident from the Assyrian royal annals. Nielsen further mentioned laws of epic literature, of which he expressly referred to the "law of repetition", the "law of the number three", and the "scenic law of the number two", proposed by A.Olrik and others as marks of orally transmitted accounts (cf. below, p.235). In addition Nielsen draws attention to textual variants. In his opinion variants indicate hearing mistakes point to oral transmission, while variants created by reading mistakes point to transmission by writing. (cf. *Oral Tradition*, p.13f). Nielsen also stressed the importance of oral tradition throughout the Ancient Near East. (cf. *Oral Tradition*, pp.18-38). Nielsen also takes up H.Ringgren's approach ("Oral and Written Transmission in the Old Testament") to argue from the differences between parallel texts in the Old Testament that these were orally transmitted.

There are, however, serious objections against the validity of these criteria. The characteristics of so-called *oral literature* are marks of orally *composed*, not necessarily of orally *transmitted* accounts. Lord's definition of *oral literature* is: "... oral epic song is narrative poetry composed in a manner evolved over many generations by singers of tales who did not know how to write; it consists of the building of metrical lines and half lines by means of formulas and formulaic expressions and of the building of songs by the use of themes" (*Singer of Tales*, p.4). It is very doubtful whether Old Testament narratives would meet such a description. Furthermore, it has not yet been demonstrated that they are *only* marks of orally composed literature and are not found in written accounts. As will become apparent below, at least some of those features can be explained as the results of redactorial treatment of written *Vorlage*, others may be valid for any narrative. As for hearing mistakes, these more probably happened during the process of dictation than that of oral transmission. The variations between parallel texts in the Old Testament are paralleled by differences between versions of Assyrian Royal Annals (cf. below, p.101, n.125). Since in the latter case the redactors presumably had written *Vorlagen*, the same origin may be assumed for those parallel texts studied by Ringgren. Nielsen did not succeed in demonstrating the primacy of oral tradition in the Ancient Near East. For the importance of transmission by writing cf. J.Læssøe, "Literacy and Oral Tradition".

C. The Investigation of Analogies

Different narratives have different plots. To be able to compare the literary development of one narrative to that of another we need to obtain descriptions of narratives or parts thereof which are independent of the narratives' individual features. This does not mean that the specific characteristics of narratives will be ignored but rather that they have to be described in a way that permits a comparison with other versions of the same narrative and with other narratives. The plot will still be needed to obtain the description.[23]

One way of describing a narrative is by its *plot profile*[24], a graph reflecting the development of the rhetorical level and the building up and resolution of tension throughout a narrative. For obtaining the *plot profile* both formal and notional criteria are important. Thus, for example, a climax, or to use R.E.Longacre's terminology a *discourse peak*[25], may be created by relating events in an unusual way. It is marked in the grammatical and syntactical structure of the narrative. Parts of narratives emphasized in this way by their narrators may be noted in a graph describing the rise and decline of the rhetorical level. However, a climax may also be created by relating *unusual* events in a form that does not necessarily differ from that of the context. Therefore, alternatively to a higher

---

23 For obtaining descriptions of narratives we have made use of some linguistic methods developed in the field of so-called *discourse analysis*. The application of such methods has to be carried out with great care, since many of these techniques have been developed by students of obscure tribal languages in South America or the Far East. Therefore, it is very difficult to check whether the techniques work in the language for the study of which they were originally developed and even more difficult to examine their applicability to texts from the Ancient Near East and the Old Testament. Nevertheless since we only use the methods for *describing* texts and not *interpreting* them, we take it as justified to make use of some techniques which seem to be valid for any language.

24 Cf. R.E.Longacre, "Spectrum and Profile Approach" and "Interpreting Biblical Stories". For the study of oral tradition J.Vansina had suggested this method of illustrating the development of tension during the recitation of a story, though his criteria for measuring tension concentrate on the narrations effect on the listener: "The ability to hold the listener's attention can be gauged for each episode, as it mainly depends on the extent to which the listener can foresee what will happen next (*Oral Tradition*, p.74)... The tension increases as the number of possible outcomes is reduced to two ... In theory, then, tension is measurable. In practice only a very rough estimate can be made ..." (p.75).

25 "Zone of turbulence" (R.E.Longacre, *Grammar of Discourse*, p.xvii).

rhetorical level the rise of tension that may be expected among hearers / readers of the narrative may also be noted. Such graphs, or *plot profiles*, established for the different versions of a given narrative enable us to study the development of the narrative structure throughout the transmission of the story and to compare it to that of other narratives with different plots, but perhaps similar profiles.

For our investigation we may further distinguish between the *main line* of a given narrative and *supportive material*. The *main line* constitutes the succession of verbs of main clauses throughout the narrative and marks the progress of the plot, whereas subordinate clauses belong to the *supportive material*. We can then investigate how the transmission of a given narrative affected its *main line* as opposed to the *supportive material*.

For the investigation of the complexity of a given narrative we shall analyze the development of the participant orientation pattern[26] and of the relationship between the sequence of narrated events and the sequence of narration. In the narratives investigated below there are up to three distinct participants in a given main-clause (A, B, and C). Their rôles may be described as *agent*, *patient*, and *benefactive*.[27] In our description of the participant orientation the

---

[26] Method and terminology are described in J.E.Grimes, *Thread of Discourse*, pp.261-271. In the present thesis, sequences of permutations have been studied, rather than permutation states. For the investigation of permutation states, each participant orientation is compared with the initial one (cf. e.g. M.R.Wise and I.Lowe, "Permutation Groups"), whereas for studying the complexity of a narrative it is more appropriate to describe each participant orientation in its relationship to that of the preceding sentence.

[27] In certain instances the evidence is ambiguous. The notional *agent* and the grammatical subject may not be identical (e.g. in passive forms). In those cases the notional *agents* have been noted. Some verbs do not describe an *action*. The fear of an enemy of an Assyrian king may be described as *imqussu ḫattu* ("fear fell upon him" - BM 113203, l.26) with an impersonal grammatical subject, or as *pulḫē melammē bēlūtīya isḫupūšu* ("the terrible splendour of my lordship overwhelmed him" - Rass. {// Chic. ii_{39}}) with the pronominal suffix *-ya* ("my") referring to Sennacherib, or as *puluḫti Aššur u Ištar ālikūt idīya isḫupšuma* ("the fear of Aššur and Ištar who walk at my side overwhelmed him" - Av_{71}) with Assyrian gods being referred to, or as *iplaḫ libbašun* ("they became afraid" - Rass {// Chic. ii_{78}}) with the enemies(' heart) as grammatical subject (for the abbreviations cf. below, pp.71f.96f). All of these expressions are roughly synonymous, but with different grammatical subjects. It may be possible to argue that the first three cases describe the cause and the last case the effect. However, there remains the dilemma that in an expression that has "the fear of A (overwhelmed B)" as grammatical subject, within the latter, A as the one feared is grammatical object. In our investigation of participant relations we have treated expressions containing references to participants like mentions of participants. Other expressions have been evaluated according to their

agent is given the first position, the *patient* the second, and the *benefactive* the third. Some narratives only have two participants, and in those which have three, not all of them are constantly mentioned. If a participant was not mentioned in a given sentence, we have assumed that he kept the rôle of the preceding sentence. The following symbols describe the different changes of the participant orientation:

"I" for "identity" (ABC > ABC) denotes a continuation of the participant orientation.

"r" for "reversal" (ABC > BAC) describes a reversal of the main relation, that between "agent" and "patient". The participants in the main relation are the same as in the previous sentence. This is different in the other operations.

"s" for "switch" (ABC > ACB) marks a greater alteration of the participant orientation. C, previously denoting the "benefactive" enters the main relation, even though it then marks only the "patient". Still greater is the change through

"rs" (ABC > BCA). All three participants take a different position. The "agent" leaves the main relation to become the "benefactive", the "patient" becomes "agent" and the "benefactive" becomes "patient". Thus A moves two places to the right. A similar operation is that of

"sr" (ABC > CAB), in which C moves two places to become the "agent". Both combinations of operations mark the beginnings of units within the narrative. The operation that describes the greatest change of participant orientation is

"srs" (ABC > CBA). The relations are reversed. Both, A and C, move two positions. "srs" denotes a major break within the course of the narrative.

Throughout a given narrative we shall further distinguish between *primary* and *secondary* participants. *Secondary* participants have no narrative function on their own, but rather act on behalf of *primary* participants. Often this is expressly mentioned in the narrative, e.g. where messengers or soldiers are sent. Both, the *primary* and their *secondary* participants, appear together (almost) exclusively in transitional passages, where one takes the function of the other. Further indication that a participant is *secondary* may be found in participant designations.[28]

context.

[28] Thus, for example, in a passage of BM 113203's account of Sennacherib's first

There is an infinite number of aspects under which the development of a narrative could be studied and compared with the development of other narratives. Thus in a certain way the choice of investigated aspects determines the result of the investigation. The aspects chosen for the present work were partly determined by the prevailing methods used in literary-critical study of Old Testament narratives, partly by the availability of linguistic methods.

The variety of aspects under which the literary development of narratives may be investigated implies that there are various possibilities of categorizing a given alteration. In such a case priority will be given to the effect the alteration had on the literary structure of the narrative rather than on the grammatical structure.

It should be noted that the methods outlined above are only used to obtain a *description* of a narrative in its different versions. At this stage no further conclusions may be drawn from the established grammatical and notional structures, because the established structures only reflect the observer's choice of criteria. This implies that they may only be used for description and not for evaluation. Their use as indication of artistry is problematic, and for demonstrating a narrative's unity they cannot serve at all.[29]

D. The Aims of the Present Study

The aims of the present study are to examine various internal criteria used for the identification of redactorial intervention in Old Testament narratives[30] and to investigate the applicability of some empirical models. The results of text-immanent research can be counterchecked against an empirical model where ear-

campaign the Assyrian army and its officers are described as "*ṣindīya* ... *ummānātēya* ... *gibšīya* ... *bēlē piḫātēya* ("my yokes ... my army ... my host ... my governors" - BM 113203, ll.19-21, cf. also l.22) with the pronominal suffix *-ya* ("my") referring to Sennacherib, which indicates that the Assyrian king is the protagonist and his soldiers function as secondary participants.

29 *Contra* R.E.Longacre, "Interpreting Biblical Stories", p.182f.

30 This includes the criteria for the identification of forms of tradition, as e.g. *Sage* or *Legende*, which are commonly held to have been determined by their modes of transmission (cf. H.Gunkel, *Genesis*, p.8, C.Westermann, *Genesis* 2, pp.40ff).

lier stages of literary development have been preserved. Both internal and external criteria may supplement each other. If only internal criteria are taken into account, several internally consistent reconstructions of the possible transmission history of a given narrative may be adduced. Consistency is a necessary condition for such a hypothesis, but it is not sufficient. Applying Occam's razor, the simplest reconstruction is to be regarded as the most probable one. However, it is important to be aware of the fact that Occam's razor and the notion of *probability* only apply to our perception of the phenomena, not to the latter themselves. The simplest explanation is the most probable one only for the phenomena considered. As for the event (of redaction) itself, the notion of *probability* loses its meaningfulness, or, as Philo states it in David Hume's *Dialogues Concerning Natural Religion*: "Every event, before experience, is equally difficult and incomprehensible; and every event, after experience, is equally easy and intelligible."[31] Plausibility and veracity must not be confused.[32] In our attempt to follow up redactorial processes we can only reach verdicts of probability, which depend on the phenomena chosen for consideration. With sets of criteria differing in quality and/or quantity probabilities, too, will be different. Even with a given set of phenomena taken into consideration the simplicity of a suggested literary development cannot be evaluated without further (external) criteria, and its plausibility will also rest on preconceptions of redactorial processes. An empirical model can serve as a touch-stone for the latter. It further may increase the amount of information on which the assessments of plausibility and probability can be based and thus increase their trustworthiness. To deny the usefulness of an analogy *in principle* would mean to renounce additional available evidence that may lead to different - possibly superior - plausibilities and probabilities.

Even though only a working hypothesis can be established through the present investigation, the picture drawn from the study of the literary development of narratives from the Ancient Near East can give valuable illustrations for the transmission of Old Testament stories, however hazy it may be. It reminds us that in the study of Old Testament texts and their transmission their historical and

---

31 Part VII (M.Bell's edition, p.93).

32 Cf. above, pp.6f, n.11.

cultural context must not be ignored. It is self-evident that any suggested analogy can only constitute a starting point for the study of a given narrative, not more. The development of any given narrative may have been atypical and different from the empirical model. The present study does not claim to present the best possible analogy but is intended as an invitation to further discussion.

II. Previously Proposed Analogies

A. Akkadian Epics[1]

As an analogy for the redactorial treatment of Old Testament narratives J.H.Tigay referred to the transmission of the Gilgameš epic.[2] *A priori*, however, there is no reason to prefer the transmission of the Gilgameš epic to that of other literary works from Ancient Mesopotamia as analogies for the transmission of Old Testament narratives. There are at least four epics whose literary development can be investigated.

The conditions, however, are far from being ideal. Of the stories about Anzu and Atraḫasīs only two main versions are extant.[3] Although of the Gilgameš epic more than two versions have been preserved, only two of them are eligible for an investigation according to our purpose and the conditions set out above.[4]

---

1 For convenience we subsume under this genre designation the stories about the theft of the tablet of decrees by the bird *Anzu* and its return by *Ninurta* ("*Anzu* epic"), about the Flood ("*Atraḫasīs* epic"), about Etana's quest for the birth plant ("*Etana* epic"), and about Gilgameš's quest for eternal life ("*Gilgameš* epic"). For a discussion of the relationship between the genres of epic and myth see K.Hecker, *Untersuchungen*.

2 Cf. J.H.Tigay, *Literary-Critical Studies*, *Evolution of the Gilgamesh Epic*, J.H. Tigay (ed.), *Empirical Models*; cf. also W.E.Rast, *Tradition History*, pp. 5-7.

3 The 11th tablet of the Neo-Assyrian version of the Gilgameš epic (Glg. XI) is not a new edition of the Atraḫasīs epic and thus has to be ignored here.

4 The facts that there is little parallelism in wording between the Old Babylonian and the Neo-Assyrian versions and that they have different orders of events have led J.R.Kupper to the conclusion that the two versions were accomplished independently ("Les différents versions", p.100). In spite of the problem of textual dependency we shall compare the two versions, regarding the Old Babylonian version as a representative of an earlier stage of literary development compared to that of the Neo-Assyrian version. For practical purposes we may ignore the question of different versions among the Old Babylonian fragments (cf. W.G.Lambert, Review, p.117; W.von Soden, *Gilgamesch-Epos*, pp.6-7).

Thus the consistency of redactorial treatment cannot be analyzed. Only of the Etana epic three main versions have been preserved, termed by J.V.Kinnier Wilson Old Version (OV), Middle Assyrian version (MAV), and Late Version (LV).[5] Thus a basic condition for the possibility of assessing the consistency of redactorial treatment is fulfilled, but for only one, possibly two, passages all three versions are extant. Furthermore, as is indicated by the agreements between OV and LV against MAV[6], the textual dependencies are obscure. MAV may not simply be regarded as LV's *Vorlage*. The time gaps between the extant versions of all four

---

We shall further exclude the "foreign" manuscripts found at Boghazköy and Megiddo, since their textual history is even more obscure than that of the version exhibited by Mesopotamian manuscripts. S.N.Kramer, "Epic of Gilgameš", p.14, n.53, has drawn attention to the fact that in the Hittite version the sun-god is mentioned as ^{d}*UTU ŠAME.E* which has a parallel in "Gilgameš and the Land of the Living", where he is continually called ^{d}*utu-an-na*, but not in any of the extant Semitic versions.
The study of the relationship between the Sumerian Gilgameš tales and the Babylonian epic exceeds the limits of the present thesis. Attempts to demonstrate that some of the known Sumerian Gilgameš tales constituted an epic with a fixed order of episodes have failed. While St.Langdon ("Sumerian Epic") did not adduce evidence for the coherence of the different tales, Matouš was forced to retract his conclusions in the light of the publication of a new fragment containing the concluding part of "Gilgameš and the Land of the Living" (cf. van J.van Dijk, "Dénouement"; L.Matouš, "Les rapports", p.89, n.3). The epic as such was compiled in Old Babylonian (cf. S.N.Kramer, "Epic of Gilgameš"; K.Oberhuber, "Gilgamesch", p.1; B.Landsberger, "Einleitung", p.32). Two, perhaps three, of the five known Gilgameš tales appear to have been used by the author, "Gilgameš and the Land of the Living" (cf. S.N.Kramer, "Gilgamesh and the Land of the Living") and "Gilgameš and The Bull of Heaven" (cf. M.Witzel, "Himmelsstier-Episode"), perhaps "The Death of Gilgameš" (cf. S.N.Kramer, "The Death of Gilgamesh"), but only the broad outlines of the Sumerian tales were taken over. A further Sumerian Gilgameš story ("Gilgameš, Enkidu, and the Netherworld") was appended to the epic in literal translation to form the 12th tablet of the Neo-Assyrian Gilgameš series (cf. S.N.Kramer, "Epic of Gilgameš", pp.19-23.83). Since the differences between the Sumerian tales and the Akkadian epic are so great it cannot be argued with any certainty that the preserved tales constituted the *Vorlage* of the epic. The problems of textual dependency are even greater than between the Babylonian versions. Even if we assume that we have two successive versions, the differences are too great to permit detailed analysis (cf. above, p.12). Furthermore, the compilation of an epic from disconnected tales was, or at least may have been, carried out under different redactorial principles and techniques. Since the preservation of the Sumerian tales and the Akkadian epic is unique it is not possible to isolate *general* developmental tendencies.

5 Cf. J.V.Kinnier Wilson, *Etana*, pp.21-23.

6 OV I/A_4 // LV II_{23}; OV I/A_{8-9} // LV II_{28-29}; OV I/C_{24-25} // LV II_{46-47}; OV I/D_3 // LV II_{113}. MAV readings not found in OV and LV: I/$A_{10-14.18-20}$; I/B_{26-30} (break).

epics would allow for several intermediate versions.[7] Thus detailed research for any one of the four epics is rendered impossible.

If, however, the differences between the extant versions could be related to those between different versions of other epics, general tendencies of redactorial intervention may nevertheless become apparent in each of them and some consistency in the literary development of these narratives may be assumed. Even then, as has already been noted, the tendencies isolated from the differences between various versions only reflect the observer's choice of phenomona to be considered. Thus they may only be applied as an empirical model for the development of the same kinds of phenomena in Old Testament narratives, not to others. If the epics' literary development led to narratives with a structure (with regard to the considered phenomena) fundamentally different from that of Old Testament texts, they have to be ruled out as empirical models.

1. The Anzu Epic

As has already been noted above, the Anzu epic with only two extant versions, an Old Babylonian (OB) and a Standard Babylonian (SB) version,[8] does not fulfill the conditions of an *explorable* analogy. It is not possible to determine whether there was any consistency of redactorial treatment in the literary development of the epic. A given difference between the two versions may not simply be equated with one alteration. It may be the result of several changes.

The following passages have been preserved in both versions:

OB	$\mathrm{II}_{1\text{-}80}{}^{\mathrm{II}}$	//	SB $\mathrm{Iiii}_{23}\text{-}\mathrm{iv}_{12}$ $\mathrm{II}_{1\text{-}37}$
	$\mathrm{III}_{3\text{-}19}$	//	$\mathrm{II}_{38\text{-}63}$
	$\mathrm{III}_{62\text{-}77}$	//	$\mathrm{II}_{108}\text{-}\mathrm{III}_{9}$

In the Anzu story, after the tablet of decrees has been stolen by Anzu, Adad is summoned and asked to retrieve the tablet. After his refusal appeals are made to Girra and Šara, who also decline, and, finally, Ninurta. Already in OB

---

7 For the Atraḫasīs epic W.G.Lambert and A.R.Millard have argued from internal evidence that the Assyrian recension is dependent on a Middle Assyrian original (*Atraḫasīs*, pp.37-38).

8 For the texts cf. J.Nougayrol, "Ningirsu"; B.Hruška, *Mythenadler*; W.W.Hallo and W.L.Moran, "First Tablet"; H.W.F.Saggs, "Additions". References to lines of Tablet I are given according to W.W.Hallo and W.L.Moran, "First Tablet".

there is some parallelism between the first three summons. The address to Adad and his reply are given in full extent in direct speech (OB II_{11-24}). Of the appeals to Girra and Šara only the introductions are given (OB II_{25-26}, OB II_{27-28}). These lines parallel the introduction of the gods' appeal to Adad (ll.11-12). The replies of Girra and Šara are not mentioned, but rather have to be inferred from the context. In SB the parallelism between the various speeches was increased by adding quotations of the appeals to Girra and Šara and their replies.[9] The corresponding speeches and their introductions resemble each other closely (SB $Iiii_{37-44.45-[55]}$ {Adad} // SB $Iiii_{[56-65].[66]-76}$ {Girra} // SB $Iiii_{77-86.87-97}$ {Šara}).

SB has further increased the correspondence between narrator's report of the theft and references to it found in the different speeches. Adad's reply to the gods' appeal according to OB contained the line *[ipparišma šad]îssu ittaši rēšīšu* ("[he flew off] and headed for his [mountain]" - OB II_{20}), which describes *Anzu's* escape. This line had no equivalent in the narrator's relation of the event. SB altered the line to *Anzu ipprišma šadûssu [igguš]*[10] ("Anzu flew off and [made his way] to his mountain" - SB $Iiii_{51}$ // iii_{72} // iii_{93})[11] and inserted it into the narrator's report (SB $Iiii_{24}$). Thus the two parallel passages, the narrator's relation of *Anzu's* escape and Adad's reference to it, were adapted to each other. In OB the narrator's report contained the phrase *nadû parṣē* ("the offices are neglected" - OB II_1 // SB $Iiii_{23}$), which had no direct equivalent in Adad's reply. Again, in SB the correspondence between the two descriptions of the event was increased by addition. The line was inserted in Adad's reply ($Iiii_{50}$ // $Iiii_{71}$ {Girra} // $Iiii_{92}$ {Šara}).

In OB III_{70-71} Ninurta is encouraged: *[libšûma libban]û parak[kīk]a [kibratam erb]ettam šitakkan māḫāzīk[a]* ("your daises [shall be there and shall be built], place your shrines across the world"). These lines either constitute part of

---

9 Equally plausible is J.Nougayrol's explanation for the missing speeches in OB: "Pour la restitution des paroles d'Anu, du refus qui suit et de l'atmosphère qu'il crée, le scribe de Suse s'en rapportait à la mémoire de ses lecteurs, alors qui celui de Ninive repétait par deux fois tout ce passage. A Suse, le «raccord» est fourni par la «faiblesse» pássagère des dieux." ("Ningirsu", p.90, n.2). There still remains, however, the adaptation of the appeal made to Ninurta to the preceding appeal(s).

10 Cf. W.W.Hallo and W.L.Moran, "First Tablet", p.82.

11 Cf. also the narration of Ninurta's advance in SB II_{29} *igrur ir[t]a'ub šadûssu igguš* ("he writhed, he raged, made his way to his mountain"; cf. H.W.F.Saggs, "Additions", p.12) // OB II_{74}: *qitrud tāḫāzim igdabuš šadîš* [...] ("mighty in battle he became proud, to the mountain [...]"; cf. J.Nougayrol, "Ningirsu", p.93).

Ea's message given to *Šarur* for Ninurta who was already fighting against Anzu (// SB $II_{121-122}$)[12] or part of *Šarur's* delivery of the message (// SB $II_{144-145}$). The narration of the gods' appeals to Adad and Ninurta in OB had contained no direct equivalent of these lines. SB increased the correspondence between the appeals to Adad, Girra, Šara and Ninurta to set out and retrieve the tablet and a later message to Ninurta by inserting the two lines in the former four passages (SB $Iiii_{41-42}$ {Adad}, $Iiii_{62-63}$ {Girra}, $Iiii_{83-84}$ {Šara}), II_{24-25} {Ninurta}).

To Mami's exhortations urging Ninurta to retrieve the tablet SB added further ones (SB II_{20-27}). Six of the eight lines (SB II_{20-25}) are paralleled in OB (III_{67-71})[13] of either Ea's advice for Ninurta given to Šarur (// SB $II_{117-122}$) or, which appears to be more probable, Šarur's delivery of the message (SB $II_{140-145}$). SB has thus adapted Mami's advice for Ninurta to Ea's and again increased the correspondence between parallel passages.[14] In SB all three passages are given in identical wording.

The progressive assimilation of corresponding passages seems to be the overriding scribal principle apparent in the redactorial treatment of the Anzu epic. There are further omissions, additions, and alterations which, however, could only with great difficulty be related to general trends. The following table indicates the extent of verbal agreements between parallel passages in SB. (Almost) identical lines are noted on the same lines in the table.

---

[12] *libšûma libbanû parakkī ina kibrāt erbetti šitakkana maḫāzīka* ("daises shall be there and shall be built, place your shrines across the world").

[13] ll.146-147 have no parallel in the extant portion of the passage in OB. The addition of ll.24.25 parallels that of SB $Iiii_{41-42}$.

[14] Cf. also J.S.Cooper, "Symmetry and Repetition", p.509. Further cases may be seen in the addition of SB $II_{62.111-116}$. SB II_{62} adds the introduction of Anzu's speech which had been missing in OB. The line is paralleled in SB $II_{78.93}$. OB equivalents of this passage and of the parallel to SB $II_{111-116}$ (SB $II_{134-139}$) have not been preserved. Thus it cannot be ruled out that all these passages were inserted by SB.
SB has also added $Iiii_{111-116}$. These lines relate *Ninigiku/Ea's* suggestion to summon the *Bēlet ilī*. The narration of the fulfillment, but not Ea's recommendation, had been present in OB (I_{36}). The wording of the suggestion proper (SB $Iiii_{112-116}$) corresponds closely to that of SB's narration of its fulfillment (ll.117-121). It should, however, be noted that ll.118.120.121 of the narration of the actual summon were added by SB. Although this alteration does not constitute an adaptation of parallel passages towards each other, it may nevertheless serve as indication of the redactor's interest in narrative symmetry.

SB	Iiii			
	appeal to Adad			
		appeal to Girra	appeal to Šara	II
	33			
	34			
	35	[56]	77	appeal to Ninurta
	36	[57]	78	
	37	[58]*[15]	79*	
	38	[59]*	80*	.
	39	[60]*	81*	.
	40	[61]*	82*	.
	41	[62]*	83*	24*
	42	[63]*	84*	25*
	43	[64]*	85*	26*
	44	[65]*	86*	27*
	Adad's reply	Girra's reply	Šara's reply	
	45	[66]*	87*	
narration	46	[67]*	88*	
of theft	47	[68]*	89*	
	48	[69]*	90*	
22	49	70*	91*	
23	50	71*	92*	
24*	51	72*	93*	
.	52	73*	94*	
.	53	74*	95*	
.	54	75*	96*	
	[55]	76*	97*	

[15] * = added by SB.

II			III
	Ninšiku's orders to Šarur	Šarur's orders to Ninurta	
			events
	105[16]	128	
	106	129	9
	107	130	10
	108	131	11
	109	132	12
	110	133	13
appeal to	111	134	
Ninurta	112	135	
	113	136	
17	114	137	
18	115	138	
19	116	139	
20	117	140	20
21	118	141	
22	119	142	
23	120	143	
24	121	144	
25	122	145	
26	123	146	
27	124	147	

events	events
29	149
30	150
31	151
32	152
33	153f
34	155

[16] The parallelism between $II_{105-124}$ and $II_{128-147}$ goes so far to give references to Ninurta in the 2nd p.sgl., although in $II_{105-124}$, properly speaking, Šarur is addressed. Cf. also below, p.27, n.17.

battle	Ninurta's orders to Šarur	Šarur's report
.	72[17]	89
.	73	90
.	74	
59	75	
60	76	91
61	77	92
62	78	93
63	79	94
64	80	95
65	81	96
66	82	97
67	83	98
68	84	99
69	85	100

2. The Atraḫasīs Epic

The best preserved version of the Atraḫasīs epic is the edition of Ku-Aya,[18] accomplished during the reign of king Ammi-ṣaduqa. Middle Babylonian fragments, as far as they are preserved, overlap with neither the Old Babylonian version nor the Late Assyrian fragments.[19] Thus between the texts that can be compared with each other, Ku-Aya's edition and three Late Assyrian fragments (S, T, and U)[20], there may be a time gap of about a thousand years! The *Vorlage* of the Late Assyrian version may have differed greatly in wording from that of Ku-Aya.[21] The following passages are extant in both versions:[22]

OB $I_{18\text{-}38}$ // S $i_{1\text{-}13}$
OB I_{71} // S i_{14}

---

[17] The parallelism between $II_{59\text{-}69}$, $II_{72\text{-}85}$, and $II_{89\text{-}100}$ even includes the use of the 3rd person for Ninurta in the latter's own speech. Cf. also K.Hecker, *Untersuchungen*, p.160 with n.1, who refers to a similar case in *Nergal and Ereškigal* where both parallel passages use 1st p.sgl. ($v_{2'\text{-}12'}$ // $v_{18'\text{-}27'}$).

[18] Cf. W.G.Lambert and A.R.Millard, *Atra-ḫasīs*, p.31.

[19] The fragment from *Ras Šamra* (RS 22.421) gives an account in the 1st pers. sgl. relating the Flood only and is thus ignored here.

[20] For the manuscripts and their designations cf. W.G.Lambert and A.R.Millard, *Atra-ḫasīs*, pp.40f and W.G.Lambert, "New Fragments", pp.71-76.

[21] Cf. above, p.22, n.7.

[22] Line count according to W.G.Lambert and A.R.Millard, *Atra-ḫasīs*.

OB $I_{118-145}$	//	S ii_{8-29}[23]
OB $I_{169-173}$	//	S ii_{1-7}
OB $I_{252-260}$	//	S iii_{0-7}
OB $I_{277-300}$	//	S iii_{8-20}
OB I_{352}-IIi_{23}	//	S iv_{1-51}
OB $IIiv_{1-17}$	//	S v_{3-33}

---

23 Sii_{1-7} and ii_{8-29} are, strictly speaking not parallels of OB $I_{169-173}$ and $I_{118-145}$. W.G.Lambert and A.R.Millard, Atra-ḫasīs, p.xii, give the following parallels:

S ii	23	...^{d}e]n-líl	(OB I_{125})
	24	...] *an-nu-gal*	(127)
	25	...E]N *tāḫazi*(*KA X ERÍN*)	(129)
	26	...*ig-ra*]-*a giš-lá*	(130)
	27	...*b*]*āb* ^{d}*en-líl*	(133?)
	28	...*a*]-*bu-šu*	(136)
	29	...] ^{d}*en-líl*	(137)

According to the fragments of the Assyrian version published by W.G.Lambert, "New Fragments", pp.71-74, l.27, corresponding to l.17 of the same col., has to be restored as [*qáb-lu i-ru-ṭa ana b*]*āb* ^{d}*en-líl* ("battle has come up to the gate of Enlil" - for *irūṭa* instead of *irūṣa* cf. W.G.Lambert, "New Fragments", p.74). Thus the line probably parallels OB I_{131} // $_{143}$. Of these lines only *qá*[*b* is preserved. The content makes clear that the line probably contained a further accusation of the Igigi. In OB $I_{81.83}$ Nusku tells Enlil: *qablum irūṣa ana bābīka* ("battle has come up to your gate" - cf. also l.110 and 114).

Sii_{28} might parallel OB I_{132}//$_{144}$ and Sii_{29} OB I_{133}//$_{145}$. OB $I_{133.145}$ like Sii_{29} end with ^{d}*en-líl*. However, ll.28-29 have no parallel in the preceding spech of *Anu*. Thus it is not probable that they constituted part of Nusku's speech. In any case, the passage preserved in Sii does not constitute an exact parallel to that of OB.

According to the latter Enlil sends Nusku to inquire the reasons for the *Igigi's* uprising (ll.118-133). Enlil's order is carried out by Nusku who repeats Enlil's message verbatim (ll.134-145). The *Igigi* reply to Nusku (ll.146-152), who returns and repeats the reply to Enlil (ll.153-165). Enlil asks *Anu* to summon one of the *Igigi* and have him killed (ll.168-174). Then *Anu* replies to this suggestion (ll.174ff). OB is only preserved up to l.170, but its text may be deduced from Late Assyrian fragments which overlap with OB from l.163 onwards. ll.182-189 are completely lost. According to LA Enlil's suggestion to kill one of the *Igigi* (Sii_{3-7}) is followed by another trip of Nusku (S ii_{8ff}), which is not reported in the preserved part of OB. From the additional fragments of the Assyrian version published by W.G.Lambert it becomes clear that Nusku is sent to the rebels, although he is not sent to speak *ina puḫri kala ilīma* ("in the assembly of all the gods" - OB $I_{122.134}$), but *ina puḫri ša ilāni rabûti* ("in the assembly of the great gods" - Sii_{10}) and that in S Nusku is dispatched by *Anu*, not *Ea* (as in OB, cf. ll.111-112).

The reference of the pronominal suffix of *a*]*būšu* ("his father") in Sii_{28} is obscure. It might refer to *Ea*, of whom a speech is preserved in ms.G. This speech repeats part of *Anu's* reply to Enlil suggestion to have one of the *Igigi* killed and has *Ea* suggest that Mami / *Bēlet-ilī* (cf. OB I_{246f}) should create mankind. With this suggestion the main version sets in again. The suffix may also refer to *Wê-ila*, the one of the *Igigi* who was killed (OB I_{223}), or even to Nusku himself.

OB $IIiv_{19\text{-}23}$	//	S $vi_{16\text{-}19}$	
OB $IIIi_{15\text{-}21}$	//	U $obv._{13\text{-}16}$	// Glg. $XI_{20\text{-}22}$
OB $IIIi_{22}$-ii_{50}	//		// Glg. $XI_{23\text{-}92}$
OB $IIIii_{51\text{-}55}$	//	U $rev._{2\text{-}3}$	// Glg. $XI_{93\text{-}95}$
	//	U $rev._{4\text{-}15}$	// Glg. $XI_{96\text{-}102}$
OB III iii_5-iv_{14}	//	U $rev._{16\text{-}23}$	// Glg. $XI_{103\text{-}123}$
OB III iv_{15}-vi_{50}	//		// Glg. $XI_{124\text{-}186}$

There are corresponding passages from almost all major parts of the epic. They cover the report of the Igigi's work and their uprising, Enlil's order to Nusku, Enlil's address to Anu, the creation of mankind by Mami, the multiplication of mankind, the imposing of the plague, Enki's advice to Atraḫasīs, the renewed multiplication of the people, their starvation, Enki's further advice, and the Flood. Since, however, parallels from only two versions of the epic have been preserved[24] the consistency of redactorial treatment cannot be analyzed and thus general tendencies of literary development cannot be isolated.

Already OB is well structured. The Atraḫasīs epic narrates that after having laboured for 40 years the oppressed Igigi gods approach Enlil (OB $I_{43\text{-}46}$ // $I_{57\text{-}60}$). Unfortunately the text immediately preceding and following $I_{33\text{-}49}$ is not preserved. Presumably the first of the two parallel passages, OB $I_{43\text{-}46}$, described

[24] As has already been pointed out (cf. above, p.20, n.3) Glg.XI has to be disregarded here, since it is not a new version of the Atraḫasīs epic and it is not clear on which edition(s) it is dependent. Glg. $XI_{99\text{-}102}$ parallel OB $IIvii_{49\text{-}53}$ and U $rev._{14\text{-}15}$. Glg. $XI_{99\text{-}100}$ // OB $IIvii_{49\text{-}50}$ have no correspondence in U. OB $IIvii_{49\text{-}53}$ relate Enki's order to create a flood. A corresponding passage relating the events may be seen in OB $IIIiii_{4\text{-}10}$, but both passages are mutilated and the preserved portions do not exhibit parallel phraseology. The passage in Glg. XI relates events, Enki's order is not mentioned. This may be due to the fact that Glg.XI has only taken over the Flood narrative and does not mention the preceding events. OB $IIIiii_{51\text{-}53}$ is paralleled in both U $rev._{14\text{-}15}$ and Glg. $XI_{101\text{-}102}$. U, however, mentions the lines in a different order from that of OB and Glg. XI. A further case of agreement of OB and Glg. XI against the Assyrian version is found in OB $IIIiii_{13\text{-}14}$ // Glg. $XI_{111\text{-}112}$, which has no equivalent in U.

On the other hand U $obv._{14\text{-}15}$ agrees with Glg. $XI_{20\text{-}21}$ against OB:

OB III_{16}: *[is]saqar ana ardīšu*
"he said to his servant"

U $obv._{14\text{-}15}$: *[izzaka]r ana kikkiši* [. . .] *kikiš kik[iš]*
"[he said] to the reed-hut ... Reed-hut! Reed-hut!"

Glg.$XI_{20\text{-}21}$: *amāssunu ušannâ ana kikkišu kikkiš kikkiš igār igār*
"he repeats their words to the reed-hut: Reed-hut! Reed-hut! Wall! Wall!"

U $rev._2$ and Glg. XI_{93} relate that Atraḫasīs / Utnapištim entered the ship, which is not mentioned in OB. The latter agreement, however, is not close enough to indicate textual dependency. That Atraḫasīs / Utnapištim did enter the ship according to OB is can be deduced from the context.

the council of the Igigi where the plan was set up to approach Enlil, whereas the second passage, ll.57-60, relates the action following the plan. Both passages are stated in (almost) identical wording. The Igigi surround Enlil's house and the latter is roused by Kalkal. Enlil commands his vizier Nusku to bar his gate and take his weapons. Enlil's order to Nusku is quoted in ll.87-88 which parallel ll.89-90 where its execution is mentioned. Nusku then advises Enlil to send for Anu (ll.97-98). Enlil follows the advice (ll.99-100) and, again, advice and fulfillment are narrated in almost identical wording.

The Anunnaki decide to send Nusku to the rebels to inquire concerning the reasons for their uprising. The order to Nusku is stated in ll.120-133. Of these ll.124-133 contain the Anunnaki's message which is delivered by Nusku to the Igigi (ll.136-145). Again order and execution are related in (almost) identical wording.

The Igigi reply to Nusku's message (ll.146-152) and Nusku passes on their reply to the Anunnaki (ll.159-165). The latter react with imposing Plague (ll.352-363)[25]. Atraḫasīs prays to Enki who gives the advice to worship no god but Namtara (ll.374-383). Atraḫasīs repeats Enlil's suggestion to the elders (ll.389-398f) who follow it (ll.401f-410f). Enki's advice, its repetition by Atraḫasīs to the elders and its execution are related in (almost) identical wording, only the narration of the execution of the plan is slightly different.[26]

Then the plague ceases, and because Enlil rest is again disturbed by the peoples' noise the cycle starts all over again. This time a famine is imposed to diminish mankind. The people's multiplication and Enlil's disturbed rest are phrased as in the first instance (IIi_{1-8} // $I_{352-359}$). Enki's second advice to Atraḫasīs ($I_{374-383}$)[27] is repeated verbatim by the latter to the elders ($IIii_8$[28]$_{-19}$ // $I_{389-398f}$). The description of its execution ($IIii_{20-38}$) again differs from the advice but coincides with the execution of Enki's first advice. The ceasing of the famine is described, as far as the passages are extant, very similarly to the ceasing of the Plague ($I_{412-413}$ // $IIii_{34-35a}$).

---

25 Ll.360-363 are not preserved.

26 Ll.374-375 (// $Q_{13'-14'}$) // 389-390, unfortunately mutilated, are not paralleled in the description of events and ll.401f // $IIii_{20}$ have no correspondence in the advice.

27 OB parallel not extant.

28 The preceding lines are not preserved.

Then three times a speech of Enlil is reported complaining that the gods' plans were not successful. Unfortunately the passages and their context are not well preserved. Apart from the fact that the Igigi are referred to once in 3rd p. (IIv$_{14-21}$ - Enlil speaks to himself) and twice in 2nd p., (IIv$_{28ff}$[29] // IIvi$_{23-30}$ - Enlil addresses the Igigi) the passages appear to be identical. The repetitive structure of the preserved portions of OB is indicated by the following table.

I

plan	execution
.	.
.	.
43	57[30]
44	58
45	59
46	60
order	execution
87	89
88	90
advice	execution
97	99
98	100
message	delivery
124	136
125	137
126	138
127	139
128	140
129	141
130	142
131	143
132	(144)
133	145

[29] The passage after IIv$_{32}$ is not extant.

[30] The preceding passage is not preserved.

reply	delivery			
146	159f			
147f	161			
149	162			
150	163			
151	164			
152	165			
			II	
Enlil disturbed			Enlil disturbed	
352			i1	
353			2	
354			3	
355			4	
356			5	
357			6	
358			7	
359			8	
Enki's advice to Atraḫasīs	Atraḫasīs' advice to elders	execution	Atraḫasīs' advice to elders	execution
374	389			
375	390			
		401f	.	20
376	391	403	.	21
377	392	404	ii 8	22
378	393	405	9	23
379	394	406	10	24
380	395	407	11*	25
381	396	408	12	26
382	397	409	13	27
383	398f	410f	14f	28f
			16	30
			17	31f
			19	33
			cessation of plague	
		412		34*
		413		35*

Enlil speeches

v14	28	vi23
15	29	24
16	30	25
17	31	26
18	32	27
19	.	28
20	.	29
21	.	30

The developmental tendency towards increasing assimilation of parallel passages can also be observed in the differences between OB and LA.

Although as was already pointed out[31] OB $I_{118\text{-}145}$ and $Sii_{8\text{-}27}$, do not directly correspond to each other, they report comparable events, and we may suspect that $Sii_{8\text{-}27}$ closely paralleled the passage in LA which properly corresponded to OB $I_{118\text{-}145}$ but which has not been preserved. Thus a comparison seems to be justified. OB $I_{118\text{-}145}$ and $Sii_{8\text{-}27}$ report that Nusku is dispatched to the rebels. In OB there is a close correspondence between Ea's message and its delivery by Nusku. OB I:

118 *Enlil piāšu ī[pušamma]*
"Enlil [opened] his mouth,"

119 *issaqar ana [šukalli Nusku]*
"he addressed [vizier Nusku],"

120 *dNusku pite [bābka]*
"Nusku, open [your gate],"

121 *kakkīka l[iqe ...*
"[take] your weapons [..."

122 *ina puḫri [kalâ ilīma]* "In the assembly of [all the gods]"	134 *[illik Nusku ana puḫri k]alâ ilīma* "[Nusku went to the assembly] of all the gods."
123 *kimis izi[z . . .]-ni* "bow down, stand up, our [. . .]"	135 *. . .] X X X ipšur* ". . .] he explained."
124 *išpuranni [abūkunu] anu* "*Anu*, [your father], sent me,"	136 *[išpuranni a]būkunu anu* "*Anu*, your father, [sent me],"
125 *malikkunu [qurādu Enl]il* "(also) your counsellor, [the hero Enlil],"	137 *[malikkunu qurā]du En[li]l* "[(also) your counsellor, the hero] Enlil,"

---

31 Cf. above, p.28, n.23.

126 *guzalûkun[u Nin]urta* "your chamberlain Ninurta,"	138 *[guzalûkunu N]inurta* "[your chamberlain] Ninurta,"
127 *u gallûkun[u En]nugi* "and your sheriff Ennugi."	139 ⌈*u*⌉ *[gallûkunu E]nnugi* "and [your sheriff] Ennugi."
128 *mannummi [. . . q]ablim* "Who [. . .] of battle?"	140 *ma[nnummi . . . q]ablim* "Who [. . .] of battle?"
129 *mannum[mi ..... tāḫ]āzi* "Who [. . .] of hostilities?"	141 *ma[nnummi . . . tāḫā]zi* "[Who . . . of hostilities?]"
130 *mannu[mmi igram t]uqumtam* "Who [declared] war?"	142 *ma[nnummi igram tuqu]mtam* "[Who declared war?]"
131 *[qablam . . .] X X X* "[battle . . .]"	143 *qa[blam . . .] X X* "[battle . . .]"
132 *[ina . . .] X X* "[in . . .]"	144 *ina [. . .] X* "in [. . .]"
133 *[ibba-. . .] X X X X Enlil* "[bring . . .] ... Enlil"	145 *ibba-[. . . Enl]lil* "bring [. . .] Enlil".

However, the correspondence between Anu's and Nusku's speech is still closer in Sii[32]:

8 *Anu pâšu īpuša iqabbi* "Anu opened his mouth, he spoke,"	
izzakar [ana Nusku] "he said [to Nusku:]"	18 *[Nusk]u annīt[a ina šemēšu* "when Nusku heard this"
9 *Nusku pete bābka*: "Nusku, open your gate,"	
kakkīka [leqe (. . .)] "[take] your weapons [. . ."	19 *kakkīšu ilt[aqe (. . .)]* "he took his weapons [. . ."
10 *ina puḫri ša ilāni rabûti*: "In the assembly of the great gods"	20 *ina puḫri ša ilāni rabûti* [: "In the assembly of the great gods"
kimi[s . . .] "bow down [. . ."	*ikmis ...]* "[he bowed down . . ."
11 *qibašunūti [...]* "Speak to them [. . ."	21 *[iqbâ]*⌈*šu*⌉*[nūti . . .]* "[He spoke to them . . .:"
12 *išpuranni A[num abūkunu]* "*Anu*, [your father], has sent me,"	22 *[išpuranni abūkunu An]um* "[Your father *Anu* has sent me,"
13 *malikkunu q[urādu Enlil]* "(also) your counsellor, [the hero Enlil],"	23 *[malikkunu qurādu E]nlil* "[(also) your counsellor, the hero] Enlil,"
14 *guza[lû]kunu Ni[nurta* "your chamberlain Ninurta,"	24 *[guzalûkunu Ninurta* "[your chamberlain Ninurta],

[u$^?$ gallûkunu$^?$ Annugal]
"[and? your sheriff? Annugal]."

15 *mann[umm]a bēl qabli*
"Who is responsible for battle?"

[mannumma bēl tāḫāzi]
"[Who is responsible for hostilities?"

16 *ya˒⸢u⸣ ilu ša ibnâ [tuqunta]*
"Which is the god who started war?"

17 *qa[bl]u irūṭa ana [bābīya]*
"Battle has come up to [my gate]."

[u? gallûkunu?] Annugal
"[and$^?$ your sheriff$^?$] Annugal.

25 *[mannumma bēl qabli*
"[Who is responsible for battle?]"

mannumma b]ēl tāḫāzi
"[Who] is reponsible for hostilities?"

26 *[ya'u ilu ša ibn]â tuqunta*
"[Which is the god who started] war?"

27 *[qablu irūṭa ana b]āb Enlil*
"Battle has come up to the gate of Enlil."

In OB only the message proper had been repeated with almost no changes. In LA, however, the correspondence is increased to include the orders given to Nusku, with the exception of 1.9a,[33] ll. 132-133, and probably their equivalent in ll.144-145, too, which are not represented in LA. Unfortunately these lines are badly mutilated. Thus no reason for their omission is apparent.

Further assimilations were achieved by the addition of S rev. iv$_3$ which adapts the description of events to Enlil's speech to the gods (cf. OB I$_{359}$ // S rev. iv$_8$) and the addition of S rev. iv$_7$ which adapts Enlil's speech to the description of events (cf. OB I$_{355}$ // S rev. iv$_2$).

Already in OB there is some correspondence between the descriptions of Enlil's complaints and the preceding events. According to OB Enlil complained to the gods:

OB I

358 *[iktabta] ⸢rigim⸣ awīlūti*
"the noise of mankind has become intense,"

359 *[ina ḫubūrīši]na uza⸢am⸣ma šitta*
"[with their tumult] I am deprived of sleep."

This has a correspondence in the preceding description of events:

355 *ina [ḫubūrīšina] ilu ⸢it⸣ta⸢˒d⸣ar*
"with [their tumult] the god got disturbed.]

356 *[Enlil išteme] ri⸢gim⸣šin*
"[Enlil heard] their noise".

---

32 For the text of ll.14-29 cf. W.G.Lambert, "New Fragments".

33 The missing repetition of Sii$_{9a}$ may be due to scribal error (haplography because of Homoioarkton {l.18}).

In LA the complaints are:

S rev. iv

6 *[ik]tabtam[a r]igim amēlūte*

"The noise of mankind has become intense."

7 *[ana*[34] *r]igmē[šin]a attādar*

"[At their] noise I have got disturbed,"

8 *[ana ḫ]u[bū]rīšina lā iṣabbatanni šittu*

"[at] their tumult sleep does not overcome me."

and events are described as:

2 *[ana] rigmēšina itta*[⌉]*[dar]*

"[At] their noise he was disturbed,"

3 *[ana] ḫubūrīšina lā iṣabbassu [šittu]*

"[at] their tumult, [sleep] did not overcome him."

Thus the correspondence between description of events and complaints has been increased and it is noteworthy that this was achieved by expansion rather than abbreviation.[35]

In the report of the fulfillment of Enlil's orders to cause the second drought LA has added S rev. $v_{5\text{-}6a}$ (// $iv_{56\text{-}57}$ {description of the first drought}). These lines had had their equivalent in Enlil's orders for the first drought (OB $IIi_{18\text{-}19}$ // S rev. $iv_{46\text{-}47}$). Thus it seems probable that LA increased the parallelism between orders and fulfillments. Although the description of the first drought and Enlil's orders for the second have not been preserved in OB the tendency towards assimilation of parallel passages becomes apparent from the close correspondence in LA between Enlil's orders for the first drought and the description of the second, which had not been found in OB.

The addition of S rev. $v_{27\text{-}30}$, introducing a conversation between Atraḫasīs and Ea after the description of the second famine, adapts this passage to the description of the first one where these lines had also been present in OB.[36]

---

34 Cf. ll.40-41 and W.G.Lambert, "New Fragements", p.74.

35 However, in the parallel passage describing the gods' next attempt to diminish mankind, OB has an exact correspondence to $IIi_{4.5.7.8}$ (Enlil disturbed by the noise), while LA only mentions Enlil's renewed complaints ($Siv_{40\text{-}41}$), which corresponds to $Siv_{7\text{-}8}$. LA only mentions Ea's advice to Atraḫasīs, but omitted a description of their fulfillment and the subsequent multiplication of mankind.

36 Cf. S $iv_{17\text{-}20}$ // OB $I_{364\text{-}367}$.

Due to *lacunae* in OB further cases cannot be adduced with certainty.[37] The following table indicates the repetitive structure of LA.

	Anu's message	delivery
Sii	9	19
	10	20
	11	21
	12	22
	13	23
	14	24
	15	25
	16	26
	17	27

Enlil disturbed, plague ordered			
S rev.iv	1		report to
	2		gods
	3		
	4		37
	5		
	6		
	7	execution	40
	8		41
	9	13	
	10	14	
	11	15	
	12	16	

[37] Another case may be the addition of S rev. $iv_{47b\text{-}51}$. These lines are part of Enlil's orders for the second attempt to diminish mankind (the first drought), which had also been mentioned in OB IIi. OB IIi_{18} parallels S rev. iv_{46} and OB IIi_{19} corresponds to S rev. iv_{47a}. OB $IIi_{20\text{-}22}$ have not been taken over by LA. Unfortunately OB IIi breaks off after l.22. That the lost portion contained an equivalent of S rev $iv_{47b\text{-}51}$ does not seem probable, since the focus of Enlil's speech had already turned from effects of the famine on nature to those on mankind in l.20. The descriptions of the taking effect of Enlil's orders in LA contained equivalents of the added passage ($iv_{57b\text{-}61}$ {first drought} and $v_{6b\text{-}9}$ {second drought}). Corresponding lines have been preserved in OB's description of the second drought:

S rev. v_{6b} // OB $IIiv_7$

S rev. v_7 // OB $IIiv_{4.8}$

S rev. v_8 // OB $IIiv_5$.

If, therefore, S rev. $iv_{47b\text{-}51}$ had had no equivalent in OB, which seems probable, the addition constitutes an adaptation of the description of the fulfillment to that of the order. OB $IIi_{20\text{-}22}$ had no parallel in the description of subsequent events and may have

Atraḫasīs prays to Ea

S rev.iv 17	S rev. v 27		
18	28		
19	29		
20	30		
famine ordered	execution		
		execution	
S rev.iv 42	52		
43	53	S rev.v (2)	
44	54	3	
45	55	4	
46	56	5	
47	57	6	
48	58	7	
49	59	8	
50	60	[9]	
51	61	[9]	
		effects of the famines on mankind	
		[11]	
		12	S rev.vi 1
		13	2
		14	3
		15	4
		16	5
		17	6
		18	7
		19	8
		20	9
		21	10
		22	11
		23	12
		24	13
		25	14
		26	15

---

been omitted for that reason.

Ass has further added S rev. v_{9-10} mentioning the peoples' barrenness because of the pestilence during the second drought. l.9 can be restored after S rev. iv_{60-61}, l.10 cannot be reconstructed. The addition of l.9 may be regarded as adaptation to the parallel passage in the description of the first drought (S rev. iv_{60-61} // iv_{50-51} {Enlil's orders}), but there, too, the line(s) might have been added (no equivalent is preserved -but OB IIi breaks off after l.22; OB IIi_{19} // S rev. iv_{47a}). Unfortunately a possible parallel passage, Enlil's orders for his first attempt to diminish mankind (OB $I_{360-363}$), is almost

Although the Atraḫasīs epic had already been well structured with repetitions and parallels in OB, we can notice a tendency to increase the prominence of this feature even further. Further general tendencies of redactorial treatment are not *apparent*.

3. The Etana Epic

Three major versions of the Etana epic have been preserved.[38] The following parallels can be noted:

OV I/A$_{1-14}$			//	LV I$_{9-16}$
OV I/C$_{1-13}$	//	MAV I/A$_{1-22}$	//	LV II$_{17-36}$
OV I/C$_{14-51}$			//	LV II$_{37-71}$
		MAV I/B$_{1-25}$	//	LV II$_{92-112}$
OV I/D$_{1-3}$	//	(MAV I/B$_{26-30}$)[39]	//	LV II$_{113}$
OV I/D$_{4-15}$			//	LV II$_{114-128}$
		MAV I/C$_{1-10}$	//	LV II$_{138-145}$.

As has already been pointed out above,[40] the textual dependencies of the extant versions are not linear. For our purpose we shall disregard this and treat the versions as if OV constituted the Vorlage of MAV and LV. Since there is only slight indication that the LV used MAV at all,[41] we shall treat those passages found in MAV and not in the other two versions as *additions* by MAV rather than as *omissions* by the LV.[42] Those cases where LV differs from MAV, and where OV is not preserved, are therefore not conclusive.[43]

---

completely lost.

38 For the texts cf. J.V.Kinnier Wilson, *Etana*.

39 No correspondence in phraseology.

40 Cf. above, p.21.

41 The only agreements between the two versions over against OV consist of MV I/A$_2$ {restored after LV} // LV II$_{22}$, MAV I/A$_6$ // LV II$_{18}$ (equivalents of which may have been present in OV in the lost portion preceding OV I/C$_1$) and the omission of OV I/D$_{1-3}$.

42 For the consequences of the uncertain textual dependency for the investigation of macrostructural development cf. the development of the accounts on Aššurbanipal's Egyptian campaigns; see below, pp.116ff.

43 In the LV there is a close agreement in wording between the eagle's and the serpent's oath of friendship and the warning spoken by the eagle's young not to breach the oath. The MAV of the warning is not extant. Thus it remains uncertain whether the omission of MAV I/A$_{5-7}$, which has no counterpart in the LV of the warning (MAV I/A$_6$ // LV II$_{18}$ // LV II$_{49}$), adapted the narration of the oath to that of the warning.
A further verbal parallelism in LV is that between Šamaš's orders to the serpent and their execution. The former have not been preserved in MAV. In the narration of the

Unfortunately there is not a single case in the Etana epic where two or more parallel passages, command-fulfillment etc., are preserved in different versions. Thus it cannot be argued with certainty that in this epic, too, the correspondence between parallel passages was increased by redactorial treatment.

Only a few examples for possible adaptation may be adduced from the Etana epic. MAV (I/A,8-9) has reworded OV I/C,6-7.[44] The two passages read:

OV: *ina ṣilli ṣerbettim u[l]lid ṣerrum erû ittalad ina ṣērīšu*

"in the shadow of the poplar the serpent begot (young), the eagle begot (young) at the top of it"

MAV: *ina appi iṣi erû ālidma ina ešdi ṣarbate ṣēru italda.*

"at the tree-top the eagle begot (young), at the foot of the poplar the serpent begot (young)"

In a later passage describing the eagle's safety from the serpent, LV (II_{44}) has *appi iṣi* ("tree-top"). Unfortunately the whole passage is missing in MAV and the corresponding line is mutilated in OV (I/C,20). Thus it cannot be argued with certainty that the alteration of *ṣērīšu* ("top of it") to *appi iṣi* ("tree-top") constitutes an adaptation to the later passage.

In the narration of eagle and serpent swearing an oath of mutual assistance and friendship the LV has replaced *utamammū* ("they had sworn" - OV I/C_4) with *itmū erṣet*[*im rabītim* ?] ("they had sworn by the [great] netherwor[ld]" - LV II_{23} // LV II_{15} {serpent's proposal}.[45] This alteration may have assimilated the narration of the serpent's proposal to swear an oath to that of the event. Unfortunately the OV of the former has not been preserved.

The parallelism between OV $I/C_{24\text{-}25}$, MAV $I/A_{1\text{-}2}$, and LV $II_{22.46\text{-}47}$ (cf. also $II_{68.70}$) may indicate another case of assimilation of parallel passages. The OV of the warning given by the eagle's young to his father not to fly down to the bull where the serpent was hiding contained the lines:

---

latter the LV has no equivalent of MAV I/B_{24} and reads *ištene*ʾʾ*i* ("he looks at" - LV II_{105} // LV II_{81}) for *ippa*[*lis*] ("he examined" - MAV I/B_{15}), *ana ku*⌈*tum*⌉ *libbi* ("to the (fatty) covering of the intestines" - LV II_{108} // LV II_{82}) for *ana karaš r*[*īmi*] ("to the stomach of the bull" - MAV I/B_{21}), and *ana li*[*bb*]*i* ("inside" - LV II_{109} // LV II_{83}) for *ana qerbuš* ("inside" - MAV I/B_{22}). LV $II_{92\text{-}93}$ (// LV $II_{78\text{-}80}$) have no equivalent in MAV. Some or all of these differences may be due to an assimilation of the descriptions of order and fulfillment, but since in the MAV only one of the two passages is extant, this cannot be argued with certainty.

44 LV caret.

45 MAV *caret*.

OV I/C

24 *[l]ā t[ākal abī ...*

"do not [eat, father ..."

25 *[gišperrū . . .*

"[the traps ..."

A corresponding passage in OV of the oath sworn by eagle and serpent is not extant, but may have been lost with the passage preceding OV I/C_1. In MAV these lines are paralleled not in the warning, but only in the description of the oath:

MAV I/A

1 *[šētu ša Šamši] [l]ibbalkissum[a]*

"may the [net of Šamaš] come down on him"

2 *[gišparrū māmīt Šamši] [li][bārūnim]m[a]*

"may [the traps of the oath of Šamaš] seize him"

In LV the narration of the warning contains both lines with a slightly different wording. Of these only the first is present in the narration of the swearing of the oath by serpent and eagle, but it contains the verb-forms of both lines of MAV:

LV II

22 *gišparrū māmīt Šamši libbalkitūšuma l[ibārūšu]*

"may the traps of the oath of Šamaš come down on him and [seize him]"

46 *lā tākal abī šētu ša Šamši ibā[rka]*

"do not eat, father, the net of Šamaš will seiz[e you]"

47 *gišparrū māmīt Šamši ibbalkitūkama ibārūnikk[a]*

"the traps of the oath of Šamaš will come down on you and seize you."

Whether MAV and LV removed (different) parts of a parallel structure or LV increased the parallelism compared to the earlier versions cannot be established with certainty or even with probability. It depends on whether the lost portion preceding OV I/C_1, narrating the oath sworn by serpent and eagle, contained equivalents of the lines in question or not. In their narrations of the oath MAV and LV mention the curses in different orders. If OV had the same order as LV, the lines would be expected in the extant portion, where they are missing. LV would thus have increased the agreement between the parallel passages of oath and warning. If, on the other hand, OV agreed with MAV in its order of mentioning the curses, the lines in question would have been present in the lost portion preceding OV I/C_1 and the parallelism in OV may have exceeded that of LV.

The alteration of OV I/D_8, describing the serpent's revenge after the eagle had devoured the serpent's young, to LV (II_{119}[46] // LV II_{86} {Šamaš's advice}) may have adapted the narration of events to that of Šamaš's advice.[47]

OV I/D

[8] *ašar mû* [...
"a place, where water ... "

LV II

[86] *mūt bubūti u ṣummi limūta*
"he shall die the death of hunger and thirst"

[119] [*mūt*] *bubūt*[*i u ṣumm*]*i imâ*[*ti*]).
"he shall die the [death] of hunger [and thirst]".

Since the narration of the serpent's revenge in OV is not extant, no firm conclusion can be reached.

From the Etana epic not a single certain case of progressive assimilation of parallel passages can be adduced. However, this may be due to the bad state of preservation of the different versions. The close correspondence of some parallel passages in LV[48] may be taken as an indication for such a tendency in the transmission of the Etana epic. Other general developmental trends are not apparent.

4. The Gilgameš epic

The development of the Gilgameš epic and its applicability to the study of Old Testament narratives have been investigated in detail by J.H.Tigay.[49]

---

46 MAV of this passage is not extant.

47 *uttaz*[*ik* (OV I/D_6) and *unakkis* ("he cut off" - LV II_{117} // LV II_{84} {*nukkis* - "cut off"}) may be different forms of the same verb and thus not be taken as indication for a further case of adaptation of parallel passages. J.V.Kinnier Wilson (*Etana*, p.46) suggests *uttazik* for **uttassik*, being derived by Metathesis from *uttakkis* (*nakāsu*). Von Soden (*Akkadisches Handwörterbuch* II, p.772), however, restores *uttaz*[*im*] (*nazāmu* Dt - "Klage führen"). The context and the corresponding passage in the LV support Kinnier Wilson's suggestion.

48 Cf.LV II_{22} // II_{47}, $II_{26\text{-}27}$ // $II_{28\text{-}29}$, $II_{30\text{-}31}$ // $II_{32\text{-}33}$, $II_{73\text{-}86}$ // $II_{87\text{-}93.108\text{-}109.117\text{-}119}$, $II_{138\text{-}140}$ // III/$A_{12\text{-}14}$ // IV/$C_{12\text{-}14}$, $II_{143\text{-}145}$ // $II_{148\text{-}150}$, IV/$B_{18\text{-}20}$ // IV/$B_{21\text{-}23}$, IV/$B_{25\text{-}27}$ // IV/$B_{31\text{-}33}$ // IV/$B_{35\text{-}37}$, IV/$C_{26\text{-}27}$ // IV/$C_{28\text{-}29}$, IV/$C_{30\text{-}31}$ // IV/$C_{34\text{-}35}$ // IV/$C_{38\text{-}39}$, IV/$C_{44\text{-}45}$, IV/$C_{46\text{-}47}$, IV/$C_{48\text{-}49}$.

49 Cf. *Evolution of the Gilgamesh Epic*, *Literary-Critical Studies*, and his essays in J.H.Tigay (ed.), *Empirical Models*.

However, the methodology of the present study differs substantially from Tigay's and requires a new investigation. Only few parallel passages have been preserved in the different versions of the epic and, as has already been mentioned above,[50] only two of them, the Old Babylonian (OB) and the Neo-Assyrian (NA) versions,[51] may be used for a comparison. Thus the consistency of redactorial treatment cannot be evaluated and all conclusions derived from the development of the Gilgameš epic must be treated with care.[52]

A first case of increasing parallelism and repetition is found in the literary development of the descriptions of Gilgameš's dreams of Enkidu.[53] In both versions Gilgameš's first dream was about a meteorite[54] falling from heaven. The people of Uruk gathered around it and kissed its feet. In his dream Gilgameš tried to lift the meteorite, but without success. According to OB he was able to raise it with the people's support and took it to his mother. According to NA he embraced[55] it "as a woman" and then took it to his mother who "made it equal" with him. In both versions Gilgameš told the contents of his dream to his mother who revealed to him that he had dreamed of a mighty friend who was to arrive. Gilgameš then had a second dream. This time he dreamed of an axe, which according to OB he embraced "as a woman" and placed at his side, but according to NA he took it to his mother, then he embraced it "as a woman", and his mother "made it equal" with him. Again, in both versions Gilgameš's mother explained to him the contents of his dream.

The descriptions of the contents of Gilgameš's dreams were assimilated by NA. Thus NA in its narration of Gilgameš's second dream has no equivalent of

---

50 Cf. pp.20f with n.4.

51 The correspondence found between a fragment from Nippur and the Neo-Assyrian version I_{30ff} is ignored here, since the former may be post-OB (cf. J.H.Tigay, *Evolution of the Gilgamesh Epic*, p.40, n.1) and the textual relationship of this fragment and the other OB texts is uncertain.

52 If no other publications are referred to the texts are taken from R.Campbell Thompson, *Epic of Gilgamish*. For further bibliographic information cf. *Gilgameš et sa légende*, pp.7-27.

53 Cf. J.S.Cooper, "Gilgamesh Dreams of Enkidu", where the texts of are given on pp.41-42. There and in the translation on p.43 OB Penn.(cf. below, p.45, n.56) i_{31} is missing (cf. M.Jastrow and A.T.Clay, *Old Babylonian Version*, p.63, and R.Campbell Thompson, *Epic of Gilgamish*, p.20.

54 *kiṣru ša Anim* ("rock {?} of Anu").

55 Cf. J.S.Cooper, "Gilgamesh Dreams of Enkidu", p.43, n.22.

OB Penn.[56] IIi_{35-36}. These lines mention that Gilgameš took the axe and placed it at his side and have no correspondence in the first dream. The action suited the object of the second dream, the axe, but not that of the first dream, the meteorite. The assimilation of the descriptions of first and second dream in NA was thus achieved by abbreviation rather than expansion. According to NA Gilgameš took both objects to his mother.

NA has further replaced ⌊*um*⌋*mi ina šāt mušītīya* ("mother, in my {dream} this night" - OB Penn. IIi_3) with *ummi šunat aṭṭalu mušītīya* ("mother, my dream which I saw this night" - NA Iv_{26}). Corresponding lines in the relations of the second dream in OB and NA read:

OB Penn. i_{26}: [*um*]⌊*mi ā*⌋*t*[*a*]*mar šanītam*
"mother, I saw a second one."

NA I vi_8: [*ummi āt*]*amar šanīta šutta*.
"[mother], I saw a second dream."

It is thus apparent that NA Iv_{26} increased the parallelism between the corresponding passages in the descriptions of the first and the second dream. *naṭālu* was employed instead of *amāru*, which is found in the corresponding passage in the second dream, presumably because of the foretelling of Gilgameš' dream in NA Iv_{24}: *Gilgameš ina lib Uruk inaṭṭala šunatēka* ("Gilgameš will in Uruk see dreams about you"). The passage has thus also been adapted to its immediate context.

NA has also omitted OB Penn. IIi_{4-5}, which do not deal with the relationship between the protagonists Gilgameš and Enkidu, resp. meteorite or axe. Neither OB nor NA exhibit correspondences to OB Penn. IIi_{4-5}. Such lines would have been positioned between NA Ivi_8 and vi_9, resp. OB Penn. IIi_{25} and i_{26}. The omission thus assimilates the relations of the two dreams.

NA has further added Iv_{36}, which narrates Gilgameš's caressing the meteorite, in its narration of Gilgameš's first dream. A corresponding line is also found in both versions in their descriptions of the second dream (OB Penn. IIi_{33-34} // NA Ivi_{14}).[57]

---

56 The "Pennsylvania Tablet"; cf. M.Jastrow and A.T.Clay, *Old Babylonian Version*, pp.62-68; R.Campbell Thompson, *Epic of Gilgamish*, pp.20-24.

57 Cf. J.H.Tigay, *Evolution of the Gilgamesh Epic*, p.88.

OB Penn. Ii_{33-34}: *arâmšuma kīma aššatim aḫabbub elīšu*
"I love it, like a woman I embrace it (*sc.* the axe)"

NA Ivi_{14}: *[arāmšum]a kī aššate elīšu aḫbub*
"[I loved it], like a woman I embraced it (*sc.* the axe)"

NA Iv_{36}: *[arāmšu kīm]a aššate elīšu aḫbub*
"[I loved it, like] a woman I embraced it (*sc.* the meteorite)."

Thus the addition constitutes an adaptation of the narration of the first dream to that of the second.

NA has further added Ivi_{10-13} to the description of Gilgameš's second dream. These lines closely parallel NA $Iv_{31-33.37}$. The addition therefore constitutes an adaptation to NA's description of Gilgameš's first dream. Since the expansions were carried out in the narrations of both dreams the trend towards harmonization alone cannot explain these alterations. We can, however, note that the verbal correspondence between the two passages is greater in NA.[58] While NA Iv_{31f} // NA Ivi_{10f} and NA Iv_{37} // NA I vi_{13} have a parallel in OB's description of the first dream and NA Iv_{32} // Ivi_{11} in OB's relation of both dreams, NA Iv_{33} // NA Ivi_{12} has no immediate correspondence in OB. Possibly this line was inserted to create an EEN-construction.[59]

OB Penn. Ii10 (first dream): *Uruk mātum paḫir elīšu*
"the land of Uruk was assembled around it"

NA Iv_{31-32} (first dream): *Uruk mātum izzaz elīšu [mātum puḫḫurat] ina [muḫḫīšu]*
"the land of Uruk stands over it, the land is assembled around it"

OB Penn. (second dream): -

NA Ivi_{10-11} (second dream): *[Uruk mā]tum izzaz elīšu [mātum puḫḫur]at ina muḫḫīšu*
"the land [of Uruk] stands over it, [the land is assembled] around it"

OB Penn. (first dream): -

NA Iv_{33} (first dream): *[idappir umm]ānu e[li ṣerīšu]*
"the people [jostle] [about it]"

NA Ivi_{12} (second dream): *idappir ummānu eli ṣērīšu*
"the people jostle about it"

OB Penn. Ii_{14} (first dream): *aššiaššuma atbalaššu ana ṣērīki*
I lifted it and brought it to you"

---

58 For the increased parallelism between the contents of the dreams and the actual events cf. below, pp.48f.

59 *Uruk mātum izzaz elīšu* (NA Iv_{10} // Ivi_{31})
mātum puḫḫurat ina muḫḫīšu (NA Iv_{11} // Ivi_{32})
idappir ummānu eli ṣērīšu (NA Iv_{12} // Ivi_{33}). Cf. below, p.48.

NA Iv_{37} (first dream): *[u a]ttadīšu ina šaplīki*
"[and I] placed it before you"

NA Ivi_{13} (second dream): *[anāku] attadīšu ina šaplīki*
"[I] placed it before you".

NA also assimilated the descriptions of the contents of the dreams and references to them given in the interpretations by Gilgameš's mother. Thus NA added Iv_{38} (narration of first dream), Iv_{46} (interpretation of first dream), and Ivi_{15} (narration of second dream). All three passages mention that Gilgameš's mother made the object found be Gilgameš "equal with him". A corresponding line had already been present in the interpretation of the second dream in OB Penn. $IIii_1$ // NA Ivi_{20}[60], whence it was taken over by NA into the descriptions and explanations of both dreams. NA has also added Iv_{41-47}. These lines have Gilgameš's mother repeating Gilgameš's narration of his dream. Thus their insertion constitutes an adaptation of the explanation of the dream to the narration of its contents.

NA further assimilated the interpretations of the dreams. The description of Enkidu in the interpretation of the first dream by *Gilgameš's* mother differs in the two versions (OB Penn. IIi_{17-23} // NA Ivi_{1-5}). Unfortunately the description of Enkidu in the interpretation of the second dream is extant only in NA, which exhibits close parallels to that of the first dream (NA Ivi_{1-3} // NA Ivi_{21-23}). The only line preserved of the interpretation of the second dream in OB has no parallel in that of the first dream. It thus seems probable that NA increased the parallelism between the two interpretations. This is also indicated by NA's reference to the meteorite (which had appeared in Gilgameš's *first* dream) in the interpretation of the *second* dream (Ivi_{23}). The interpretation of the first dream also resembles the relation of the dream and passages in other parts of the epic. NA Ivi_4, describing Gilgameš's attraction towards the friend whose arrival was foretold in the dream, refers back to $Iv_{36(//47)}$. NA Ivi_{2-3} resume the description of Enkidu given in $Iiii_{3-4}$. The express declaration of the dream as favourable (NA Ivi_6)[61] parallels Vii_{38-39}.[62] Unfortunately no OB parallel of the latter is preserved, which, too, could

60 Cf. J.H.Tigay, *Evolution of the Gilgamesh Epic*, p.88.

61 *[damqat šuqu]rat šunatka* ("favourable, precious is your dream"; cf. B.Landsberger, "Zur vierten und siebenten Tafel", p.116.

62 *[ib]ri damqat šuna[tka] [š]uttum šuqurat* ("friend, favourable is your dream, the dream

thus have been added there. If so, then the positive evaluation of the dream by Enkidu in the later passage would anticipate the outcome of the encounter with Ḫumbaba and the addition would thus have been that of a prolepsis.[63] The same function may be assumed for NA Ivi$_{1.5}$ which remind of NA IIIi$_{4\text{-}5.9}$.[64]

In NA the speech-introductions for Gilgameš's relations of the dreams and their interpretations by his mother were harmonized. The speech-introductions in OB are:

OB Penn. IIi$_{2f}$: *itbēma Gilgameš šunatam ipaššar izzakkaram ana ummīšu*
"Gilgameš arose, he explains the dream, says to his mother"

OB Penn. IIi$_{15f}$: *ummi Gilgameš mūdiat kalāma izzakaram ana Gilgameš*
"Gilgameš's mother, who knows all, said to Gilgameš"

OB Penn. IIi$_{25}$: ⌊*it*⌋*bi ītawâm ana ummīšu*
"he arose, told it to his mother"

OB Penn. IIi$_{37f}$: ⌊*ummi*⌋ *Gilgameš mūdât* ⌊*kalā*⌋*ma [izzakkaram ana Gilgameš]*
"Gilgameš's mother, who knows all, [said to Gilgameš]".

In NA the verbal agreement betweent the various speech-introductions was increased:

NA Iv$_{25}$: *itbīma Gilgameš šunata ipaššar izakkara ana ummīšu*
"Gilgameš arose, he explains the dream, says to his mother"

NA Iv$_{39}$: *[ummi Gilgameš emqet mū]dât kalāma īdi izakkar ana bēlīša*
NA Iv$_{40}$: *[sinnišat rīmat Ninsun] emqet mūdât kalāma īdi izakkar ana Gilgameš*
"[Gilgameš's mother, wise,] understanding, who knows all, says to her lord,
[the woman, wild cow Ninsun,] wise, understanding, who knows all, says to Gilgameš"

NA Ivi$_{7}$: *[Gilgameš šaniš izakkar] ana ummīšu*
"[a second time Gilgameš speaks] to his mother"

NA Ivi$_{16}$: *[ummi Gilgameš] emqet mūdât kalāma īdi izakkara ana mārīša*
NA Ivi$_{17}$: *[sin]nišat rīmat Ninsun emqet mūdât kalāma īdi izakkara ana Gilgameš.*
"[Gilgameš's mother,] wise, understanding, who knows all, says to her son"
"the woman, wild cow Ninsun, wise understanding, who knows all, says to Gilgameš"

The additional appositions to the mention of Gilgameš's mother in NA Iv$_{39f}$.vi$_{16f}$ are paralleled in NA IIIi$_{17}$, where Gilgameš's mother is described as *Ninsun emqet mūdât kalāma īdi*. Unfortunately no OB parallel of this passage has

is precious" - line count according to R.Campbell Thompson, *Epic of Gilgamish*; B.Landsberger, "Zur vierten und siebenten Tafel", pp.98.117, regards Campbell Thompson's col. ii as col.i.

63 Cf. OB Penn. IIIiv$_{27.28}$, NA IIIi$_{9}$ vi$_{8}$ IVvi$_{38}$.

64 // NA IIIvi$_{8}$ (cf. IVvi$_{38}$); OB Penn IIIvi$_{27}$.

been preserved.[65] Thus it remains uncertain whether this expansion, too, may be due to a trend towards increasing verbal parallelism.

NA further assimilated the description of Gilgameš's dreams and the narration of events foretold there. The expansion of OB Penn. Ii_{10}, describing the people's reaction to the arrival of the meteorite, to NA $\mathrm{Ii}_{31\text{-}33}$ has already been noted above as an example for the assimilation of the descriptions of Gilgameš's two dreams about Enkidu. The added lines (+ NA Ii_{34}) also correspond to the description of Enkidu's arrival in Uruk as found in NA $\mathrm{II}_{38\text{-}42}$. Already in OB there is some correspondence between the narrations of the people's actions in the second dream (OB Penn. $\mathrm{Ii}_{27\text{-}30}$) and the later events (OB Penn. $\mathrm{Iv}_{11\text{-}13}$):

OB Penn. $\mathrm{Ii}_{27\text{-}30}$ (second dream): *...]e-mi-a ina sūqim [ša Uru]k ribītim ... elīšu paḫru*
"... in the streets of broad-marted [Uru]k ..., around it they assembled"

OB Penn. $\mathrm{Iv}_{12\text{-}13}$ (events): *izzizamma ina sūqim ša Uruk ribītim paḫrāma nišū*
"as he stood in the streets of broad-marted Uruk the people were assembled".

The correspondence, however, is far greater in NA.

NA Iv_{31} (first dream): *Uruk mātum izzaz elīšu*
"the land of Uruk stands over it"

NA $\mathrm{Ivi}_{10\text{-}11}$ (second dream): *[Uruk mā]tum izzaz elīšu*
"[the la]nd [of Uruk] stands around it"

NA IIii_{38} (events): *Uruk mātu izzaz [elīšu]*
"the land of Uruk stands [around it]"

NA Iv_{32} (first dream): *[mātum puḫḫurat] ina [muḫḫīšu]*
"[the land is assembled around it]"

NA Ivi_{11} (second dream): *[mātum puḫḫur]at ina muḫḫīšu*
[the land is assemb]led around it"

NA IIii_{39} (events): *mātu puḫḫurat [ina muḫḫīšu]*
"the land is assembled [around it]"

NA Iv_{33} (first dream): *[idappir umm]ānu e[li ṣerīšu]*
"[the peo]ple [jostle] [about it]"

NA Ivi_{12} (second dream): *idappir ummānu eli ṣērīšu*
"the people jostle about it"

NA IIii_{39} (events): *idappir ummāni [eli ṣērīšu]*
"the people jostle [about it]"

NA Iv_{34} (first dream): *[eṭlūtu uk]tammaru elīšu*
"[the men ga]ther around it

---

[65] In OB Penn. IIvi_{33f} Gilgameš's mother is referred to as *rīmtum ša supūri Ninsun* ("wild cow of the fold, Ninsun").

NA Ivi (second dream): -
NA $IIii_{40}$ (events): *eṭlūtu uktammaru* [*elīšu*]
"the men gather [around it]."

Thus the expansion may be regarded as an adaptation of the dream to the narration of events foretold in it. Even though the wording of the narration of Enkidu's arrival differs in NA from OB Penn., and it is not possible to reconstruct the exact course of literary development, it is important to note that the verbal correspondence between the relations of dream(s) and event is greater in NA than in OB.

The mutual assimilation of parallel passages was achieved by alteration, omission, addition, expansion, and abbreviation. It is difficult to see any basic tendency behind all these alterations apart from that of increasing the verbal correspondence of parallel passages. The following table indicates the correspondences between parallel passages in OB and NA.[66]

Old Babylonian version[67]				Neo-Assyrian version[68]			
first dream		second dream		first dream		second dream	
Dream	Interpr.	Dream	Interpr.	Dream	Interpr.	Dream	Interpr.
		24					
i 1f	15f	25	37[69]	v 25	39-40	7	16f
3		26		26		8	
4f							
6				27	41		
7		27-		28	42	9a	18
8		-30				9b	
9				29	43		
10				30			
				31		10	
				32		11	
				33		12	
				34			
11	21	31		35			
12f	20.22	32f		36	47	14	19
14	23	34f		37	45	13	20
				38	46	15	
	17		ii 1				
	18						
	19						

66 Parallel passages are noted in the same lines of the table.
67 OB Penn. cols.i.ii.
68 NA Iv.vi.
69 Ll.38f not preserved.

vi 1	21
2	22
3	23
4[70]	
5	
6	

A further case where NA has harmonized the narration of parallel events is that of Gilgameš's encounters with Siduri (an "ale-wife"), Sursunabi (OB) / Uršanabi (NA- Utnapištim's boatman), and, finally, Utnapištim himself.[71] Unfortunately the former two passages are mutilated in OB and the latter is completely lost. However, enough has been preserved to show NA's tendency towards unification. In OB there is only slight verbal agreement between the corresponding passages.

Thus, for example, Sursunabu's question

OB Me. Xi$v_{5'}$: *mannum šumka qibiam yâšim*
"What is your name, tell me?"

OB Me. Xi$v_{6'}$: *anāku Sursunabu ša Utanapištim rūqim*
"I am Sursunabu, of Utnapištim the Faraway"

is answered by

OB Me. Xi$v_{8'}$: *Giš šumī anāku*
"My name is Gilgameš, I,"

OB Me. Xi$v_{9'}$: *ša allikam ištu Uruk Eanni*
"who came from Uruk-Eanna,

OB Me. Xi$v_{10'}$: *ša asḫuram*[72] *šadî*
"who traversed the mountains,"

OB Me. Xi$v_{11'}$: *urḫam rēqetam waṣi Šamši*
"a distant journey, Šamaš's way".

The agreement between corresponding passages is far greater in NA. Extant, though mutilated, are Siduri's questions and Gilgameš's answers, Uršanabi's questions and Gilgameš's answers, and Gilgameš's answers to Utnapištim[73]:

---

70 // v_{47}.

71 For OB cf. B.Meissner, "Altbabylonisches Fragment" (henceforth OB Me.); A.R.Millard, "Gilgamesh X" (henceforth OB Mi.); W.von Soden, "Kleinere Beiträge", pp.189-192.

72 Cf. W.von Soden, "Kleinere Beiträge", p.20.

73 According to R.Campbell Thompson, *Epic of Gilgamish*, p.58, the beginning of col.v, which contained Utnapištim's question, should be restored according Xi_{33}-ii_{14}. Gil-

lament[74]/ narrative	Gilg.	Siduri	Gilg.	Uršan.	Gilg.	Utnapišt.	Gilg.
		i_{39}		iii_{1}	iii_{8}	broken	
	i_{a}[75]	i_{40}					
	i_{37}	i_{41}					
	i_{38}	i_{42}					
		i_{43}					
		i_{44}		iii_{2}	iii_{9}		broken
		i_{45}		iii_{3}	iii_{10}		[v_{1}]
IXi_{4} Xi_{8}		i_{46}[76]		iii_{4}	iii_{11}		[v_{2}]
i_{9}		i_{47}		iii_{5}	iii_{12}		[v_{3}]
		i_{48}		iii_{6}	iii_{13}		[v_{4}]
VIII		i_{49}		iii_{7}	[iii_{14}]		[v_{5}]
ii_{8}		broken			[iii_{15}]		[v_{6}]
ii_{9}					[iii_{16}]		[v_{7}]
ii_{10}					[iii_{17}]		[v_{8}]
ii_{11}					[iii_{18}]		[v_{9}]
ii_{12}					iii_{19}		[v_{10}]
							[v_{11}][77]
					iii_{20}		[v_{12}]
					iii_{21}		[v_{13}]
					iii_{22}		
					iii_{23}		[v_{14}]
							[v_{15}]
			broken		iii_{24}		[v_{16}]
			ii_{7}		iii_{25}		[v_{17a}]?
IXi_{5}			ii_{8a}				[v_{17b}]
			ii_{8b}		iii_{26}		[v_{18a}]?
			ii_{9}		iii_{27}		[v_{18b}]
			ii_{10}		iii_{28}		[v_{19}]
			ii_{11}		iii_{29}		[v_{20a}]
			ii_{12}		iii_{30}		[v_{20b}]
			ii_{13}		iii_{31a}?		[v_{21a}]
			ii_{14}		iii_{31b}?		[v_{21b}]
			ii_{15}		iii_{32}		
			ii_{16}		iii_{33}		
			ii_{17}		iii_{34}		
			ii_{18}		iii_{35a}		
			ii_{19}		iii_{35b}		

---

gameš's answer has also been preserved on a Neo-Babylonian fragment, BM 35546 (cf. D.J.Wiseman, "Additional Neo-Babylonian Gilgamesh Fragments"). BM 35546, l.2' (the last line of Utnapištim's question - l.1' is not legible), however, disagrees with NA Xii_{14} (the last line of Siduri's question) and the preserved parallel passages of NA. Wiseman therefore regards Campbell Thompson's suggestion as unlikely ("Additional Neo-Babylonian Gilgamesh Fragments", p.131, n.1). Since BM 355546 is a Neo-Babylonian fragment and ll.3'ff agree with NA Xv_{22ff}, it has nevertheless been assumed here that the beginning of col.v corresponds to parallel passages in cols.i-iii, unless the

Since the beginning of Gilgameš's speech to Siduri in OB (Me.)Xii is lost, it is not possible to determine how many and which lines were added by NA. Unfortunately in OB Gilgameš's lament for Enkidu at his friend's death-bed (// NA VIII) is not extang. Thus we do not know whether NA has increased the agreement between the lament and Gilgameš's references to Enkidu's death in Tablet X. It is, however, apparent that the parallelism between the questions, between the answers, and between questions and answers, was increased. The only extant parallel between the addresses to Gilgameš is: *Giš êš balāṭam ša tasaḫḫuru lā tutta* ("Gilgameš, whereto (do you go), the life you seek you shall not find" - Me Xi$_{7'-8'}$ {Šamaš} // Me Xiii$_{1'-2'}$ {Siduri}).

Gilgameš's answer to Siduri in NA may be reconstructed with the help of parallel passages (NA Xiii$_{20-23}$[78] {Gilgameš's answer to Uršanabi} and NA Xv$_{12-15}$[79] {Gilgameš's answer to Utnapištim}) and agrees comparatively closely with OB (Me. Xii$_{1'-13'}$). Unfortunately, the beginning of passage is not extant in OB.

---

remains of col.v indicate deviation.

74 The corresponding passage in OB is not extant.

75 i$_{a-49}$ are taken from BM 34193 (cf. R.Campbell Thompson, *Epic of Gilgamish*, pl.42), a Neo-Babylonian fragment representing a different version. Identification of its position within the epic and line count are given according to A.Schott, "Übersetzung", pp.132-133; cf. also D.J.Wiseman, "Additional Neo-Babylonian Gilgamesh Fragments", p.128-130.

BM 34193	Xiii	Xv
Gilgameš's exploits (i$_{a-38}$)		
repeated by Siduri (i$_{39-43}$)		
Siduri's questions (i$_{44-49}$)	Uršanabi's questions (1-7)	[Utnapištim's questions]
[repeated by Gilgameš]	repeated by Gilgameš (8-14)	repeated by Gilgameš (...1-5)
	Gilgameš and Enkidu's exploits (15-19)	Gilgameš and Enkidu's exploits (6-11)
[Enkidu's fate and its effects on Gilgameš]	Enkidu's fate and its effects on Gilgameš (20-31)	Enkidu's fate and its effects on Gilgameš (12-21...)

Since in the repetition of Gilgameš's exploits by Siduri in BM 34193 2nd p.sgl. is used (Xi$_{40-43}$), 1st p.sgl. may have been used in Gilgameš's narration of his achievements (Xi$_{a-38}$, which differs from the parallel passage in Xv, where, as is indicated by 1.9 (...]*a ninârū* [... {"we slew"} - K 3382; cf. R.Campbell Thompson, *Epic of Gilgamish*, pl.42; cf. also NA VIIIii$_{11}$), 1st p.pl. was employed.

76 The 3rd p.sgl. suffix in *karšīšu* ("*his* mind") probably is a scribal error influenced by Xi$_8$ // IXi$_4$ // Xiii$_4$ // Xiii$_{11}$ // Xv$_2$ (corresponding passages in Gilgameš's and Utnapištim's speeches are lost).

77 Unfortunately it is not possible to determine which line of Xv$_{5-11}$ was added.

78 Cf. R.Campbell Thompson, *Epic of Gilgamish*, pl.40.

79 Cf. R.Campbell Thompson, *Epic of Gilgamish*, pl.42.

OB	NA
$ii_{1'}$: *ittīya ittallaku kalû marṣ[ātim]* "who went with me through all difficulties,"	*ibrī* [. . .] *kalû marṣāti* "my friend [. . .] all difficulties,"
$ii_{2'}$: *Enkidu ša arâmūšu danniš* "Enkidu, whom I loved dearly,"	*EN.KI* [. . .]*lakū KI.MIN* "Enki[du . . . who went] dto."
$ii_{3'}$: *ittīya ittallakū kalû marṣātim* "who went with me through all difficulties."	
$ii_{4'}$: *illikma ana šīmātu awēlūtim* "He went to the fate of mankind,"	*ikšu[d*[80] . . . "overwhelmed [. . ."
$ii_{5'}$: *urri u mūši elīšu abki* "day and night I wept over him."	*VI urr[i* . . .] *elīšu abki* "six days [. . .] I wept over him"
$ii_{6'}$: *ul addiššu ana qebērim* "I did not give him for burial,"	*u[l . . . q]ebēri*[81] "not [. . . for b]urial"
$ii_{7'}$: *ibrīman itabbiam ana rigmīya* "if my friend should rise at my lament,"	
$ii_{8'}$: *sebet ūmim u sebe mušiātim* "seven days and seven nights,"	
$ii_{9'}$: *adi tūltum imqut ina appīšu* "until a worm fell out of his nose."	*adi* [. . .]*šu* "until [. . .] his"
$ii_{10'}$: *ištu warkīšu ul ūta balaṭam* "Since he died I have not found life"	
	adurma [. . .] *ib*$^?$ [. . .] "I feared [. . ."
$ii_{11'}$: *attanaggiš kīma ḫābilim qabaltu ṣēri* "I roam like a hunter in the midst of the steppe"	*mūta ap[laḫma arappud ṣ]ēri*: "[I was frightened] by death [and roamed over the st]eppe,"
	amāt ibrīy[a (nad)a$^?$*-]at elīya* "the matter of my friend [rests] upon me."
	urḫa rūqāta arappud ṣēri: "On distant paths I roam the steppe"
	amāt EN.KI.DU ibrīya[82] *KI.MIN* "the matter of Enkidu, my friend, dto."

---

80 $Xiii_{22}$ (Gilgameš's answer to Uršanabi) - not in Gilgameš's answer to Utnapištim! Cf. the table above, p.51, and below, n.81.

81 Xv_{15} (Gilgameš's answer to Utnapištim) - not in Gilgameš's answer to Uršanabi! Cf. the table above, p.51, and above, n.80. R.Campbell Thompson's reconstruction of NA Xii contains parallels of both NA $Xiii_{22}$ and Xv_{15} (*Epic of Gilgamish*, p.56).

82 Restored after NA Xv_{19} (R.Campbell Thompson, *Epic of Gilgamish*, pl.42). Campbell Thompson's restoration of Xii_{9} has only *ibri* ("friend"; cf. *Epic of Gilgamish*, p.56).

ḫarrānu rū[qātu] arappud [ṣēri]
"On di[stant] roads I roam the [steppe]"

$ii_{12'}$: *inanna sābītum attamar pānīki*
"Now, ale-wife, I have seen your face,"

$ii_{13'}$: *mūtam ša atanaddaru aiāmur*
"death, which I fear, let me not see".

Apart from the trend towards increasing harmonization it is difficult to see any strict method or general trend behind these alterations. The redactors have added passages, retained, omitted or reworded others. NA has contracted OB Me. $Xii_{5'-8'}$ to one line, but expanded OB Me. Xii_{11}. Sentences of similar contents ($Xi_{8'}$. $ii_{10'}$. $iii_{2'}$) have been omitted and the retained material has been reworded. NA Xi_{43} as part of Siduri's speech mentions one of Gilgameš's exploits, but is without equivalent in the extant portion of the preceding speech of Gilgameš. If the order of mentioning was not changed in Siduri's answer, the ale-wife mentioned one of Gilgameš's and Enkidu's feats which Gilgameš had not told her before. The line has a parallel in $VIIIii_{11}$ (Gilgameš's lament for Enkidu) // $Xiii_{18}$ (Gilgameš's speech to Uršanabi) // Xv_{9} (Gilgameš's speech to Utnapištim). No reason for the addition of NA Xi_{43} is apparent. Possibly the equivalent was accidentally omitted from the preceding speech of Gilgameš. Xi_{48-49}, belonging to Siduri's description of Gilgameš's appearance, have no equivalent in the extant narrative portions of the epic. No reason for their addition is apparent.

A further possible case of assimilation may be found in the narrations of Gilgameš's encounter with Sursunabi / Uršanabi, where NA has replaced *[leq]ēma Gilgameš ḫaṣṣinnam ina qātīka* ("[ta]ke the axe in your hand, Gilgameš" - OB $Mi.iv_{11}$') with *išši Gilgameš ḫaṣṣinna ana i[dīka* ("raise the axe in your h[and], Gilgameš" - NA $Xiii_{40}$). The text of NA agrees with NA Xii_{33}, *iši Gilgameš ḫaṣṣinna ana [idīš]u* ("Gilgameš raised the axe in [hi]s [hand]") for which no OB parallel is extant.[83] The alteration may constitute an adaptation to the earlier passage, but because of the bad state of preservation of OB no final conclusion can be reached.

The only general tendency apparent from the present analysis of the redactorial treatment of Akkadian epic literature is that of increasing parallelism and

[83] Cf. also NA $Xiii_{44}$.

repetition.[84] It dominates the literary development of all epics investigated above. According to the methodological requirements to be fulfilled by valid empirical models, the *late* version of the suggested analogy and the present versions of narratives in the Old Testament have to be comparable with regard to the criteria for which the empirical model is adduced. With a few exceptions (e.g. 2 Kgs.1_{9ff} 2_{1ff}) the effects of such a general tendency to describe parallel passages with identical wording are not found in Old Testament narratives. Thus the redactorial principles dominating the transmission of Akkadian epics are not to be regarded as an appropriate empirical model for the transmission of Old Testament narratives.

Furthermore, since the general tendency is towards harmonization of different passages, which implies the removal of certain individual features, earlier developmental stages are irrecoverably lost. If the transmission of Akkadian epics is used as an empirical model, the exact reconstruction of the literary pre-history of a given narrative is impossible. Only broad outlines could be suggested.

It may be objected against the present negative evaluation of the usefulness of the transmission of Akkadian epics that we would reject valuable illustrations for what may have happened to narratives on their way into the Old Testament and ignore possible confirmation for already existing literary-critical hypotheses. However, any alteration *may* have been carried out. If the purpose of an empirical model is merely to illustrate what *may* have happened, it does not increase our

---

84 K.Hecker has treated parallelisms and repetitions in Akkadian epics as techniques of composition (cf. *Untersuchungen*, pp.154-160; cf. also M.E.Vogelzang, "Kill Anzu!"). Similarly B.Alster argued that the repetitions are a mark of oral transmission and were employed as a poetic device by oral poets (*Dumuzi's Dream*). Although, of course, it cannot be ruled out that parallelisms and repetitions could be employed as literary devices, the fact that they increase in number and extent through the process of transmission must not be ignored. Thus parallelisms and repetitions should be regarded as *developmental* tendencies unless it can be demonstrated that they were deliberately used as literary devices. The dominance of verbatim repetition over adaptation in grammar and contents (cf. J.S.Cooper, "Gilgameš Dreams of Enkidu", p.40) of the added parallel passages to their new context may indicate that expansions were carried out rather mechanically. With Alster's interpretation of parallel passages as signs of oral poetry there are major problems. How are we to imagine that the recitations of oral poets were committed to writing? Devices used in recitation may not have been necessary in dictation, which would have been much slower than the actual recitation. Why did parallelisms increase? Are we to regard the different versions as written copies of different recitations? Unless these questions can be satisfyingly answered, Alster's suggestion is to be rejected.

knowledge above the present hypotheses. The fact that a certain alteration was carried out during the transmission of a suggested empirical model does not mean anything for the transmission of Old Testament narratives - unless it conforms to a general tendency which can be related to the transmission of Old Testament narratives. It is thus one of the basic objections to be raised against the approach for which the work of J.H.Tigay is representative that it is content with showing what *may* have happened. To be sure, the *illustrative* value of the transmission of the Akkadian epics should not be ignored. However, the claim that it is of *demonstrative* value has to be rejected.

B. The Biblical Books of Samuel-Kings and Chronicles

The Old Testament itself provides examples of the literary development of narratives. In a comparative study of parallel texts[85] H.Ringgren[86] has, though not convincingly,[87] argued that the differences between them are to be taken as indications of oral transmission. Since direct dependency of one of these parallel texts on the other may not *a priori* be assumed and their relative temporal order is obscure we have to disregard them in our investigation. The case is different for the Biblical books of Samuel-Kings (Sam.-Kgs.) and Chronicles (Chr.). That the Chronicler's version is, at least generally, secondary compared to that presented in Sam.-Kgs. can hardly be doubted. The use of the Chronicler's work as an analogy for the transmission of Old Testament narratives in general was recently revived by W. Johnstone[88]. In principle, if the Chronicler's work can be shown to provide a permissible analogy, the fact that it is within the Old Testament would give it priority to others. However, the question remains whether the Chronicler's treat-

---

85 Ps.18_{2-51} // 2 Sam.22_{2-51}, Ps.14_{1-7} // Ps.53_{2-7}, Ps.40_{14-18} // Ps.70_{2-6}, Pss.57_{8-11}.60_{10-12} // Ps.$108_{2-5.10-12}$, Pss.105_{5-15}.96_{1-13}.106_{47} // 1 Chr.16_{8-36}, Is.2_{2-4} // Mi.4_{1-3}, Is.16_{6-12} // Jer.48_{29-36}, Is.37_{22-35} // 2 Kgs.19_{21-34}, Ob.1-6 // Jer.$49_{14-16.9-10}$, Jer.6_{12-15} // Jer.8_{10-12}, Jer.6_{22-24}.49_{19-21} // Jer.50_{41-46}, Jer10_{12-16} // Jer.50_{41-46}.

86 "Oral and Written Transmission".

87 Some of the deviations between these parallel texts can be explained by scribal error, others resemble those between Assyrian campaign accounts in their different versions, where they are not to be related to oral transmission; cf. below, p.101, n.125.

88 "Reactivating the Chronicles Analogy".

ment of his *Vorlage can* serve, or better: *should* serve, as an illustration of how narratives generally were transmitted.

Only two developmental stages are available for investigation, Sam.-Kgs. and Chr. Thus no general developmental tendencies can be isolated.[89] Furthermore, it is an open question whether the Chronicler aimed to *supersede* Sam.-Kgs. or whether he rather intended to *supplement* it. If the latter is true, we cannot even properly speak of two versions of the same work.[90] A third basic difficulty in investigating the Chronicler's editorial techniques lies in the establishment of his *Vorlage*. The similarity of narratives in Chr. to those in Sam.-Kgs. indicates that there is some kind of literary relationship between them, but the exact nature of this relationship is obscure.

The agreements of the Massoretic Text of Chr. (Chr.$_{MT}$) with the LXX of Sam.-Kgs.[91] (Sam.-Kgs.$_{LXX}$) indicate that the Chronicler's *Vorlage* was not identical with the MT of Sam.-Kgs. (Sam.-Kgs.$_{MT}$). On the other hand, there are also agreements of Chr.$_{MT}$ with Sam.-Kgs.$_{MT}$ against the Sam.-Kgs.$_{LXX}$. Further indication that the Chronicler's *Vorlage* differed from Sam.-Kgs.$_{MT}$ is provided by 4QSam^a. Unfortunately the fragments have not yet been properly published and thus we have to rely on the judgements and identifications of F.M.Cross and his pupils. Furthermore, only for a small part of the books of Samuel fragments appear to have been identified.[92]

Apart from the expected agreements of the MT of Sam. (Sam.$_{MT}$) and 4QSam^a against Chr.$_{MT}$,[93] there is a substantial number of agreements of Chr.$_{MT}$ and 4QSam^a against Sam.$_{MT}$,[94] Sam.$_{LXX}$ and Chr.$_{MT.LXX}$ against Sam.$_{MT}$,[95] and Sam.$_{MT}$ and Chr.$_{MT}$ against 4QSam^a.[96] In some of the cases where Chr.$_{MT}$ and

---

89 Cf. above p.12.

90 Indications for this may been seen in the Chronicler's different modes of referring to his sources. See below pp.66f.

91 Cf. M.Rehm, *Textkritische Untersuchungen*, pp.28-30.

92 Differences between Sam.$_{MT}$, 4QSam^a, and Chr.$_{MT}$ are listed below in appendix I, table 1.

93 Cf. below, appendix I, table 1, nos.3.5.6.7.11.12.15.17.22.23.30.31.32.33.(34.)35. 50.52.

94 Cf. below, appendix I, table 1, nos.1.2.4.8.14.18.20.24.25.26.27.28.29.37.38.39.40. 41.43.44.45.46.47.48.49.53.

95 Cf. below, appendix I, table 1, nos.8.9 (also against 4QSam^a).

96 Cf. below, appendix I, table 1, nos.16 (Sam.$_{LXX}$ agrees with 4QSam^a).42.

4QSam^{a} agree against Sam.$_{MT}$ the text of 4QSam^{a} is further supported by the LXX's text of the books of Samuel (Sam.$_{LXX}$).[97] The close relationship between the text of 4QSam^{a} and the LXX's *Vorlage* is indicated by a case like the one noted in appendix I, table 1, no.34 where 4QSam^{a} and Sam.$_{LXX}$ have the same erroneous reading[98] (2 Sam.7$_{23}$):

Sam.$_{MT}$: וֵאלֹהָיו

Sam.$_{LXX}$: *καὶ σκηνώματα* (וְאֹהָלִים)

4 QSam^{a}: ואהלים.

There are further instances, where all three Hebrew versions disagree with each other.[99] Passages, where Sam.$_{LXX}$[100], 4QSam^{a}[101], or Chr.$_{MT}$[102] appear to have combined the readings in Sam.$_{MT}$ and Chr.$_{MT}$ may be taken as indication for their secondary character compared to Sam.$_{MT}$, but a case like appendix I, table 1, no.10 (2 Sam.5$_{11}$ // 1 Chr.14$_{1}$), where Sam.$_{MT}$ appears to have combined readings represented by Sam.$_{LXX}$ and 4QSam^{a} // Chr.$_{MT}$ hints that a simple and consistent stemma of manuscripts cannot be established:

Sam.$_{MT}$: וְחָרָשֵׁי עֵץ וְחָרָשֵׁי אֶבֶן קִיר וַיִּבְנוּ

Sam.$_{LXX}$: *καὶ τέκτονας ξύλων καὶ τέκτονας λίθων καὶ ᾠκοδόμησαν*
(וְחָרָשֵׁי עֵץ וְחָרָשֵׁי אֶבֶן וַיִּבְנוּ)

4QSam^{a}: חרשי קיר [וי]בנו

Chr.$_{MT}$: וְחָרָשֵׁי קִיר וְחָרָשֵׁי עֵצִים לִבְנוֹת

Chr.$_{LXX}$: *καὶ οἰκοδόμους τοίχων καὶ τέκτωνας ξύλων τοῦ οἰκοδομῆσαι.*

Of the three possible *Vorlagen* for the Chronicler which are accessible, Sam.$_{MT}$, 4QSam^{a}, and the reconstructed *Vorlage* of Sam.$_{LXX}$, none agrees constantly with either Chr.$_{MT}$ or Chr.$_{LXX}$ against the others. Thus it is not probable that any one of them constituted the actual *Vorlage* for the Chronicler's work.[103] The matter is further complicated by the fact that for 2 Sam.11$_{2}$-1 Kgs.2$_{11}$ and 1 Kgs.22-2 Kgs.25 the *codex Vaticanus* does not exhibit the Old Greek transla-

---

97 Cf. below, appendix I, table 1, nos. 8.26.37.40.41.53.

98 Cf. also below, appendix I, table 1, no.16.

99 Cf. e.g. appendix I, table 1, nos.9.10.15.17.19.21.36.51.53.54. Certainly in nos.19. 51.53, perhaps in no.11, too, the reading of 4QSam^{a} is supported by the Sam.$_{LXX}$.

100 Cf. below, appendix I, table 1, nos.22.25.

101 Cf. below, appendix I, table 1, nos.51.53.

102 Cf. below, appendix I, table 1, no.8.

103 Cf. also W.E.Lemke, "Synoptic Problem".

tion.[104] Whether the Old Greek translation of these passages may have survived in a stratum of "Lucianic" mss. (LXX^{L}) is debated.[105] Thus it is apparent that differences between Sam.-Kgs.$_{MT}$ and Chr.$_{MT}$ may not simply be attributed to alterations carried out by the Chronicler,[106] indeed, not even to his *Vorlage*.

Further difficulties arise from the fact that both Sam.-Kgs. and Chr. were further transmitted after the Chronicler had used material paralleled in Sam.-Kgs. There is indication of deliberate alteration of the text of Sam., where the Chronicler has preserved an older text form. One well known example is that of the names of David's, Saul's, and Jonathan's sons:

Sam.$_{MT}$	Sam.$_{LXX}$	Chr.$_{MT}$	Chr.$_{LXX}$
אִישׁ בֹּשֶׁת[107]	Ιεβοσθε[108]	אֶשְׁבַּעַל[109]	Ασαβαλ[110] / Ισβααλ[111]
מְפִ(י)בֹשֶׁת[112]	Μεμφιβοσθε[113]	מְרִיב בַּעַל[114] / מְרִי־בַעַל	Μεριβααλ / Μαριβααλ
אֱלְיָדָע[115]	Ελιδαε	בְּעֶלְיָדָע[116]	Βαλεγδαε
יֹשֵׁב בַּשֶּׁבֶת[117]	Ιεβοσθε[118]	יָשָׁבְעָם[119]	Ιεσεβααλ

[104] Cf. H.St.J.Thackeray, *Septuagint and Jewish Worship*; D.Barthélemy, *Devanciers d'Aquila*, pp.91-143.

[105] Cf. D.Barthélemy, *Devanciers d'Aquila*, pp.126f; F.M.Cross, "History of the Biblical Text"; E.Tov, "Lucian and Proto-Lucian".

[106] This constitutes a fundamental objection against Brunet's (cf. "Le Chroniste I.II") or Th.Willi's (cf. *Chronik als Auslegung*) investigations of the Chronicler's editorial methods.

[107] 2 Sam.2$_{8.10.12.15}$ 3$_{7(pc\ mss).8.14.15}$ 4$_{5.8.12}$. For the Greek versions of the name in 2 Sam.4 cf. below.

[108] 2 Sam.2$_{8.10.12.15}$: Ιεβοσθε (LXX^{L}: Μεμφειβοσθε {boc$_2$}; Εισβααλ / Εισβαλ {e$_2$}), 2 Sam.3$_{7.8.11(>MT).14.15}$: Μεμφιβοσθε.

[109] 1 Chr.8$_{33}$ 9$_{39}$.

[110] 1 Chr.8$_{33}$.

[111] 1 Chr.9$_{39}$. S: Ισβααλ; B: Ιεβααλ; A: Βααλ.

[112] 2 Sam.4$_1$(only in 4Q Sam^a {מפיב[...}, MT: בֶּן־שָׁאוּל,).$_4$ 9$_{6.10.11.12.13}$ 16$_4$ 19$_{25.26.31}$ 21$_{7.8}$.

[113] 2 Sam.4$_{1.2(>MT).5.7(>MT).8.12}$ 4$_4$ 9$_{6.10.11.12.13}$ 16$_{1.4}$ 19$_{25.26.27(>MT).31}$ 21$_{7.8}$. (LXX^{L}: Μεμφιβααλ). In 2 Sam.4$_{5.8.12}$ the MT reads אִישׁ בֹּשֶׁת.

[114] 1 Chr.8$_{34}$ 9$_{40}$.

[115] 2 Sam.5$_{16}$.

[116] 1 Chr.14$_7$.

[117] 2 Sam.23$_8$.

[118] LXX^{L}: Ιεσβααλ.

[119] 1 Chr.11$_{11}$.

Further cases are:

בֵּית עַשְׁתָּרוֹת[120]	τὸ ᾿Ασταρτεῖον	בֵּית אֱלֹהֵיהֶם[121]	ἐν οἴκῳ θεοῦ αὐτῶν
עֲצַבֵּיהֶם[122]	τοὺς θεοὺς αὐτῶν[123]	אֱלֹהֵיהֶם[124]	τοὺς θεοὺς αὐτῶν

It is hardly conceivable that בֹּשֶׁת in the names of Saul's (and Jonathan's) sons would have been altered to בעל, whereas it is much more likely that בעל was replaced by the polemic בֹּשֶׁת. The same is true for the alteration of the name of one of David's sons from בְּעֶלְיָדָע to אֶלְיָדָע, whereby the offending reference to a foreign god would have been removed from the name of the great king's son. The Greek equivalents of יֹשֵׁב בַּשֶּׁבֶת and יָשָׁבְעָם indicate that the original form of the name probably was יִשְׁבַּעַל. While ישבעם can be regarded as a corruption of ישבעל, ישב בשבת is best explained by a scribal error following a deliberate alteration of ישבעל to יש בשת. Similarly אֱלֹהֵיהֶם, referring to the Philistine gods, was replaced by עֲצַבֵּיהֶם.[125] In the Chronicler's account of David's wars against the Philistines in 1 Chr.$14_{8\text{-}17}$ אֱלֹהִים, God, occurs six times.[126] Thus it seems unlikely that the Chronicler would have replaced עֲצַבֵּיהֶם by אֱלֹהֵיהֶם and thus have created a possible ambiguity. Again, the Chronicler's reading appears to be the older one.

While the Chronicler, if he does not retain the divine name from Sam.-Kgs., usually replaces יהוה with אֱלֹהִים,[127] there are a few instances where he has יהוה whereas Sam.-Kgs. have אֱלֹהִים.[128] In some passages יהוה or אֱלֹהִים is used

---

120 1 Sam.31_{10}.

121 1 Chr.10_{10}.

122 2 Sam.5_{21}.

123 Usually עָצָב is represented by the LXX with *γλυπτός* (Ps. $106_{36.38}$ Is.46_1) or *εἴδωλον* (1 Sam.31_9 1 Chr.10_9 2 Chr.24_{18} Ps.115_4 135_{15} Hos.4_{17} 8_4 13_2 14_9 Mi.1_7 Za.13_2 Is.10_{11} and only in 2 Sam.5_{21} with *θεός*.

124 1 Chr.14_{12}.

125 2 Sam.5_{21} // 1 Chr.14_{12}. Sam.$_{LXX}$ (*τοὺς θεοὺς αὐτῶν*) preserved the older reading.

126 Vv.10.11.13(2x).15.16. The Tetragrammaton is used once (v.16). The parallel passage in 2 Sam.$5_{17\text{-}25}$ consistently has יהוה (vv.19{2x}.20.23.24.25).

127 2 Sam.23_{17}//1 Chr.11_{19}, 2 Sam.6_5//1 Chr.13_8, 2 Sam.$6_{9(2x)}$//1 Chr.$13_{12(2x)}$, 2 Sam.6_{11}//1 Chr.13_{13}, 2 Sam.5_{18}//1 Chr.14_{10}, 2 Sam.5_{20}//1 Chr.14_{11}, 2 Sam.5_{23}//1 Chr.14_{14}, 2 Sam.5_{24}//1 Chr.14_{15}, 2 Sam.5_{25}//1 Chr.14_{16}, 2 Sam.$6_{17(2x)}$//1 Chr.$16_{1(2x)}$, 2 Sam.7_3//1 Chr.17_2, 2 Sam.7_4//1 Chr.17_3, 2 Sam.7_{18}//1 Chr.17_{16}, 2 Sam.7_{19}//1 Chr.17_{17}, 2 Sam.24_{10}//1 Chr.21_8, 2 Sam.24_{17}//1 Chr.21_{17}, 1 Kgs.3_5//2 Chr.1_7, 1 Kgs.6_1//2 Chr.3_3, 1 Kgs.7_{48}//2 Chr.4_{19}, 1 Kgs.7_{51}//2 Chr.5_1, 1 Kgs.8_{11}//2 Chr.5_{14}, 1 Kgs.8_{63}//2 Chr.7_5, 1 Kgs.10_9//2 Chr.9_8 (אֱלֹהֶיךָ), 1 Kgs.12_{15}//2 Chr.10_{15}, 1 Kgs.15_{15}//2 Chr.15_{18}, 1 Kgs.22_6//2 Chr.18_5 (הָאֱלֹהִים > אֲדֹנָי), 2 Kgs.11_3//2 Chr.22_{12}, 2 Kgs.11_{10}//2 Chr.23_9, 2 Kgs.22_{19}//2 Chr.34_{27}.

128 2 Sam.6_{12}//1 Chr.15_{25}, 2 Sam.6_{17}//1 Chr.16_1, 2 Sam.7_2//1 Chr.17_1, 1 Kgs.12_{22}//2

consistently by Sam.-Kgs., but not in Chr.[129] No reason is apparent why the Chronicler should have removed this uniformity. We either have to assume that in these cases the Chronicler's *Vorlage* differed from Sam.-Kgs.,[130] or that he was not consistent in his redactorial treatment, or that he was in a certain way consistent, but we are unable to follow his intentions. Each of these conclusions presents problems for using the Chronicler's work as an empirical model for the literary development of Old Testament narratives in general, since, as is demanded by the methodological requirements pointed out above, only general tendencies of redactorial treatment may be referred to.

The Chronicler's references to non-extant literary works[131] indicate a further difficulty for an investigation of the his way of treating his *Vorlagen*.

Chr.11_{2}.

129 2 Sam.5_{19}(יהוה in vv.19{2x}.20) // 1 Chr.14_{10} (יהוה in v.10, אֱלֹהִים in vv.10.11), 2 Sam.$24_{10.17}$ (יהוה in vv.1.3 {יהוה אֱלֹהֶיךָ}.10{2x}.11.12.14.15.16.17.18.21.23 {יהוה אֱלֹהֶיךָ}.24 {יהוה אֱלֹהַי}.25{2x}) // 1 Chr.$21_{8.17}$ (יהוה in vv.2.9.10.11.12{2x}.13.14.15 {2x}.16.17{יהוה אֱלֹהַי}.18.19.26.27. 28.29.30; 22_{1}{יהוה הָאֱלֹהִים}; אֱלֹהִים in vv.8.15. 17), 1 Kgs.6_{1} (יהוה in vv.1.3) // 2 Chr.3_{3} (יהוה in v.1, הָאֱלֹהִים in v.3), 1 Kgs.$7_{48.51}$(בֵּית יהוה in vv.45. 48.51{2x}) // 2 Chr.4_{19} 5_{1}(בֵּית יהוה in 6_{16} 5_{1}, בֵּית הָאֱלֹהִים in 4_{19} 5_{1}), 1 Kgs.8_{11}(יהוה in vv.10.11{2x}.12) // 2 Chr.5_{14} (יהוה in vv.13{3x}. 14, הָאֱלֹהִים in v.14), 1 Kgs.8_{63}(יהוה in vv.62.63{2x})//2 Chr.5_{14}(יהוה in vv.4.6{2x}, הָאֱלֹהִים in v.5), 1 Kgs.10_{9} (יהוה in vv.1.5.9{יהוה אֱלֹהֶיךָ}.9.12) // 2 Chr.9_{8}(יהוה in vv.4.8{2x יהוה אֱלֹהֶיךָ}.11, אֱלֹהִים in v.8{אֱלֹהֶיךָ}), 1 Kgs.12_{15}(2x יהוה) // 2 Chr.10_{15} (הָאֱלֹהִים ,יהוה), 1 Kgs.15_{15} (יהוה in vv.14.15) // 2 Chr.15_{18} (יהוה in vv.8.9{יהוה אֱלֹהָיו}.11.12{יהוה אֱלֹהֵי אֲבוֹתֵיהֶם}.13{לַיהוה אֱלֹהֵי־יִשְׂרָאֵל}.14.15, אֱלֹהִים in v.18), 1 Kgs.22_{6}(אֲדֹנָי)$_{.14}${יהוה in vv.5.{6.}7.8.11.12.14 {2x}.15.16.17.19{2x}.20.21{2x}.23{2x}.24. 28) // 2 Chr. $18_{5.13}$(יהוה in vv.4.6.7.10.11. 13.15.16.18{2x}.19.20{2x}.22.23.27, אֱלֹהִים in vv.5.13{אֱלֹהַי}, 2 Kgs.$11_{3.4.10}$(יהוה in vv.3.4{2x}.6.10.13.15) // 2 Chr.2_{12} $3_{2.3.9}$(יהוה in vv.5.6{2x}12.14, ìëäîà אֱלֹהִים in 2_{12} $3_{3.9}$), 2 Kgs.22_{3-5} (בֵּית יהוה in vv.3.4.5{2x}) // 2 Chr.34_{8-10}(בֵּית יהוה in vv.8. 10 {2x}, בֵּית אֱלֹהִים in v.9), 2 Kgs.22_{19}(יהוה in vv.15. 16.18.18{יהוה אֱלֹהֵי יִשְׂרָאֵל}.19) // 2 Chr.34_{27} (יהוה in vv.23{יהוה אֱלֹהֵי יִשְׂרָאֵל}.24.26 {יהוה אֱלֹהֵי יִשְׂרָאֵל}, אֱלֹהִים in v.27).

130 As for at least the books of Samuel, there is strong indication that the Chronicler's *Vorlage* did indeed differ from the MT; cf. above.

131 It is noteworthy that the Chronicler does not state expressly that he used these texts as *sources*. The fact that he does not always refer to their contents, and in those cases where he mentions specific contents he often refers to matters which are dealt with in Chronicles only briefly or not at all, rather suggests that the Chronicler intended to refer to these texts for further information. This is also shown by his reference to יֶתֶר / שְׁאָר which indicates that these texts for certain matters provided more information than his work. It seems nevertheless plausible that the Chronicler incorporated or at least claimed to have incorporated material from these works in his and since they are commonly referred to as the Chronicler's "sources" we shall use this term. The Chronicler's major *source* references are given below in appendix I, table 2.

While for David's reign the description of the Chronicler's sources (1 Chr.29_{29-30}) might indeed match the account in Sam.-Kgs., the case is different for the succeeding kings. Already a superficial comparison of the Chronicler's remarks on the contents of the quoted *sources* with the those of Kgs. shows that the former and the latter cannot be identical.[132] The "Book of the Kings of Judah and Israel is quoted for the reigns of Asa (2 Chr.16_{11} -סֵפֶר הַמְּלָכִים לִיהוּדָה וְיִשְׂרָאֵל), Amaziah (2 Chr.25_{26} -סֵפֶר מַלְכֵי־יְהוּדָה וְיִשְׂרָאֵל), and Ahaz (2 Chr.28_{26} - סֵפֶר מַלְכֵי־יְהוּדָה וְיִשְׂרָאֵל). In each case the Chronicler's account is more extensive than that of Kgs. It is, therefore, hardly conceivable that the Chronicler would refer to the Biblical books of Kings for additional information. Thus, although for Hezekiah's reign Kgs. provides a more detailed account than the Chronicler, the fact that the "Book of the Kings of Judah and Israel" contained "the vision of Isaiah, the prophet, the son of Amoz" (2 Chr.32_{32} - הִנָּם כְּתוּבִים בַּחֲזוֹן יְשַׁעְיָהוּ בֶן־אָמוֹץ הַנָּבִיא עַל־סֵפֶר מַלְכֵי־יְהוּדָה וְיִשְׂרָאֵל) rules out the possibility that with the mention of the former a canonical source is referred to.

The same is true for the "Book of the Kings of Israel and Judah" (סֵפֶר מַלְכֵי־יִשְׂרָאֵל וִיהוּדָה), which is mentioned by the Chronicler as having contained accounts of Jotham's wars (2 Chr.27_{7}), which are not found in Kgs. The same *source* is cited for more information on Jehoiakim's reign (2 Chr.36_{8}), for which the accounts in Chr. and Kgs. are of about the same length. Only for Josiah's reign the description of the Chronicler's *source* (חֲסָדָיו - 2 Chr.35_{26-27}) might match the account in Kings, but the identification of one with the other is already ruled out by other references to the same work.

The "Acts of the Kings of Israel" (דִּבְרֵי מַלְכֵי יִשְׂרָאֵל) are mentioned by the Chronicler as having contained Manasseh's prayer and the speeches of seers (תְּפִלָּתוֹ אֶל־אֱלֹהָיו וְדִבְרֵי הַחֹזִים הַמְדַבְּרִים אֵלָיו בְּשֵׁם יְהוָה אֱלֹהֵי יִשְׂרָאֵל - 2 Chr.33_{18}). A prayer by Manasseh has not been preserved in Kgs. There is a summary of

---

[132] The only possible exception is quoted in 2 Chr.9_{29} for Solomon's reign: וּשְׁאָר דִּבְרֵי שְׁלֹמֹה הָרִאשֹׁנִים וְהָאַחֲרוֹנִים הֲלֹא־הֵם כְּתוּבִים עַל־דִּבְרֵי נָתָן הַנָּבִיא וְעַל־נְבוּאַת אֲחִיָּה הַשִּׁילוֹנִי וּבַחֲזוֹת יֶעְדִּי הַחֹזֶה עַל־יָרָבְעָם בֶּן־נְבָט. As the repetition of the prepositions עַל and בְּ shows, three distinct works are referred to. While a speech of Nathan is found in 1 Kgs.1_{22-27} and a prophecy of Ahijah in 1 Kgs.11_{26-39}, Iddo is not mentioned in the canonical Book of Kings. It is interesting to note that only in this *source* reference שְׁאָר is used instead of the more common יֶתֶר.

prophetic speeches in 2 Kgs.21_{10-15}, which was not taken over into Chr. The passage in Kgs. is introduced with וַיְדַבֵּר יְהוָה בְּיַד־עֲבָדָיו הַנְּבִיאִים לֵאמֹר (2 Kgs.21_{10}), but the Chronicler mentions his *source* as having contained both the prophetic speeches and Manasseh's prayer. The plural form דִּבְרֵי הַחֹזִים would have suited several speeches better than one summary. דִּבְרֵי חוֹזָי are mentioned as having contained Manasseh's prayer, building operations and other deeds (2 Chr.33_{19}). The striking similarity between דברי החזים (V.18) and דברי חוזי (V.19) may indicate textual corruption of this passage, which thus originally may have contained only one *source* reference.

The "Midrash of the Book of Kings" (מִדְרַשׁ סֵפֶר הַמְּלָכִים) is mentioned as having contained information on Jehoash's son, taxes introduced by him, and his building operations in the Temple (2 Chr.24_{27}). Since these are not described in Kgs. the מִדְרַשׁ is not to be regarded as part or whole of the latter.

The Chronicler mentions the "Words of Shemaiah the prophet and of Iddo the Seer" (דִּבְרֵי שְׁמַעְיָה הַנָּבִיא וְעִדּוֹ הַחֹזֶה - 2 Chr.12_{15}) as *source* for his account on Rehoboam's reign. No details about the contents of this *source* are stated. A reference to wars between Rehoboam and Jeroboam (מִלְחֲמוֹת רְחַבְעָם וְיָרָבְעָם כָּל־הַיָּמִים - 2 Chr.12_{15}) given immediately after the mention of the *source* has a parallel in 1 Kgs.14_{30} (וּמִלְחָמָה הָיְתָה בֵין־רְחַבְעָם וּבֵין יָרָבְעָם כָּל־הַיָּמִים) where it is found in the same position. Since, however, the information provided in Kgs. does not exceed that given by the Chronicler himself, it does not seem probable that the Chronicler referred to part or whole of Kgs.

The Chronicler's accounts of Abijah's (2 Chr.13), Jehoshaphat's (1 Chr.17-21_1), and Uzziah/Azariah's (2 Chr.26) reigns are more extensive than their counterparts in Kgs. (1 Kgs.15_{1-8}, 1 Kgs.22_{1-51}, 2 Kgs.14_{21f}.15_{1-7}). Thus the "Midrash of the Prophet Iddo" (מִדְרַשׁ הַנָּבִיא עִדּוֹ - 2 Chr.13_{22}), the "Words of Jehu, Son of Hanani" which are described as having been inserted in the "Book of the Kings of Israel" (דִּבְרֵי יֵהוּא בֶן־חֲנָנִי אֲשֶׁר הֹעֲלָה עַל־סֵפֶר מַלְכֵי יִשְׂרָאֵל - 2 Chr.20_{34}),[133] and the Acts of Uzziah, Written by Isaiah, Son of Amos, the Prophet (דִּבְרֵי עֻזִּיָּהוּ הָרִאשֹׁנִים וְהָאַחֲרֹנִים כָּתַב יְשַׁעְיָהוּ בֶן־אָמוֹץ הַנָּבִיא - 2 Chr.26_{22}) cannot be identified with part or whole of Kgs.

---

133 The "Book of the Kings of Israel" is also mentioned in 1 Chr.9_1 as having contained genealogies of all of Israel.

Various solutions to this *synoptic problem* have been suggested. The common features and the differences have been thought to be best explained by the assumption that Sam.-Kgs. and Chr. go back to a common source, the "Book of the Kings of Judah and Israel" / "Book of the Kings of Israel and Judah" (referred to in Chr.) being equated with[134] or regarded as being dependent on[135] "the Book of the Chronicles of Judah" plus "the Book of the Chronicles of Israel" (referred to in Kgs.),[136] which Sam.-Kgs. and Chr. used independently. This would imply that the Chronicler's *Vorlage* can be reconstructed only where Chr. agrees with Sam.-Kgs. Material in Chr., not found in Sam.-Kgs. might have been abbreviated by the Chronicler and omitted by Sam.-Kgs. or added by the Chronicler. In such cases where Sam.-Kgs. and Chr. differed from each other, it would be impossible to determine which is closer to the common *Vorlage*. Thus any attempt to analyze the Chronicler's editorial method would have to disregard the greatest part of the Chronicler's work. No firm conclusions would be possible. However, this suggestion does not take account of the fact that there is a marked stylistic and grammatical difference in Chr. between the passages paralleled in Sam.-Kgs. and the Chronicler's *Sondergut*[137] and that the Chronicler's *source* references, with the exceptions of 1 Chr.$29_{29\text{-}30}$ and 2 Chr.$35_{26\text{-}27}$, appear in the same place within the account of a given king's reign where they are found in Kgs., even in those cases, where the *source* reference is not given at the end of the account (2 Chr.16_{11}//1 Kgs.15_{23}, 2 Chr.20_{34}//1 Kgs.22_{46}, 2 Chr.25_{26}//2 Kgs.14_{15}). For the accounts of Jehoiachin's and Zedekiah's reigs neither in Kgs. nor in Chr. a *source* reference is given. This renders it improbable that the Chronicler's *Sondergut* should stem from a *common Vorlage*.

---

134 Thus C.F.Keil, *Biblischer Commentar über die nachexilischen Geschichtsbücher*, p.25; E.König, *Einleitung*, pp.270-272, who further assumes that the Chronicler used Kgs., too.

135 Thus E.Bertheau, *Chronik*, p.XLf.

136 The fact that Chronicles concentrates on Judean affairs would render the "Book of the Chronicles of Israel" unnecessary as a source for the Chronicler but, as has been pointed out by de W.M.L. de Wette (*Kritischer Versuch*, p.37) against J.G.Eichhorn, it is unlikely that the Chronicler would have replaced "Judah" in the source's title with "Judah and Israel".

137 Cf. S.R.Driver, *Introduction*, pp.535-540, and "Speeches"; A.Kropat, *Syntax*; R.Polzin, *Late Biblical Hebrew*, pp.28-84.

A.Klostermann therefore suggested that the Chronicler used an enlarged and supplemented version of Kgs.[138] If this should be true, the lost intermediate stage between Kgs. and Chr. would provide a serious obstacle for analyzing the Chronicler's editorial method. His sources for enlarging Kgs., if there had been any, would have been lost. Again, material found in Chr. but not in Kgs. may have been abbreviated from the *Vorlage* rather than added.

This difficulty can be avoided if a direct dependency of Chr. on Kgs. is presupposed. The similarity in style between the Chronicler's *Sondergut* and alterations carried out by him and the fact that the Chronicler, with only a few exceptions, gives his references parallel to the *source* references in Kgs., has prompted the conclusion that material peculiar to Chr. was created by the Chronicler himself and that his *source* references are imaginary.[139] It is, however, difficult to find a motive for the Chronicler's inclusion of imaginary *source* references. That the reference to sources was an element of Deuteronomistic style adopted by the Chronicler[140] or a claim of having used the sources referred to in Kgs.[141] or their interpretation[142] cannot be demonstrated. If the Chronicler followed Deuteronomistic style, why did he not take over the reference formula prominent in Kgs.,

יֶתֶר דִּבְרֵי ... ([וְ{כָל} גְּבוּרָתוֹ] {וְכָל} אֲשֶׁר עָשָׂה) ?[143]

On the other hand, the Chronicler's הָרִאשֹׁנִים וְהָאַחֲרֹנִים[144] is not found in

---

[138] "Chronik", pp.96f, followed by W.Rudolph, *Chronikbücher*, p.Xf; O.Eißfeldt, *Einleitung*, p.725.

[139] Thus C.C.Torrey, "Chronicler", p.223; J.Becker, *1 Chronik*, p.7; K.Galling, *Chronik*, p.8; Th.Willi, *Chronik als Auslegung*, p.233ff; R.Smend, *Entstehung des Altes Testaments*, p.228f.

[140] Cf. M.Noth, *Überlieferungsgeschichtliche Studien I*, p.175; K.Galling, *Chronik*, p.8; H.G.M.Williamson, *1 and 2 Chronicles*, pp.17-19.

[141] Cf. R.Smend, *Entstehung des Altes Testaments*, p.228f; Th.Willi, *Chronik als Auslegung*, p.233.

[142] Cf. J.Becker, *1 Chronik*, p.7; Th.Willi, *Chronik als Auslegung*, p.233.

[143] Of the references paralleled in Chronicles the complete formula is present in: 1 Kgs.15_{23} 2 Kgs.20_{20},
(. . .) missing in: 2 Kgs.14_{18},
[. . .] missing in: 1 Kgs.11_{41} 1 Kgs.14_{29} 1 Kgs.15_{7} 2 Kgs.12_{20} 2 Kgs.15_{6} 2 Kgs.15_{36} 2 Kgs.16_{19} 2 Kgs.21_{17} 2 Kgs.23_{28} 2 Kgs.24_{5},
{ . . . } missing in 1 Kgs.22_{46} 2 Kgs.15_{36} 2 Kgs.16_{19}.

[144] Cf. 1 Chr.29_{29-30} 2 Chr.9_{29} 2 Chr.12_{15} 2 Chr.16_{11} 2 Chr.20_{34} 2 Chr.25_{26} 2 Chr.26_{21} 2 Chr.28_{26} 2 Chr.35_{26-27}.

the parallel passages in Kgs. Furthermore, there is not a single case where the names of the *sources* mentioned in Kgs. and Chr. agree. The same is true for the description of their contents. Where these are described in Kgs., the Chronicler's *Sondergut* generally does not match them.[145] This is not to argue that the Chronicler could not have used Kgs.' sources, but the suggestion that he *claimed* to have used them is not tenable. It is difficult to see how the Chronicler's readers should have been able to recognize that he claimed to have used the *sources* mentioned in Kgs. or why and how he should have interpreted the *source* references given there. The fact that the Chronicler followed the order of narration in Kgs. shows his dependency on his *Vorlage* but does not necessarily devaluate the authenticity of the sources to which he referred. From the fact that the Chronicler's extra-canonical sources are not extant does not follow that they never existed.[146]

Two main features of the Chronicler's *source* references need to be explained: 1. the Chronicler's main source, 'Sam.-Kgs.'[147], is not mentioned and 2. there is a linguistic unevenness between the passages paralleled in Sam.-Kgs. and the Chronicler's *Sondergut*, which reflects his style. A possible solution to both problems is the assumption that the Chronicler used two different modes of reference. He referred to 'Sam.-Kgs.' by quoting it (almost) verbatim with hardly any modernization of syntax or vocabulary. He may have been able to assume that his readers knew from where he was quoting, whereas he treated his other sources in a different manner, using his own style and vocabulary[148], and referred to them

---

[145] The "Book of the Chronicles of Judah" (סֵפֶר דִּבְרֵי הַיָּמִים לְמַלְכֵי יְהוּדָה) is described in Kgs. as having contained names of cities built by Asa (1 Kgs.15_{23}). In 1 Kgs.15_{22} // 2 Chr.16_{6} the building of Geba is mentioned. Since 2 Chr.$14_{6\text{-}7}$ do not give names of the cities built, there is no reason to assume that the Chronicler claimed to have used Kgs.' sources. For Manasseh's reign the source reference in Kgs. mentions expressly Manasseh's sin (2 Kgs.21_{17}). Contrarily Chronicles places much emphasis on Manasseh's conversion. There only remains the case of Kgs.' source reference for Hezekiah's reign, where the building of the pool, the conduit, and the bringing of water into the city is noted (2 Kgs.21_{17}). This is indeed reported in 2 Chr.$32_{3\text{-}4}$.

[146] *Contra* Th.Willi, *Chronik als Auslegung*, p.232.

[147] Quotation marks are used to indicate that the Chronicler's *Vorlage* was related to but not identical with the the Masoretic Text of Sam.-Kgs.

[148] Thus S.R.Driver's assumption that if the Chronicler used the quoted sources these "must have been composed at a date scarcely earlier that that of Chronicles itself, and by an author writing in a similar style and with a similar aim" (*Introduction*, pp.530f),

by mentioning their title so that his readers could consult them for further information.[149] This, however, is mere speculation.

The difficulties outlined above indicate that a comparison between Sam.-Kgs. and Chr. *on its own* cannot yield a valid empirical model for the transmission of narratives in general. However, a general agreement of the Chronicler's editorial methods with tendencies of redactorial treatment apparent in a suggested empirical model would constitute further confirmation of the appropriateness of the latter as a possible analogy to the transmission of Old Testament narratives. Like the literary development of Akkadian epics the Chronicler's treatment of his *Vorlage* may be of illustrative, even of confirmative, but not of demonstrative value. We shall thus, in spite of the methodological problems involved, examine the differences between Sam.-Kgs. and Chr. below in comparison with those between different versions of another possible empirical model, Assyrian campaign accounts.

III. A New Analogy: Assyrian Royal *Annals*

There is a third body of literature which, according to our methodological considerations outlined above, is better suited to provide an analogy to the kind of literary development that may have occurred in the transmission of Old Testament narratives - Assyrian Royal *annals*.[1] The relative order of the extant manuscripts, and in many cases even their dates, can be established. Their close temporal sequence renders it probable that (almost) successive versions are available. The decisive advantage, however, lies in the fact that the *late* versions of Assyrian

---

is possible, but not necessary.

[149] This is supported by the presence of יֶתֶר and שְׁאָר in the references to extra-canonical material.

[1] This term will be used for convenience although campaign accounts were also presented in geographic or thematic order.
M.Liverani suggested that the royal titulary provides a good opportunity to follow up the redactors' intentions and that "every variation in it is always the result of a decision deeply considered and not at all casual" ("Critique of Variants", p.231). However, it seems more likely that in titularies compared to campaign accounts proper we would find a higher ratio of stock-expressions which could be altered and exchanged without "deeply considered" motivations.

annals and Old Testament narratives do not exhibit significant differences in structure.[2] First the literary developments of Sennacherib's and Aššurbanipal's campaign accounts will be analyzed and in the light of the results obtained the differences between Sam.-Kgs. and Chr. will then be evaluated.

A. The Macrostructural Development of Assyrian Royal *Annals*

The purpose of this part of the present investigation is to analyze the changes that occurred in the process of continuous rewriting or re-editing of Assyrian *annals*. The fact that Assyrian campaign accounts may not serve as an analogy for changes that may have occurred during the process of oral transmission which is commonly regarded as having played an important rôle in the formation of Old Testament narratives does not render them invalid as an empirical model. It only means that we have to concentrate on the process of transmission after the narratives were committed to writing, which accords with the methodology of the present investigation.[3]

An analysis of the development of the narrative structure of Assyrian *annals* is faced with various difficulties. The narratives in the *annals* of the Assyrian kings are generally brief, which means that rise and decline of tension - if it is traceable at all - takes place within a small amount of space and that only few rhetorical devices are employed to mark a narrative climax. Various accounts, especially among those of Aššurbanipal's campaigns, relate a conflict and its resolution without significant differences in the rhetorical level throughout the narrative. Already in their earliest extant versions they are reduced to a minimum of content.

A further obstacle is provided by the fact that the campaign accounts are not freely composed narratives, but are pre-shaped by the events which they describe. Their primary purpose is not to entertain but rather to convey information.

---

2 The decision which differences between narratives are taken as *significant* is, of course, necessarily subjective. For our purpose a difference between the *late stages* of two narratives may be regarded as *significant* if it can be related to trends of redactorial treatment which cannot be imagined as having produced Old Testament narratives in their present form, e.g. the difference between Old Testament narratives and the *late stages* of the epics investigated above.

3 Cf. above, pp.13-14.

Thus within the narratives there are lists of enemies, booty, captives *etc.* which seem to disturb the progression of the plot. Since these texts were written in a different culture, ideology and personal preferences of authors and listeners as well as literary conventions are likely to have been different from ours. Some remarks may have increased attention among listeners/readers merely by their contents and we may not be able to discern these.[4]

It has already been mentioned that only few rhetorical devices to mark the discourse *profile* are employed in the texts under question. Although conclusions thus might be based on little information, one may expect that these devices were employed in those parts of the text which the author wanted to emphasize. Criteria used here for the identification of a narrative climax are, for example:

Form:

- accumulation of verbs[5]
- accumulation of adverbs, adverbial phrases[6]
- accumulation of nouns, adjectives[7]
- direct speech[8]
- parallelisms[9]
- EEN constructions[10]
- unusual reports of common events[11]

---

4 Examples may be seen in the mentions of the scattering of salt (Fv_{56} // Avi_{79} // Tv_7; DT 257 {cf. Th.Bauer, *Inschriftenwerk*, p.61}, K 13755 {cf. Th.Bauer, *Inschriftenwerk*, p.60}, K 4455 {cf. Th.Bauer, *Inschriftenwerk*, p.61} and of horses as tribute by IT (cf. below, p.152f, n.314).

5 Accumulation of verbs corresponds to R.E.Longacre's "change of pace", which is one of the possibilities to mark a surface structure *peak*. Either these verbs are almost synonymous, which means that the narrator *rests* at a point of a narrative or they describe successive action. The plot *accelerates*.

6 In narratives verbs are of special importance. Thus adverbs and adverbial phrases, describing and intensifying the related actions, are likely to be employed at points of special emphasis (cf. R.E.Longacre, *Grammar of Discourse*, p.28).

7 This corresponds to the accumulation of verbs. A high ratio of nouns or adjectives retards the narrative.

8 Direct speech, if not employed to extensively, increases the vividness of a narrative. It is likely to be quoted in such part the narrator wishes to emphasize (cf. R.E.Longacre, *Grammar of Discourse*, pp.30-32.

9 Parallelisms denote a higher level of speech and thus are likely to be used at points of importance.

10 EEN stands for *e̲llu, e̲bbu, n̲amru*, ("clear, bright, shining") one of the examples used by H.Ehelolf to demonstrate the principle of ordering words or phrases according to increasing length, which he discovered in Assyrian texts (cf. *Wortfolgeprinzip*). Fales, "A Literary Code", uses the term with a different reference. He employs it for any construction consisting of three or more parts, regardless of length or meaning of the com-

Content:

- immediate confrontation of the main participants[12]
- resolution of conflict[13]
- unusual events reported.[14]

Furthermore, it is presumed here that the distinction between *main line* which is generally characterized by verbs in Preterite Indicative, and *supportive material* conforms with different levels of importance and emphasis. It is the *main line* that carries the narrative forward.[15]

Because of space limitations and to avoid unnecessary repetition, the developments of five campaign accounts (Sennacherib's first campaign,

---

ponents. Here it is used only for those constructions the parts of which a) belong to the same *category* and b) are of increasing length. Both features are essential. Ehelolf discovered that the principle worked for single words as well as for phrases. Since a series of single words may be triggered by the mention of the first of these, (e.g. booty items) and such series are not uncommon, they will not receive special attention here. The case is different with EEN constructions that involve phrases or sentences. Belonging to the same category means that either they are *descriptive* with roughly the same meaning or function, or they are *narrative* carrying the plot forward. The increasing length means increasing emphasis, with the last member stressed most. Such constructions can consist of short components, eg. the common expression *appul / aqqur / ina išāti aqmu* ("I destroyed / I devastated / I burned with fire" {e.g. Chic. i_{18f}}), or longer ones as, for example:

rēmu aršīšuma
māru ṣīt libbīšu utīrma arîmšu
ḫalṣē ša [e]li Baʾli šar Ṣurri urakkisu apṭur
ina tâmtim u nābali gerrētīšu mala uṣabbitu apti
"I took pity on him,
his own son I graciously gave back to him,
the fortifications which against Baʾlu, the king of Tyre, I had built, I tore down;
by sea and land his approaches, as many as I had seized, I opened" ($Bii_{59\text{-}64}$ - for the designations of mss. cf. below, pp.71f.96f).

11 In the accounts of the various campaigns of Sennacherib and Aššurbanipal certain events are repeatedly narrated, e.g. the arrival of a messenger at the Assyrian court reporting the rebellion of a vassal, or the mustering of the Assyrian army. When these events are described with unusual vivdness, prolexity and/or vocabulary we might suspect that the narrator wanted to place emphasis on them. The same is true for the reports of unusual events, which, however, may be difficult to identify.

12 This contrasts with R.E.Longacre's reference to a "crowded stage" as indication of *peak* sections (cf. *Grammar of Discourse*, p.27).

13 The movement of the two major opponents towards each other causes an increase in tension, which is resolved in the mention of a battle and/or an Assyrian victory.

14 Cf. above, p.69, n.4.

15 Evidence for the validity of this assumption can be found e.g. in Bull 4's treatment of its sources. There the *main line* has received far less alteration than the *supportive material*; cf. below.

Aššurbanipal's two Egyptian campaigns, and the accounts of the submissions of Gyges and of Ba'alu, Mugallu, Iakinlu, and Sandišarme)[16] serve as examples. Corresponding and contrasting phenomena in the development of further accounts will be noted briefly. *Participant orientation* patterns and *discourse profiles* of the latter will be presented with short comments in appendices. The five accounts have been selected because of their variety in structure and contents and because they constitute clear examples for developmental trends.

The conditions for an investigation of the redactorial trends underlying the alterations carried out between the different versions of accounts of Sennacherib's first campaign are excellent. A sufficient number manuscripts of the same kind, namely Cylinder(s) and Prisms, which were used as foundation deposits[17] are preserved which renders it possible to explore the consistency of redactorial treatment. Reports on Sennacherib's campaigns are also given as Bull inscriptions, and the text version of one of them, too, will be considered.[18]

1. Sennacherib's First Campaign

The earliest extant account of Sennacherib's first campaign,[19] in the course of which he defeated Merodach-baladan is that of BM 113203[20]. Presumably written shortly after this campaign and before the next one, it only relates this campaign. The so-called "Bellino Cylinder"[21] (K 1680), which is dated to 702 B.C.,[22] exhibits accounts of the first two campaigns. Reports of the first three campaigns are furnished by the so-called "Rassam Cylinder"[23] (87-7-19,1),

---

16 We shall also refer to the developments of accounts of Sennacherib's second and third campaigns, and Aššurbanipal's campaigns against Kirbit, Aḫšeri, Urtaku, Teummān, Ummanaldasi, Dunanu, and against Arabs.

17 Cf. R.Ellis, *Foundation Deposits*, pp.108-113.

18 For the texts of the accounts for Sennacherib's first campaign cf. R.Borger, *Babylonisch-Assyrische Lesestücke*, pp. 68-71, and D.D.Luckenbill, *Annals*, pp. 49-55 (BM 113203), pp.55-60 (Bellino Cylinder), pp.23-26 (Chicago-Taylor Prisms), pp.66f (Borger's "Bull 4"); for the designations of mss. cf. below.

19 For the chronology of this period cf. J.A.Brinkman, "Merodach-baladan II", pp.22-27.

20 For manuscripts duplicating the text of Sennacherib's inscriptions quoted here cf. R.Borger, *Babylonisch-Assyrische Lesestücke*, pp.64-67.

21 Henceforth "Bell.".

22 Cf. D.D.Luckenbill, *Annals*, p.20.

23 Henceforth "Rass.". The line-count is given according to parallel passages in the Chicago prism.

which is dated to 700 B.C.[24] Other mss. reporting three campaigns only will not be taken into consideration. Of importance are, however, the accounts of the Chicago- and the Taylor-prisms, dated in 689 B.C., resp. 691 B.C., reporting eight campaigns.[25] These two manuscripts differ from each other only in orthography and will therefore be treated here as a single text version.[26] The Bull inscription mentioned above is that of Bull 4, written after Sennacherib's sixth campaign.

Before the literary development of reports on Sennacherib's first campaign can be investigated the literary dependencies of the manuscripts have to be established. For the accounts of Sennacherib's second campaign L.D.Levine[27] suggested the following stemma:

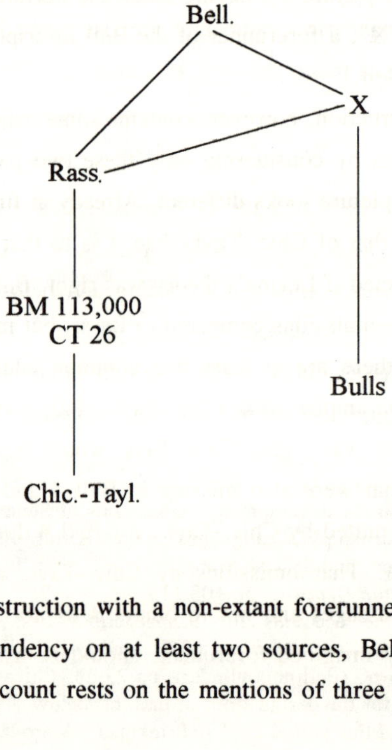

Levine's reconstruction with a non-extant forerunner of the Bull inscriptions and Rass.'s dependency on at least two sources, Bell. and a non-existent source "X", for one account rests on the mentions of three cities in varying con-

24 Cf. D.D.Luckenbill, *Annals*, p.20.
25 Cf. D.D.Luckenbill, *Annals*, p.21.
26 Henceforth "Chic.-Tayl.".
27 Cf. "Second Campaign".

texts. The oldest extant account for Sennacherib's second campaign, that of Bell., refers to the city of Bīt-Kilamzaḫ as being captured during an expedition to the Zagros mountains (1.22). Later (1.24) Bell. mentions that deportees were settled there. Bell., 1.25 narrates that Sennacherib settled captured escapees, who had been brought down from the mountains, in Ḫardišpi and Bīt-Kubatti. These two cities were thus evidently situated on the plain. Rass., 1.5a, and Chic. i_{72} mention all three cities together in the context of the mountain expedition as being conquered. The reports of deportations to the three cities are given, as in Bell., separately. Bull 4, too, narrates the conquests of all three cities (1.10), but mentions deportations only to Bīt-Kilamzaḫ (1.12). Levine argued that while Bull 4's text can be explained by the its tendency towards abbreviation, Rass. is seen as presenting "a muddled picture",[28] having taken the narration of the conquests of the three cities from "X", a forerunner of the Bull inscriptions, and the mentions of deportations from Bell.

Levine's construction, however, contains some major weaknesses. He had reached his conclusions by considering only these two passages in the differing versions. The overall picture looks different. Already at first glance the text-form of Bull 4 is closer to that of Chic.-Tayl. than it is to that of Rass. The opposite would have been expected if Levine's theory was right. Bull 4 and Chic.-Tayl. do not only have the same omissions compared to Rass., but in their accounts of Sennacherib's campaign there are at least two common additions to Rass.[29] Thus Levine's reconstruction implies that Chic.-Tayl., too, would have used "X". If Levine's reconstruction was right, Chic.-Tayl. would have omitted from Rass. only those passages that were also missing in Bull 4 and Bull 4 wuld have not retained any passage omitted by Chic.-Tayl., for Bull 4 does not give information missing in Chic.-Tayl. That omissions by Chic.-Tayl. would only have been carried out in those passages and not in others does not seem likely. Therefore Bull 4, as well as any imagined forerunner, should be assumed to be secondary

---

28 Cf. "Second Campaign", p.315.

29 *šadâšu īmid* ("he fled to his mountain" = "he died" - Chic. ii_{40}, Bull 4, 1.19), (*ša*) *la iknušū ana nīrīya* ("who did not submit to my yoke" - Chic. iii_{19}, Bull 4, ll.27f). Chic. iii_{39} // Bull 4, 1.31 and Chic. iii_{41} // Bull 4, 1.31 are of too little significance to be considered.

compared at least to Rass., probably also to Chic.-Tayl. But there are even more reasons to dismiss Levine's suggestion. In all those cases where Rass. (and Chic.-Tayl) and Bull 4 provide additional information compared to Bell.,[30] these additions would have been made by the forerunner of Bull 4, not by Rass. Rass. and the Bull inscriptions would have retained all additions made by "X". In one case (Chic. $ii_{30b\text{-}32}$) the forerunner of Bull 4 would have added 2 1/2 lines. According to Levine, however, the tendency of that forerunner was to abbreviate. Indeed, Bull 4 is much shorter than the other versions. Thus the assumption of a non-extant forerunner "X" of Bull 4, which is regarded as having been used by Rass., creates more problems than it can solve. It is quite conceivable that Rass. could mention the three cities together without any dependence on a written source. The stemma with the greatest probability is that of a simple dependency of Bell. on BM 113203, Rass. on Bell., Chic.-Tayl. on Rass., and Bull 4 on (a forerunner of) Chic.-Tayl.[31] Although it cannot be assumed with any certainty that any of these inscriptions or even text forms actually constituted the *Vorlage* for the subsequent one, the close agreements between them indicate that the existence of identical copies or intermediate stages in the textual development would only distribute the alterations among more manuscripts, but not affect the results of this investigation substantially. A provisional stemma for the accounts of Sennacherib's first three campaigns thus would be:

BM 113203

Bell.

Rass.

Chic.-Tayl.

Bull 4

[30] Chic. i_{22}, i_{50}, ii_{20}, ii_{22}, ii_{30} parr.

[31] Bull 4, containing the reports of six campaigns, is, indeed, earlier than Chic.-Tayl.,

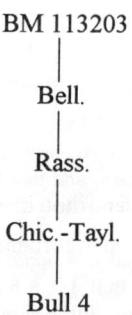

It should, however, be mentioned that some difficulties remain, which cannot be explained by the provisional stemma suggested here, but there are not significant enough to require a different stemma.[32]

Having established the order of dependency of the text-forms under consideration we can now proceed to investigate the differences between them. The conditions for our analysis of the literary developments are excellent. The earliest extant account was written shortly after the events narrated and the succeeding versions not significantly later, as is evident from the fact that Bell. narrates only Sennacherib's first and second campaigns and Rass. only the first three campaigns and from the dates of the manuscripts. The availability of five versions in combination with a simple stemma enables us to examine the consistency of redactorial treatment. Especially this last point is of crucial importance for our search for *general* tendencies of literary development.

a) The Structure of the Earliest Extant Version

The first four lines of BM 113203's account introduce Sennacherib and give a royal titulary, the actual account begins with line 5, which gives the first time reference to the text. Since BM 113203 only reports the first campaign there is no difficulty in identifying the end of the account.

An analysis of participant relations is of threefold importance. Firstly, the development *within* a given account can help us to identify *peak* sections and enables us to establish a description of the narrative which is independent of its specific contents. Secondly, participant relations belong to the most important

---

narrating eight campaigns. Nevertheless, the fact that the text of Bull 4 is closer to Chic.-Tayl. than to Bell. or Rass. and that Chic.-Tayl. is closer to Bell. and Rass. than Bull 4 is indicates that the order of text-forms is different from the chronological order of the manuscripts.

32 Thus Rass. and Chic.-Tayl read *sīsê ṣumbī* ("horses, wagons" - Chic. i_{25}) whereas BM 113203, l.29, Bell., l.7, and Bull 4, l.5 have the reverse order. BM 113203, l.57 and Bull 4, l.8 (*mandattašu* - "his gift") agree against Bell., l.17, Rass., and Chic. i_{57} (*tāmartašu* - "his tribute"). Adaptation of the reports to changed political circumstances does not seem probable, but cannot be ruled out (for the meanings of *tāmartu* and *mandattu* cf. W.J.Martin, "Tribut", p.45 {with p.24}, J.N.Postgate, *Taxation*, p.154). A further difficulty might be found in Chic. $i_{32\text{-}33}$ parr. BM 113203, l.32, and Chic.-Tayl. mention *zammerē zammerāti* ("male singers, female singers"). These are not noted in the booty-lists in Bell. and Rass.

criteria for the identification of *Sage* or *Legende* as opposed to historical accounts. An analysis of the participant orientation pattern may thus test the appropriateness of such criteria. Thirdly, alterations of the *participant orientation pattern* may indicate redactorial trends. Since our investigation deals with narratives we shall concentrate on the *main line* as opposed to the *supportive material*.

The *main line* reads as follows:

	Main Line	agent	patient	benefactive	operation[33]	Bell.	Rass.	Chic.-Tayl	Bull 4
						-	+[34]	+	+
l. 7	*isḫurma*	B[35]	C	(A)		-	-	-	-
	"brought over (to his side"								
	ušatlimšuma	B	C	(A)	⇒ I	-	-	-	-
	"gave him"								
	ēterrissu	B	C	(A)	⇒ I	-	-	-	-
	"he demanded of him"								
l. 9	*išpura*	C	B	(A)	⇒ r	-	-	-	-
	"he sent"								
l.15	*upaḫḫirma*	B	C	(A)	⇒ r	-	-	-	-
	"he gathered"								
	ušakṣer	B	C	(A)	⇒ I	-	-	-	-
	"he assembled"								
l.16	*ušannūnimma*	A'	A	(B/C)	⇒ r	-	-	-	-
	"they reported"								
	annadirma	A	(B/C)		⇒ I	-	-	-	-
	"I raged"								
	aqṭibi	A	B(/C)		⇒ I	-	-	-	-
	"I commanded"								

33 In the present analysis of participant orientation operations we have concentrated on major participant relations and assumed as few changes as possible. Therefore, *primary* and *secondary participants* (e.g. A and A') have neither been distinguished nor counted separately. The transition from *uma"irma* (l.34 - "I sent", *agent*: A, *patient*: A', *benefactive*: B) to "*uba"ûšūma*" (l.34 - "they searched", *agent*: A', *patient*: B) is instructive. This transition is been evaluated as "I", although in fact *agent*, *patient*, and *benefactive* have all changed. With regard to the main conflict, that between Sennacherib and Merodach-baladan, however, the participant relation has remained the same. The fact that mentions of secondary participants were altered to those of primary participants corroborates this mode of description.

34 *aštakan* ("I accomplished", *agent*: A, *patient*: B/C).

35 "A" stands for Sennacherib, "A'" for his generals, "B" for Merodach-baladan, and "C" for the latter's allies.

1.17	*išmēma*	B(/C)	A		⇒ r	-	-	-	-
	"he heard of"								
1.18	*udannin*	B	C	(A)	⇒ I	-	-	-	-
	"he strengthened"								
	ušēribma	B	C	(A)	⇒ I	-	-	-	-
	"he brought (them) into"								
	ušanṣir	B(/C)	A		⇒ I	-	-	-	-
	"he installed a watch"								
1.19	*uštešsera*	A	(B/C)		⇒ r	-	-	-	-
	"I prepared"								
	aṣbatma	A	(B/C)		⇒ I	-	-	-	-
	"I set out"								
	ul ušadgil	A	(B/C)		⇒ I	-	-	-	-
	"I did not hold back"								
	ul ūqi	A	(B/C)		⇒ I	-	-	-	-
	"I did not wait"								
1.20	*uma''ir*[36]	A	A'	(B/C)	⇒ I	-	-	-	-
	"I sent"								
1.21	*ēmurma*	B(/C)	A'		⇒ r	-	-	-	-
	"he saw"								
	ūṣâmma	B(/C)	(A')		⇒ I	-	-	-	-
	"he went out"								
	ēpuš	B(/C)	A'		⇒ I	-	-	-	-
	"he did"								
1.22	*idninma*[37]	B(/C)	A'		⇒ I	-	-	-	-
	"it was mighty"								
	ul ili'û	A'	B(/C)		⇒ r	-	-	-	-
	"they did not succeed"								
	išpurūni	A'	A	(B/C)	⇒ I	-	-	-	-
	"they sent to me"								
1.23	*aškunma*	A	C(/B)		⇒ s	-	-	-	-
	"I made (an assault)"								
	utibbiḫma	A	(C/B)		⇒ I	-	-	-	-
	"I slaughtered"								
	aṣṣabat	A	C(/B)		⇒ I	-	-	-	-
	"I seized"								

36 + direct speech.

37 Impersonal subject (*qitrub tāḫāzi nakri* - "the enemy's approach for battle") referring to Merodach-baladan.

1.24	*ušēṣâmma*	A	C(/B)		⇒ I	-	-	-	-
	"I brought out"								
	amnu	A	C(/B)		⇒ I	-	-	-	-
	"I counted (as spoil)"								
1.25	*annadirma*[38]	A	(C/B)		⇒ I	-	-	-	-
	"I raged"								
	allabib	A	(C/B)		⇒ I	-	-	-	-
	"I stormed"								
	aštakan	A	B(/C)		⇒ s	-	-	-	-
	"I set (my face)"								
1.26	*ēmurma*	B(/C)	A		⇒ r	-	-	-	-
	"he saw"								
	imqussu[39]	A	B(/C)		⇒ r	-	-	-	-
	"it fell upon him"								
	ēzibma	B	B'(/C)	(A)	⇒ r	r	r	r	-[40]
	"he forsook"								
					-	I[41]	I	I	r
	innabit	B(/C)	A		⇒ I	I	-	-	-
	"he fled"								
					-	I[42]	-	-	-
					-	I[43]	I	I	-
1.27	*aškunma*	A	C(/B)		⇒ rs	-	-	-	-
	"I accomplished"								
	uparrir	A	C(/B)		⇒ I	-	-	-	-
	"I shattered"								
1.28	*aṣbat*	A	C(/B)		⇒ I	-	-	-	-
	"I seized"								
1.29	*ikšudā*[44]	A	C(/B)		⇒ I	r[45]	r	r	r
	"(my hands) captured"								

---

38 Cf. l.16.

39 Impersonal subject (*ḫattu* - "terror"). Since immediately before it is reported that Merodach-baladan saw *akāmu girrīya* ("the cloud of dust of my campaign" - with the pronominal suffix *-ya* {my} referring to Sennacherib), the implied *agent* has been evaluated as "A".

40 Cf. below pp.94f.

41 *ipparšidma* ("he escaped").

42 *ērumma* ("he went into").

43 *ēṭir* ("he saved {his life}").

44 The grammatical subject is *qātāya* ("my hands").

45 Because of the omission of BM 113203, ll.27-28, the grammatical subject of *umašširū* ("he abandoned" - Bell., l.7) is Merodach-baladan, whereas in BM 113203, l.29 (*ša qereb tamḫāri muššurū* - "which they had abandoned during the battle") the *agents* are

1.30	*aḫīšma*	A	B(/C)		⇒ s	-	-	-	-
	"I hastened"								
	ērub	A	B(/C)		⇒ I	I[46]	I	I	I
	"I entered"								
1.31	*aptēma*	A	B(/C)		⇒ I	I	I	I	I
	"I opened"								
1.33	*ušēṣâmma*	A	B(/C)		⇒ I	I	I	I	-
	"I brought out"								
	amnu	A	B(/C)		⇒ I	I	I	I	I[47]
	"I counted (as spoil)"								
1.34	*urriḫma*	A	B(/C)		⇒ I	I[48]	-	-	-
	"I hurried"								
	uma''irma	A	A'	B(/C)	⇒ I	I	-	-	-
	"I sent"								
	uba''ûšūma	A'	B(/C)		⇒ I	I[49]	-	-	-
	"they searched"								
	ul innamir[50]	A'	B(/C)		⇒ I	I	-	-	-
	"was not found"								
1.35	*upaḫḫir*	A	B(/C)		⇒ r	-	-	-	-
	"I gathered"								
ina mētiq girrīya									
	"in the course of my campaign"								
1.50	*alme*	A	C		(⇒ s)	(rs)	(s)	(s)	-
	"I surrounded"								
	akšud	A	C		⇒ I	I	I	I	(s)
	"I conquered"								
	ašlula	A	C		⇒ I	I	I	I	I
	"I took as spoil"								
1.51	*ušākil*	A	C		⇒ I	-	-	-	-
	"I had (my troops) devour"								
	appul	A	C		⇒ I	-	-	-	-
	"I destroyed"								

his allies (cf. ll.27-28). This causes a change of *patient*. Consequently the operation is "r", not "rs".

46 Cf. above, pp.78f, n.45.

47 *ašlula* ("I took as spoil").

48 *aṣbatma* ("I seized").

49 *iparūnimma* ("they searched").

50 Although the grammatical subject is impersonal (*ašaršu* - "his place") with the pronominal suffix *-šu* ("his") referring to Merodach-baladan, Sennacherib's generals

	aqqur "I devastated"	A	C		⇒I	-	-	-	-
	aqmu "I burned"	A	C		⇒I	-	-	-	-
	utīr "I turned into (forgotten heaps of rubbish)"	A	C		⇒I	-	-	-	-
1.52	*ušēṣâmma* "I brought out"	A	C		⇒I	I	I	I	I
	amnu "I counted (as spoil)"	A	C		⇒I	I	I	I	I
1.53	*ušākil* "I had (my troops) devour"	A	C		⇒I	-	-	-	-
1.54	*aštakan* "I installed"	A	A'	C	⇒I	I	I[51]	-	-
					-	-	I[52]	-	-
					-	-	I[53]	-	-
					-	-	I[54]	-	-
	ina tayyartīya "on my march back"								
1.56	*akšudma* "I captured"	A	C		(⇒ I)	(I)	(I)	(I)	(I)
	ašlula "I took as spoil"	A	C		⇒I	I	I	I	I
	ina mētiq girrīya "in the course of my campaign"								
1.57	*amḫur* "I received"	A	C		(⇒ I)	(I)	(I)	(I)	(I)
1.58	*ušamqitma* "I slew"	A	C		⇒I	I	I	I	I
	ul ēzib "not (a soul) escaped"	C	(A)		⇒r	r	r	r	r
					-	-	r[55]	r	-
					-	-	I[56]	-	
1.59	*aṣbat* "I reorganized"	A	C		⇒r	r	I	I	r

---

constitute the notional *agent* of the passive verbal form.

51 *ušēšib* ("I installed").

52 *ušadgil* ("I let {his face} see" = "I entrusted him with the government").

53 *aškunma* ("I installed").

54 *ēmissunūti* ("I imposed").

55 *ālulma* ("I hung").

56 *ušalme* ("I surrounded").

ukīn "I imposed"	A	C	⇒I	I	I	I	I
l.60 *atūra* "I returned"	A	C	⇒I	-	-	-	-
l.62 *ušamqitma* "I slew"	A	C	⇒I	-	-	-	-
ālul "I hung"	A	C	⇒I	-	-	-	-

34 x I (69.39 %), 11 x r (22.45 %), 3 x s (6.12 %), 1 x rs (2.04%) / 11 x I / 1 x I/ 5 x I, 2 x r.

The formulae *ina mētiq girrīya* ("in the course of my campaign") and *ina tayyartīya* ("on my march back") divide BM 113203's account into four parts. The setting, or *stage*, of the first part is provided by ll.5-15. First a time reference is given (l.5), then the enemy's *sin* is described; first in general terms (l.6) then more specifically (l.7). A list of the enemy's allies is given in ll.8-15. The *stage* is clearly dominated by Sennacherib's enemy. Merodach-baladan is the grammatical subject of all of its *main line* verbs. Then the *inciting event* is presented: Sennacherib learns about the rebellion (l.16). The significance of this part of the narrative structure is shown by the description of Sennacherib's emotional response which is intensified by an adverb (*labbiš* - "like a lion", l.16). The *inciting event* leads to an increase of tension. The rhetorical level is higher than that of the *stage* and both opponents have entered the narrative. The scope then switches back to Merodach-baladan, whose preparations for battle are described (ll.17-18). Again, Merodach-baladan dominates all *main line* verbs of this section. Thereafter the Assyrian advance is reported (ll.19-20). Here all *main line* verbs are dominated by Sennacherib. The absolute time reference loosens the connection of the following sentences with the previous ones and renders them less dependent on the context. Thereby the information previously given is somewhat reduced in its importance. It is interesting to note that the narrations of the opponents' preparations for battle differ from each other. While that of Sennacherib's enemies describes the enemies as *šū imdi gallî lemni* ("he, prop of an evil demon"), *ša lā īdû mī*[*tū*?]*tu* ("who do not know death {?}"), *emūqi lā nībi ittīšunūtima* ("a countless host was with them"), that of Sennacherib himself contains no subordinate clauses or appositions but concentrates more on action. In l.19 a comparison, *kīma rīmi gapši* ("like a mighty bull"), and a parallelism, *pān gipšīya ul ušadgil* ("I did not hold back the vanguard of my host") / *arkâ ul ūqi* ("for the rearguard I did not wait"), are employed. L.20 contains direct speech. Thus the Assyrian advance is depicted on a higher rhetorical level than that of Merodach-baladan. Next in BM 113203's account is the mention of the battle between the Assyrian and the allied armies (ll.21-22a). Of the battle it is only mentioned that it took place and that the Assyrian army had to withdraw. No adverbial phrases are used to intensify verbs. The rhetorical level thus is comparatively low. This conforms with the fact that after the outcome of the battle is known, tension declines; but only to rise again with the mention of a messenger sent to Sennacherib (l.22b). Now Sennacherib himself enters the scene, whereby the function of the account of the previous events is almost reduced to that of a *stage*. This is accompanied by a rise of the rhetorical level (*ina uggat libbīya* - "in the anger of my heart", *ṭabāḫu* - "to slaughter",[57] *asliš* - "like sheep").

After the mention of the successful assault upon Kutha booty and captives taken are listed (l.24). Then the report on the progression of the campaign is resumed and the rhetorical level increases even further (*labbiš annadirma alabib abūbiš* - "I raged like a lion, I stormed like a flood", l.25). *labbiš annadirma* ("I raged like a lion") had already been used in l.16 to describe Sennacherib's reaction to his learning of Merodach-baladan's rebellion. But in l.25 it is intensified by the parallel expression *alabib abūbiš* ("I stormed like a flood"). Now Merodach-baladan's reaction is mentioned (l.26; cf. l.17). Again, both major opponents take part in the story plot and tension increases. The battle itself is not described. The mention of the Assyrian victory is intensified by the parallel expression *uparrir el<las>su* ("I shattered his army").[58] The next two lines again mention the booty and captives taken by the Assyrians. Again the narrative rests. But thereafter (l.30) action is resumed on a high rhetorical level: *ina ḫūd libbi u numur pāni* ("in joy of heart and with a radiant face"), *aḫīšma* ("I hastened"). L.30 contrasts sharply with l.16 (*labbiš annadirma* - "I raged like a

---

[57] usually *dâku* ("to kill").

[58] Usually only *taḫtašun* / *abiktašun aškun* ("I administered their defeat").

lion") and l.25 (*labbiš annadirma alabib abūbiš* - "I raged like a lion and stormed like a flood") and marks the *dénouement* of the notional structure. The following lines describe the booty taken from Merodach-baladan's treasure house (ll.31-33). Tension declines, but increases again with the narration of the hunt for Merodach-baladan (l.34), though not to the level it had reached before; *arāḫu* ("to hurry") which is more intensive than *alāku* ("to go") is used, but no adverb or adverbial phrase is employed. The mention of the failure of the search (l.34b) and the report on the gathering of Merodach-baladan's scattered forces concludes this section of BM 113203's account.

The other episodes within the account of the first campaign (ll.36-51; 52-54; 55-56; 57-59) do not exhibit great increase or decrease of tension. With the exception of the negated *ul ēzib* ("not {a soul} escaped"), Sennacherib dominates all *main line* verbs. Emphasis is on taking booty and ravaging the enemy's country.[59] For the main section a *discourse profile* can be established.

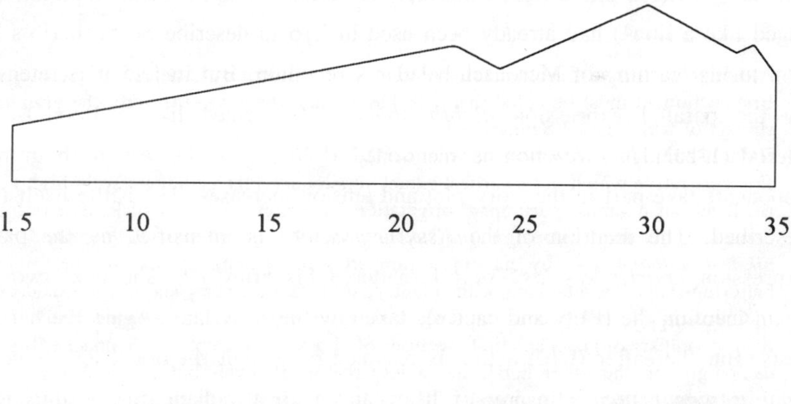

59 Cf. the EEN-constructions *alme akšud ašlula šalassun* ("I besieged, I conquered, I took their spoil", l.50), *appul aqqur ina girri aqmu ana tillē mašûti utīr* ("I destroyed, I devastated, I burned with fire, and turned (them) into forgotten tells", l.51).

The participant orientation pattern parallels the differences of rhetorical level between the various sections of the account. In the first section we can note:

I	34x	69.39%
r	11x	22.45%
s	3x	6.12%
rs	1x	2.04%
	49x.	

The other sections exhibit a stronger prevalence of the I-function (11 x I / 1 x I / 5 x I, 2 x r).[60] The substantial number of *reversals* in the first section mirrors the vividness of the narration. We further note that towards the beginning of the account B and C are mentioned with separate functions within a sentence. Thus not only the main participant relation, that between Sennacherib and his enemies, receives attention, but also that between the enemies themselves. Four times Sennacherib's messengers or generals appear as *main-line agents* and seven (+ one)[61] times as *patients*. The alternation between primary and secondary participants, too, contributes to the story's liveliness. Even at a relative *peak*, the report on the first battle, secondary participants for Sennacherib are mentioned.

The narrative structure and the participant orientation pattern of BM 113203's account may thus be described as complex,[62] whereas the time organization is simple.

---

60 Although in this last section the *percentage* of r-functions is nearly as great as in the first section, it must be noted that it is due to only *one main-line* verb, the grammatical subject of which is not Sennacherib.

61 BM 113203, 1.21: *ūṣâmma* ("he went out").

62 For a narrative which in its earliest extant version exhibits a comparatively high rhetorical level but a simple participant orientation pattern cf. section 4 of Rass.'s account of Sennacherib's third campaign (*ina šukbus arammē u qitrub šupê mitḫuṣ zūk šēpē pilši niksi u kalbānāte* - "by having a rampart built {stamped} and by bringing near battering-rams, by attacking with infantry, by breaches, cuts, and scaling ladders {?}" // Chic. iii_{21-23} {EEN-construction}, *kīma iṣṣūr quppi* - "like a caged bird" // Chic. iii_{27} {comparison}). The first section of Rass.'s account of Sennacherib's third campaign, on the other hand, has a low rhetorical level, but a complex participant orientation pattern (cf. appendix III, table 2). Finally, there are narratives with a unified *main line* and a low rhetorical level already in their earliest extant version. With the exception of two verbs Sennacherib dominates the complete *main line* of Bell.'s account of Sennacherib's second campaign. There are only two *reversals* and secondary participants do not occur on the *main line* (cf. appendix III, table 1). Bell.'s rhetorical level there is low compared with BM 113203's narration of Sennacherib's first campaign, only two *main line* verbs are intensified by an adverb or an adverbial phrase. EEN-constructions are of the more common kind. Cf. also sections 2 and 3 of Rass.'s

b) The Structural Development

The following diagram indicates the passages retained by Bell. with regard to the discourse profile of BM 113203's account of Sennacherib's first campaign.

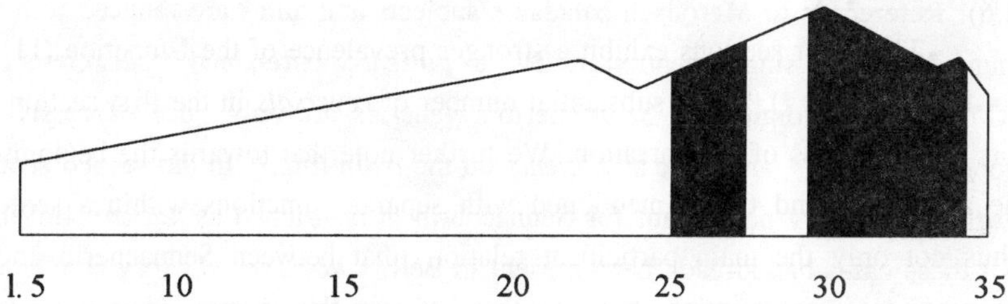

■ retained by Bell.

Bell. has omitted the complete *stage*, *inciting event* and the remarks on the first battle, as well as those on the assault upon Kutha with the list of booty taken (BM 113203, ll.5-24). Only the decisive victory is mentioned. By Bell.'s alterations the *profile* of the narrative was made simpler - one *relative peak* wa omitted.

The alterations' effects on the *main line* of the narrative are significant. The number of *reversals* was reduced from eleven (+ one *rs*) to two,[63] one at the beginning of a section relating Merodach-baladan's escape and one at the beginning of the passage relating Sennacherib's victory and conquest. Thus, rather than reflecting the narrative's vividness the *reversals* function as markers of the borders of narrative sections. Both *reversals* had already been present in BM 113203. Thus the *participant orientation pattern* of the first section was simplified by Bell.'s redactorial activity. The further sections' *participant orientation patterns*

account of Sennacherib's second campaign.

63 This is more important than the percentage reduction of *reversals* (22.45% > 15.4%). Comparable cases are Bull 4's omission of *išâṭ* ("he bore {my yoke}", Chic. ii_{68}), the only verb in the third part of Chic.-Tayl.'s account of Sennacherib's third campaign not governed by the Assyrian king as *agent*, and of Chic. $ii_{80\text{-}81}$, whereby a *reversal* is removed. Bull 4 has further omitted *āṣê abul ālīšu utirra ikkibuš* ("the one coming out of the gate of his city I turned back to his misery", Chic. iii_{30}) and thus unified the line of *patients*. Cf. also the Rass.' omission of Bell. l.12 which contains three different *main line agents*.

had already been unified in BM 113203. As in BM 113203, in these paragraphs only one main clause, *napištu ul ēzib* ("not a soul escaped"), interrupts the domination of the *main line* by Sennacherib as *agent*. The omissions in the first section primarily affected the passages dealing with the actions of Sennacherib's enemies. Thus of Merodach-baladan it is only told that he fled and saved his life (1.6). References to Merodach-baladan's subjects and allies are reduced to a minimum. While the single mention of "B'" as *patient* was retained,[64] all references to "C" have been omitted.[65] Sennacherib's generals are only once expressly mentioned as *agents*[66] and once as *patients* on the *main-line*.[67] In the second section a further secondary participant for Sennacherib is mentioned as *patient*: Bel-ibni.[68] All these cases had already been present in Bell.'s *Vorlage*. We may conclude that in the first section Bell. concentrates on the major conflict, that between the primary participants Sennacherib and Merodach-baladan.[69] As has been mentioned above, the other sections exhibited a clear participant orientation pattern already in BM 113203.

The alterations also affected the *time organization* within the narrative. A chronological order of narration has given way to a more thematic one. Proleptic remarks also suppress an increase of tension. While the narrative structure has been simplified, the opposite is true for the time organization. The report in BM 113203 seems to adhere closely to the chronological order.[70] It does not anticipate

---

64 *ellatīšu ēzibma* ("he forsook his army", BM 113023, l.26) ⇒ *ēzib karāssu* ("he forsook his camp", Bell. l.6).

65 However, in a sentence added by Bell. at the beginning of the campaign account, the outcome of the conflict is stated and both, "B" and "C" are mentioned as *patients*. For the effect of the omissions cf. also above, pp.78f, n.45.

66 *iparūnimma* ("they searched", l.10). For an additional case, where Sennacherib's generals constitute the notional, but not the grammatical, subject cf. above, pp.79f, n.50.

67 *umaʾʾir* ("I sent", l. 10 // BM 113203, l.20).

68 *aštakan* ("I installed", l.13 // BM 113203, l.54).

69 The trend towards focussing on primary participants may also be responsible for the alteration of the reference to the warriors of *Ḫirimmu*, *ša ultu ulla ana šarrāni abbēya lā iknušū* ... ("who from old had not submitted to the kings, my fathers"; BM 113203, l.58), to *ša ultu ulla ana nīrīya lā iknušū* ("who from old had not submitted to my yoke"; Bell., l.18). This alteration does not affect the overall structure of the narrative. For similar cases cf. below, p.91, n.81.

70 This is also true for the earliest extant account of Sennacherib's second campaign (Bell.), and the first two sections of Rass.'s narration of Sennacherib's third campaign.

events which happened later in the course of the campaign. This is different in Bell. where the writer knew which of the events reported in BM 113203 were important for the main course of narration. Thus the account of Bell. starts with *ina rēš šarrūtia ša Marduk-apal-iddina šar Karduniaš adi ummānāt Elamti ina tamirti Kiš aštakan taḫtâšu* ("at the beginning of my kingship I established the defeat of Merodach-baladan, king of Babylonia, together with the army of Elam in the plain of Kish") mentioning right at the beginning the outcome of the conflict. In Bell. Merodach-baladan's escape is mentioned thereafter, introduced by *ina qabal tamḫāri šuātu* ("in the midst of that battle"), whereas according to BM 113203 Merodach-baladan fled before the battle took place (ll.25-27). The remark on the Assyrian victory in Bell. is thus to be regarded as anticipatory and more emphasis is placed on the outcome of the campaign.

A comparison of the passages relating the escape of Merodach-Baladan is instructive.

BM 113203 reads:

> *u šū ēpiš lemnēti akāmu girrīya ana rūqēti ēmurma imqussu ḫattu gimir ellatīšu ēzibma ana Guzummani innabit* (l.26).
>
> "and when that evil-doer saw the cloud of dust of my campaign from afar, terror fell upon him, he forsook all of his troops and fled to the land of Guzummanu".

Bell. reads:

> *ina qabal tamḫāri šuātu ēzib karāssu ēdiš ipparšidma ana Guzummani innabit qereb agamme u appārāte ērumma napištuš ēṭir*" (l.6).
>
> "in the midst of that battle he forsook his camp, escaped alone to the land of Guzummanu and went into the swamp and marshes and saved his life".[71]

Bell. thus anticipates later events. In BM 113203 the escape of Merodach-baladan is reported before the Assyrian victory is mentioned, in Bell. the order is reversed. The "swamp and marshes" were originally mentioned later in the account (BM 113203, l.34). Likewise the success of his escape is stated by Bell. (*napištuš ēṭir* - "he saved his life") before the pursuit of Merodach-baladan is reported. It might be argued that, since in Bell. the report of the hunt is retained, *napistuš ēṭir* ("he saved his life") may only refer to a first escape. However, the fact, that *qereb agamme u appārāte ērumma* ("he went into the swamp and mar-

Cf., however, below, p.95, n.101.

71 For further comments on this passage cf. below pp.179f.

shes") was taken from BM 113203's report of the hunt (l.34)[72] into Bell., l.6 indicates that in Bell. the failure of the search is implied.[73]

Further redactorial activity took place in Bell., l.12. In this passage Bell. adds "Kutha" to the list of cities given in BM 113203, l.52. In BM 113203 the conquest of Kutha is reported separately, after Sennacherib's generals had lost the first battle. By this addition Bell. compensated for the omission of this passage from the original context.[74] The remarks on Bel-ibni (BM 113203, l.54) and the list of peoples captured introduced by *ina tayyartīya* "on my march back", are retained by Bell. without any alteration.

Bell. then gives the total amount of booty taken to Assyria with wording and some of the numbers differing from BM 113203's version. For these changes no reason is apparent. The mention of the tribute imposed upon Nabu-bel-šumate is taken over from BM 113203 almost verbatim. The only alteration carried out by Bell. is the replacement of *mandattu* ("gift") by *tāmartu* ("tribute").[75]

Bell. has transferred the mention of the total amount of booty taken[76] by Sennacherib which in BM 113203 is followed only by a remark on the punishment of Sennacherib's unsubmissive enemies, to a position before the mention of the tribute from Nabu-bēl-šumāte, which is introduced in both versions by ina *ina mētiq girrīya* ("in the midst of my campaign"). Thus Bell. has changed the chronological order towards a thematic one.[77]

The anticipatory and summarizing remarks prevent a great increase and decrease of tension. This accords with the generally lower rhetorical level, a result of the omission of adverbs and adverbial phrases.

In Bell. twenty-two lines of BM 113203 (ll.16-27) are summarized in one single sentence: *ina rēš šarrūtīya ša Marduk-apal-iddina šar Karduniaš adi*

72 BM 113203 mentions *ana Guzumanni* ("to the land of Guzummanu") in both passages (ll.26.34).

73 Comparable is Rass.'s addition of *uṣaḫḫir māssu* ("I diminished his land" // Chic. ii_{22}, cf. Bell. l.31) which anticipates Chic. $ii_{23ff.}$

74 Cf. also Rass. additional mention of *Ḫardišpi* and *Bīt Kubatti* (// Chic. i_{72}, see above, p.73).

75 Cf. above, p.75, n.32.

76 BM 113203, l.60: *itti ... atūra ana qereb Aššur* ("with ... I returned to Assyria"), Bell., l.16: *ašlula ana Aššur* ("I took as spoil to Assyria").

77 For the different order between the two mss. cf. the participant orientation pattern above, pp.79ff. One reason for the alteration of the order might be that Bell. wanted to

ummānāt Elamti ina tamirti Kiš aštakan taḫtâšu ("at the beginning of my kingship I established the defeat of Merodach-baladan, king of Babylonia, together with the army of Elam in the plain of Kish", l.5). Here information of very diverse origin is packed closely together. Sentences of that kind are not found in BM 113203's account. The mention of Sennacherib's accession (BM113203, l.5) was omitted from the time reference by Bell., giving thus more attention to the king's feats. Further omissions by Bell. have already been mentioned.[78] To these should be added that considerable alteration took place in the account of Sennacherib's entering the palace of Merodach-baladan's:

BM 113203 l.30: *ina ḫūd libbi u numur pāni ana Babili aḫīšma ana ekal Marduk-apla-iddina aššu paqād būši u makkūri qerebša ērub.*

"in joy of heart and with a radiant face I hastened to Babylon and entered Merodach-baladan's palace to take charge of the property and belongings in it."

Bell. l.8: *ana ekallīšu ša qereb babili ḫadîš ērumma ...*

"his palace which is in Babylon I entered joyfully".

The text of Bell. is much shorter. Two adverbial phrases of BM 113203, *ina ḫūd libbi u numur pāni* ("in joy of heart and with a radiant face") are represented in Bell. only by a single adverb, *ḫadîš* ("joyfully"). Furthermore, Bell. does not mention that Sennacherib *hastened* to Merodach-baladan's palace, but only that he *entered* the palace, which was the more important of the two actions. Bell. also omits the adverbial phrase *aššu paqād būši u makkūri qerebša* ("to take charge of the property and belongings in it"), for the information given there was also contained in the following sentences narrating that Sennacherib entered the treasure house. These alterations reduced the rhetorical level of the passage.

We can note that the most *vulnerable* parts of BM 113203's narration were the *stage* and pre-*peak*-episodes. The whole account in Bell. was put on a lower rhetorical level than it had been in BM 113203; it is less vivid and the rise and decline of tension is much smaller. This is partly due to the use of anticipatory remarks and partly to the reduced number of participants. The effect of the major alterations on the *discourse profile* was that the number of *relative*

---

conclude the account of the first campaign with the mention of tribute paid regularly.

78 Cf. above, p.85.

peaks was reduced. Thus the course of the narrative was much simpler in its second edition than it had been in the first.

Since Rass.'s *Vorlage* was a secondary version already, alterations to the same extent as those between BM 113203 and Bell. were not to be expected. As a major abbreviation we can note a further reduction of *discourse profile peaks*. Rass. omits the reference to the destination of Merodach-baladan's escape, part of which had been added by Bell., and to his escape into the "swamp and marshes", which had been added by Bell. Consequently the report of Sennacherib's pursuit of Merodach-baladan, too, is omitted by Rass. Perhaps the omission of the latter prompted that of the former. By the omission of the report of the hunt for Merodach-baladan a relative *peak* was omitted. This provides further indication that the omissions carried out by Bell. and Rass. conform to a general tendency of redactorial treatment. The remark that Merodach-baladan saved his life was, presumably because he continued to be a major opponent of Sennacherib[79], retained by Rass. In Rass.'s version there is only one *discourse peak*, the narrative structure is simpler concentrating only on the main conflict and its resolution. The following diagram shows the progressive simplification of the narrative structure:

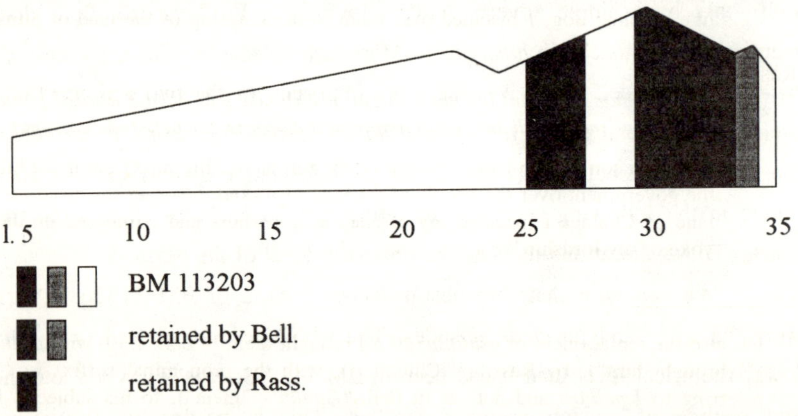

Alterations have also affected the participant orientation. Rass. has added *rēṣīšu* ("his ally")[80] to identify the Elamites as allies of Merodach-baladan and

79 Cf. the mention of Merdach-baladan's flight during Sennacherib's fourth campaign in Chic. iii_{59-65}.

80 // Chic. i_{22}; cf. Bell. l.5.

thus mentions their rôle in the conflict expressly. It joins Sennacherib's opponents and thus clarifies the participant orientation, which in Bell. had already been indicated by *Marduk-apal-iddina šar Karduniaš* ***adi*** *ummānāt Elamti* ("Merdoach-baladan, king of Babylonia, *together with* the army of Elam"). With the omission of the report of the hunt for Merodach-baladan mentions of Sennacherib's generals (secondary participants) as *agent*s were removed. Thus we can note a further concentration on primary participants.[81] Similarly in a reference to captured Chaldean cities Rass.[82] has replaced *ālāni dannūti* ("strong cities") with *ālānīšu* ("his cities"). By the addition of a personal suffix the internal coherence of the narrative has, though only slightly, increased.[83]

In the altered reference to Bēl-ibni mentions of secondary participants have been added, which disagrees with the development of the participant orientation pattern from BM 113203 to Bell. The difference, however, can probably be explained by another redactorial tendency, that of updating.

BM 113203, 1.54 // Bell., 1.13:

> *Bēl-ibni mār Rab-bāni per'i Babili ša kīma mīrāni ṣaḫri qereb ekallīya irbu ana šarrūt māt Šumeri u Akkadî aštakan elīšun.*
>
> "Bēl-ibni, son of Rab-bāni, a scion of Babylon, who had grown up in my palace like a young dog, I installed over them to the kingship of the land of Sumer and Akkad."

Rass.[84]:

> *Bēl-ibni mār Rab-bāni ina kussî šarrūti ušēšib nišē māt Akkadî ušadgil pānussu eli gimir nagê māt Kaldi šūt-rēšīya ana pāḫati aškunma nīr bēlūtīya ēmissunuṭi.*
>
> "Bēl-ibni son of Rab-bāni, I placed on the throne of kingship. I entrusted him with the government over the people of the land of Akkad. Over all the disctricts of the land of Chaldea I installed my officers as governors and I imposed on them the yoke of my lordship".

---

81 Cf. also the replacement of *ušālikšunūti* ("I brought them" - Bell. 1.30) with *ušālikšuma* ("I brought him"), by Rass. (// Chic. ii_{22}), with the pronominal suffix *-šu* ("him") referring to *Ispabāra* and not, as in Bell. (*-šunūti* - "them"), to his subjects. By the omission of Chic. ii_{46}, Bull 4 has removed all references to secondary participants from the first section of Chic.-Tayl.'s account of Sennacherib's third campaign. From the third unit Bull 4 has omitted the references to the Egyptian army as *main line agents* (Chic. ii_{80-81}).

82 // Chic. i_{36}.

83 The omission of *dannūti* ("strong") as a correspondence to *ṣiḫrūti* ("small") might have been accidental; usually *ālāni ṣiḫrūti* ("small cities") is preceded by a reference to *ālāni dannūti* ("strong cities"); Chic.-Tayl. has *ālānīšu dannūti* ("his strong cities"; i_{36}).

84 The passage is between the equivalents of Chic. i_{42} and i_{43}.

The alteration probably reflects the situation in Babylonia prior to or even during Sennacherib's fourth campaign. Sennacherib reports that during his fourth campaign he defeated Šuzubu, "the Chaldean" (Chic. iii_{52f}). The passage in Rass., *eli gimir nagê māt Kaldi šūt-rēšīya ana pāḫati aškunma* ("over all the districts of the land of Chaldea I installed my officers as governors") possibly reflects this. After his victory over Merodach-baladan and the king of Elam Sennacherib installed his son Aššur-nadin-šum as king of "Sumer and Akkad"[85], which suits Rass.'s remark *nīr bēlūtīya ēmissunūti* ("the yoke of my lordship I imposed on them"). The alterations may thus constitute an update of the information provided by Bell.[86] implying a resolution of the chronological order of narration.[87]

Due to the omission of the reference to the pursuit of Merodach-baladan one of the indications for Bell.'s secondary character was not taken over, since from the context in Rass. it is not clear that *napištuš ēṭir* ("he saved his life")

---

85 ... *ina kussî bēlūtīšu ušēšibma rapaštum Šumeri u Akkadî ušadgil pānussu* ("... I placed on the throne of his {Merodach-baladan's} lordship, with the wide land of Sumer and Akkad I entrusted him", Chic. iii_{72f}).

86 Cf. L.D.Levine, "Manuscripts", pp.63f, where comparable cases are suggested. M.Liverani, "Critique of Variants", p.256, regards only the omission of *Šumeri* as a factual variant indicating that Bēl-ibni lost territory to Merodach-baladan. He interprets the causative verbal forms *ušēšib* ("I placed") and *ušadgil* ("I entrusted") in Rass. as a "definition of the subordinate rôle of Bel-ibni". However, the causatives also appear in the report of Aššur-nadin-šum's installation (cf. Chic. iii_{73f}) where no reference to the Assyrian administrative system is made. The omission of *Šumeri* in Rass.'s mention of Bēl-ibni's installation may be significant. The Babylonian Chronicle I reports that in his third year Bēl-ibni was taken bound to Assyria (ii_{27}) and that *Sin-aḫḫe-ēriba ana Akkadî ūrdamma ḫubut Akkadî iḫtabat* ("Sennacherib went down to Akkad and carried of the booty of Akkad"; cf. A.K.Grayson, *Assyrian and Babylonian Chronicles*, p.77). The omission thus may reflect a reduction of territory controlled by the Assyrians. Cf. also J.A.Brinkman, *Prelude to Empire*, pp.58-60, and "Merodach-Baladan II", pp.26f.

87 The added reference to the punishment of rebels at Ḫirimme (Chic. i_{58-60}) may reflect later events, but possibly it was prompted by a similar passage in the account of Sennacherib's third campaign (Chic. iii_{10}). The remarks were not retained by Bull 4. Rass. (// Chic. ii_{30-32}) adds a note of the settlement of deported peoples in Kar Sennacherib to Bell.'s account of Sennacherib's second campaign. The settlement may have taken place at a later time. Comparable are Chic.-Tayl.'s insertion of a remark on Lule's death, which updates the narration of his escape (ii_{40}) and the additional mentions of Sippar in Chic. i_{41} and Išqaluna in Chic. iii_{32}. Rass. (// Chic. ii_{30ff}) adds references to the settlement of deportees in Elenzaš, the handing over of the city to the governor of Ḫarḫar, and the resulting extension of Assyrian territory. These remarks, too, might reflect later events. Cf. also the addition of *gammalē* ("camels") by Rass. (// Chic. ii_{20}) to a list of booty items taken from Ispabara's country and below, p.116, n.209.

anticipates the outcome of a later search. It is noteworthy that in this case the number of indications of a secondary character of a text did not increase progressively with further editions.

Two alterations may be taken as having affected the time structure of the narrative. Whereas Bell. had taken over the introduction with the royal epithets without alteration, Rass. added one epithet to the list: *šar kiššati* ("king of the world" // Chic. i_2). Rass. also replaced *ina rēš šarrūtīya* ("at the beginning of my kingship") by *ina maḫrê girrīya* ("in my first campaign") which corresponds to *ina šanê girrīya* ("in my second campaign"), already present in Bell. (l.20).

The developmental tendencies apparent in the previous redactions can also be seen in the differences between Rass. and Chic.-Tayl. It was noted above that already in Bell. mentions of Sennacherib's enemies' actions were reduced to a minimum. In Chic.-Tayl. a passage describing these actions has been added to the royal titulary before the account of the first campaign thus summarizing and anticipating later events:

ultu tâmti elēnīti ša šalām šamši adi tâmtim šaplīti ša ṣīt šamši gimri ṣalmāt qaqqadi ušakniš šēpū'a u malkī šipṣūti ēdurū tāḫāzi dadmēšun izzibūma kīma sutinni iṣṣūr nigiṣṣi ēdiš ipparšū ašar lā âri

"from the upper sea of the sunrise to the lower sea of the sunset all mankind he brought in submission to my feet and mighty kings feared my war-fare, left their dwellings; like a bat, the bird of the crevice, they fled alone to an inaccessible place" (ll.13-19).

In the following campaign accounts the reported actions of Sennacherib's enemies are almost restricted to those mentioned in the summarizing introduction. The actions mentioned in the introduction are:

(*iknušū* -	"they submitted")[88]	i_{15}
ēdurū	("they feared")	i_{16}
izzibū	("they left")	i_{17}
ipparšū	("they fled")	i_{19}.

Actions mentioned in the accounts of the first three campaigns are:

ezēbu	("to leave")	i_{23}[89], i_{59}[90]
naparšudu	("to escape")	i_{24}[91], ii_3[92]

---

88 The text has the causative *ušakniš* with the god Aššur as grammatical subject. The implied action of Sennacherib's enemies is that of *kanāšu* ("to submit to").

89 The *agent* is Merodach-baladan.

90 The verb is negated with *ēdu* ("a single one") as *agent*.

91 The *agent* is Merodach-baladan.

92 The *agents* are the "people of the land of the Kassites and the Yasubi-gallai".

wašāru	(D "to leave")	i_{26}[93], ii_{14}[94]
kanāšu	("to submit to")	$i_{49.67}$, $ii_{61,72}$, iii_{19}[95]
nābutu	("to flee")	ii_{14}[96], ii_{40}[97]

Exceptions are found in Chic.-Tayl's account of the third campaign and in those passages which report that peoples submitted to the Assyrians and paid tribute. That exceptions are found in the account of the third campaign[98] (and in later ones) is due to the fact that these show fewer signs of redactorial activity. The exceptions are mainly found in passages describing internal participant relations.

The reference to Bēl-ibni, who in the meantime had been taken to Assyria (Bab.Chr. ii_{27}) was completely omitted by Chic.-Tayl., thus adapting the account to political circumstances at the time the redaction took place. The omission also removes a mention of a secondary participant as *patient* and conforms to the tendency to concentrate on primary participants.

Bull 4 followed this trend and with the alteration of *ina qabal tamḫāri šuāti ēzib karāssu* ("in the midst of that battle he {sc. Merodach-baladan} forsook his camp" - Chic. i_{23}) to *šū ana šūzub napištīšu* ("that one, to save his life"; Bull

---

93 The *agent* is Merodach-baladan.
94 The *agent* is Ispabara.
95 All listed occurrences of this verb are negated.
96 The *agent* is Ispabara.
97 The *agent* is Lule.
98 Actions of Sennacherib's enemies in Chic.-Tayl.'s account of his third campaign are:

Lule	*innabit* ("he fled", ii_{40}),
	īmid (with *šadâšu*, "he fled to his mountain" = "he died", ii_{40}),
vassals	*iššûnimma* ("they brought", ii_{60}),
	unaššiqū (with *šēpēya*, "they kissed my feet", ii_{60}),
Šarruludari	*išâṭ* (with *abšānī*, "he bore my yoke", ii_{68}),
Sidqa	*iknušū* ("who submitted", negated, ii_{72}),
people of Ekron	*iddûma* ("who had thrown {Padi, their king ... into fetters ...}", ii_{75}),
	iddinūšu ("who had given him {over to Hezekiah}", ii_{77}),
	ikterūnimma ("they called upon {the Egyptian kings}", ii_{81}),
Egyptians	*illikū* ("they came {to their aid}", ii_{81}),
	uša''alū ("they sharpened {their weapons}", iii_{1}),
people of Ekron	*ušabšū* (with *ḫiṭṭu*, "they committed sin", iii_{8f}),
Hezekiah	*iknušū* ("who submitted", negated, iii_{19}),
	ušēribūma ("which he had brought in", referring to *Urbi u ṣābēšu damqūti* {"the Urbi and his picked troops"}, iii_{39}),
	ušēbilamma ("he had {them} bring {tribute after me}", iii_{48}).

4, 1.4) the last reference to secondary participants (*karāssu* - "his camp" {B'}) has disappeared from the main-line of the account.

We can thus note that at least for the development of Sennacherib's campaign accounts common trends are apparent. The narrative structure and participant orientation pattern have become progressively simpler.[99] The narrative was edited with its outcome in view. The redactors thus resolved the chronological order of the first version.

If we take the development of Sennacherib's campaign accounts as empirical model serious obstacles for literary-critical research into the pre-history of Old Testament narratives arise. Hypotheses as those outlined above[100] have not found support. To the contrary, the omitted portions could not be reconstructed without the presence of earlier manuscripts. Without the latter it is also difficult to establish the order of events as compared to the order of narration. Even if this could be done, we cannot *a priori* assume that both necessarily agreed in the earliest version.[101] We have noted that editors revised their sources with the narrative's outcome in view. We thus have to reckon with harmonizing changes, removing difficulties from the narrative. Again, from a harmonized exemplar it is not possible to deduce the original differences. Since several of the narrative features which can be related to redactorial intervention are also present in *early versions* of other stories, their absence may be taken as indication for an *early stage* of literary development but their presence does not permit unequivocal deductions. The effects of alterations carried out in the transmission of Sennacherib's campaign accounts may permit to identify a given narrative with a simple time

---

99 In the case of Sennacherib's second campaign where already the earliest extant version (Bell.) exhibited a simple narrative structure and participant pattern these were not significantly altered. This is also true for sections 2,3, and 4 of Rass.'s narration of Sennacherib's third campaign. The treatment the first section of Rass.'s account by later versions shows that narratives with a complex participant orientation pattern were not necessarily simplified (see tables 1.3-5 in appendix III).

100 Cf. pp.2f, n.7; pp.6f, n.11.

101 In Rass.'s account of Sennacherib's third campaign Padi's release and the siege of Jerusalem are related in separate sections, which implies a resolution of the chronological order. The release of Padi (*ultu qereb Urusalimmu ušēṣâmma* ("I brought out of Jerusalem", with Sennacherib as *agent* - // Chic. iii_{15}) is not likely to have taken place before the beginning of the siege of Judean cities (// Chic. iii_{18ff}) or even of Jerusalem (// Chic. iii_{28}). But even within the sections the order of narration is not chronological (cf. Rass. // Chic. ii_{74-77}, $iii_{27.39-40}$).

organization, a complex participant orientation pattern, references to secondary participants, and a complex narrative structure as being preserved in an *early stage* of literary development, but the opposite conclusion from the absence of these features cannot claim any certainty.[102]

2. Aššurbanipal's Campaign Accounts

The second set of *annalistic* literature to be investigated is provided by Aššurbanipal's campaign accounts. Again a stemma has to be established first. The dates of the main editions taken as basis here are those established by A.K.Grayson.[103] These are:

E	665 B.C.(?)[104]
B	649 B.C.[105]
C	646 B.C.[106]
F	c.646 B.C.[107]
A	c.643/2 B.C.[108]

---

102 Although in our investigation we have to concentrate on the differences between the versions, it must not be ignored that in a number of cases accounts were retained without significant alteration (cf. appendix III).

103 "Chronology". Cf. also H.Tadmor, "The Three Last Decades" (E: 665 B.C.(?), B: 649 B.C., C: 647 B.C., F: 645 B.C., A: 643 B.C.).

104 For the text cf. A.C.Piepkorn, *Historical Prism Inscriptions*, pp.10-16 (A 7919, A 7920, K 1821, K 1828), R.Campbell Thompson, "A Selection" (BM 134445 {no.20}, BM 121018 {no.21}, BM 134455 {no.23}), A.R.Millard, "Fragments" (BM 127923 {pl.20}, BM 127940 {pl.19}, BM 128230 {pl.19}, BM 128306 {pl.20}, BM 134454 {pl.20}, BM 134481 {pl.20} + 128305 {pl.19}). A.Spalinger, "Assurbanipal and Egypt", p.317, dates the sack of Thebes to 664 and thus ed. E to a later date. A.K.Grayson, "Chronology", p.245, argues for 663 B.C. However, taking up M.Cogan's and H.Tadmor's suggestion ("Gyges and Ashurbanipal") he assumes the existence of two earlier editions of E, E_1 (666/5 B.C.) and E_2 (665/4 B.C.). In this respect the latters' conclusions are not supported by the evidence available. The relative order of mss., however, is not affected by a slightly later date of E.

105 For the text cf. A.C.Piepkorn, *Historical Prism Inscriptions*. A.Spalinger, "Assurbanipal and Egypt", dates B to 648 B.C. The text of prism D does not differ significantly from that of ed. B (cf. A.C.Piepkorn, *Historical Prism Inscriptions*, pp.94-95) and thus has been disregarded in our comparison.

106 For the text cf. R.D.Freedman, *Assurbanipal's "Annals"*; cf. also R.D.Freedman, *Cuneiform Tablets*.

107 For the Text cf. J.M.Aynard, *Prisme*.

108 For the text cf. M.Streck, *Assurbanipal* II.

Further important editions are H_1 (c.639 B.C.)[109], H_2[110], K and T (646 B.C.)[111] An early and important version of Aššurbanipal's early campaigns is found on K 228(+)[112]

In a study of Aššurbanipal's campaigns in Egypt[113] A. Spalinger established the following stemma:

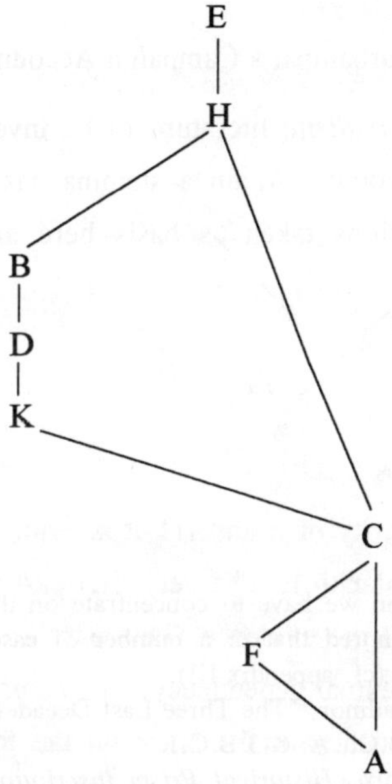

As was already evident in the case of Sennacherib's *annals*, considerations based only on a part of the available evidence do not permit final conclusions. A

---

[109] Cf. A.K.Grayson, "Chronology", p.245. For the text cf. E.Nassouhi, "Prisme d'Assurbanipal".

[110] Cf. Weidner, "älteste Nachricht".

[111] Cf. R.Campbell Thompson, *Prisms*, pp.29-36. pll.14-18.

[112] Cf. M.Streck, *Assurbanipal* II, pp.158-174; henceforth HT (Harran Tablets, after the place for which they were composed). Although HT is a votive inscription and thus does not constitute an *annal* edition, because of its closeness to ed. E and the similar case of K 2802(+) and VAT 5600(+) (cf. M.Weippert, "Kämpfe", pp.74-81) for Assurbanipal's campaigns against Arabs, it will nevertheless be treated like an *annal* edition. Since HT contains reports of the Arvad and Tabal affairs, not present in E, HT was probably written later than E (cf. A.Olmstead, *Assyrian Historiography*, pp.54f and A.Spalinger, "Assurbanipal and Egypt", pp.317f.). Further indications will be given below in our discussion of developmental tendencies.

[113] "Assurbanipal and Egypt".

comparison of the whole texts of the various editions was carried out by R.D.Freedman[114] and led to different results:

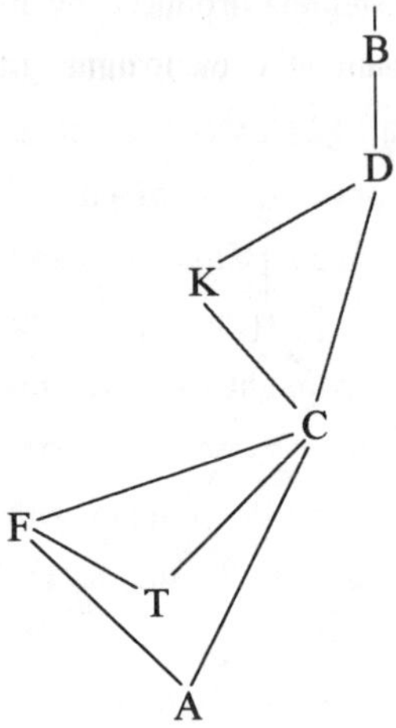

From the great similarity of E and HT it is evident that HT depends on E or at least on a text very similar to E. The very first part of Spalinger's stemma is without doubt justified by all the evidence. This part was not covered by Freedman's reconstruction of the textual dependency. The nature of similarities between HT and B indicates a dependency of the latter on the former. Thus Spalinger's reconstruction is correct in this part, too. B also has readings in common with E against HT. $Biii_{11}$ has *ālu šuātu* ("that city") which is also found in $Eiii_{28}$,[115] whereas HT has *Kirbit*. This instance by itself however, would not be sufficient evidence for a literary dependency. The difference between the two readings could well be due to the different contexts in the three manuscripts. Two more cases can be adduced. $Biii_{12}$ provides the information that the leader of the city of Kirbit was taken to Nineveh. A reference to this is also made in $Eiii_{5}$,[116] but not in HT. It must, however, be said that not only the wording is different but also the name of the deported leader. The second case is found in HT rev.12, where HT has

114 *Assurbanipal's "Annals"*, p.138.
115 BM 134445, BM 121018 (cf. R.Campbell Thompson, "A Selection", pp.100-102, nos.20.21).
116 BM 134481 (Millard, "Fragments", pl.20), K 1821 (A.C.Piepkorn, *Historical Prism Inscriptions*, p.14 {as iv_5}).

kišittī qātēya ("captives of my hands") which is found in neither E nor B. The latter have similar readings in this passage. A dependency of C on HT is also traceable.[117] With regard to this the stemma produced by Freedman is somewhat misleading. Furthermore, a dependency of C on E might be indicated by the presence of *arkānu* ("afterwards") in Cii_{105}, which is present in Eii_{27}, but missing in HT. Unfortunately the bad state of preservation of ed. C does not allow to adduce more evidence. Aii_9 and Eiv_{19}[118] read *aškun* ("I established {a treaty with him}") whereas HT has *ašpur* ("I wrote {a treaty with him}" - obv.54).[119] The corresponding passage in C is lost but might have had the same reading as A, coinciding with E against HT. Numerous agreements of eds. F and C indicate that F is dependent on C. F has also a reading in common with B against C. Fi_{40} has the same text as Bii_{22} *ana qereb Ni' innabit* ("he fled to Thebes"). Cii_{83} has a different word-order in this passage: *innabit ana qereb N*[*i'*]. This, however, may be regarded as insufficient evidence to postulate literary dependence.

With regard to A's *Vorlagen* it is important to note that A is not only dependent on C and F as Spalinger's and Freedman's stemmata might suggest. $Aii_{98.104}$ // HT rev.16f.20 indicate that A is also dependent on HT and, if Cogan and Tadmor are right, and their reconstruction of the extent of edition E[120] appears to be reasonable, then A might also have used a text of edition E as a source. A and B share a reading against F in $Bvii_{48}$ (// Aiv_5). The readings of A and B are, however, not entirely identical. B has a main clause, whereas A has a subordinate clause. Since the common reading is a stock-phrase,[121] the textual situation could be explained without the assumption of literary dependence. The case is different with $Bvii_{58\text{-}61}$, which is retained in $Aiv_{12\text{-}15}$. The word order is different, but the information common to B and A does not consist of stock-phrases. Thus either A is dependent on B or they have used very similar sources. It is interesting to note that the reading of A also occurs in B_5.[122]

---

117 Cii_{105}-iii_3 parallels HT obv.33-41.43-47, which has no equivalent in ed.B.

118 BM 128305 (cf. A.R.Millard, "Fragments", pl.19).

119 Cf. Th.Bauer's correction of Streck's reading in *Inschriftenwerk*, p.33, n.3.

120 Cf. "Gyges and Ashurbanipal", p.70, n.18; cf. below, pp.137ff.

121 *ul išāl šulum šarrūtīya* ("he did not inquire after the well-being of my kingship" - B), *lā išālu šulum šarrūtīya* ("who did not inquire after the well-being of my kingship" - A).

122 Cf. A.C.Piepkorn, *Historical Prism Inscriptions*, p.79, n.28. B_5 has an additional "ša". Cf. also B_5 (//$Bviii_{53}$) // Aiv_{10} (cf. A.C.Piepkorn, *Historical Prism Inscriptions*,

The following stemma may be suggested:[123]

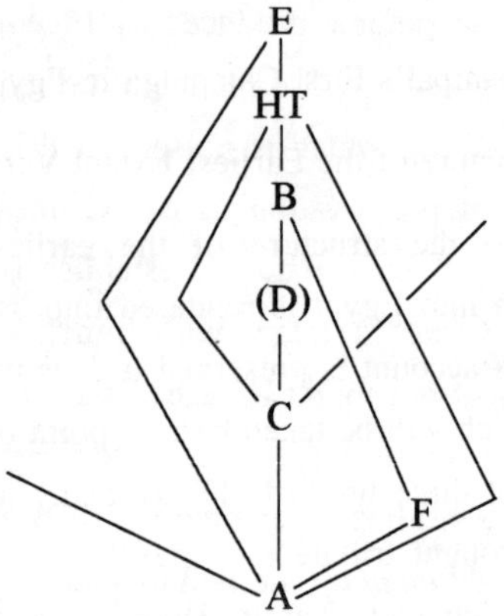

As in the case of Sennacherib's *annals*, this stemma can only present a distorted picture. It cannot claim to represent actual and direct dependences. The stemma indicates as a dependence on several sources what in fact may have been a more complex literary history with several non-extant manuscripts, each depending on only one *Vorlage*. It is only because of the preservation of ed. E and HT that we know that B and later versions did not expand their *Vorlagen* but omitted from a more extensive source. Without the actual *Vorlagen* any comparison between different editions is thus necessarily preliminary. However, the substantial similarities between the extant editions justify the present investigation. We further have to allow for the author's / redactor's personal preferences[124] which may have been responsible for some changes not corresponding to or even contradicting the general course of literary development. It is important to recognize that even where earlier sources are extant some of the alterations cannot be related

---

p.79, n.24).

[123] Only the main versions are mentioned. There were, of course, other sources, e.g. the list of Esarhaddon's vassal kings which was used by ed. C. Cf. below, p.126, n.233.

[124] We may note A's extensive description of Šamaš-šum-ukīn's rebellion here (cf. Aiii$_{70-135}$ iv$_{41-10}$). To B's account of the campaign against Ummanigaš C has added two references to Aššurbanipal's brother (Cviii$_{15.45}$).

to general tendencies, the redactor's reasons for changing the text of the *Vorlage* remain obscure.[125]

a) Aššurbanipal's First Campaign in Egypt

(1) The Structure of the Earliest Extant Version

An investigation into the structure of the earliest extant account of Aššurbanipal's first campaign into Egypt is rendered impossible by E's bad state of preservation. As far as E's account is preserved it does not seem to differ substantially from that of HT which will be taken here as point of departure.

Unfortunately the first three lines of HT are badly mutilated.[126] The next line[127] narrates that kings brought tribute to Nineveh and kissed Aššurbanipal's feet. L.2 introduces a new character, Tarqu. Here, contrary to l.15, he is not called *šar Kusi* ("king of Kusi"). This suggests that he had been mentioned in the first three lines of HT. Nevertheless, l.2 constitutes the beginning of a new paragraph. There appears to be no link in form or content between this line and the previous one.

---

[125] A has inserted narrations of Šamaš-šum-ukīn's uprising (iii_{70-127}), Aššurbanipal's campaign to quell the rebellion ($iii_{128-135}$), of a famine in Babylon, Šamaš-šum-ukīn's death, and the sack of Babylon (Aiv_{41-109}). These accounts were inserted in two sections, both introduced with *ina ūmēšu* ("in these days" - $Aiii_{70}$, iv_{41}). The first section anticipates the second with $iii_{130-134}$ and the second section refers back to the first with iv_{42f} // $iii_{79.106}$. The description of the famine parallels C's account in contents but differs in wording (resemblences are found in Aiv_{43-45} // $Cviii_{115-117}$, A_{51-52} // Cix_{29-34}, Aiv_{59} // Cix_{16-18}, Aiv_{62-63} // Cix_{36-37}, Aiv_{64-65} // Cix_{38-44}). A's accounts include the description of a seer's dream which closely corresponds to that of the later events (iii_{122f} // iv_{43} - cf. also iii_{79}); iii_{125} // iv_{59}, $iv_{50f.58.60}$, iii_{135}·$iv_{43.59.80}$; iii_{126} // iii_{134}·iv_{79}). For the differences between C and A no reason is apparent. We can only note that in A the narrations of prophecy and fulfillment correspond to each other.
In those parts of B's account of Tammaritu's dethronement ($Bvii_{45-57}$) which have been taken over by F and/or A ($Fiii_{12-20}$ // Aiv_{3-22}), virtually every phrase has been slightly altered. No reason for this is apparent. It is interesting to note that the differences between B and F/A correspond to those found between Biblical parallel accounts, from which H.Ringgren "Oral and Written Transmission") deduced a period of oral tradition. The variations between Aššurbanipal's campaign accounts show that such differences are perfectly compatible with transmission by writing.

[126] Cf. Th.Bauer, *Inschriftenwerk*, p.33, n.3.

[127] M.Streck's line 1 (cf. above, p.96, n.108). Streck's line counting will be used hence.

The rhetorical level of HT's account is high. Already ll.2-4, the *stage* of the narrative, contain an EEN construction:

danān Aššur bēlīya emêšma
ittakil ana emūq ramānīšu
[epš]ēt maruštu ša abu banû'a ēpušuš ul ibbalkit ina libbīšu.

"he ignored the power of Aššur, my lord,
he trusted in his own strength,
the harmful deed, which the father who begot me inflicted upon him, he did not remember."

The same is true for the narration of the *inciting event* (ll.5-7):

illikamma
qereb Mimpi ērumma
ālu šuātu ana ramānūšu utīr

"he went,
entered Memphis,
took this city for himself,"

ana *dâki*
ḫabāti
šalāli
uma''era ummānšu

"To kill,
loot,
plunder
he sent his army".

Aššurbanipal's emotions are described in a chiastic parallelism:

libbī īgugma
issariḫ kabittī

"my heart became enraged,
my liver seethed" (l.10).

The narrative rests for a moment, only to go on in intensified form. The rise of tension is paralleled by an accumulation of adverbs in ll.13-14.[128] The tension reaches its climax in ll.16-18, where the opposition of Aššurbanipal's and Tarqu's forces is expressed in another parallel construction:

ana epēš *qabli*
kakkē tāḫāzi ummānātēšu idkâ
isdira miḫrit ummānātēya

---

128 *urruḫiš* ("hastily), *šamriš* ("furiously"), *ḫanṭiš* ("swiftly"). A similar function of adverbs my be adduced for E's description of the destruction of Kirbit and some other cities (*abūbiš* {"like a flood" - iii_{23}}, *imbariš* {"like fog" - iii_{32}}, *ḫuḫariš* {"as with a bird-trap" - iii_{33}}); cf. BM 134445, BM 121018 (R.Campbell Thompson, "A Selec-

"to do battle,
fighting with arms, *his* troops he mustered,
he drew up (his battle lines) before *my* troops"

(l.16).

Overlay[129] is employed to slow down the narrative and prepare for the resolution of the conflict. The outcome of the battle is introduced by a comparatively extensive reference to divine support (l.17). The narrative rests for a moment to describe the Assyrian victory (l.18). The resolution of the conflict is stated and tension declines. The narration of Tarqu's fate parallels ll.10ff. A description of feelings precedes the report of actions. While the rise of tension was expressed by EEN-constructions with increasing length, it is interesting to note that Tarqu's escape is related in sentences of decreasing length:

ultu Mimpi[130] *āl šarrūtīšu ašar tukultīšu uṣṣīma*
ana šūzub napištīšu qereb eleppi irkabma
karāssu umašširma
ēdiš ipparšidma
qereb Niʾ ērub

"from Memphis, his royal city, his strong point, he went out,
to save his life he boarded a ship,
he left his camp,
escaped alone,
entered Thebes."

The mentions of the capture of Tarqu's ships (l.23)[131] and of another *mār-šipri* ("messenger") sent to Aššurbanipal (l.24) conclude the first section of the campaign account. HT obv.24 constitutes a transition passage concluding the first section by transferring the scope back from secondary participants to Aššurbanipal himself, and simultaneously initiating another episode by prompting the Assyrian king to intervene again. The structure of this episode corresponds to that of the first one, conforming to a similar course of events. The overall rhetorical level, however, is lower. Aššurbanipal's emotions are only indirectly referred to by *bussurat ḫadê* ("joyful message" - obv.24). Aššurbanipal sends his army, Tarqu learns about it and flees. Rhetorical devices are employed far less extensively. No

---

tion", pp.100-102, nos.20.21).

129 Each member of the construction repeats part of the preceding member; cf. J.E.Grimes, *Thread of Discourse*, pp.292ff.

130 Cf. l.5.

131 Cf. below, pp.110f, n.167.

adverbs are used, the march of the army is referred to by one *main line* verb only, *illikū* ("they went"), and Tarqu's escape is described less extensively than the first time with *āl dannūtīšu umašširma Iaru'u ēbirma* ("he left his strong city, crossed the Nile" - obv.31). The lower rhetorical level conforms to the fact that the decisive event, the defeat of Tarqu's army, had already taken place.

The introduction of a different grammatical subject in 1.33, *Niku Šarruludari Pakruru*, indicates the beginning of a second unit,[132] the rhetorical level of which is comparatively high.

The first part of this section narrates a plot against the Assyrians in which Egyptian vassal rulers were involved, giving in direct speech their plan and their message to Tarqu (- 1.40). Already the introduction is formed in a chiastic parallelism:

adê Aššur u ilāni rabûti bēlēya ētiqūma
iprusū māmīssun

"the oaths of Aššur and the great gods, my lords, they transgressed,
they broke their treaty."

The quotation of direct speech slows down the narration and since direct speech is not very commonly employed in Aššurbanipal's *annals* it denotes a rise of the rhetorical level. In the rebels' message to Tarqu rhetorical underlining is used and HT obv.39b-40 constitute an EEN-construction:

nindaggara aḫāmeš
māt aḫennâ nizuzma
ai ibbaši ina bīrini šanûmma bēlum.

"let us help one another,
let us divide the land amongst each of us,
there shall not be another lord amongst us."

The parallelism in ll.41-42 summarizes the allies' plans and clarifies the major conflict by expressly mentioning the Assyrians as the target of the aggression:

ana ummānāt Aššur gabšātīya	*ištene''û amāt lemuttim*
ana šūzub[133] *napištīšun*	*ikrimū ḫulluqû adi lā bašê*

"against the Assyrian army, my multitudes, they devised an evil plan,
to save their lives, they held back complete destruction".

---

132 Ed. E (ii_{27} // Cii_{105} // Ai_{118}) further separates the units by *arkānu* ("afterwards").
133 Eii_{47}: *nakās* ("to cut"); cf. Piepkorn, *Historical Prism Inscriptions*, p.14.

There is still no progress of events. The intensifications *gapšatīya* ("my multitudes") and *adi lā bašê* ("until non-existence") led to a further increase of tension. For the *dênouement* of the story the narration is resumed, though again very slowly, in parallel constructions and with the use of *overlay*:[134]

šūt-rēšīya amāti annāti	*išmûma*	*ikkilū niklassun* (l.43)
rakbêšun	*iṣbatūnimma*	*ēmurū epšet surrātīšun* (l.44)
Šarruludari Niku	*iṣbatūnimma*	
ina birēti parzilli išqāti parzilli	*utammeḫū qātā u šēpā* (l.45)	
māmīt Aššur šar ilāni	*ikšussunūtima ša iḫṭū ina adê* <*ilāni*>[135] *rabûti* (l.46)	

"My officers *heard* of these matters, *saw through* their cunning plan,
they *seized* their mounted messenger, *discovered* their rebellious plot,
they *seized* Šarruludari, Niku
they *bound* (their) hands and (their) feet with iron shackles (and) iron bonds.
The oath of Aššur, king of the gods, captured them, who had sinned against the treaty of the great <gods>".

While the second parts of ll.43.44 correspond to each other (*ikkilū* {"they saw through"} - *ēmurū* {"they discovered"}), the first parts denote progress of events (*išmûma* {"they heard of"}, *iṣbatūnimma* {"they seized"}). *iṣbatūnimma* ("they seized") in l.45a refers back to the same word in l.44, and l.45b only intensifies the first part of the line.[136] It is the grammatical object that changes from l.44 to l.45 and the grammatical subject from l.45 to l.46. Ll.46-50 form the *Coda* of the narrative. Ll.46-48, intensified by l.49, describe the punishment of the rebels and resemble the report of the *inciting event*:

ll.34-35	ll.46-48
adê Aššur u ilāni rabûti bēlēya...	*māmīt Aššur šar ilāni ...*
iprusū māmīssun	*ša iḫṭû ina adê* <*ilāni*>[137] *rabûti*
ṭābti ša abu bānīya...	*ṭābti ... ša ēpušūšunūti dunqu*
libbašunūti ikpud limuttam	*u nišē ālāni mala ittīšunu* [*šaknū*] *ikpudū amāt limutti*
"the oath of Aššur and the great gods my lords..."	"the treaty of Aššur, king of the gods..."
"they broke their treaty"	"who had sinned against the oath of the great gods"
"the favour of the father, who begot me..."	"the favour ... the kindness which I had shown to them"
"their heart plotted evil"	"and the inhabitants of the cities,

---

[134] Cf. above, p.103, n.129.
[135] Cf. Ai$_{133}$.
[136] *parzilli* ("iron") contrasts with *ḫurāṣi* ("golden") in ll.56.57.58.
[137] Cf. above, n.135.

as many as had joined them
(and) had plotted evil."

In l.50 the setting switches back to Nineveh.[138] This concludes the section. In this passage l.47 is of special significance. This sentence describes the result of a gradual development. L.44 narrates the capture of the enemies' messenger by Aššurbanipal's generals (A' - C'), l.45 the capture of the rebels themselves (A' - C), l.46 refers to divine intervention (A*[139] - C) and, finally, l.47 describes the resolution of the conflict with the express mention of the primary participants (A - C). The participant orientation thus gradually approaches and culminates in the main participant relation.[140] This has led to the sudden appearance of a verb in 1st p.sgl., *(qātuššun) uba''īma* ("I called them to account" - l.47) with Aššurbanipal as *agent*, although, as is evident from l.50, the Assyrian king is still in Nineveh.[141] Consequently in obv.49f again 3rd p.pl. is employed.[142]

---

[138] Cf. II.1.9.

[139] An asterisk will be used henceforth to indicate references to divine participants.

[140] Similarly in B's account of Aššurbanipal's campaign against Dunanu (cf. appendix III, table 11) the participant relation in a first resolution of the conflict is A'- B'/C' (vii_{30-35}). In the final resolution of the conflict which was achieved by divine intervention the participant relation is A* - B (vii_{40-42}). In E's version of the Kirbit affair (cf. appendix III, table 6), and B's accounts of Aššurbanipal's campaign against Teummān (cf. appendix III, table 8, and below, pp.115f, n.208) the main participant relation with the Assyrian king as *agent* does not occur on the *main line* at all. Several cases may be adduced, where *late stages* omitted references to secondary participants, especially in *peak* sections (cf. below, pp.122f, n.224).

[141] Cf. the interesting parallels in 2 Sam.12_{26-30} // 1 Chr.20_{1-2}, 2 Kgs.12_{18-19} // 2 Chr.24_{24}.

[142] HT obv.47 is paralleled in E (BM 121018 iv_3 {cf. R.Campbell Thompson, "A Selection", no.21}). Cf. also the transition from E (K 1821 {cf. A.C.Piepkorn, *Historical prism inscriptions*, p.14}) iv_6, *ublūni* ("they brought"), to iv_7, *assuḫ* ("I tore away"). Of particular interest is further the participant orientation pattern of B's account of the campaign against Aḫšeri. In the first part of the narrative (iii_{16-30}; cf. below, appendix II, pp.248ff), secondary participants for both Aššurbanipal and Aḫšeri appear as *agents* of *main line* verbs. Neither 1st p.sgl. nor 3rd p.pl. are consistently used. In $Biii_{29}$ the Assyrian army suddenly becomes *agent* (cf. l.22). In the second part (iii_{31ff}), this has suddenly changed back without transition. C has altered *umallū* ("they filled" - $Biii_{30}$) to *umalli* ("I filled" - Civ_{58}) and thus mentions Aššurbanipal as *agent* in the description of the Assyrian victory. F has omitted the first part of the account and thus removed the inconsistency. In F's account of Aššurbanipal's second campaign against Ummanaldasi 1st p.sgl is used until Fv_{43} (// Avi_{64}), then the Assyrian army is introduced as *main line agent* (Fv_{48} // Av_{69}), and from Fv_{49} (//Av_{70}) onwards the account resumes 1st p.sgl. narration.

Further examples can be adduced from accounts of Aššurbanipal's campaigns against

Noteworthy is also the difference between *ṭābti ša abu bānīya* ("the favour of the father who begot me" - l.35) and *ṭābti ... ša ēpušūšunūti dunqu* ("the favour ... the kindness which I had shown to them" - l.47), conforming to the tendency to mention primary participants in *peak* sections.[143]

u anāku Aššur-bān-apli ("and I, Aššurbanipal" - l.51) introduces the concluding section of HT's account of Aššurbanipal's first Egyptian campaign. The Assyrian king clearly dominates the *main line* for the remainder of the account. Almost no progress of events is apparent. Ll.55-59 describe Aššurbanipal's gifts to Niku, who had been pardoned by the Assyrian king (ll.52-54). The mention of the lavish presents (*ḫurāṣu* {"gold"} in ll.56.57.58)[144] constitutes another climax of the narrative. The campaign account ends with the mentions of Niku's and his son's re-installations (ll.61-65) and a reference to the fate of Tarqu (l.66), thereby closing the circle to l.2.

Arabs. B's participant orientation pattern exhibits several abrupt changes from primary to secondary participants in $\text{Bviii}_{5\text{-}6\text{-}7.(15\text{-}16.)26\text{-}28}$. According to Bviii_7 Assyrian troops are dispatched *ṣēruššu* ("against *him*"), but Bviii_8 notes *abiktašunu iškunū* ("they accomplished *their* defeat"). Bviii_{27} mentions the punishment according to *adêšun* ("*their* oath"), which was inflicted on (*ištmū*)-*šu* (-"*him*"). VAT 5600+ ll.44-60 (// $\text{Avii}_{105\text{-}124}$) have the Assyrian army as *main line agents*, whereas in col. IV suddenly the Assyrian king is grammatical subject. Additional cases of sudden changes are found in $\text{Avii}_{93.100}$ and $\text{Aviii}_{102.104}$. Since it is not probable that VAT 5600+ would have altered 1st pers. sgl. into 3rd pers. pl., we may assume that A has preserved an earlier version of the account.

The preserved portions of K 2652 (cf. M.Streck, *Assurbanipal* II, pp.188-194) appear to have a sudden change of grammatical subject from rev.8-10 to rev.11 (cf. appendix II, pp.252f, n.12).

A further inconsistency created by the difference between primary and secondary participants is found between Bvi_1 where Aššurbanipal claims to have decapitated Teummān and $\text{Bvii}_{60\text{-}61}$ where he(!) ascribes this to a soldier of his army.

We can also note inconsistencies of participant designations. In B Uaite᾽ is introduced as *šar Qadaru* ("king of Qedar", vii_{94}). His subjects, however, are designated as "Arabs" (cf. $\text{Bviii}_{4.8.23}$). A has altered the introduction to *šar Aribi* ("king of Arabia" - vii_{83}) and has thus removed the inconsistency. In another section, however ($\text{Aix}_{1\text{-}2}$, not paralleled in B), the participant designations were not harmonized (*u Qidraya Uaite᾽ ... šar Aribi* {"and the Qidrai of Uaite᾽ ... king of Arabia"}). Cf. also below, p.155.

143 A has *ṭābat ... ēpussunūti* ("the favour ... which I had shown to them") in both passages ($\text{Ai}_{119.133}$).

144 Cf. also l.63.

The following diagram shows the *discourse profile* of HT's version:

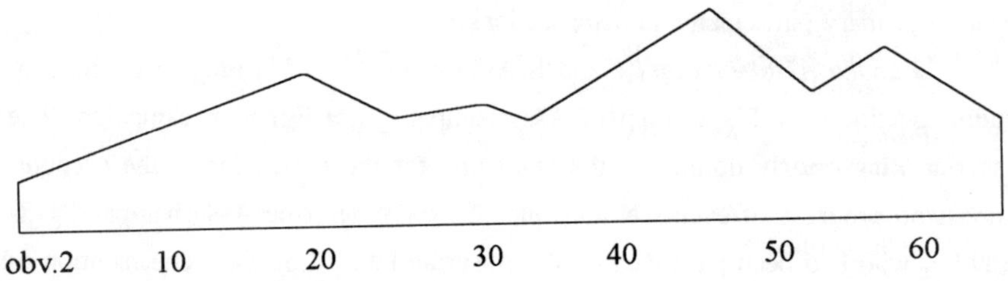

The order of narration appears to be roughly chronological, with the exception of several subordinate clauses,[145] most of which refer to Esarhaddon. In Ei the installation of Egyptian vassal kings by Esarhaddon had been reported on the *main line* before the actual campaign account. The following table represents the participant orientation pattern for the account on Aššurbanipal's first campaign in its different versions.

				HT	B	C/A
					+[146]	+
l.2	*uštamṣâ*[147] "he set about"	B	(A)		-	-
l.3	*emēšma* "he forgot	B	A*[148]	⇒ I	r	r
	ittakil "he trusted"	B	(A)	⇒ I	I	I
l.4	*ul ibbalkit* (with *ina libbīšu*) - "he did not remember"	A*[149]	B	⇒ r	-	
l.5	*illikamma* "he went"	B	A'	⇒ r	I[150]	I

---

[145] Cf. ll.4.33.47.48.52.61. Cf. also in B's account of Aššurbanipal's campaign against Aḫšeri the subordinate clauses in $iii_{18\text{-}19.53\text{-}54.74\text{-}75}$ $iv_{5.10\text{-}15}$ which do not follow the chronological order.

[146] *lu allik* ("I went") - A [B].

[147] For the text cf. M.Streck, *Assurbanipal* II, pp.158-174.

[148] *danān Aššur bēlīya* ("the power of Aššur, my lord"); cf. above, p.106, n.139.

[149] Grammatical subject: *epšēt marušti ša abu bānû'a ēpušuš* ("the harmful deed which the father, who begot me, inflicted upon him").

[150] *illaka* ("he went")- corresponds to *uma''era ummānšu* ("he sent his army", HT obv.8).

	ērumma "he entered"	B	A'		⇒ I	I	I
	utīr "he took"	B	A'		⇒ I	I[151]	I
1.8	uma''era "he sent"	B	B'	A'	⇒ I	-	-
1.9	illikamma "he went"	A'	A	(B)	⇒ r	r	r
	ušannâ "he notified"	A'	A	(B)	⇒ I	I	I
1.10	ēgugma "(my heart) became enraged"	A	(B)		⇒ I	I	I
	issariḫ "(my liver) seethed"	A	(B)		⇒ I	I	I I[152] I[153] I[154]
1.11	alsīma "I called"	A	A'	(B)	⇒ I	-	-
1.13	aškunšunūti "I gave them (order)"	A	A'	(B)	⇒ I	I[155]	I I[156] I[157]
	ušaškina (with šēpāšun) - "I ordered them to march"	A	A'	(B)	⇒ I	-	I[158]
1.14	irdū "they marched"	A'	(B)		⇒ I	I[159]	I
	illikū "they went"	A'	(B)		⇒ I	I[160]	I
1.15	išme "he heard"	B	A'		⇒ r	r	r

---

[151] ūšib ("he took up residence") - B [A].
[152] aššu ("I lifted up {my hands}") - A A* [B] (Ai₆₅, not in ed.C).
[153] uṣalli ("I implored") - A A* [B] (Ai₆₅, not in ed. C).
[154] ušteššera (ḫarrānu) ("I took the road" - A [B].
[155] adki ("I mustered").
[156] iššûnimma ("they brought") - A' A [B].
[157] unaššiqū ("they kissed") - A' A [B].
[158] urḫu padānu ušaṣbissunūti ("I had them take path {and} road") - A A' [B]
[159] ardīma ("I marched") - A [B].
[160] allik ("I went") - A [B].

1.16	*idkâ*	B	B'	A'	⇒ I	I	I
	"he mustered"						
	isdira	B	B'	A'	⇒ I	-	-
	"he drew up"						
1.18	*iškunū*	A'	B		⇒ r	r[161]	r
	"they accomplished (his defeat)"						
	urassibū	A'	B'		⇒ I	-	-
	"they slew"						
						r[162]	r
1.19	*imqussuma*	A[163]	B		⇒ I	r[164]	r
	"they fell upon him"						
	illiku	B	(A)		⇒ r	r	r
	(with *maḫḫutiš*) "he went mad"						
1.20	*uṣṣīma*	B	(A)		⇒ I	-	-
	"he went out"						
1.21	*irkabma*	B	(A)		⇒ I	-	-
	"he boarded (a ship)"						
						r[165]	r
1.22	*umašširma*	B	(A)		⇒ I	r	r
	"he left"						
	ipparšidma	B	(A)		⇒ I	I[166]	I
	"he escaped"						
	ērub	B	(A)		⇒ I	-	-
	"he entered"						
1.23	*uṣabbitū*[167]	A'	B'		⇒ r	-	-
	"they captured"						

---

161 *aškuna* ("I accomplished {the defeat of his troops}") - A B'.

162 *išmâ* ("he heard of") - B A.

163 Grammatical subject: *ḫattu puluḫtu* ("terror, fear"). Cf. *ḫattu puluḫtu bēlūtīya isḫupšuma* ("terror, fear of my dominion overwhelmed him") in 1.66, with the pronominal suffix *-ya* ("my") referring to Aššurbanipal.

164 *isḫupūšuma* ("they overwhelmed him") - A* (*namrīrī Ašur u Ištar* - "the splendour of Aššur and Ištar") B.

165 (*melammē šarrūtīya*) *iktumūšuma* ("{the majesty of my kingship} covered him") - A B.

166 *innabit* ("he fled") - B [A].

167 According to Eii$_{4-5}$, HT obv.23 should be emended to *eleppēti qarābi mala ittīšu* <*u*> *ṣābē tāḫāzi*<*šu*> *uṣabbitū ina qātā* ("the warships, all that were with him, they captured with {their} hands"). The *agents* of *uṣabbitū* ("they captured") are the Assyrian troops (cf. 1.16). For HT obv.24 M.Streck, *Assurbanipal* II, p.160, n.a) suggested the emendation of *DA-A-UD*(*PAR*)*-RA* to *iš*(?)*-ta*(?)*-a-par-ra* ("he sent" {?}). The corresponding passage in Eii$_8$, however, has *ša a-tam-ra* ("that I should behold" ?). Since Streck's emendation does not render the text meaningful, a scribal error (*DA* for *ŠA*)

					-	r[168]	r
					-	I[169]	I
					-	I[170]	I
					-	I[171]	I
					-	I[172]	I[173]
					-	I[174]	I
					-	I[175]	I
					-	I[176]	I
					-	-	I[177]
					-		I[178]
1.24	*iqbâ*	A'	A	(B)	⇒ I	-	-
	"he said"						
1.29	*uraddīma*	A	A'	B	⇒ I	-	-
	"I added"						
	ašpur	A	A'	(B)	⇒ I	-	-
	"I sent"						
	illikū	A'	B		⇒ I	-	-
	"they went"						
1.31	*išme*	B	A'		⇒ r	-	-
	"he heard"						
	umašširma	B	A'		⇒ I	-	-
	"he left"						
1.32	*ēbirma*	B	(A')		⇒ I	-	-
	"he crossed (the river)"						
	iškuna	B	(A')		⇒ I	-	-
	"he set up (a camp)"						
1.34	*ētiquma*	C	A*[179]		⇒ srs[180]	-	rs[181]
	"they transgressed"						

seems more probable.

168 *aṣbat* ("I seized") - A B(').

169 *ušērib* ("I let {my troops} enter {that city}") - A A' [B].

170 *ušēšib* ("I let {my troops} dwell {in that city}") - A A' [B].

171 *utīrma* ("I restored") - A A' [B].

172 *ulzissunūti* ("I installed them") - A A' [B].

173 *apqissunūti* ("I appointed them") - A A' B.

174 (*ana eššūti*) *aṣbat* ("I reorganized") - A A' [B].

175 *udannin* ("I made stronger") - A A' B.

176 *urakkisa* ("I bound {their bonds}" ⇒ "I organized"?) - A A' B.

177 *utīr]amma* ("I turned {my yoke} around") - A (Cii_{103}, not in ed.A).

178 *atūra* ("I returned") - A.

179 Grammatical object: *adê Aššur u ilāni rabûti bēlēya* ("the oaths of Aššur and the great gods, my lords").

180 C has been treated as virtual *benefactive*.

181 *iḫṭû* ("they sinned") - C (the vassal kings have become primary participants) A(*).

	iprusū "they broke"	C	A*[182]		⇒ I	-	-
1.35	*imšûma* "they forgot"	C	A*[183]		⇒ I	-	I
	ikpud "(their heart) plotted"	C	(A)		⇒ I	-	I
1.36	*idbubūma* "they spoke"	C	(A)		⇒ I	-	I
	imlikū "they decided"	C	(A)		⇒ I	-	I
1.38	*uma’’erū* "they sent"	C	B	(A)	⇒ s	-	I
1.41	*ištene’’û* "they devised"	C/B	A		⇒ I	-	I
1.42	*ikrimū* "they held back"	C/B	(A)		⇒ I	-	-
1.43	*išmûma* "they heard of"	A’[184]	C/B		⇒ r	-	r
	ikkulū "they saw through"	A’	C/B		⇒ I	-	-
1.44	*iṣbatūnimma* "they seized"	A’	C’/B’		⇒ I	-	-
	emurū "they discovered"	A’	C’/B’		⇒ I	-	I
1.45	*iṣbatūnimma* "they seized"	A’	C		⇒ I	-	I
	utammeḫū "they bound"	A’	C		⇒ I	-	I
1.46	*ikšussunūtima* "it reached them"	A*[185]	C		⇒ I	-	I
1.47	*uba’’īma* (with *qātuššun*) "I called them to account"	A	C		⇒ I	-	I
					-	I[186]	-

[182] Grammatical object: *māmīssun* ("their treaty").
[183] Grammatical object: *ṭābti abi bānīya* ("the favour of the father, who begot me").
[184] Cf. below, p.114, n.204.
[185] Grammatical subject: *māmīt Aššur šar ilāni* ("the treaty of Aššur, king of the gods").
[186] *akšud* ("I conquered") - A B’.

1.49	*ušam[qitū* "they slew"	A'	C'	⇒ I	I[187]	I[188]
	lā ēzibū "they did not spare"	A'	C'	⇒ I	-	I
				-	I[189]	I[190]
				-	I[191]	I[192]
				-	I[193]	I[194]
1.50	*ublūni* "they brought"	A'	C	⇒ I	s[195]	I[196]
	(?)				-	-
1.53	*aršīšuma* (with *rēmu*) "I showed mercy"	A	C	⇒ I	-	I
	[ad?]dissuma "I gave (?)"	A	C	⇒ I	-	I[197]
1.54	*[ušaṭirma]*[198] "[I had written]"	A	C	⇒ I	-	I
	aškun "I imposed"	A	C	⇒ I	-	I
1.55	*ušarḫissuma* "I made confident"	A	C	⇒ I	-	-
	ulab]bissuma "I clothed him"	A	C	⇒ I	-	I
1.56	*aškunšu* "I put on him"	A	C	⇒ I	-	I
1.57	*u[rakkisa]*[199] "I p[ut] (on his fingers)"	A	C	⇒ I	-	I
1.58	*[ašṭurma]*[200] "[I wrote]"	A	(C)	⇒ I	-	I

---

187 *anīr* ("I slaughtered") - A B'.
188 *ušamqitūma* ("I slew") - A B'.
189 *ālul* ("I hung") - A B'.
190 *īlulū* ("they hung") - A' C'.
191 *ašḫuṭ* ("I flayed") - A B'.
192 *išḫ]uṭū* ("they flayed") - A' C'.
193 *uḫallip* ("I covered") - A B'.
194 *uḫallipū* ("they covered") - A [C'].
195 *aṣbat* ("I seized") - A C(B'?); cf. below, p.120, n.216.
196 *ubilūni* ("they brought") - A C(B'?).
197 *uballiṭ* ("I saved {his} life") - A C.
198 Cf. Aii_{9}.
199 Cf. Aii_{11}.
200 Cf. Aii_{13}.

	addinšu "I gave"	A	C		⇒I	-	I
1.59	*aqissu* "I gave"	A	C		⇒I	-	I
1.60	*ašpur* "I sent"	A	A'	C	⇒I	-	I
1.62	*utīršu* "I returned him"	A	C		⇒I	-	I
					-	-	I[201]
1.63	*ušātirma* "I increased"	A	C		⇒I	-	I
	ēpussu "I did"	A	C		⇒I	-	I
1.65	*aškun*[202] "I installed"	A	C'		⇒I	-	-
1.66	*isḫupšuma* "it overwhelmed him"	A[203]	B		⇒s	s	s
	illik (with *namušīšu*) "he made off"	B			⇒r	r	r

62 x I (82.76 %), 10 x r (13.33 %), 2 x s (2.67 %), 1 x srs (1.33 %)

The participant orientation pattern of HT's account of Aššurbanipal's first Egyptian campaign is comparatively complex. The most vivid section is the first one (ll.2-32; 28 x I {77.78 %}, 8 x r {22.22 %}). Three major *agents* (Aššurbanipal {A}), Tarqu {B}, and Niku, Šarruludari, and Pakruru {C}) with their secondary participants are mentioned.[204] However, only for the Assyrian

201 *apqid* ("I stationed") - A C' (corresponds to *aškun* {"I installed", HT obv.65}).

202 Cf. above, n.201.

203 Grammatical subject: *ḫattu puluḫtu bēlūtīya* ("terror, fear of my dominion", cf. 1.19).

204 It must, however, not be ignored that HT does not constitute the earliest extant version. There is a small difference between E and HT which is not without significance for the development of the participant orientation pattern. In HT the uncovering of the plot against the Assyrians is ascribed to "an officer" (obv.43; cf. $Eiii_{49}$). A more detailed report on the events is provided by BM 82-5-22,10. Unfortunately the text is fragmentary. A.Spalinger, "Assurbanipal and Egypt", pp.320f, argued that Pišanḫuru, who figured prominently in the account in BM 82-5-22,10, is identical with the officer mentioned in ed.E. If his suggestion is correct, then the development would be from a primary to a secondary participant and, by the alteration of sgl. to pl. into further anonymity (cf. however below, p.120, n.216). Since the conspirator's message has the same wording in both BM 82-5-22,10 and E/HT, Spalinger's claim that the tradition of the former was not used by the latter cannot be upheld.

king do secondary participants appear as *agents* on the *main line*.[205] Even in ll.17-18, constituting a first relative *peak*, the participant relation is A' - B, A' - B'. This resembles BM 113203's account of Sennacherib's first campaign.[206]

Further parallels between the two narratives may be seen in the comparatively extensive references to enemies actions[207] and internal participant relations between primary and their secondary participants.[208]

---

[205] For further accounts with complex participant orientation pattern and comparatively many references to secondary participants cf. also B's account on Aššurbanipal's campaign against Urtaku (Biv$_{18-86}$, esp.iv$_{29-30}$ {Assyrian officers}$_{.35-37.43-44}$ {messenger}). B's version also exhibits a high rhetorical level with direct speech (Biv$_{46-48}$), parallelisms (Biv$_{19-20.20-21.69-70}$, cf. also the parallel structure between ll.66-68 and ll.69-73), a comparison (Biv$_{46}$), and an EEN-construction (Biv$_{56-58}$). The account has no equivalent in F and A, and the accounts of C, K, and H are not well preserved. Thus a detailed comparison with B is not possible.
Comparatively many references to secondary participants, but with a simple participant orientation pattern, are present in *early versions* of Aššurbanipal's campaigns against Kirbit (ed. E {cf. appendix III, table 6}), against Aḫšeri (Biii$_{16-33.43-51.66.69.82-85}$; iv$_{9-17}$ {cf. appendix III, table 7, and comments in appendix II,1}), against Dunanu (Bvi$_{50-69.70-75.87-89}$; vii$_{3-42.43-76}$ {cf. appendix III, table 11}), against Teummān (Biv$_{87}$-vi$_{15}$ {cf. appendix III, table 8, and comments in appendix II,2 - apart from the protagonists, Aššurbanipal and Teummān, and secondary participants for both of them, various gods, a seer, unnamed messengers, and impersonal subjects are mentioned as *agents*), against Yauta' (Bvii$_{93}$-viii$_{22}$ {cf. appendix, table 13). In E's account of the Kirbit campaign secondary participants for both A and B appear as *agents*, in the *peak* section the participant relations are A' - B' and A' - B. The account contains no passage with a *main line participant orientation* A - B.
There are also *early versions* of accounts with a unified line and no or only a few references to secondary participants. F's versions of Aššurbanipal's campaigns against Ummanaldasi (iii$_{33}$-iv$_{16}$, iv$_{17}$-vi$_{21}$ {cf. appendix III, tables 9 and 10}), the accounts of the submissions of Mugallu and Iakinlu (HT), Ba'alu (B) and Sandišarme (A {see discussion below}), and various episodes from Aššurbanipal's campaigns against Arabs (with the exception of Bvii$_{93}$-viii$_{22}$ {cf. appendix III, table 12}).

[206] Cf. above, p.82.

[207] Extensive descriptions of enemies' actions as a sign of early stage of development are also found in B's accounts of Aššurbanipal's campaigns against Urtaku (iv$_{27-34.45-48}$) and Ummanigaš (vii$_{3-29}$), omitted in F and A. Cf. also the narration of Aḫšeri's advance in Biii$_{23-27}$. In ed. F Aḫšeri's rôle has become an entirely passive one. He learns of Aššurbanipal's advance, flees, and is killed by his subjects (see below, appendix II,1; appendix III, table 7).

[208] Cf. also Bvii$_{20-22.54-57}$ (Aššurbanipal's campaign against Dunanu) and B's account on Aššurbanipal's campaign against Teummān. Substantial parts of the latter narrative are not concerned with the main participant relation A - B / B - A, but rather deal with internal participant relations A - A' / A' - A, A - A* / A* - A, A*' - A, B - B'. The complex participant orientation pattern is also reflected in the succession of speeches in B's account. Aššurbanipal receives intelligence by unnamed messengers (Bv$_{21-24}$ {A' -

(2) The Structural Development

With regard to the *discourse profile* the most important change from HT to B is the drastic abbreviation of the report of the conspiracy and the omission of that of Niku's re-installation.[209] In ed. B only one sentence is devoted to the former (Bii$_{3-6}$). Thus the number of *peaks* was reduced and the narrative structure simplified. Not the overall *peak*, but rather the passage relating the final resolution of the conflict was retained. B has altered the EEN-construction from HT obv.2-4, added *Ištar u ilāni rabûti* ("Ištar and the great gods") to the first member, and omitted the third, the only one negated and not having Tarqu as grammatical subject. Thus the *main line* of this passage was unified.[210] The EEN-construction of HT's report of the *inciting event*, however, was retained as

A}). Within the report Teummān is quoted (B - A). Thereupon the Assyrian king prays to Ištar (Bv$_{29-46}$ {A - A*}), again mentioning the Elamite king's plot (B - A). Ištar comforts Aššurbanipal (Bv$_{47-49}$) and in the relation of the seer's dream (Bv$_{52-75}$ {A*' - A / A* - A*'}) she is quoted as having set her face against Teummān (A* - B). While the actual speeches are between primary and secondary participants, they reflect the main participant relation. It is also noteworthy that although Ištar speaks directly to Aššurbanipal (Bv$_{47-49}$) the major part of her message to the Assyrian king is given in the relation of a seer's dream (Bv$_{52-75}$) and thus by a secondary participant.

209 The reference to Niku's participation in the plot against the Assyrians and his pardoning by Aššurbanipal may have been omitted because Niku remained Assyrian vassal king at least of Saïs after his reinstallation, possibly of Memphis, too (cf. Ai$_{90}$).
A's insertion of subordinate clauses referring to a previous capture of Bīt-Imbi by Sennacherib (iv$_{126-131}$) may also reflect circumstances at the time of the redaction. It is interesting to note that ed.A commemorates the restoration of the Bīt-Ridūti, which had been built by Sennacherib (Ax$_{53-54}$; cf. also Aiv$_{71}$ referring to Sennacherib's death). A further reason for the additions may have been that Sennacherib's wars against Merodach-baladan were regarded as prototypes of Aššurbanipal's wars against the Elamites (cf. Avii$_{16,28}$, where Nabū-bēl-šumātē is introduced as Merodach-baladan's grandson). Cf. also above, p.92, n.87, and below, pp.217f, n.212 and p.121, n.221.

210 Unification of the *main line* can also be observed in F's version of Aššurbanipal's campaign against Dunanu. In F's Tammaritu section (iii$_{12-31}$) up to the mention of Indabigaš's rebellion, Tammaritu (iii$_{19}$) is the only *main line agent* (*išmû* {"they heard"}, Fiii$_{18}$, probably is subjunctive). Later in the account F has omitted Bvii$_{73-74}$ with various gods as *agents* and altered *ulzissunūti* ("I stationed them", Bvii$_{76}$) with Aššurbanipal as *agent* to *izzizma* ("he stood", Fiii$_{30}$), with Tammaritu, who also dominates the preceding *main line* verbs, as grammatical subject. F has further replaced *ana dalāl ilūtīšun rabīti* ("to revere their great divinity", Bvii$_{66}$), with all Elamite escapees as *agents*, by *idallala qurdi ilānīya dannūti* ("he revered the power of my strong gods", Fiii$_{31}$), with Tammaritu as *agent*. In F's version of Aššurbanipal's campaign against Teummān, there are no *reversals* at all. The Assyrian king dominates

ana *dâki*
ḫabā[ti
u ekēm Mu]ṣur[211]

"to kill,
loo[t,
and seize Eg]ypt" (i_{59}),

The rhetorical level of the narration of Aššurbanipal's intervention was significantly reduced by B.[212] Of the three adverbs, which were used in the cor-

---

all *main line* verbs. H has omitted Biii$_{95f}$ from the account of Ualli's submission and thus reduced the number of *reversals* to one. Aššurbanipal is only mentioned at the end of the passage. Cf. also below, pp.123f, n.227.

211 Restored after ed. D.

212 Several further examples with effects on the narrative structure can be adduced. The overall *peak* of B's account of Aššurbanipal's campaign against Aḫšeri is found in the description of the ravaging of Mannean territory which constitutes an EEN-construction (Biii$_{50-51}$, see below appendix II,1, p.249). Of this construction F has only retained the final member. From B's report of the campaign against Teummān F omitted Teummān's speech (v$_{21-24}$), Aššurbanipal's prayer (v$_{25-46}$), Ištar's reply (v$_{47-49}$), the seer's dream (v$_{50-74}$), and the description of the seizure and distribution of booty (vi$_{10-16}$). F's redaction thus resulted in an *episodic* account with hardly any rise or fall of tension. Noteworthy is also F's replacement of B's description of Aššurbanipal's return from the campaign against Dunanu (Bvi$_{47-49}$) by *ana Aššur* ("to Assyria", Fii$_{83}$ // Aiii$_{67}$). From the EEN-construction describing the destruction of Sapibel (Bvi$_{43-44}$) F has omitted the last member. F and A have also drastically compressed the Ummanigaš section. They have omitted the comparatively extensive description of Ummanigaš's advance and only retained some of the subordinate clauses, relating Ummanigaš's "sin" (F has parallels to Bvii$_{3-4.6}$ {// Fiii$_{6-8}$} and added Fiii$_{9}$; A has parallels to Bvii$_{4.8-9}$ {//Aiii$_{136-138}$}) and the narration of Tammaritu's uprising and thus reduced the rhetorical level to a minimum.
In opposition to this general tendency A has raised the rhetorical level in several passages by the insertion of speeches (Aiii$_{5-7}$ iv$_{16-20}$ v$_{37-38}$ v$_{95-103}$). The first passage, a promise by the goddess Ištar, clarifies the participant relation since it becomes apparent that Aḫšeri's servants act on her behalf. The second and third passages, emphasizing the persistently hostile attitude of Elamite kings, reflect a second campaign of Aššurbanipal against Ummanaldasi (Fiv$_{17}$-vi$_{21}$ // Av$_{63}$-vii$_{8}$) and another expedition shortly before A was written (cf. Ax$_{6-39}$; for the date cf. A.K.Grayson, "Chronology", p.231). This may also explain the addition of Av$_{36-38}$ to F's version (cf. also Ax$_{17-39}$). The fourth of the noted passages relates a dream *ina šât mūši* ("in that night", Av$_{97}$) in which Ištar encouraged Aššurbanipal's troops to a dangerous crossing of the river Idide. Both F and A had reported that Ummanaldasi fled to the city Dur-Undasi and used that river as defence line (Fiv$_{25-27}$ // Av$_{72-75}$). A's alteration is particularly interesting, since F had stated explicitly that Aššurbanipal did not hesitate to cross the river (Fiv$_{46f}$: *ištēn ūmi šina ūmī ul ūqi pān arkê ul adgul ina ūmēšūma ēbir nāri* - "one day, two days I did not hesitate, for the rearguard I did not wait; on that day I crossed the river"). A thus appears not only to have contradicted a preceding version but also to have added a comparatively extensive reference to secondary participants (*ēbir* {"I crossed", Fiv$_{47}$} ⇒ *ēbirū* {"they crossed", Av$_{103}$}).

responding passage in HT and marked an increase of tension there, only *urruḫiš* ("hastily") has been retained. Likewise Tarqu's preparations for battle have received less attention in B. By the omission of *isdira* ("he drew up {his battle lines}"; l.16), which constituted a parallelism to *idka* ("he mustered"; l.16), the effect of overlay was reduced. The description of Tarqu's fear, however, was expanded in B. After the reference to Tarqu's defeat (i_{77}) B adds *Tarqu ina qereb Mimpi išma taḫtê ummānātēšu* ("Tarqu in Memphis heard of the defeat of his troops"; $i_{78\text{-}79}$). This addition creates a contrast to $i_{72\text{-}74}$. Tarqu learns of events

Tarqu šar Muṣur u Kūsi	*qereb Mimpi alāk girrīya išmēma ...*
"Tarqu, king of Muṣur and Kusi	in Memphis heard of the progress of my campaign"
(ll.71-72),	
Tarqu	*ina qereb Mimpi išmâ taḫtê ummānātēšu ...*
Tarqu	in Memphis heard of the defeat of his troops (ll.78-79),

and reacts. B has shifted the emphasis from Tarqu's first reaction to the second, the decisive one.[213] This was accomplished by an expansion of the description of Tarqu's fear from two to three members:

Another purpose of the additions may have been to emphasize the futility of the enemies' plans. This is apparent in the expansion in the account of the campaign against Dunanu. There Tammaritu complains: *Ummānigaš kī unaššiq qaqqaru ina pān mārē šipri ša Aššur-bān-apli šar Aššur* ("Ummanigaš, how did he kiss the ground in front of the envoy of Aššurbanipal, king of Assyria", $Aiv_{18\text{-}20}$). But Tammaritu has to face a rebellion and flees to Assyria. Then A's account remarks: *Tammaritu šēpā šarrūtīya unaššiqma qaqqaru ušēšir ina ziqnīšu* ("Tammaritu kissed my royal feet, he swept the ground with his beard", $Aiv_{28\text{-}29}$); cf. also $Aiv_{114\text{-}115.123}$ $v_{21.35}$ $vii_{56\text{-}57.78}$. In the account of Aššurbanipal's first campaign against Ummanaldasi A has added a speech in which Tammaritu mentions the looting of Elam by the Assyrians ($v_{25\text{-}28}$). This, too, has correspondences in later reports (cf. $Av_{59\text{-}62}$ v_{132}-vi_{57} $vi_{81\text{-}97}$). Whatever the purpose of these insertions may have been, it is significant that all of them have been carried out by the same addition and that all of them comprise direct speech. A further case may be seen in VAT 5600+ (cf. M.Weippert, "Kämpfe", pp.74-81) II,13-22 (// $Aix_{65\text{-}74}$), which are not paralleled in B and which quote Arabs admitting that the famine from which they were suffering was inflicted upon them, because they had broken treaties with the Assyrians. The textual relationship between B, VAT 5600+ and A is, however, uncertain (cf. below, appendix III, pp.287f, n.109).

213 Various alterations show that redactors edited narratives with their outcome in view. Apart from the insertion of anticipatory remarks (see below, p.121 with n.221) cf. e.g. the replacement of *ana katārišu* ("to ask {me} to help him", $Bvii_{72}$) with *aššu epēš dīnīšu alāk rēṣūtišu* ("to do justice {and} come to his aid", $Fiii_{29}$ // Aiv_{32}; cf. $Fiii_{37}f$ // Aiv_{30}, $Fiii_{70f}$ // Aiv_{21f}). By the addition of *anāku Aššur-bān-apli libbu rapšu lā kāṣir ikki mupassisu ḫiṭâte ana Tammaritu rēmu aršīšuma* ("I, Aššurbanipal, magnanimous, lenient, forgiving sin, showed mercy to Tammaritu") to F's description of the pardoning of Tammaritu ($Aiv_{37\text{-}39}$) ed. A may also prepare for the description of

namrīrī Aššur u Ištar isḫupūšuma
illika maḫḫūtaš
melammē šarrūtīya iktumūšuma ...
the splendour of Aššur and Ištar overwhelmed him,
he went mad,
the majesty of my kingship covered him".

This is supplemented by a change in the participant orientation pattern. In HT the participant relation in the narration of the battle had been A' - B', A' - B. Ed.B in the corresponding section (i_{75-77}) has A - B', which prepares for A - B in the sentence added to the description of Tarqu's fear.[214] Thus the *peak* has moved from the narration of a conflict to the relation of its effects.[215]

B further noted the occupation of Memphis, which had been presupposed but not expressly mentioned in HT. The *main line* verbs (*aṣbat* {"I took"}, *ušērib*

Aššurbanipal's showing mercy to the inhabitants of Babylon (Aiv_{94}). The alteration of the campaign formula from *eli Teummān šar Elamti lu allik* ("against Teummān, king of Elam, I marched") to *ana Elamti uštešsera ḫarrānu* ("to Elam I took the road") may reflect that after the expedition against Teummān further campaigns were necessary. It also corresponds to the fact that the *peak* section described the conquest of Elam (cf. appendix II,2). Noteworthy is further the alteration of *Dunanu aḫḫēšu* ("Dunanu, his brothers", Bvi_{25}) to *Dunanu Samgunu* ("Dunanu, Samgunu", Fii_{79}). Of Dunanu's brothers only Samgunu is mentioned later (cf. B_3's addition to Bvi_{51}: *qaqqad Ištarnandi ina kišād* [*Samgunu*] *aḫi Dunanu tardennu* [*ālul*], "the head of Ištarnandi [I hung] around the neck of [Samgunu], the younger brother of Dunanu" {cf. A.C.Piepkorn, *Historical Prism Inscriptions*, p.94} // $Kiii_{70-71}$, Bvi_{76}).
According to VAT 5600+ (cf. M.Weippert, "Kämpfe", pp.74-81) III,12 Aššurbanipal conducted a second campaign against Uwaiteʾ because of the latter's conspiracy with Natnu. According to $Aviii_{65ff}$, however, it was Abiateʾ who had conspired with Natnu. Ed.A further inserted a reference to Abiateʾ in $viii_{94-95}$ (// VAT 5600+ III,33). While the first part of the campaign was only of limited success (Uwaiteʾ escaped), the second part achieved its aim. Abiateʾ and Aimu were captured and carried to Assyria (Aix_{15-24} // VAT 5600+ IV,22-28), escapees were punished (Aix_{25-41} // VAT 5600+, IV,29ff {text mutilated}).

[214] In the mention of Tarqu's death B has replaced *ḫattu puluḫtu bēlūtīya* ("terror, fear of my dominion", HT obv.66) with *rašubbat kakki Aššur bēlīya* ("the dread of the weapon of Aššur, my lord", ii_8).

[215] B's additional text to the narration of the punishment of rebellious cities (Bii_{1-2}) is paralleled in C (not extant) / Aii_{3-4}. On the other hand C/A (i_{134}-ii_2) agree with HT obv.48-49 // E (BM 134481 ii_{1-2}; cf. A.R.Millard, "Fragments", pl.20) against Bi_{98-99}. The fact that in ed. A 3rd p.pl. is used and in B 1st p.sgl. may either be explained by the assumption that C/A being dependent on a non-extant source, possibly older than E/HT, have preserved the older text or that C/A have adapted their *Vorlage* to the new context in C/A. Therefore, we cannot decide whether B has expanded the passage or HT has abbreviated it.

{"I let enter"}, *ušēšib* {"I let dwell"}; $Bi_{85\text{-}86}$) parallel the narration of Tarqu's conquest of the same city (*ērumma* {"he entered"}, *ūšib* {"he took up residence"}; Bi_{60}). Mentions of the punishment of rebellious cities,[216] the capture of Šarruludari, and Tarqu's death conclude the account.

The following diagram shows the *discourse profile* of B's version of the account of Aššurbanipal's first campaign in Egypt.

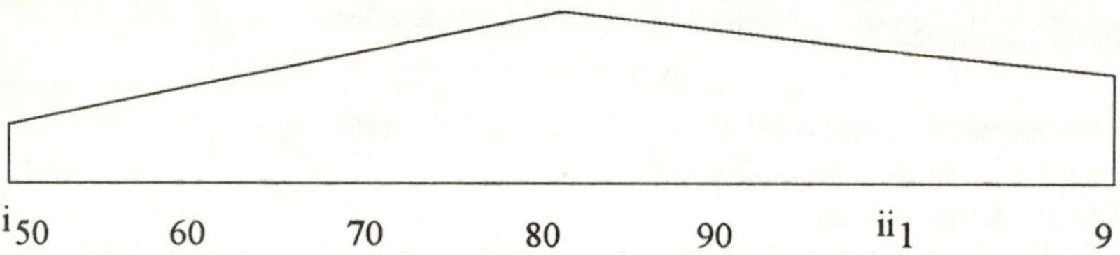

With regard to the time structure of the campaign account, there are only two minor alterations apparent, the insertion of a campaign formula: *ina maḫrê girrīya ana* [*Ma*]*kan u* [*Meluḫḫa*] *lu allik* ("in my first campaign I went to [Ma]kan and [Meluḫḫa]", $Bi_{50\text{-}51}$)[217] and the designation of Tarqu as [*šar Muṣur u*][218] *Kūsi* ("[king of Muṣur and] Kūsi", i_{52}). In HT Tarqu had been introduced as

---

216 The names of these cities are given as *Sa-a-a Bi-in-ṭi-ṭi Ṣa-ʾ-nu*. According to Ai_{91} Šarruludari ruled over a city called *Ṣi-ʾ-nu*, while *Ṣa-ʾ-nu* was governed by a certain Puṭubišti. In Ai_{134} (// Bi_{95}) *Ṣa-ʾ-nu* and *Ṣi-ʾ-nu* are variant readings. Possibly the two names refer to the same city and the list in $Ai_{90\text{-}109}$ may mention Šarruludari and Puṭubišti as successive rulers (thus von Zeissl, quoted in A.Spalinger, "Assurbanipal and Egypt", p.319, n.25 *contra* Spalinger), as may have been the case with the rulers of *Na-at-ḫu-ú* (cf. $Ai_{92.97}$). The king of the latter city named first is Pišanḫuru, who figured prominently in BM 82-5-22,10. Possibly, he, too, was deposed by Aššurbanipal after the unsuccessful revolt. If the two names do not refer to the same city *Ṣiʾnu* may be identified with Pelusium (Sin; thus K.A.Kitchen *Third Intermediate Period*, p.393, n.877).

217 Cf. also A's addition of a campaign formula ($Avii_{82\text{-}84}$) to the account(s) of Aššurbanipal's campaigns against Arabs (cf. $Bvii_{93ff}$).

218 Restored after prism D.

king of *Kūsi*[219], who intended to conquer *Muṣur*.[220] The designation in ed. B is thus proleptic.[221] It further leads to the literary difficulty that Tarqu as [*šar Muṣur u*] *Kūsi* ("king of Muṣur and Kūsi"; i_{52}) sets off *ana* ... [*ekēm Mu*]*ṣur* ("to [seize Mu]ṣur", i_{59}). Such a creation of literary inconsistencies is of particular interest since their presence belongs to the most important criteria for the recognition of redactorial intervention. In the present case the creation of the inconsistency may be related to a trend towards increasing harmonization of participants' designations. The literary development of Aššurbanipal's *annals* demonstrates that inconsistencies in *late* versions cannot simply be ascribed to only one particular mode of origin.[222]

---

219 Cf.ll.15.30.38.66 and above, p.101.

220 Obv.2; cf. also obv.28.

221 Cf. also A's expansion of description of Uwaite''s insubmissiveness in which several sentences are anticipatory (cf. $Avii_{94-95}$ // $ix_{53-57.75-89}$ // $viii_{31ff}$ and above, pp.118f, n.213). While B had stated that the Assyrian army dispatched against Uwaite' killed *nišē Aribi mala itbûni* ("the people of Arabia, as many as had come", $Bviii_{8f}$) and only from a later passate ($Bviii_{23}$) it is apparent that Uwaite' escaped, VAT 5600+ I,50 added *ittīšu* ("with him" // $Avii_{117}$) and thus indicated that Uwaite''s fate was different. Because the transfer of the descriptions of the wealth of the booty taken and the famine among the Arabs to a different passage, A mentions Uwaite''s escape *ana ruqēti* ("to a distant place") immediately after the defeat. The second reference to Uwaite''s flight ($Bviii_{31}$) had already been updated in VAT 5600+ II,23f by the addition of *ana Nabayate* ("to Nabatea" // $Avii_{124}$).
As in the case of Sennacherib's annals (cf. above, p.95, n.101) there are also narratives which already in their earliest extant version contain proleptic remarks. Thus *attallaka šaltiš* ("I advanced victoriously"; $Biii_{33}$) may anticipate the success of Aššurbanipal's campaign against Aḫšeri.
In B's account of Aššurbanipal's campaign against Urtaku the mention of the Elamite king's breach of peace ($Biii_{19-20}$) is followed by a description of Aššurbanipal's support for Elam in times of famine (iii_{20-26}). The relation of Urtaku's rebellion in $Biii_{27ff}$ indicates that the remarks in $Biii_{19-20}$ are anticipatory. The reference to Sin plotting evil for Teummān (Bv_{4-5}) may be regarded as prolepsis of the signs given by Sin and Šamaš ($Bv_{5-8.9}$).

222 The creation of literary inconsistencies by omission can be exemplified in HT's abbreviation of E's account of Aššurbanipal's campaign against Kirbit. Although HT mentions only the capture of one city, Kirbit, a *plural* reference was retained in rev.12 (*ālāni šâtūnu* {"these cities"} // Eiv_7: *ālāni šunūti* {"these cities"}). In the preceding line HT had used a sgl. reference (*nišēšu* {"its inhabitants"}). Cf. also *bēl ālānīšunu* ("lord of their cities"; HT rev.8 - Th.Bauer, *Inschriftenwerk*, p.33, n.3), which in $Biii_7$ // Civ_{33} was altered to *bēl ālīšunu* ("lord of their city") and thus adapted to the further course of narration. HT further retained *ikšudū* ("they conquered", rev.11 // $Eiii_{23}$), but added *kišittī qātīya* ("captives of *my hands*") to the reference to the cities captured.
The difference between eds. E and B with regard to Tandayya's fate may be due to

Developmental tendencies can also be observed in the alteration of the participant orientation pattern. The increase of the percentage of *reversals* from 13.52 % (HT) to 29.73 % (B) is somewhat misleading. B's participant orientation pattern contains 11 *reversals*. Of these one had been created by the addition of the campaign formula and eight more are found in a single paragraph Bi_{70-86}. B has omitted the second section of HT's account, in the third section relating the revolt and subsequent punishment of the rebels B has no *reversals* at all, and in the final section both HT and B have one *reversal*. It is only in the first section that the number of *reversals* increases from HT to B. Two of the additional *reversals* are created by B's adaptation of i_{78ff} to i_{71ff}, the remaining two by the expansion of the description of Tarqu's fear (i_{82}).[223] Both alterations can be related to general tendencies of development. Thus this case does not contradict the trend towards a reduction of *reversals*. It rather demonstrates that other tendencies may have prevailed against it.

It has been noted above that in HT many secondary participants appear on the *main line*. In B, however, the only secondary participant functioning as *agent* is the messenger sent to Aššurbanipal. It is the Assyrian king himself, who, according to B, leads his army to Egypt (Bi_{66ff}), defeats Tarqu's army (i_{77ff}), and even captures Šarruludari (ii_6).[224] Since for the references to Aššurbanipal's

---

aberratio occuli (Ta-an-da-a-a / A-ku-da-a-a). $Biii_{12}$ mentions *Tandayya bēl ālīšunu* ("Tandayya, the lord of their city") as being taken to Assyria, whereas according to ed.E *Tandayya bēl āli* ("Tandayya, lord of the city") was killed by the Assyrian troops (iii_{34}), who captured *Akudayya nāgiršunu* ("Akudayya, their leader") alive and and brought him before Aššurbanipal (iv_5).

A further cause for inconsistencies can be related to the tendency to emphasize primary participants. Thus while according to B's account the Moabite king defeated Ammuladdi ($Bviii_{48-50}$), in A Aššurbanipal claims the victory for himself (*abiktašu aškun* {"I established his defeat"}, $Aviii_{23}$). In the narration of Ammuladdi's capture, however, 3rd p.pl. is used (*iṣbatūnimma ubilūni adi maḫrīya* - "they seized him (and) brought him into my presence" {$Aviii_{26}$} // *uṣabbit ... adi maḫrī*[*ya ušēbila*] - "he captured {them} ... and [had them brought] into [my] presence", with the Moabite king as grammatical subject {$Bviii_{48-50}$, restored after prism D}).

For examples of literary inconsistencies in *early versions* cf. above, pp.106f, n.142.

223 Cf. above, pp.16f, n.27.

224 Cf. also the alteration of *meḫret ummānātēya* ("opposite to my army", HT obv.16) to *ana maḫrīya* ("against me", Bi_{74}). For further alterations cf. the participant orientation table above, pp.108ff. Similar changes have also been carried out in other campaign accounts. In their version of the Kirbit campaign B/C have have altered all verbs with the Assyrian army as *agents* to 1st p.sgl. and thus reduced the number of participants in

enemies the same trend is apparent[225] these alterations should not be (solely) attributed to the egocentricity of the Assyrian kings.[226] B has also reduced the number of primary participants. None of the rebels (C) appears as *agent* of a *main line* verb.[227]

---

the *main line*. For the mention of the capture of Kirbit (and other cities) we can note a development of participant designations from ... *ikšudū išlulā* ... ("they captured ..., they took as spoil ..."); $Eiii_{23}$, HT rev.11), referring to the Assyrian army, to *kišitti qātīya* ("captives of my hands", HT rev.12), to *akšud* ("I captured", $Biii_{11}$ // Civ_{32}) with the Assyrian king as *agent*. As a consequence of B's abbreviations the participant relation in $Biii_{12}$ is A - B. Ed. F omitted the first part of B's account of Aššurbanipal's campaign against Aḫšeri ($Biii_{16-30}$), where secondary participants for the Assyrian king appeared as *main line agents*. F also omitted all references to secondary participants and consequently to all internal participant relations, too, from the *main line* of its account of Aššurbanipal's campaign against Teummān (see below, appendix III, table 8). The Assyrian king is the only *main line agent*. In its account of Aššurbanipal's campaign against Dunanu B narrates that Tammaritu's servants rebelled ($Bvii_{54}$), and mentions that Indabigaš, who had instigated the revolt, took the throne ($Bvii_{56-57}$). F and A, however, relate that it was Indabigaš, who defeated Tammaritu ($Fiii_{20}$ // Aiv_{12}). In the narration of Tammaritu's escape A has further replaced *iṣbatū šēpē šarrūtīya* ("they took hold of my royal feet", $Bvii_{70}$), with all refugees as grammatical subject, with *šēpē šarrūtīya unaššiqma* ("he kissed my royal feet", Aiv_{28}), even though in iv_{115} and v_{21} A refers to this incident with *ša ... iṣbata šēpēya* ("who took hold of my feet"). *unaššiq* ("he kissed") and Aiv_{29} correspond to the contents of Tammaritu's speech (cf. above, pp.117f, n.212). For additional alterations of references to participants in this account see above pp.116f, n.210. In the report of the first campaign against Uwaite' A has replaced all mentions of the Assyrian army as *main line agents* by references to Aššurbanipal (cf. appendix III, table 12). In the report of Ammuladdin's defeat VAT 5600+ has omitted the reference to the Moabite king ($viii_{43-45}$), but replaced [*iddima*] ("he put"; $Bviii_{49}$, restored after D) with *addišuma* ("I put him"; VAT 5600+, II,43). The addition of the sgl. suffix is noteworthy, since in B the context implied that Ammuladdin and his subjects were taken to Assyria (cf. $viii_{46}$). Consequently ... *ana Ninua adi maḫr*[*īya ušēbila*] ("he had [them brought] to Nineveh into my presence"; $Bviii_{50}$) was replaced by *ūrâ ana Aššur* ("I led to Assyria"; VAT 5600+ II,44). The Ištar Temple Tablet (henceforth IT; cf. R.Campbell Thompson and M.E.L.Mallowan, "Excavation at Nineveh", pp.80-90) has further abbreviated this passage by omitting the mention of Ammuladdi's fight against the Amurrite kings, which in $Aviii_{16}$ are introduced as secondary participants for Aššurbanipal (*ša Aššur Ištar u ilāni rabûti ušadgila pānū'a* - "whom Aššur, Ištar, and the great gods had placed under my dominion"). Cf. also above pp.121f, n.222.

225 Cf. the alteration of *uma''era ummānšu* ("he {sc. Tarqu} sent his army", HT obv.8) to *illaka* ("he went", Bi_{60}).

226 *Contra* S.Mowinckel, "Königs- und Fürsteninschriften", p.285.

227 Šarruludari, a third primary participant apart from Aššurbanipal and Tarqu, appears once as the *patient* of *aṣbat* ("I seized", Bii_6). Secondary participants for C are not mentioned. The cities punished by Aššurbanipal are referred to with *ša ibbalkitū itti Tarqu iškunū pīšun* ("which had revolted, with Tarqu set their mouth {=made common cause}", Bi_{96-97}; HT obv.48: *mala ittīšunu* [*šaknū*]" - "as many as [had joined] them",

Related to the tendency to concentrate on primary participants is the trend to clarify their relationship. Thus B has altered the order of narration of *stage* and *inciting event*. According to HT Tarqu first moves to Memphis (obv.5) and then sets off to fight against the Assyrians (obv.6ff). In B his intentions are stated first

Related to the tendency to concentrate on primary participants is the trend to clarify their relationship. Thus B has altered the order of narration of *stage* and *inciting event*. According to HT Tarqu first moves to Memphis (obv.5) and then sets off to fight against the Assyrians (obv.6ff). In B his intentions are stated first (i_{57-60}) and his move to Memphis is supplemented by [*ṣīruššun*][228] ("[upon them]") (Bi_{60}), where the reference of the suffix may include Niku. In any case, it is expressly mentioned at the beginning of the account that Tarqu's actions are directed against the Assyrians.

The next extant edition, that of C and A[229], exhibits an intermediate stage between E and HT on the one side and B on the other. C and A follow ed. B in the first part of the account, narrating that the Assyrian king himself led his army, but agree with HT in ascribing the capture of the rebels to Aššurbanipal's officers.[230] Between the two events C and A have inserted a reference to

restored after ed. A, with the pronominal suffix *-šunu* ("them") referring to the rebels). In its report of Aššurbanipal's campaign against Dunanu, F has reduced the number of participants by changing the remark that Tammaritu had fled before the "weapon of Aššur and Ištar" ($Bvii_{64f}$) to "before Indabigaš" ($Fiii_{23}$). By the omission of the reference to the decapitation of one of Teummān's generals (Bvi_{39-42}, participant relation: A C') F and A have reduced the number of participants and unified the *main line*. F and A have further omitted the description of the ravaging of Gambulu (Bvi_{45-46}) and only retained a description of the conquest and destruction of Sapibel, where Dunanu and his brother(s) were captured (cf. below, appendix III, table 11). To be noted further is HT's omission of the reference to the settlement of foreign peoples in Kirbit, which did not concern the main conflict and denoted a *switch* in the participant orientation pattern. For further cases cf. also above, pp.122f, n.224.

In its account of the campaign against Aḫšeri ed.A has added a note of the killing of Aḫšeri's relatives ($Aiii_{10}$). Thus it might constitute a witness for an intermediary stage between F and A. Aḫšeri's relatives are, however, mentioned with pronominal suffixes *-šu* ("his") referring to Aḫšeri (*aḫḫēšu qinnūšu zēr bīt abīšu* {"his brothers, his family, the descendents of the house of his father"}). The presence of this line in BM 82-3-23,5218 (cf. Th.Bauer, *Inschriftenwerk*, p.58) may indicate that A took it over from its source and that B may have omitted it from its *Vorlage*.

228 Restored after D and A.

229 Prism F omits Aššurbanipal's first Egyptian campaign.

230 Cf. also C/A's narration of the punishment of rebellious cities, where C/A partly agree with B against HT, and partly with HT against B. See above, p.119, n.215.

Aššurbanipal's return to Nineveh. The literary relationships of the various versions are thus complex. Either we have to assume that C and A were dependent on a non-extant *Vorlage* or that they combined different sources. In any case, for an analysis of the structural development C and A have to be compared with HT rather than B. On the other hand, since C, A and B agree in the first parts of their accounts, the statements made above on the development of time structure and participant orientation are valid for C and A, too, and need not be repeated here.

C and A do not narrate the second, unsuccessful, expedition against Tarqu (HT obv.24-32) and thus have reduced the number of *peaks*. We can therefore note a simplification of the narrative structure from originally four *peaks* (HT) to two (C and A) and to one *peak* (B). This parallels the development of the account of Sennacherib's first campaign.[231] The following diagram shows the *discourse profile* of HT's account of Aššurbanipal's first Egyptian campaign and indicates the portions retained by eds. B and C/A.

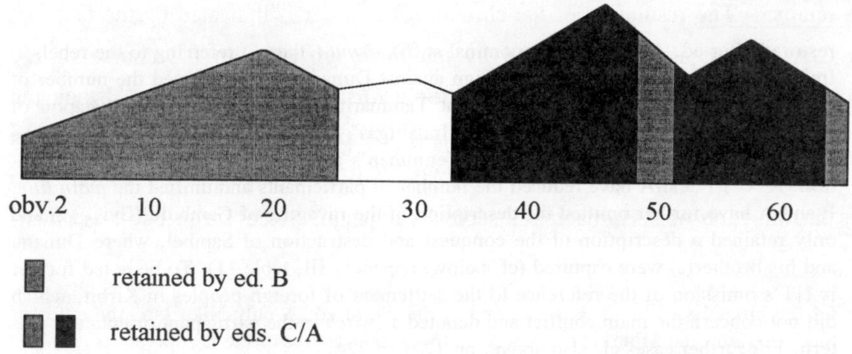

Both C and A have lists not present in the preceding editions. C adds a list of vassal kings from *aḫi tâmtim qabal tâmtim u nābali* ("the coast, the midst of

231 Similarly F has omitted narrative sections containing *peaks* from B's versions of Aššurbanipal's campaigns against Aḫšeri (cf. appendix II/1) and against Teummān (Bv_{89}-vi_{13}, cf. appendix II/2).

the sea, and the dry land", ii_{60f}) who were sent by Aššurbanipal to support the Assyrian troops, whereas A has a list of Egyptian vassal kings reinstalled after Tarqu had been defeated by the Assyrians. From the narrative point of view the only purpose apparent for the addition of these lists is preservation of information, the effect of their inclusion on the narrative structure is thus difficult to evaluate. They turn attention away from the course of events.[232] For the establishment of *plot profile*s we have disregarded these insertions the existence of which we, nevertheless, have to take notice.

The kings from *aḫi tâmtim qabal tâmtim u nābali* who were sent to Egypt by Aššurbanipal[233] are probably identical with those from *eber nāri* ("across the river {Euphrates}") who are mentioned in HT obv.25, but not in B. C/A and HT, however, differ considerably in wording. Furthermore, the position of this episode within the course of the narrative is different. In HT the kings were sent to Egypt after Tarqu's army had been defeated and the Ethiopian king had fled to Thebes. In C/A, however, they are sent to Egypt at the beginning of the campaign. Since C/A have Aššurbanipal himself leading his army to Egypt and have omitted the narration of Tarqu's second escape, the original position of the passage could not be retained. The resolution of the chronological order is indicated by the fact that in C/A the passage is introduced by *ina mētiq girrīya* ("in the course of my campaign").[234] The addition of *ana Muṣur u Kūsi ušteššera ḫarrānu* ("I took the road to Muṣur and Kūsi", Cii_{36} // Ai_{67f}) identifies the meaning of *Makan u Meluḫḫa* in the campaign formula ($[C]/Ai_{52}$ // Bi_{50}) and creates a parallelism to the introduction of Aššurbanipal's second campaign. Since Tarqu had been men-

---

[232] Of the kings listed in ed. C none, and of the list in ed. A only Niku (and the cities of Saïs, Pindidi, and Ṣi'nu) is mentioned in the further course of the narrative.

[233] While C mentions the names of the kings, A only states their number. The names given in ed. C are very similar to those mentioned in an inscription of Esarhaddon (cf. R.Borger, *Inschriften Asarhaddons*, p.60). Apart from orthographic variants all but two names are identical. C has *Ia-ki-in-lu* for *Ma-ta-an-ba-'a-al* and *Am-mi-na-ad-bi* for *Bu-du-ilu*. The alterations may constitute updates. The different purpose of the list in the two inscriptions may indicate that C Esarhaddon's prism did not constitute C's immediate *Vorlage*.

[234] *ina mētiq girrīya* is also used by F to mark an insertion of an account of the Bit-Imbi affair into its report of the first campaign against Ummanaldasi (cf. below, p.151, n.311).

tioned as [*šar Muṣur u*] *Kūsi* ("[king of Muṣur and] Kūsi", i_{52}) the participant orientation has been further clarified.

A has expanded the description of Aššurbanipal's reaction to Tarqu's attack to an EEN construction:

libbi ēgugma
iṣṣaruḫ kabitti
ašši qātīya uṣalli Aššur u Ištar aššurītu
"my heart became enraged,
my liver seethed,
I lifted up my hands and implored Aššur and the Assyrian Ištar" (i_{64-65})[235]

and thus adapts the passage to $Ai_{56.66f.84}$. This further simplifies the participant orientation, since it becomes apparent that Aššur and Ištar act on Aššurbanipal's behalf.[236]

b) Aššurbanipal's Second Campaign in Egypt

(1) The Structure of the Earliest Extant Version

The oldest of the major editions for Aššurbanipal's campaign against Tandamanē[237] is that of HT, which will be taken as point of departure. HT has separated this section from the previous one only by the introduction of a new grammatical subject (*Tandamanē*, HT obv.67). The new paragraph is linked with the previous one by referring back to Tarqu with a pronominal suffix.[238]

Only very few literary devices are employed. This conforms to the fact that the Assyrian king does not dominate a single *main line* verb in this account. There is, therefore, no substantial rise or fall of the rhetorical level. Tension

---

235 Without equivalent in C.

236 Clarification of the participant relations can also be observed in A's version of Aššurbanipal's campaign against Aḫšeri. A has added a promise of Ištar to the narration of Aḫšeri's death. Through Ištar's statement *mītūtu Aḫšeri šar Mannayya kīma ša aqbu eppuš* ("the death of Aḫšeri, king of Mannayya, I shall bring about, as I have said", $Aiii_{6-7}$) it becomes apparent that Aḫšeri's servants act as secondary participants for the Assyrian goddess. In ed. B this could only be deduced from *Aššur u Ištar imnûšu ina qātā ardānīšu* ("Aššur and Ištar counted him into the hands of his servants", $Biii_{83}$).

237 Ed.B: *Tašdamanē*.

238 *mār aḫātīšu* ("son of his sister", obv.67; cf. R.Borger, *Babylonisch-Assyrische Lesestücke*, p.92). M.Streck, *Assurbanipal* II, p.164, erroneously has *mār aššatīšu* ("son of his wife"), but gives the correct translation ("Schwestersohn").

increases with the report on Tandamanē's preparations for war, but decreases quickly after the outcome of the decisive battle is mentioned (obv.71). The tension rises again with the report on the Assyrian army pursuing Tandamanē. The overall surface structure *peak* of this narrative is found in the description of the capture of Thebes with the intensifying supplements *ana siḫirtīšu* ("in its totality") and *abubiš* ("like a flood") in obv.74. The enumeration of booty taken from Thebes and the parallelism *ušēṣûnimma* ("they led out") / *ana šallatiš imnû* ("they counted as spoil", rev.4) slows down the narration and the decrease of the rhetorical level. The mention of the safe return of the Assyrian troops (rev.ll.5-6) concludes this section. The following diagram shows the *discourse profile* of HT's account of Aššurbanipal's second Egyptian campaign.

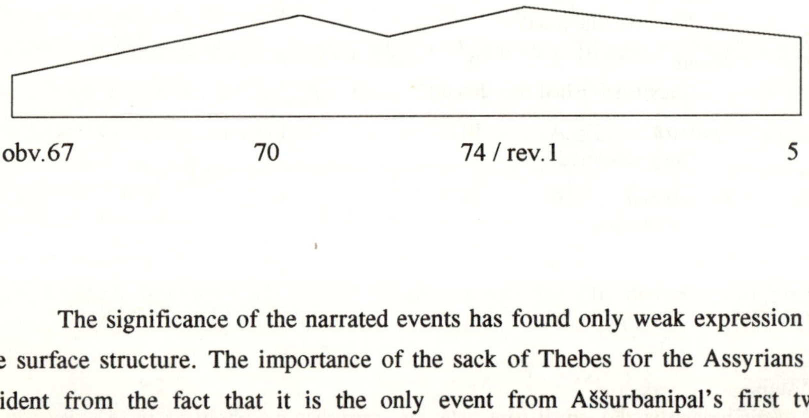

The significance of the narrated events has found only weak expression in the surface structure. The importance of the sack of Thebes for the Assyrians is evident from the fact that it is the only event from Aššurbanipal's first two campaigns to be mentioned by IT[239] (l.80). The same is true for ed. H, which has introductory remarks in ll.1-6, then mentions the capture and looting of Thebes in l.7, and continues with the mention of Ba'alu of Tyre.[240]

The account in HT appears to follow a chronological order. Because of its briefness statistical data have to be treated with care.

---

[239] Cf. above, pp.122f, n.224.

[240] Cf. also K 3127+4435 (Th.Bauer, *Inschriftenwerk*, pp.66f.).

The *main line* reads:

					HT	B	F
obv.l.67	*ūšibma* "he ascended (to his throne)"	B				+	-
	umaʾʾir "he ruled"	B	B'		I	-	-
l.68	*iškun* "he established"	B	B'		I	I	-
	upaḫḫir "he assembled"	B	B'		I	I	-
					-	I[241]	-
					-	I[242]	-
					-	I[243]	-
					-	r[244]	-
					-	I[245]	-
					-	r[246]	+[247]
					-	r[248]	r
l.69	*ušatbâ* "he prepared"	B	(B')	A'	I	-	-
	iṣbata "he took (the road)"	B	A'		I	-	-
l.71	*iškunū* "they established (his defeat)"	A'	B		r	-	-
	uparrirū "they shattered"	A'	B'		I	-	-
l.72	*ipparšidma* "he escaped"	B	(A')		r	I[249]	I
	ērub "he entered"	B	(A')		I	I[250]	I
					-	r[251]	r

241 *idkâ* ("he mustered") - B B'.
242 *ēsirma* ("he encircled") - B A'.
243 *iṣbata* ("he seized") - B A'.
244 *illikamma* ("he came) - A' A [B].
245 *iqbâ* ("he told") - A A' [B].
246 *ašnīma* ... *uštešsera* ... ("a second time I took {the road to ...}") - A [B].
247 Without *ašnīma* ("I did again").
248 *išmēma* ("he heard") - B A.
249 [*umašširma*] ("[he left]", restored after prism D) - B [A].
250 *innabit* ("he fled") - B [A].
251 *illikūnimma* ("they went") - A' A [B].

				-	I[252]	I
				-	I[253]	I
l.73	*illikū* "they went"	A’	B	r	I[254]	I
				-	r[255]	r
				-	I[256]	I
l.74	*ikšudū* "they conquered"	A’	B’	I	r[257]	r
	ispunū "they crushed"	A’	B’	I	-	-
rev.l.4	*ušēṣûnimma* "they led out"	A’	B’	I	I[258]	I
				-	I[259]	I
	imnû "they counted (as spoil)"	A’	B’	I	I[260]	-
				-	I[261]	-
				-	I[262]	-
l. 5	*iššûnimma* "they carried"	A’	A	s	I[263]	-
	unaššiqū "they kissed"	A’	A	I	-	-

(12 x I [75 %], 3 x r [18.75 %], 1 x s [6.25 %])

The participant orientation pattern in HT exhibits only few *reversals*. Secondary participants for both protagonists appear on the *main line*. There are, however, only two *agents*, the Assyrian army and Tandamanē. Aššurbanipal is not mentioned as *agent* even in transitional passages. In the passage containing the overall *peak*, the participant relation is between secondary participants (A’ - B’).

252 *unaššaqū* ("they kissed") - A’ A [B].
253 *aṣbat* ("I took {the road}") - A B.
254 *allik* ("I went") - A [B].
255 *umašširma* ("he left") - B [A].
256 *innabit* ("he fled") - B [A].
257 *ikšudā* ("{my hands} conquered") - A B’.
258 *assuḫma* ("I tore out") - A B’
259 *alqâ* ("I took") - A B’.
260 *ašlula* ("I despoiled") - A B’.
261 *ušamrirma* ("I sharpened {my weapons}") - A B’.
262 *aštakan* ("I established {authority}") - A B.
263 *atūra* ("I returned") - A.

(2) The Structural Development

There is evidence that B's *Vorlage* differed from HT. Tandamanē's siege of Memphis, which had not been mentioned by HT is also referred to in the Kushite king's Dream Stele[264]. Possibly B was dependent on a source earlier than HT.[265] Any analysis of the differences between the editions is thus only provisional. Until further finds clarify the textual dependence between the various manuscripts we shall nevertheless regard HT's text as B's source.

The table above shows that ed. B has substantially expanded HT's account. Most of the events added by B to HT's version of Aššurbanipal's second campaign to Egypt are standard in Assyrian campaign accounts and have parallels in the accounts of the first Egyptian campaign. The alterations also follow the tendency to have the *main line* dominated by primary participants.

The arrival of a messenger at the Assyrian court corresponds to Bi_{63} parr. As in its account of Aššurbanipal's first campaign, B has the Assyrian king himself leading his army to Egypt. The phraseology resembles Ai_{67f}. In B, both Tarqu's and Tandamane's actions are preceded by a reference to their learning of events:

Tarqu ... alāk girrīya išmēma ... idkâ tāḫāzīšu

"Tarqu ... heard of the progress of my campaign ... he mustered his forces" (Bi_{71-73})

Tarqu ... išmâ taḫtê ummānātēšu ... Mimpi umašširma ana šūzub napištīšu innabit ana qereb Niʾ

"Tarqu ... heard of the defeat of his army ... he left Memphis (and) to save his life he fled to Thebes" (i_{78-85}).

Tašdamanē [*alāk girrīya*] *išmēma ... Mimpi* [*umašširma ana šūzub napištīšu*] *innabit an*[*a qereb Niʾ*][266]

---

[264] Cf. A.Spalinger, "Assurbanipal and Egypt", pp.324f.
From the parallel between HT obv.30 and obv.73

ana Niʾ āl dannūti Tarqu šar Kūsi illikū mālak arḫi X ūmē

"to Thebes, the strong city of Tarqu, king of Kusi, they went a distance of one month and ten days" (obv.30)

mālak arḫi X ūmē urḫi pašqūti arkāšu illikū adi qereb Niʾ

"a distance of one month and ten days on difficult roads they went after him as far as Thebes" (obv.73)

it could be deduced that the battle between Tandamanē's and Aššurbanipal's forces took place near Memphis.

[265] Cf. above, pp.98f.

[266] Restored according to eds. C and A.

"Tašdamanē heard of [the progress of my campaign] ... [he left] Memphis [(and) to save his life] he fled [to Thebes]" (ii_{20-22}).

tīb tāḫāzīya ēmurma Niʾ umaššir innabit [ana Kipkipi][267]
"he saw the advance of my forces, left Thebes, fled [to Kipkipi]" (ii_{27-28}).

B's report of Tandamanē's second flight to Kipkipi may constitute an update of the account.[268] It also parallels HT's mention of Tarqu's second escape.[269] According to prism B, after Tandamanē's defeat and escape the Egyptian vassal kings paid homage to Aššurbanipal. A counterpart may be seen in C/A's version of Aššurbanipal's campaign against Tarqu where a reference to the submission of kings from *aḫi tâmtim qabal tâmtim u nābali* ("the coast, the midst of the sea, and the dry land") is related (i_{68-71}).[270]

The parallelism between B's accounts of Aššurbanipal's first and second campaigns has also found its expression in *ašnīma ana Muṣur [u Kūsi] uštešśera ḫarrānu*[271] ("a second time I took the road to Muṣur [and Kūsi]", Bii_{18-19}) which refers back to *ina maḫrê gi[rrīya] ana [Ma]kan u [Meluḫḫa] lu allik* ("in my first cam[paign] I went to [Ma]kan and [Meluḫḫa]", Bi_{50-51}).[272] The formal beginning of the campaign narrative is thus to be found in Bii_{18-19} parr.

The assimilation of narrations of comparable events which were already noted for B's version of Aššurbanipal's first campaign has reached a higher level here. Not only passages within a narrative were assimilated but a complete narrative was adapted to another one. This has at least two very important implications. For the attempt to trace earlier stages of development in *late versions*, it means that in this case it is not possible to reconstruct the altered passages. The con-

---

267 Restored according to eds. C and A.

268 Cf. e.g. the insertion of a reference to Lule's death by Chic.-Tayl. (cf. above, p.92, n.87). Comparable is further the addition of *ana Nabayyate* ("to Nabatea") by VAT 5600+ II,23f to the narration of Uwaiteʾ's escape (cf. $Bviii_{31}$).

269 *Tarqu ša alāk ummānātēya išme Niʾ ... umaššir Iaruʾu ēbir[ma* ... ("Tarqu, who heard of the advance of my army, left Thebes ..., crossed the river Iaruʾu", obv.31-32).

270 Since, however, the two passages have different functions within the accounts - in the report on the first Egyptian campaign the vassal kings are sent to Egypt to support the Assyrian troops, whereas in B's version of the second Egyptian campaign the Egyptian vassal kings submit to the victorious king - the comparison is a weak one. It is also possible that Bi_{24} reflects HT rev.5.

271 Restored after eds. C and A.

272 The next campaign, against Baʾalu of Tyre, is referred to as Aššurbanipal's third campaign (Bii_{41}).

sequences for the treatment of suspected *doublets* are of even greater importance. We cannot *a priori* assume that two similar narratives constitute alternative versions of one story. In the light of the literary development of Assyrian annals the assimilation of originally different accounts with common features seems more probable. Further examples will be given below.

The conception of the crushing of Tandamanē's rebellion as a campaign of the Assyrian king has led to an increasing separation of this account from the previous one. In B the insertion of *arkānu* ("afterwards") marked the beginning of the new section. The adaptations also affected the *discourse structure*. In B *stage* and *inciting event* are marked and separated from the account of the campaign proper by the mention of a messenger arriving in Nineveh. The description of Tandamanē's preparations is downgraded by the replacement of the two sentences containing *ušatbâ* ("he prepared") and *iṣbata ḫarrāna* ("he took the road") with the more usual *idkâ* ("he mustered").[273] The battle between Tandamanē's forces and the Assyrians is not mentioned in B. The resolution of the conflict with the Assyrian king as *agent* is therefore found in the description of the conquest and looting of Thebes, which contains the overall *peak* of B's account. HT's *ispunū abūbiš* ("they crushed {this city} like a flood") is omitted, but the looting is described with three *main line* verbs (*assuḫma* - "I tore out"}, *alqâ* - "I took", *ašlula* - "I despoiled; ll.35-36).

B's summarizing remarks (ii_{37-38}) reflect the tendency towards placing more emphasis on results than on a sequence of events.[274] The account is concluded with the mention of Aššurbanipal's return to Nineveh (Bi_{39}).

---

[273] Cf. HT obv.16 parr.; Bi_{66} parr.

[274] Similarly, VAT 5600+ has omitted the mention of a victory against Ammuladdin ($Bviii_{43-45}$), but rather concentrated on the result, Ammuladdin's capture (II,40-44). IT further left out the references to Ammuladdi's fight against the Amurri and narrates only that Ammuladdi was captured alive and brought before Aššurbanipal (l.114). Cf. also IT's remarks on the submission of Uwaite''s (ll.113.119-121.123-126, see below, pp.135f, n.276) and Natnu (ll.123.124).
This trend can also be recognized in HT's omissions from E's account of the Kirbit affair. HT has only retained the narration of the destruction of Kirbit and the capture of its mayor (rev.11-12), but left out references to prior events. The preference of mentioning results to relating a sequence of events implies a reduction of tension and thus HT's account is *episodic*. This is also true of F's version of the campaign against Teummān, where the tendency is underlined by an alteration of the order of narration (cf. below, pp.135f, n.276) and an expansion of the description of the conquest of

With regard to the development of the participant orientation pattern, B's adaptation of the account to the preceding one and to the usual sequence of events runs against the tendency to reduce the number of *reversal*s on the *main line* (HT: 3xr - 13.33 %; B: 6 x r - 24 %). B's *main line* is generally dominated by primary

---

Elam (Fii_{62-66} // Bv_{93-98}; cf. below, appendix II, table 8, and appendix III, figure 3 with comments). By the omissions F has created a historical inaccuracy. F retained the time denotation of Bv_{77ff} (// Fii_{57}), but left out its reference, the mustering of the Assyrian army. In F, therefore, *ina ulūl* ...("in the month of Ulūl") relates to the conquest of Elam.

A has expanded the narration of Aḫšeri's death by inserting a parallel line ($Aiii_9$), a reference to Aḫšeri's relatives ($Aiii_{10}$), and a quotation of Ištar's promise ($Aiii_{6-7}$) and thus placed more emphasis on the resolution of the conflict. Unfortunately IT's version is mutilated, but since l.87 concludes IT's version of Gyges' submission and l.89 mentions Ualli, there remains only one line for the Aḫšeri episode. From the account of the campaign against Dunanu IT has only retained that Aššurbanipal captured Sapibel and took Dunanu with rich spoil to Assyria (ll.105-107).

A part of the last section of F's account of Aššurbanipal's first campaign against Ummanaldasi is paralleled by the text of a prism represented by ND 4378B, 5527, 5529, and 5533 (cf. E.E.Knudsen, "Fragments", pll.xxi, xxiv, xxv, xxvi), assigned by Knudsen to ed. C. R.D.Freedman, however, argued convincingly that the prism belongs to a different edition (cf. *Assurbanipal's "Annals"*, p.8f). Since the fragments' text agrees with C against F and A in other passages (Cix_{66ff}, without equivalent in F and A), we shall assume that they present an earlier version compared to F and A. ND 4378B+ ll.x+1-x+11 correspond to Fiv_{8-16} (// Av_{53-62}). Up to *ašlula ana Aššur* ("I took as spoil to Assyria", ll.x+12) the text is identical with that of editions F and A. Then the prism continues to give a summary of Aššurbanipal's conquests and the booty taken and mentions the distribution of the spoil among Assyrians. This is narrated in neither F's nor A's account on the first campaign against Ummanaldasi, but a similar passage is found later in the two editions (Fvi_{12ff} // Avi_{125ff}) in the context of a second expedition against the Elamite king, the last campaign reported in ed.F. A briefly mentions a further expedition against the Elamite king (Ax_{6-16}). Since the similarities of the descriptions could be due to the subject and there are also differences (ll.x+12-31.40-44 are not represented in F/A; F/A add *Nusku* to the list of gods in l.x+36, A further adds *Adad* to l.x+34, and the texts of Fvi_{16-21} // Avi_{3-8} are not present in the preserved parts of the prism). The evidence does not require the assumption of a textual dependency, but on the other hand it cannot be ruled out. It is quite conceivable that F transferred parts of this passage from the end of a first campaign against Ummanaldasi to the end of the report of a second campaign against the same king. Of B's account of Aššurbanipal's campaign against Ummanigaš ($Bvii_{3-42}$) F and A have only retained that Ummanigaš who had accepted a bribe from Šamaš-šum-ukīn was killed by Tammaritu ($Fiii_{6-11}$ // $Aiii_{136}$-iv_2). Similarly A has transferred the account of the wealth of booty taken during a first campaign against Uwaite' and of a famine among the Arabs to a passage after the report of a second campaign against the Arab king ($Bviii_{12-31}$ // VAT 5600+ I,54-II,22 {cf. above, pp.117f, n.212} // Aix_{42-74})

A's addition of v_{15-16} may appear as an exeption to the rule, but the added lines provide necessary background information on a participant who had been introduced in v_{15}.

participants. Only in the reports of the arrival of a messenger and of the submission of vassal kings do secondary participants appear as *agents*. The participant relation in the passage containing the overall *peak* is A B'.[275]

In the description of the booty taken from Thebes B has resolved the chronological order by adding that Aššurbanipal took two obelisks to Assyria (Bii_{33-35}). Four lines later the Assyrian king's return to Nineveh is mentioned. B has combined similar passages describing the taking of booty and thus resolved the chronological order of narration to a thematic one.[276]

---

[275] The development of the participant designations at this point is significant. While HT had 3rd p.pl. (*ikšudū* - "they conquered", HT obv.74) referring to the Assyrian troops, B - followed by C/A, and F - has retained the pl. (*ikšudā* - "they conquered", Bii_{29}) with *qātāya* ("my hands") as grammatical subject. The pronominal suffix *-ya* ("my") refers to Aššurbanipal. The development ends with the use of 1st p.sgl. (*akšud* - "I conquered") in ed. H (ii_7).

[276] A thematic rather than a chronological order can also be observed as a result or redactorial intervention in F's version of Aššurbanipal's campaign against Elam (Biv_{87-88}: "against Teummān"). The order of narration is according to importance; first the victory over Elam, then the killing of the Elamite king and then that of his soldiers. Thereafter the account returns to the description of the extent of Aššurbanipal's victory which is thus stressed twice. F has transferred the remarks on Ummanigaš's and Tammaritu's escape to the passage narrating their enthronement ($Fii_{68.70}$), thus further altering the chronological order of narration towards a thematic one (cf. $Biv_{74-86.89-96}$). This purpose may also be responsible for the twofold mention of Uwaiteʾ's punishment ($Aviii_{1-14}$, Aix_{97-114}). The insertion of the first passage may have been prompted by the mention of Uwaiteʾ's escape, whereas the second passage introduces the description of punishments inflicted by the Assyrian king on insubmissive enemies.
Several of IT's accounts can be adduced. Unfortunately IT's report of the campaign against Teummān / Elam is only poorly preserved. The extant portions are different from the preceding versions. IT l.100 mentions the cities *Šušan Pi-*[*dil-ma*]. Since the next line narrates the taking of booty, the cities probably are mentioned as having been conquered. This took place during Aššurbanipal's second campaign against Ummanaldasi ($Fiv_{36.38}$ // $Av_{84.87}$). IT l.102 relates the installation of Tammaritu as king of Ḫidāli, which in eds. B, F, and A is mentioned after the campaign against Teummān. Thus IT appears to have put together information from several campaigns against the Elamites. IT's order of narration of Aššurbanipal's expeditions against Arabs differs from that of the major editions: Ammuladdi (l.114), Natnu (ll.123-124), Uaiteʾ (ll.113.119.[124]-126). The narration of Šamaš-šum-ukīn's fate may have prompted the first mention of Uaiteʾ (l.113 *Uaiteʾ* [*ša pī it*]*tīšu iššaknu* - "Uaiteʾ, [who] had made [common cause wi]th him"). The second mention (l.119: *Iauteʾ*) is part of a list of kings humiliated in Nineveh (cf. Ax_{17-30}). The list notes Elamite kings first and follows a reference to Aššurbanipal's conquest of Elam (ll.115-118). The third mention (l.124 - king's name not preserved) followed the narration of the submission of Natnu, king of Nabatea (*ša ana N*]*abayā*[*ti ittak*]*lu u tā*[*martišu* ... - "[who had trust]ed [on N]aba[tea] and his gi[fts ...") . It is interesting to note that ll.113.119 have both

The text of C/A is almost identical with that of B.[277] A has replaced *mār aḫātīšu* ("son of his sister", ii_{10}) with *mār Šabaku* ("son of Šabaku") and inserted *ina šane girrīya* ("on my second campaign") after the mention of the messenger, thus omitting the back-reference and separating the two accounts more clearly from each other.

Edition F has the account of the campaign against Tandamanē as its first campaign account[278] and thus concentrates on the final confrontation between the Assyrian and a Kushite king. F further has omitted the *stage* of B's version including the mention of the messenger, B's summarizing remarks, and the reference to Aššurbanipal's return to Nineveh.[279] Thus in F no conflict is introduced and there is consequently only one *peak*, the conquest and looting of Thebes.

---

orthographic forms of the name, although the extant possible *Vorlagen* of this passage use only one. Uwaite''s support of Šamaš-šum-ukīn is mentioned by $Avii_{99}$ (Uwaite') and VAT 5600+ I,42-44 (Uwaite'). Uwaite''s humiliation is narrated in A (Uwaite', cf. Ax_{21ff}). Cf. also below, p.288, n.112. Both passages in IT mention him as king of *Sumu-ili*, which has no equivalent in B, VAT 5600+, C or A.

A resolution of the chronological order of narration is also recognizable in A's resumption of Aimu's capture in Ax_{1-4} (// ix_{19-22}). The redactor presumably placed Aimu's execution (Ax_5) in its historical context rather than mentioning a separate event (*contra* M.Weippert, "Kämpfe", p.49). It is noteworthy that the first part of the later passage is narrated in subordinate clauses. A has also inserted the account of Abiate''s entronement between the report of the latter's support for Šamaš-šum-ukīn against Aššurbanipal and that of another conspiracy together with Natnu ($Aviii_{48-51.68ff}$; cf. below, p.249, n.2), both of which had not been reported in the preceding versions. Whether Abiate' was re-installed or B and VAT 5600+ omitted the former incident cannot be decided from the texts.

Thematic order is, however, not necessarily a sign of redactorial intervention. In the case of Aššurbanipal's first campaign against Ummanaldasi it is already present in the earliest extant account, that of ed. F. F's account begins with the submission of cities ($Fiii_{39-61}$) and then turns to individuals ($Fiii_{62ff}$).

For the presence of *resumptive repetition* in *early versions* and its employment by redactors to mark secondary insertions cf. below, appendix II, p.249 with n.2.

277 For minor alterations cf. below.

278 Consequently the Egyptian vassal kings are described with *ša Aššur-aḫḫa-iddina šar Aššur abu bānû'a ištakan qereb Muṣur* ("whom Esarhaddon, king of Assyria, the father who begot me had installed in Egypt", Fi_{41}), whereas B reads *ša qereb Muṣur aškun* ("whom I had installed in Egypt", ii_{23}).

279 An abbreviation of the *stage* is also apparent in HT's treatment of E's account of Aššurbanipal's campaign against Kirbit (see appendix III, table 6) Even though E's text is badly mutilated, enough has been preserved to indicate that that E's *stage* was far more extensive than that in HT (rev.8-9). B/C have further abbreviated HT's *stage* by leaving out rev.7, which paralleled rev.8. They also omitted the *inciting event*, the

As has been noted above, Ed. H has retained only the *peak* section. The following diagram shows the *discourse profile* of B's account of Aššurbanipal's second Egyptian campaign indicating the passages retained by eds. F and H.

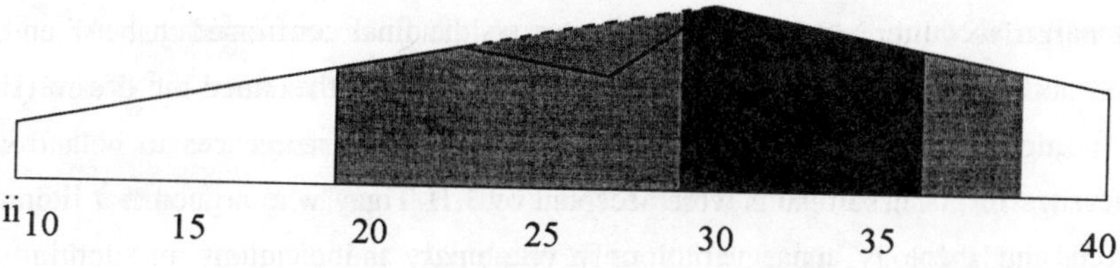

c) The Gyges Affair

In the discussion about appropriate usage of Ancient Near Eastern material for literary criticism applied to Old Testament narratives, A's account of the submission of Gyges to the Assyrian king has received special attention. In Aii$_{100f}$ we find a twofold mention of a messenger sent by the Lydian king to Aššurbanipal. It is the presence of two practically synonymous terms, *rakbû* ("{mounted} messenger") and *mār-šipri* ("messenger"), that caught attention. K.A.Kitchen argued that this passage and others indicate that the presence of varying terminology cannot serve as evidence for conflation of sources.[280] On the other hand M.Cogan and H.Tadmor have argued that A was dependent on two different versions of ed.

---

request for Aššurbanipal's intervention by the inhabitants of Dēru (HT rev.10). Comparable is furthermore F's omission of the first part of B's account of Aššurbanipal's campaign against Ašḫeri (Biii$_{18-32a}$; cf. appendix III, table 7). The omitted passage narrates a first battle between Assyrian and Mannean forces before Aššurbanipal entered Aḫšeri's territory. F has drastically abbreviated B's account of Aššurbanipal's campaign against Teummān by compressing B's *stage* into one subordinate clause (*ša ikpudū limuttu* - "who had plotted evil", Fii$_{61}$) and omitting the *inciting event* (Bv$_{15-24}$).
The expansion the description of Uaite’’s "sin" by ed. A (vii$_{86.88.90f.104-106}$) may have been prompted by Uaite’’s capture and punishment (cf. Aix$_{97-114}$).

280 Cf. *Ancient Orient and Old Testament*, p.124.

E, E_1 and E_2.[281] While E_1 is argued to have used *rakbû*, E_2 had *mār-šipri*. Further differences between the versions are claimed to be recognizable in the fact that in E_1 the messenger could not be understood because he spoke a "barbaric" language, whereas E_2 presupposes that he spoke a "mutually intelligible language".[282] Cogan and Tadmor also ascribed to E_2 the development of the dream sequence in the narration of the Gyges affair. From this reconstruction of the narrative's literary development Cogan and Tadmor concluded that HT and A used both versions of E.[283] HT preferred *rakbû* (E_1) but retained the dream (E_2). A is said to have conflated both versions by including references to both *rakbû* and *mār-šipri*. These results were accepted by J.H.Tigay who argued that literary-critical methodology, using variations in vocabulary as indications for sources was thus corroborated.[284]

There are, however, various difficulties with Cogan and Tadmor's reconstruction of the literary history of the Gyges story. They have convincingly shown that the length of a col. of E_2 was 80 lines.[285] If the mention of the *mār-šipri* in BM 134454 col. B, l.2' belongs to the account of the Gyges affair then the whole account must have comprised more than one complete col., for BM 134454, col. A contains part of the narrative. Of those at the very least 80 lines are (partially) preserved:

BM 134454 col. A:	11 lines
BM 134445 + 121018:	14 lines
BM 134455 + 127923:	14 lines
BM 134454 col. B:	2 lines
	41 lines.

This leaves at least 39 lines of E_2 which are completely lost. There is no reason to exclude the possibility that these lines could have contained the mention of a *rakbû*. Of ed. E_1 even less is preserved. Thus the distinction between two hypothetical versions of ed. E is not as certain as Cogan and Tadmor have argued.

281 Cf. "Gyges and Ashurbanipal".
282 Cf. "Gyges and Ashurbanipal", p.74.
283 Cf. "Gyges and Ashurbanipal", pp.77f.
284 "Stylistic Criterion", pp.154f.
285 Cf. "Gyges and Ashurbanipal", p.70, n.18. Ed. E (cf. above, p.96, n.104) probably did not contain the list of the Egyptian vassal kings found in Ai_{90ff} (partially paralleled in C). Both E and HT have a relative clause narrating that Assurbanipal's father had installed these kings. A and C do not have this clause since the information had already

Their reconstruction also ignores the agreements between A and other editions. A would have used E_1, E_2, B, and perhaps HT and C, too, for an account of 14 lines. In A's account of Gyges' downfall and his son's accession both terms are used ($Aii_{111.122}$). As in the account of Gyges' submission a *rakbû* is (not) sent *ana ša'āl šulmēya* ("to inquire after my well-being") and the *mār-šipri* delivers a message. A difference in meaning between the two terms could provide enough reason for A's additional reference to a *mār-šipri* relating Gyges' dream. The parallelism does not necessarily imply that according to ed. A two distinct envoys were sent by the Lydian king. The construction may rather be regarded as *overlay* and might reflect E's high rhetorical level in the narration of the messenger's arrival at the Assyrian court.

ūmu šuttu annītu ēmurū	*rakbûšu*	*išpura ana maḫrīya ana ša'āl šulmēya*
šuttu *annītu ša ēmurū ina qātā*	*mār-šipri*	*išpuramma ušannâ yâti*

("the day he had seen the dream	he sent his rider to me to inquire after my well-being;	
the dream, he had seen, through a	messenger	he sent to relate it to me", $Aii_{100\text{-}102}$).

In any case the two different terms cannot possibly be used for the identification of different sources of ed. A![286] The same is true for the presence of the dream. The bad state of preservation of the supposed E_1 does not permit the exclusion of the possibility of a dream episode in E_1.

The preserved portions indicate that E's account(s) were far more extensive than those of the later versions. The extant parts of E's *main line*(s) read:

K 1821// A 7920:[287]

1.3	*itḫâ* "he reached"	B'	A	
1.4	*īmurūšuma* "they saw him"	A'	B'	⇒ r
1.5	*iqbûšu* "they said to him"	A'	B'	⇒ I

been given together with the names of the kings (Ai_{110} // Cii_{84} {// B/D}). HT did not have the list. It is thus not probable that it was present in E.

286 Since Cogan's and Tadmor's study was used by J.H.Tigay ("Stylistic Criterion", p.154) as basis for his argumentation for an empirical model for Pentateuchal criticism the point made above has to be emphasized. The case is different with the two variant forms of a proper name occurring in IT; cf. above, pp.135f, n.276.

287 Cogan and Tadmor's E_1.

1.9	*ubilūniššu* "they brought him"	A'	B'	A	⇒ I
1.12	*ul ibšīma* "there was no (interpreter)"	A'			⇒ I
1.14	*lā išemmû* "they did not understand (his words)"	A'	B'		⇒ r
1.16	*ūbila* "he brought"	B'			⇒ r

BM 134454, BM 134445, BM 134455, BM 127923[288]:

BM 134454	col.	$A_{11'}$	[*lā išmû*] "[they had not heard of]"	[A']	
		$A_{17'}$	*ušamqi*[*tū*] "they defeated"	C B(')	
BM 134445 / BM 121018	col.	$C_{9'}$	*ušannīma* "he related to me"	?	
BM 134455 / BM 127923	col.	C_{12}	*u*]⌜*šē*⌝*bilamma* "he sent"	B A	
			amḫur "I received"	A (B)	⇒ r

It is evident that in E's version(s) the rhetorical level was comparatively high. E's participant orientation pattern exhibits comparatively many reversals and references to internal participant relations. Secondary participants like the Lydian messenger or the inhabitants of Assyria figured prominently. All this has changed in HT. The account was compressed to five *main line* verbs. HT has drastically reduced the rhetorical level. Only one passage contains direct speech. Correspondingly HT has simplified the participant orientation pattern. There are only two *main line agents* (Aššur and Gyges) and only one *reversal*.

In HT the beginning of the account of the Gyges episode is marked by the mention of a new participant. The introduction sentence is comparatively "heavy". Much emphasis is placed on the fact that Gyges country was *ašru rūqu* ("a distant place"). Gyges had not been a vassal of Aššurbanipal and therefore this account does not deal with the crushing of a rebellion. This provides an explanation for

[288] Cogan and Tadmor's E_2.

the fact that neither Aššurbanipal nor his generals are mentioned as grammatical subjects on the *main line*. The introductory line mentions that Aššur appeared to Gyges in a dream. The exhortations given by Aššur to the Lydian king are mentioned in HT's account in a construction, which consists of 3+1 members. It is noteworthy that they are given in direct speech:

ša Aššur-bān-apli … šēpē rubûtīšu ṣabatma
šarrussu pitluḫma
ṣulla bēlūssu
ša ēpiš ardūti u nādin mandatti lillikūš suppûka

"seize the princely feet of Aššurbanipal …,
fear his kingship,
implore his lordship,
as a servant and tributary let your supplications come to him" (rev.17f).

Thus the contents of the dream are emphasized and with the rhetorical level tension increases. This is also evident from the fact that the actual reason for Aššur's appearance to Gyges has not yet been told in the account. This is different from the usual (strictly chronological) order. It is only from a subordinate clause and after the conflict is solved that the reader learns what had happened before. Unfortunately, due to the bad state of preservation of manuscripts belonging to ed.E, we do not know whether this deviation from the expected order constitutes a secondary development. The time denotation *ūmu šuttu annitu ēmuru* ("the day he had seen the dream", rev.19) links the second section of the account with the first. Contrary to the first section the second is narrative rather than descriptive. HT plainly narrates that, after Gyges had sent a messenger to Aššurbanipal, he defeated his enemies and sent (them ?) with tribute to Nineveh. The rhetorical *peak* of HT's version of the account of the Gyges affair is found near the beginning in the retelling of Gyges' dream. It coincides with neither the point of highest tension nor that of the *dénouement*. In the structuring of the dream section, too, the greatest emphasis is placed on the first member. It is noteworthy that Assyrian intervention is mentioned only in the dream section.

HT's *main line* reads:

				HT	B	F	A	IT
rev.15 *ušabrīšuma* "he showed him"	A*	B			+	+	+	[+]
rev.19 *išpura* "he sent"	B	B'	A	⇒r	r	r	r[289]	[ ][290]
				-	-	-	I[291]	-
				-		-	I[292]	-
rev.20 *ikšuda* "he captured"	B	C		⇒s	-	-	s[293]	-
				-	s[294]	s	I	-
rev.21 *ušēbila* "he sent"	B	C	A	⇒I	I	I	I	r[295]
unaššiq "he kissed"	B	A		⇒s	-	-	-	I
				-	-	-	+[296]	-

In the report of the Gyges affair the literary development appears to be inconsistent. B, C, and F have an abbreviated version of HT's account, whereas A has a more extensive report. But since ed.A relates the contents of Gyges' dream, paralleled in E and HT but not in B, C and F, we may regard the text of A as the earlier one compared with that of B, C, and F.[297]

B has omitted from HT the quotation of Aššur's exhortations, that part of the narrative in which the highest rhetorical level had been found, and replaced HT's *ikšuda* ("he captured") with *utammeḫma* ("he bound", iii_2). B retained the

---

289 *išpuru* (subjunctive), but Var.: *išpura*.

290 R.Campbell Thompson, "Excavation at Nineveh": [*išpuru* ...] ("[who had sent] ...", l.87).

291 *išpuramma* ("he sent") - B B' A.

292 *ušannâ* ("he related") - B A.

293 *ikšud* ("defeated").

294 *utammeḫma* ("he bound") - B C.

295 *tāmartīšu kabit*]*ti ušēbilamma* ("he sent his [hea]vy [tribute]") - B A.

296 A then continues to narrate Gyges' rebellion, his downfall and the accession of his son ($Aii_{111-125}$).

297 Cf. also the agreements of a variant reading to Aii_{97} with HT rev.15 (*nibīt šarrūtīya kabti* - "the mention of my heavy kingship", A: *nibīt šumīya* - "mention of my name") and of a variant reading to Aii_{100} with HT rev.19 (*išpura* - "he sent", A: išpuru - "who sent") noted in M.Streck, *Assurbanipal* II, p.20, nn.f and g, against B, C, and F. *ušannâ* ("he related", Aii_{102}) may have a parallel in E (BM 134445 l.9': *ušannīma* - "he related"). E is, however, too mutilated, and the parallel of too a common kind to permit conclusions with regard to literary dependencies.

relative clauses and appositions of HT and further amplified *utammeḫma* by adding a mention of the instruments used. Since the expression used by B is common,[298] it does not constitute a substantial rise of the rhetorical level. At the end of the narrative B has omitted the remark on the kissing of Aššurbanipal's feet, but added a different phrase, *atammaru danān Aššur u Marduk* ("that I saw the might of Aššur and Marduk"). The addition, however, was not retained in the later editions. The tendency to abbreviate prevailed. Thus C like B does not have the mention of the kissing of Aššurbanipal's feet. C has also omitted B's final phrase.

A followed HT more closely than B, C, and F had done. Thus a direct quotation of the dream contents is given, though it differs in wording from HT. The exhortations of Aššur as narrated in A comprised only two commands. The first one, *šēpā Aššur-bān-apli ṣa[batma]* ("seize the feet of Aššurbanipal"), constitutes an abbreviation of HT's first command, *ša Aššur-bān-apli šar Aššur ... šēpē rubûtīšu ṣabatma* ("seize the princely feet of Aššurbanipal, king of Assyria ...", rev.17). A has not taken over any of the other commands, but has added a different one, *ina zikir šumīšu kušud nakrēka* ("invoking his name conquer your enemies"), emphasizing Aššurbanipal's importance rather than Aššur's, whereby the contents of the dream (*kušud* - "conquer", cf. Aii_{98f}), are linked to the narration of the later events (*ikšud* - "he conquered", cf. Aii_{103f}). A has not only retained the reference to the conquest (*ikšud*), which was already found in HT rev.20 (*ikšuda*), but also *utammeḫma* ("he bound") from B and C as a link between *ikšud* and *ušēbila* ("he brought"). Like C and F, A has not taken over B's additional remark at the end of the narrative. In A the account of the Gyges affair does not end with the reference to Gyges paying tribute to Aššurbanipal, but continues to report the following changes of the relations between Lydia and Assyria.

IT, too, exhibits an account of the Gyges affair. It omits the description of Lydia as a "distant place ...". The reference to Gyges' dream is retained, though the word order is different. R.Campbell Thompson has *šumīya* ("my name") in square brackets. If IT indeed read so, it agreed with A against HT, B, C, F, which all read *šarrūtīya* ("my kingship").[299] IT also quotes the first exhortation of

---

298 Cf. $Aii_{131}.iii_{60}$.

299 HT + *kabti* ("heavy").

Aššur to Gyges in the same phraseology as A, apart from the omission of *šar Aššur* ("king of Assyria") after the mention of Aššurbanipal. Unfortunately the remainder of this sentence is mutilated in IT. Campbell Thompson only gives *-ka* ("your" / "you"). If IT l.86 indeed was identical with Aii$_{99}$, Aššur's second exhortation, we would have another case of assimilation of the descriptions of command and fulfillment, for the extant part of IT l.86 (events) corresponds closely to Aii$_{99}$ (command). The development of the correspondence between the relations of dream and event would thus be:

HT rev.17	*ša Aššur-bān-apli šar Aššur ... šēpē rubûtīšu ṣabatma* ("seize the princely feet of Aššurbanipal, king of Assyria ...")	-
rev.20	-	*Gimiraya ... ikšudā qātāšu* ("his hands captured ... the Cimmerians")
A ii$_{98f.103f}$	*šēpā Aššur-bān-apli šar Aššur ṣabatma* ("seize the feet of Aššurbanipal, king of Assyria")	*ultu libbi ūmē ša iṣbatu šēpē šarrūtīya* ("from the day he seized my royal feet")
	ina zikir šumīšu kušud nakrēka ("invoking his name conquer your enemies")	*Gimiraya ... ikšud* ("he conquered ... the Cimmerians")
IT ll.85f	*šēpā Aššur-bān-apli ṣa[batma] [ina zikir šumīšu kušud nakrē]ka* ("seize the feet of Aššurbanipal, [invoking his name conquer] your [enemies]")	*ina zikir šumīya nakrēšu ikšud* ("invoking my name he conquered his enemies")

IT has, however, omitted the correspondence to *šēpā Aššur-bān-apli ṣa[batma]* ("se[ize] the feet of Aššurbanipal"). The development of this passage, especially the treatment of HT by A, resembles that of Akkadian epic literature with its tendency towards progressive assimilation of corresponding passages. In IT's version of this passage the Assyrian king is mentioned only by his proper name, agreeing with *šumīšu / šumīya* ("his / my name"). It is, however, noteworthy that the tendency to abbreviate prevailed.

d) The Mugallu Affair, the Iakinlu Affair, and Aššurbanipal's Campaign against Ba'alu of Tyre

In HT the report of the Gyges affair is followed by the account of the submission of Mugallu, king of Tabal (rev.22-26). As in the Gyges-episode, Aššurbanipal did not directly intervene in the course of events.[300] No rise or fall of tension is apparent in the short narrative. The participant orientation pattern is unified. There is only one *reversal* at the end of the section. No internal participant relations are described and no secondary participants are introduced.

The account of the submission of Iakinlu, king of Arvad (rev.27-31) is similar. Again the Assyrian king does not intervene, the submissive king lives far away,[301] and the account is brief and *episodic*. It narrates the last incident reported in HT.

However, the literary relationship between the extant versions is complex. On the one side there is reason to assume that A's account represents an intermediate stage between HT and B[302], on the other side there is slight indication that it is secondary compared to B.[303]

We shall thus regard both eds. B and A as being dependent on HT's version, but disregard their mutual relationship. A's version indicates that the report

---

300 Tabal is described as *huršānu šadû pašqātu* ("highlands, difficult mountains", HT rev.22). Cf. the description of Lydia as *nagû neberti tâmti ašru rūqu ša šarrāni ālikūt maḫri abbēya lā išmû zikri šumīšu* ("a district across the sea, a distant place, the mention of the name of which the preceding kings, my fathers, had not heard"; HT rev.14-15).

301 *Ikkilu ... āšib rapašti qabal tâmtim ša kīma nūni ina mê lā nībi [ina gi(?)p]iš edê danni šitkunū šubtu ša eli tâmtim gallati ilûma* ("Ikkilu ..., living in the midst of the wide sea, who like a fish in countless waters took up his residence, in the torrent of the mighty flood, who had gone to the surging sea", HT rev.27-29).

302 As HT, ed.A has separate accounts of the submissions of the two rulers (+ Sandišarme, king of Ḫilakka) and mentions horses as tribute only for Mugallu (HT rev.26 // Aii$_{73-74}$). In B the reports are drawn together into one unit.

303 B in its summarizing remarks at the beginning of its account mentions *šadê šaqûti* ("high mountains", ii$_{68}$) which is paralleled in HT (rev.22), but not in A. Thus B's *Vorlage* probably differed from A. Furthermore, A has a difficult text in Aii$_{73ff}$: *eli Mugalli sīsê rabûti mandattu šattišamma ukīn ṣērussu* ("on Mugallu I imposed as annual tribute great horses on him"). Either *eli Mugalli* ("on Mugallu") or *ṣērussu* ("on him") is redundant or we have to regard *eli Mugalli* as the introduction of a new participant ("as for Mugallu"). However, Mugallu is already the grammatical subject in

of Sandišarme's submission probably existed in an independent form. We shall assume this for B's *Vorlage*.

For convenience the texts will be given here.

HT rev.22-31	Bii_{67-81}	Aii_{63-80}
	malkī qabal tâmtim u *šarrāni āšibūti šadê šaqūti* *danān epšētīya annāti* *ēmurūma iplaḫū bēlūti*	
Mugalli šar [Tabal] āšib *ḫuršāni šadî pašqūti ša ana* *šarrāni abbēya kakkē* *šitpuru ētappalu daṣāti* *qereb mātīšu ḫatti* *imqussuma puluḫti* *šarrūtīya išḫupšuma balu* *epēš qabal kakkē tāḫāzi ana* *Ninua išpuramma uṣalla* *bēlūti sīsê rabûti [mad]attu* *nadān mātīšu ukīn ṣīrussu*	*Iakinlu šar Aruadda*[304] *Mugallu šar Tabala* *Sandišarme Ḫilika ša ana* *šarrāni abbēya lā kanšū* *iknušū ana nīrīya mārāte ṣīt* *libbīšunu itti nudunnê* *ma'adi u tirḫati ma'assi*[305] *ana epēš abrakkūti ana* *Ninua ūbilūnimma unaššiqū* *šēpēya eli Mugalli sīsê* *rabûti madattu šattišamma* *ukīn ṣērussu*	*Iakinlu šar Aruadda āšib* *qabal tâmtim ša ana* *šarrāni abbēya lā kanšu* *iknuša ana nīrīya mārassu* *itti nudunnê ma'adi ana* *epēš abrakkūti ana Ninua* *ūbilamma unaššiqa šēpēya*
Ikkilu šar Aruada āšib *rapašti qabal tâmtim ša* *kīma nūni ina mê lā nībi* *[ina gi?p]iš edê danni* *šitkunu šubtu ša eli tâmtim* *gallati ilûma lā kitnušu ana* *nīrī bēlūtī [uṣal]lûma ana* *epēš ardūtīya iknušma išūṭa* *abšāni ḫurāṣē šipāte samāte* *šipāte ṣalmāte nūnē iṣṣūrē* *šattišamma ukīn elīšu*		*Mugallu šar Tabal ša itti* *šarrāni abbēya idbubu* *daṣāti bintu ṣīt libbīšu itti* *terḫāti ma'assi ana epēš* *abrakkūti ana Ninua* *ūbilamma unaššiq šēpēya* *eli Mugalli sīsê rabûti* *mandattu šattišamma ukīn* *ṣīrussu*
		Sandišarme Ḫilakka ša ana *šarrāni abbēya lā iknušū lā* *īšūtū abšānšun mārtu ṣīt* *libbīšu itti nudunnê ma'adi* *ana epēš abrakkūti ana* *Ninua ūbilamma unaššiq* *šēpēya*

the preceding passage. The same sentence also occurs in B, where the passage preceding *eli Mugalli* had had a compound grammatical subject.

[304] Fi_{70} adds *āšib qabal tâmtim* ("living in the midst of the sea", cf. HT).

[305] *tirḫati ma'assi* ("great gift") > F.

HT rev.22-31	Bii$_{67-81}$	Aii$_{63-80}$
	Princes in the midst of the sea, kings, living on high mountains, saw the power of these deeds of mine, they feared my dominion.	
Mugalli, king of [Tabal], living on the highlands, difficult mountains, who had sent weapons against the kings, my fathers, (and) continually harassed (them) - in the midst of his country the fear of my kingship fell upon him. Without armed conflict (or) battle he sent to Nineveh, implored my lordship. I imposed on him great horses as tribute, as the gift of his country.	Iakinlu, king of Arvad, Mugallu, king of Tabal, Sandišarme of Cilicia, who had not been submissive to the kings, my fathers, submitted to my yoke. They brought daughters, their own offspring, with great dowries and great gifts to Nineveh to be ladies-in-waiting; they kissed my feet. As for Mugallu, I imposed on him great horses as annual payment.	Iakinlu, king of Arvad, living in the midst of the sea, who had not been submissive to the kings, my fathers, submitted to my yoke. He brought his daughter with great dowries to Nineveh to be a lady-in-waiting; he kissed my feet.
Ikkilu, king of Arvad, living in the midst of the wide sea, who like a fish in countless waters took up his residence, in the torrent of the mighty flood, who had gone to the surging sea, who had not submitted to my yoke, implored my lordship, to act as my servant he humbled himself, he submitted, he drew my yoke. As annual (payment) I imposed on him gold, brown wool, black wool, fish, birds.		Mugallu, king of Tabal, who had harassed the kings, my fathers, brought (his) daughter, his own offspring, with great dowries to Nineveh to be a lady-in-waiting; he kissed my feet. As for Mugallu, I imposed on him great horses as annual payment
		Sandišarme of Cilicia who had not submitted to the kings my fathers, who had not drawn their yoke, brought (his) daughter, his own offspring with great dowries to Nineveh to be a lady-in-waiting; he kissed my feet.

A has adapted the different accounts to each other and placed them after an account of Ba'alu's submission which had not been related in HT. The order of narration was changed in A. The account which bears the greatest similarity to that of Ba'alu's submission, the Iakinlu-episode,[306] is placed first. A has retained elements present in both of HT's accounts and, we may assume, probably in A's Sandišarme-*Vorlage*, too: a reference to the kings' former insubmissiveness and their later obedience.[307] A has retained only few distinct elements of the accounts[308] and has thus increased their mutual similarity.

HT (Mugalli):	HT (Ikkilu) :	A (Mugallu):	A (Iakinlu):	A(Sandišarme):
Mugalli šar [Tabal] āšib ḫuršāni šadî pašqūti	*Ikkilu šar Aruada āšib rapašti qabal tâmtim ša kīma nūni ina mê lā nībi [gib?]iš edê danni šitkunu šubtu ša eli tâmtim gallati ilûma*	*Mugallu šar Tabal*	*Iakinlu šar Aruadda āšib ------ qabal tâmtim*	*Sandišarme Ḫilakka*
ša ana šarrāni abbēya kakkē šitpuru ētappalu daṣāti qereb mātīšu ḫatti imqussuma puluḫti šarrūtīya isḫupšuma balu	*ša lā kitnušu ana nīr bēlūti [uṣal]lûma*	*ša itti šarrāni abbēya idbubu daṣāti*	*ša ana šarrāni abbēya lā kanšū*	*ša ana šarrāni abbēya lā iknušu lā īšutu abšānšun*

306 Cf. *āšib qabal tâmtim* ("living in the midst of the sea", $Aii_{50.63}$).

307 Cf. table below. The replacement of *ša … lā kitnušū ana nīrī* ("who … had not submitted to my yoke") in the Ikkilu section referring to Aššurbanipal as a primary participant by *ša ana šarrāni abbēya la kanšū* ("who had not been submissive to the kings, my fathers") apparently disagrees with the usual development. The Mugallu sction in HT contained the phrase *ša ana šarrāni abbēya kakkē šitpurū* ("who had sent weapons against the kings, my fathers") which has not been taken over by A. HT thus contained both a reference to the enemies insubmissiveness to Aššurbanipal's predecessors (Mugallu-section) and to the king himself (Ikkilu-section). In ed. A the descriptions of the enemies' insubmissiveness were harmonized.

308 From the Iakinlu-episode, which had contained the most extensive description of the geographical location, A took over *āšib qabal tâmtim* ("living in the midst of the sea") and from the Mugallu-episode A retained the mention of *sīsê rabûti* ("great horses") as tribute (cf. below, pp.152f, n.314).

epēš qabal kakkē tāḫazi ana Ninua išpuramma uṣalla bēlūti				
	ana epēš ardūtīya iknušūma īšūta abšāni ḫurāṣē šipāte samāte šipāte ṣalmāte nūnē iṣṣūrē		*iknušu ana nīrīya*	
		bintu ṣīt libbīšu itti terḫāti ma'assi ana epēš abrakkūti ana Ninua ūbilamma unaššiq šēpēya eli Mugalli	*mārassu itti nudunnê ma'adi ana epēš abrakkūti ana Ninua ūbilamma unaššiq šēpēya*	*mārtu ṣīt libbīšu itti nudunnê ma'adi ana epēš abrakkūti ana Ninua ūbilamma unaššiq šēpēya*
sīsê rabûti [mad]attu nadān mātīšu ukīn ṣērussu	*šattišamma ukīn elīšu*	*sīsê rabûti madattu šattišamma ukīn ṣērussu*		
HT (Mugalli):	HT (Ikkilu) :	A (Mugallu):	A (Iakinlu):	A(Sandišarme):
Mugalli king of [Tabal], living on the highlands, difficult mountains,	Ikkilu, king of Arvad, living in the midst of the wide sea, who like a fish in countless waters took up his residence, in the torrent of the mighty flood, who had gone to the surging sea,	Mugallu, king of Tabal	Iakinlu, king of Arvad, living in the midst of the sea,	Sandišarme of Cilicia
who had sent weapons against the kings, my fathers, (and) continually harassed (them) - in the midst of his country the	who had not submitted to my yoke,	who had harassed the kings, my fathers,	who had not been submissive to the kings, my fathers, submitted to my yoke.	who had not submitted to the kings my fathers, who had not drawn their yoke,

fear of my king-ship fell upon him. Without armed conflict (or) battle he sent to Nineveh, implored my lordship.				
	implored my lordship, to act as my servant he humbled him-self, he submit-ted, he drew my yoke.			
		brought (his) daughter, his own offspring, with great dowries to Nineveh to be a lady-in-waiting; he kissed my feet. As for Mugallu, as	He brought his daughter with great dowries to Nineveh to be a lady-in-waiting; he kissed my feet.	brought (his) daughter, his own offspring with great dowries to Nineveh to be a lady-in-waiting; he kissed my feet.
As tribute, as the gift of his country I im-posed on him	As annual (pay-ment) I imposed on him gold, brown wool, black wool, fish, birds.	annual payment I imposed on him		
great horses.		great horses.		

A has also added material to the Mugallu- and Iakinlu-episodes. The phrase *unaššiq šēpēya* ("he kissed my feet", Aii$_{66.72(80)}$) may have been taken from A's *Vorlage* of the account of Sandišarme's submission or from HT's summarizing remarks (rev.33). By the insertion of *mārassu* (// *bintu* // *mārtu*) *ṣīt libbīšu itti nudunnê ma'di* (// *terḫāti ma'assi*) *ana epēš abrakkūti ana Ninua ūbilamma* ("he brought his daughter [// daughter // daughter], his own offspring, with great dowries [// great gift] to Nineveh to be a lady-in-waiting", Aii$_{65\text{-}67.70\text{-}72.78\text{-}80}$), A adapted the accounts to that of Ba'alu's submission (Aii$_{56\text{-}57}$ {// Bii$_{53\text{-}54}$}: *mārtu*[309] *ṣīt libbīšu … ana epēš abrakkūti ūbila adi maḫrīya*; "the daughter, his own off-

309 Bii$_{53}$: *mārassu* ("his daughter").

spring, ... he brought before me to be a lady-in-waiting").[310] The mutual assimilation of the accounts does not necessarily imply that the added elements are not historical. It is interesting to note that in IT the accounts of the submissions of Iakinlu and Sandišarme were combined whereas that of Mugallu is given separately. IT mentions only in the latter section, not even in the account of Baʾalu's submission, that the king's daughter was sent to Aššurbanipal. This may be regarded as a complete distortion of the actual events, but it also may be due to a different *Vorlage*.

B has contracted all three accounts into one[311] which is preceded by generalizing anticipatory remarks.[312] The submission of the three kings is related

---

310 Comparable is C's addition of: *ana rēṣū[t Šamaš-šum-ukīn]* ("to the aid of [Šamaš-šum-ukīn]", $viii_{15}$) to B and K. The addition increases the parallelism between the Ummanigaš- and the Tammaritu sections in the account of Aššurbanipal's campaign against Ummanigaš ($Bvii_{49}$ // $Cviii_{46-47}$), which had already been linked by *kīma šâšuma ṭaʾāti imḫur* ("like him he accepted bribes", $Bvii_{47}$ // $Bvii_{7-8}$).

311 The order of narration agrees with that of ed.A against HT.
A further example for the incorporation of originally separate accounts is provided by F's inclusion of the Bīt-Imbi episode in its account of Aššurbanipal's first campaign against Ummanaldasi (cf. iii_{33-36}). BM 134436 notes this incident as Aššurbanipal's 11th campaign ($x_{65a-65b}$: *ina 11-ê girrīya ālik ana Bīt-Imbi āl tukult[i ša Elamti]* - "on my eleventh campaign I went to Bīt-Imbi, the fortress city [of Elam]"). Whether the inscription belongs to ed. C (thus Freedman - BM 134436 overlaps with ND 5406, K 1794 and ND 814, even though the account is missing in K 1794) or ed. K (thus M.Cogan and H.Tadmor, "Asshurbanipal's Conquest", p.234) is not of primary importance for our question. We note that a separate account was appended at the end of an annal edition and later incorporated into a larger unit. Unfortunately BM 134436's account breaks off at the equivalent to $Fiii_{55}$. Thus the length of the original account is not known. R.D.Freedman in his reconstruction adds only two lines up to the mention of Aššurbanipal's return (x_{65k} //$Fiii_{57}$). F then continues to narrate the capture of Teummān's wife and sons (-$Fiii_{61}$) in Bīt-Imbi. The mention of Ummanaldasi ($Fiii_{62}$) starts a new paragraph. The incorporation may have been prompted by the mention of the subjection of various Elamite cities ($Fiii_{39-45}$). It is important to note, that in F the insertion was marked as such by the formula *ina mētiq girrīya* ("in the course of my campaign", $Fiii_{46}$; cf. above, p.126).
F and A have incorporated the originally separate account of Aššurbanipal's campaign "against Dunanu" (cf. Bvi_{17}-vii_{1}) into their narration of a campaign "against Elam" (Fii_{33ff} // $Aiii_{27ff}$). They have marked the insertion with: *ultu kakkē Aššur u Ištar eli Elamti ušamriru aštakkanu danānu u lītu ina tayyartīya* ... ("after I had made bitter the weapons of Aššur and Ištar against Elam and established might and victory, *on my return* ...", Fii_{72-76} // $Aiii_{50-53}$).

312 These are missing in F, where, as in ed. A, the mention of Iakinlu is followed by *āšib qabal tâmtim* ("living in the midst of the sea", i_{70}). It is therefore not probable that F is dependent on B, but rather that both have a common *Vorlage*.

as an example of these. Of the distinct elements only the mention of Mugallu's tribute was retained. The proleptic remarks draw upon the phraseology of the two accounts in HT. ***malkī qabal tâmtim u šarrāni āšibūti šadê šaqūti*** ("princes in the midst of the sea and kings, living on high mountains", Bii_{67-68}) resembles HT rev.22, ***āšib ḫuršāni šadê pašqūti*** ("living on the highlands, difficult mountains"), and HT rev.27 ***āšib rapašti qabal tâmtim*** ("living in the midst of the wide sea"). Bii_{69} refers back to the account of the campaign against Ba'alu. Bii_{70}, ... ***ēmurma iplaḫū bēlūtīya*** ("... they saw, they feared my dominion") resembles HT rev.24, ***puluḫti šarrūtīya isḫupšuma*** ("the fear of my kingship fell upon him").

B continues with a report of events after the death of Iakinlu which probably had not taken place at the time HT was composed. The account is very similar in eds. B, C, F, and A. Discrepancies between the versions include the use of different expressions to describe Iakinlu's death, the additional mention of names of Iakinlu's sons, the abbreviation of ***itti tāmartīšunu kabitti illikūnimma unaššiqū šēpēya*** ("with their heavy tribute they came, they kissed my feet") to ***itti tāmartīšunu unaššiqū šēpēya*** ("with their tribute they kissed my feet") which is only found in ed. F (ii_4) and the alteration of the description of Aššurbanipal's treatment of Iakinlu's sons by C and A.

C and F in their accounts about Mugallu and Iakinlu follow B closely. They have taken over the report of Ba'alu's submission before narrating the events concerning Mugallu and Iakinlu. They have, however, omitted the lines with which B had linked the two sections, thus removing a sign of secondary literary development.

IT has combined the accounts of the submissions of Iakinlu and Sandišarme (ll.83-84),[313] but has a separate report of the Mugallu-affair which is related in a different context (ll.138b-140). This indicates that IT had separate accounts as *Vorlage*. Thus we note that both B and IT (independently) combined accounts with similar contents and parallel structures. In IT all three accounts (including that of Ba'alu's submission) are very brief and do not give additional information. In view of the briefness of IT's reports it is noteworthy that the reference to Mugallu's tribute was retained.[314]

---

[313] Placed after the narration of Ba'alu's submission (ll.81-83).
[314] The following booty items are mentioned in IT: ***sīsê rabûti*** (l.89, from Ualli - the con-

B's report of the campaign against Tyre is more extensive than those about Mugallu and Iakinlu, presumably because of actual Assyrian involvement. In B, (C,) F, and A it is introduced as a separate campaign. B's version presents an *episodic* account, there is no substantial rise or decline of tension. Ba'alu's "sin" is mentioned in the *supportive material*, no *inciting event* is narrated, and the Assyrian king dominates the *main line* up to the mention of tribute. Nevertheless, the account is related on a comparatively high rhetorical level. Parallelisms with two or three members are present in $Bii_{44\text{-}45.54\text{-}56}$ (two) and $Bii_{45\text{-}47.51\text{-}52}$ (three). The highest rhetorical level is probably found in the passage describing Aššurbanipal's withdrawal of the siege of Tyre which constitutes an EEN-construction:

rēmu aršīšuma
māru ṣīt libbīšu utīrma arīmšu[315]
ḫalṣē ša [e]li Ba'li šar Ṣurri urakkīsu apṭur
ina tâmtim u nābali girretīšu malā uṣabbitu apti

"I took pity on him,
his own son I graciously gave back to him,
the fortifications which against Ba'lu, king of Tyre, I had built, I tore down;
by sea and land his approaches, as many as I had seized, I opened" ($Bii_{59\text{-}64}$).

The participant orientation pattern is simple. There are no secondary participants and no internal participant relations on the *main line*.[316] The following table represents the participant orientation patterns of accounts of Aššurbanipal's campaign against Ba'alu.

	B		B	C	F	A	H	IT
ii_{42}	*lu allik* "I went"	A B		+	+	+	-	
ii_{44}	*urakkis* "I built"	A B	⇒ I	I	I	I	I	I
ii_{45}	*udannin* "I strengthened"	A B'	⇒ I	I	-	-	-	-
ii_{46}	*uṣabbit* "I seized"	A B	⇒ I	I	I	I	I	I

---

text is mutilated, other items may have been mentioned), *sīsê rabûti* (1.140, from Mugallu), *sīsê rabûti* and various other goods (1.154, from Dugdanu). Thus apparently the *sīsê rabûti* ("great horses") were of special importance. Their mention, however, is not marked in the surface structure of the account.

315 Eds. F and A and K 1705 (ed. B) have *addinšu* ("I gave him").

316 Ba'alu's sons and daughters do not function as participants (cf. $ii_{53\text{-}58.60\text{-}61}$).

ii47	*aprus* "I cut off"	A B ⇒ I	I			-	-
ii49	*ušāqir* "I made precious"	A B' ⇒ I	I	-	-	-	-
ii50	*ēsiršunūti* "I surrounded them"	A B' ⇒ I	I	-	-	-	-
ii51	*usīq* "I confined (their lives)"	A B' ⇒ I	I	I	I	I	-
	ukarri "I brought (them) in distress"	A B' ⇒ I	I	I	I	I	-
ii52	*ušaknissunūti* "I subjected them"	A B' ⇒ I	I	I	I	I	I
ii54	*[ūbi]la* "he brought"	B A ⇒ r	r	r	r	r	I
ii56	*iššâ* "he brought"	B A ⇒ I	[I]	I[317]	I[318]	I[319]	I[320]
ii58	*amḫuršu* "I received"	A B ⇒ r	r	r	r	-	-
ii59	*aršīšuma* (with *rēmu*) - "I took pity on him"	A B ⇒ I	I	I	I	-	-
	utīrma "I gave back"	A B ⇒ I	I	I	I	-	-
	arīmšu "I showed mercy to him"	A B ⇒ I	I[321]	I[322]	I[323]	-	-
ii63	*apṭur* "I tore down"	A B ⇒ I	I	-	-	-	-
	apti "I opened"	A B ⇒ I	I	-	-	-	-
	amḫuršu "I accepted"	A B ⇒ I	I	-	-	-	-
		-	I[324]	-	-	-	-
ii66	*atūra* "I returned"	A ⇒ I	I	-	-	-	-

B, C, F, and A employ the standard campaign formula *ina ... girrīya eli ... lu allik* ("in my ... campaign I marched against ..."). The Assyrian king

317 *ušēbila* ("he caused to bring").

318 *ušēbila*.

319 *ušēbila*.

320 *ušēbila*.

321 *addinšu* ("I gave him").

322 *addinšu*.

323 *addinšu*.

324 *utīramma* ("I turned". A.C.Piepkorn, *Historical Prism Inscriptions*, p.43, notes [*pān nī*]*rīya utīramma* ("I turned my [chariot's ?] yoke") for B_4. However, R.D.Freedman, *Assurbanipal's "Annals"*, p.8, has identified Piekorn's B_4 as belonging to ed. C.

dominates the *main line* of this campaign narrative. Only two *main line* verbs have a different grammatical subject. They describe Ba'alu's sending of his daughter and his son to Nineveh. The participant orientation pattern indicates the alternation of *patients* from primary to secondary participants. The latter had been introduced as *nišēšu* ("his people") in ii_{45}, but thereafter in ll.46 and 47 the sgl. suffix referring to Ba'alu is used; in l.48 they are referred to with *-šunu* ("their"). This may be taken as an example that literary inconsistencies do not necessarily indicate redactorial intervention.

C has followed B faithfully. The only apparent significant alteration is the addition of [*pān nī*]*rīya utīramma*[325] by which the the correspondence between the description of the siege and its withdrawal was increased (cf. *ana nīrīya ušaknissunūti* - "I subjected them to my yoke", Bii_{52})

F, followed by A, has omitted $Bii_{45.47\text{-}50.62\text{-}70}$, a part of the description of the siege and the narration of its withdrawal. The lifting of the siege could be deduced from *rēmu aršīšuma* ("I took pity on him") and the lack of a reference to a capture of Tyre.[326] The omission of Bii_{45}, which contained a mention of *nišēšu* ("his people") has left the plural suffixes in Fi_{62} without reference.

H has abbreviated the account even further. The introductory formula was not taken over. BM 123425,[327] related to ed. H, mentions that Ba'alu's son was sent to Nineveh, but does not narrate what had happened afterwards. Thus H's account contains only one *reversal*.

IT has drastically shortened the account of Ba'alu's submission (ll.81-83). It only mentions that the king did not keep Aššurbanipal's command, that Aššurbanipal besieged Tyre, and that Ba'alu submitted. Thus IT has adapted the account of Ba'alu's submission to that of Iakinlu's submission. IT's *main line* contains no *reversal* at all. Aššurbanipal dominates the complete *main line*.

325 Cf. above, p.154, n.324.

326 This is paralleled in Sennacherib's account of the siege of Jerusalem, where the highest rhetorical level is found in the description of the siege and where no conquest of that city is mentioned.

327 Cf. A.R.Millard, "Fragments", p.108.

B. An Example of the Chronicler's Editorial Methods: The Account of Sennacherib's Siege of Jerusalem

Having established a pattern of redactorial methods applied in the transmission of Assyrian campaign accounts we shall now compare the results of our investigation with the Chronicler's treatment of his sources. Fundamental problems with this undertaking have already been outlined above: 1. The Chronicler's *Vorlage* is not extant,[328] 2. The Chronicler's different modes of referring to his sources[329] may be taken as indication that he did not aim to produce a new version of 'Sam.-Kgs.' but rather to supplement it. He thus may be regarded as an author rather than a redactor. We therefore have to allow for a larger number of alterations due to his personal preferences and style than in the Assyrian royal inscriptions. A comparison of Sam.-Kgs. and Chronicles can be of illustrative or confirmative value, but not on its own serve as an empirical model.

We shall confine our brief survey of the Chronicler's methods to his treatment of the account of Sennacherib's invasion into Judah. The two versions of the narrative (2 Kgs.18_{17}-19_{37}, 2 Chr.32_{1-23}) show substantial differences in structure and wording. Therefore a comparison can only be carried out in very general terms.

For practical purposes we shall ignore here, as far as possible, the question whether the narrative in Kgs. itself might constitute a secondary version. However, there are good reasons to disregard 2 Kgs.18_{14-16} in our comparison. These verses have no correspondence in the parallel account in Is.36. Since 2

---

328 Even if we accept the MT or the LXX of Kings, whichever is closer to the MT or LXX of Chronicles, as the Chronicler's *Vorlage*, the problem remains that extra-biblical sources have not been preserved. Only where the Chronicler has retained or abbreviated Sam.-Kgs. can we assume with some certainty that the Chronicler's *Vorlage* is extant. Wherever the Chronicler presents a more extensive account which can not be explained by a literary dependency on Sam.-Kgs., as e.g. of Josiah's passover (2 Chr.35_{1-19}, cf. 2 Kgs.23_{21-23}), this may be taken from a non-extant source and thus is impossible to investigate. The fact that large scale expansions by the Chronicler cannot be *demonstrated* does, of course, not imply that they did not take place. It does, however, imply obstacles and uncertainties for any investigation of the Chronicler's editorial method. We further have to note that the Chronicler took over comparatively few narratives, often with only few significant alterations. Thus only few examples for the structural development of narratives can be adduced from his work.

329 Cf. above, pp.66f.

Kgs.$18_{13\text{-}16}$ correspond to vv.9-12 and 2 Kgs.18_{17ff} do not refer back to a previous campaign, we regard 2 Kgs.$18_{13\text{-}16}$ and 2 Kgs.18_{17ff} as reports of the same event. The first passage gives a general overview, the second a more detailed account with emphasis on the theological significance of the events. The division is supported by differences in the participant orientation pattern. While the *main line* of $18_{14\text{-}16}$ contains solely references to the main participant relationship, the *main line* of $18_{13.17ff}$ has it only once (וַיִּשְׁלַח, 2 Kgs.18_{17}). Even in this single sentence the main participant relation is only given via a secondary participant (B-B'-A). Furthermore, 2 Kgs.$18_{13\text{-}16}$ refer to the Judean king with חִזְקִיָּה, whereas 2 Kgs.18_{17}-19_{37} have חִזְקִיָּהוּ.[330] On the other hand, 2 Kgs.18_{17ff} presuppose information provided by 2 Kgs.18_{13f}.[331] We have thus included both passages in the participant orientation table below.

The narrative as presented in Kgs. has a complex structure which is reflected by the participant orientation pattern. There are comparatively many and extensive speeches.[332] In the table below different levels of quotation have been set out in different columns. The leftmost column gives the *main line* of Kgs.' account with participant orientations. The other columns contain contain the *main lines* of speeches, with quotations within speeches indented.

Ch.18

v.13	עָלָה	B-A'[333]			
	וַיִּתְפְּשֵׂם	B-A'	⇒ I		
v.14	וַיִּשְׁלַח	A-B	⇒ r		
				חָטָאתִי	A-B

---

[330] Since a dependency of the Chronicler on vv.14-16 is not evident, these verses may not have been present in his *Vorlage*. Since, however, v.14 and v.17 begin with וַיִּשְׁלַח, omission because of *homoioarkton* cannot be ruled out.
Further common source divisions of 2 Kgs.18_{17}-19_{37} into two strands B_1, 2 Kgs.18_{17}-$19_{9a.36f}$, and B_2, 2 Kgs.$19_{9b\text{-}35}$ (cf. e.g. B.Stade "Anmerkungen", pp.173-183; L.L.Honor, *Sennacherib's Invasion*, pp.45-48; B.S.Childs, *Assyrian Crisis*, pp.69-103; P.E.Dion, "Sennacherib's Expedition"; F.J.Gonçalves, *L'expédition*, pp.351ff) will be ignored here because a) they are hypothetical and would rely on criteria which are to be examined in the present thesis and b) it would be extremely difficult to demonstrate that the Chronicler was dependent on a source of Kgs. rather than on the Kgs.-version itself.

[331] 2 Kgs.18_{13} provides the *stage* for the narrative and in v.14 it is mentioned that Sennacherib camped at Lachish (cf. v.17).

[332] An interesting parallel to the general course of events is found in B's version of Aššurbanipal's campaign against Teummān (Biv_{87ff}).

[333] B - Sennacherib, A - Hezekiah.

				שׁוּב	B-A				
				אֶשָּׂא	A-B				
	יָשֶׂם	B-A	⇒ r						
v.15	וַיִּתֵּן	A-B	⇒ r						
v.16	קִצֵּץ	A	⇒ I						
	וַיְּתַנֵּם	A-B	⇒ I						
v.17	וַיִּשְׁלַח	B-B'-A	⇒ r						
	וַיַּעֲלוּ	B'(-A)	⇒ I						
	וַיָּבֹאוּ	B'(-A)	⇒ I						
	וַיַּעֲלוּ[334]	B'(-A)	⇒ I						
	וַיָּבֹאוּ[335]	B'(-A)	⇒ I						
	וַיַּעַמְדוּ	B'	⇒ I						
v.18	וַיִּקְרְאוּ[336]	B'-A	⇒ I						
	וַיֵּצֵא	A'-B'	⇒ r						
v.19	וַיֹּאמֶר	B'-A'	⇒ r						
				אִמְרוּ	A'-A				
						אָמַר	B(-A)		
								(בָּטָחְתָּ	A)
v.20								אָמַרְתָּ	A
								בָטַחְתָּ	A
								מָרַדְתָּ	A-B
v.21								בָּטַחְתָּ	A-C
v.22								תֹאמְרוּן[337]	A/C-B
								הֵסִיר	A-A*
								וַיֹּאמֶר	A-A'
v.23								הִתְעָרֶב נָא	A-B
								וְאֶתְּנָה	B-A
								תּוּכַל	A-B
v.24						תָּשִׁיב	A-B'[338]		
v.25								עָלִיתִי	B-A
								אָמַר	A*-B
v.26	וַיֹּאמֶר	A'-B'	⇒ r						
				דַּבֶּר־נָא	B'-A'				
				וְאַל־תְּדַבֵּר	B'-A'				
v.27	וַיֹּאמֶר	B'-A'	⇒ r						
				שְׁלָחַנִי	B-B'				
v.28	וַיַּעֲמֹד	B'	⇒ I						
	וַיִּקְרָא	B'-A'	⇒ I						
	וַיְדַבֵּר	B'-A'	⇒ I						
	וַיֹּאמֶר	B'-A'	⇒ I						

---

334 > pc mss, LXX.

335 > pc mss, LXX.

336 > Is.36_3.

337 A further speech is quoted.

338 Although the context would rather point towards a speech by Sennacherib (יהוה אָמַר אֵלַי עֲלֵה עַל־הָאָרֶץ הַזֹּאת וְהַשְׁחִיתָהּ, v.25), the mention of אֲדֹנִי (v.24) makes it clear that Rabshakeh is speaking.

				שְׁמְעוּ	A'				
v.29				אָמַר	B-A'				
						אַל־יַשִּׁיא	A-A'		
v.30						אַל־יַבְטַח	A-A'		
v.31						אַל־תִּשְׁמְעוּ	A'-A		
				אָמַר[339]	B-A'				
						עֲשׂוּ	A'-B		
						וּצְאוּ	A'-B		
						וְאִכְלוּ	A'		
						וּשְׁתוּ	A'		
v.32						וִחְיוּ	A'		
						וְלֹא תָמֻתוּ	A'		
						אַל־תִּשְׁמְעוּ	A'-A		
						יַסִּית[340]	A-A'		
								יַצִּילֵנוּ	A*-A/A'
v.33						הַהִצִּילוּ	C*-C-B		
v.34						הַהִצִּילוּ	C*-C-B		
v.35						הַהִצִּילוּ	C*-C-B		
						יַצִּיל	A*-A-B		
v.36	וְהֶחֱרִישׁוּ	A'(-B')	⇒ r						
	וְלֹא־עָנוּ	A'-B'	⇒ I						
	וַיָּבֹא	A'-A	⇒ I						
	וַיַּגִּידוּ	A'-A	⇒ I						
Ch.19									
v.1	וַיְהִי כִּשְׁמֹעַ	A	⇒ I						
	וַיִּקְרַע	A	⇒ I						
	וַיִּתְכַּס	A	⇒ I						
	וַיָּבֹא	A-A*	⇒ I						
v.2	וַיִּשְׁלַח	A-A'-A*'	⇒ I						
v.3	וַיֹּאמְרוּ	A'-A*'	⇒ I						
				אָמַר	A-A*'				
						יִשְׁמַע	A*-B'		
v.4						וְהוֹכִיחַ	A*-B		
						וְנָשָׂאתָ תְפִלָּה	A*'-A*		
v.5	וַיָּבֹאוּ	A'-A*'	⇒ I						
v.6	וַיֹּאמֶר	A*'-A'	⇒ I						
				תֹאמְרוּן	A'-A				
						אָמַר	A*-A		
								אַל־תִּירָא	A-B'
v.7								נֹתֵן	A*-B
								וְשָׁב	B
								וְהִפַּלְתִּיו	A*-B
v.8	וַיָּשָׁב	B'	⇒ r						
	וַיִּמְצָא	B'-B	⇒ I						
v.9	וַיִּשְׁמַע	B-C	⇒ s						

339 Grammtically subordinated to אַל־תִּשְׁמְעוּ.
340 Grammtically subordinated to אַל־תִּשְׁמְעוּ.

				יָצָא	C-B				
	וַיָּשָׁב וַיִּשְׁלַח[341]	B-B'-A	⇒ s						
v.10				תֹאמְרוּן	B'-A				
						אַל־יַשִּׁאֲךָ	A*-A		
						בֹּטֵחַ	A-A*		
								לֹא תִנָּתֵן	A*-A'-B[342]
v.11						שָׁמַעְתָּ	A-B		
						תִּנָּצֵל	A*-A[343]		
v.12						הַהִצִּילוּ	C*-C		
v.14	וַיִּקַּח	A-B'	⇒ r						
	וַיִּקְרָאֵם	A-B'	⇒ I						
	וַיַּעַל	A-A*	⇒ I						
	וַיִּפְרְשֵׂהוּ	A-B'-A*	⇒ I						
v.15	וַיִּתְפַּלֵּל	A-A*	⇒ I						
	וַיֹּאמַר	A-A*	⇒ I						
				עָשִׂיתָ	A*				
v.16				הַטֵּה	A*-A				
				וּשֲׁמָע	A*-A				
				פְּקַח	A*-B				
				רְאֵה	A*-B				
				וּשְׁמַע	A*-B				
v.17				הֶחֱרִיבוּ	B-C				
v.18				וְנָתְנוּ	B-C*				
v.19				הוֹשִׁיעֵנוּ	A*-A/A'-B				
				וְיֵדְעוּ	C-A*				
v.20	וַיִּשְׁלַח	A*'-A	⇒ I						
				אָמַר	A*-A				
						שָׁמַעְתִּי	A*-A		
v.21						בָּזָה	A'-B		
						הֵנִיעָה	A'-B		
v.22						חֵרַפְתָּ	B-A/A'		
						וְגִדַּפְתָּ	B-A/A'		
						הֲרִימוֹתָ	B-A/A'		
						וַתִּשָּׂא	B-A*		
v.23						הֵרַפְתָּ	B-A*		
						וַתֹּשמֶר	B		
								עָלִיתִי	B
								וְאֶכְרֹת	B
								וְאָבוֹאָה	B
v.24								קַרְתִּי	B
								וְשָׁתִיתִי	B
								וְאַחְרִיב	B
v.25						שָׁמַעְתָּ	B-A*		

---

[341] Is.37_9: וַיִּשְׁמַע may be due to scribal error prompted by several occurrences of וַיִּשְׁמַע in the context. Both readings are found in IQIs[a] (וישמע וישוב // LXX: *καὶ ἀκούσας ἀπέστρεψεν*).

[342] The notional *agent* is אֱלֹהֶיךָ.

[343] The notional *agent* is אֱלֹהֶיךָ.

			הֲבֵיאתִיהָ	A*(-B)
			וּתְהִי	(B-)C
v.26			חַתּוּ	C'
			וַיֵּבֹשׁוּ	C'
			הָיוּ	C'
v.27			יָדָעְתִּי	A*-B
v.28			וְשַׂמְתִּי	A*-B
			וַהֲשִׁבֹתִיךָ	A*-B
v.29			אָכוֹל	A
			זִרְעוּ	A'
			וְקִצְרוּ	A'
			וְנִטְעוּ	A'
			וְאִכְלוּ	A'
v.30			וְיָסְפָה	A'
			וְעָשָׂה	A'
v.31			תֵּצֵא	A'
			תַּעֲשֶׂה	A*[344]
v.32	אָמַר	A*-B		
			לֹא יָבֹא	B-A'
			לֹא־יוֹרֶה	B-A'
			לֹא־יְקַדְּמֶנָּה	B-A'
			לֹא־יִשְׁפֹּךְ	B-A'
v.33			יָשׁוּב	B
			לֹא יָבֹא	B-A'
v.34			וְגַנּוֹתִי	A*-A

v.35	וַיְהִי[345]	(A*'[-B]	⇒ s)
	וַיֵּצֵא	A*'-B'	⇒ I
	וַיַּךְ	A*'-B'	⇒ I
	וַיַּשְׁכִּימוּ	B'	⇒ r
v.36	וַיִּסַּע	B	⇒ I
	וַיֵּלֶךְ	B	⇒ I
	וַיָּשָׁב	B	⇒ I
	וַיֵּשֶׁב	B	⇒ I
v.37	וַיְהִי	B	⇒ I
	הִכֻּהוּ	B'/A*'-B	⇒ I[346]
	נִמְלְטוּ	B'	⇒ I
	וַיִּמְלֹךְ	B	⇒ I

---

[344] Grammatical subject: קִנְאַת יהוה.

[345] It is noteworthy that the מַלְאַךְ יהוה is not introduced in a transition passage as being sent by the Lord.

[346] The participant relation is ambiguous. The *agent* is introduced as אַדְרַמֶּלֶךְ וְשַׂרְאֶצֶר בָּנָיו (ק״, LXX; cf. $Is.37_{38}$) with the suffix referring to Sennacherib. According to 2 $Kgs.19_7$, however, Sennacherib's sons may be regarded as secondary participants for the Lord.

The participant orientation pattern exhibits several features which in Sennacherib's and Aššurbanipal's annals we could associate with *early* stages of literary development. The table above indicates that there are extensive references to secondary participants and internal participant relations. Noted are, apart from the protagonists Hezekiah and Sennacherib (and the Lord), Rab-shakeh, Tartan, and Rab-saris as secondary participants for the Assyrian king, Sennacherib's sons,[347] the king of Egypt, the inhabitants of Jerusalem, Eliakim, Shebna and Joah as secondary participants for Hezekiah, and Isaiah and the angel[348] as secondary participants for the Lord. It is noteworthy that Tartan and Rab-saris have no narrative function,[349] the two *main line* verbs dominated by the inhabitants of Jerusalem mention that they did *not* answer,[350] and none of the three servants of Hezekiah mentioned by name plays a special rôle. This is also true for Tirhakah, who does not intervene in the course of events.

The main participant relationship, Sennacherib - Hezekiah, is introduced indirectly at the beginning of the story (B-B'-A, 2 Kgs.18_{17}) and is not reversed on the *main line*. It is directly found in Rab-shakeh's first speech comprising a recitation of Sennacherib's first message to Hezekiah (18_{19-25}, cf. table above). The same is true for A*-B.

The version of Kgs. contains a formal inconsistency. Hezekiah receives סְפָרִים (19_{14}), reads *them* (וַיִּקְרָאֵם), but then suddenly the sgl. is used (וַיִּפְרְשֵׂהוּ). We can further note the ambiguity in Rab-shakeh's speech as to whether תָּשִׁיב (2 Kgs.18_{24}) is part of Sennacherib's message to Hezekiah or not.[351] The speeches with their different levels of quotation contribute to the complexity of the narrative. Thus in 2 Kgs.18_{22} Hezekiah is quoted twice and in v.30 once in Sennacherib's speech recited by Rab-shakeh; in v.25 Sennacherib's message quotes the Lord. In fact, almost all speeches are recited by secondary participants. Sennacherib's messages to Hezekiah and the inhabitants of Jerusalem are delivered by

---

347 Cf. above, p.161, n.346.

348 The מַלְאַךְ יהוה is not introduced by a transition passage as being sent by the Lord (cf. 19_{35}).

349 The parallel passage in Is.36_2 only mentions Rab-shakeh and omits וַיִּקְרְאוּ אֶל־הַמֶּלֶךְ (2 Kgs.18_{18}).

350 הֶחֱרִישׁוּ, לֹא־עָנוּ (18_{36}).

351 Cf. above, p.158, n.338.

Rab-shakeh, Hezekiah's messages to Isaiah are delivered by his servants, the Lord's messages to Hezekiah by Isaiah and Hezekiah's servants. Only Hezekiah's prayer ($19_{14\text{-}19}$) is spoken directly to the Lord. It is interesting to note that Hezekiah sent to Isaiah to ask the prophet to pray ($19_{2\text{-}4}$), but also prayed himself.[352]

The *main line* of the Kgs.-version contains:

41 x I	-	73.21 %	(40 x I	-	78.43 %)[353]
12 x r	-	21.43 %	(8 x r	-	15.69 %
3 x s	-	5.36 %	(3 x s	-	5.88 %)

If we treat the references to the Lord (and Isaiah and the angel) separately, the percentage of *reversals* is still greater:

36 x I	-	64.28 %	(35 x I	- 68.63 %)
14 x r	-	25.00 %	(10 x r	- 19.61 %
5 x s	-	8.93 %	(5 x s	- 9.80 %)
1 x srs	-	1.79 %[354]	(1 x srs	- 1.96 %)

With the exception of 19_5 the narrative appears to follow the chronological order.

The evaluation of the discourse profile is, of course, affected by our division of the Kgs.-version into two units. If the Kgs.-version is regarded as one coherent narrative, the number of *peaks* increases by one. We shall, however, concentrate on $18_{13.17ff}$. The narrative is related on a high rhetorical level. Speeches figure prominently ($18_{19\text{-}25.26.27\text{-}35}$, $19_{3\text{-}4.6\text{-}7.10\text{-}13.15\text{-}19.20\text{-}34}$). The account begins with the introduction of the protagonists, but the participant functions are immediately transferred to secondary participants (מֶלֶךְ אשׁוּר > רַב־שָׁקֵה, רַב־סָרִיס, תַּרְתָּן; הַמֶּלֶךְ חִזְקִיָּהוּ > יְרוּשָׁלַם {18_{17}}). The narrative then continues to relate the encounter between envoys of the two kings (18_{18}). The mention of the primary participants in Rab-shakeh's speech leads to a rise in tension. The speech is structured clearly. Rab-shakeh gives four reasons why it would be better for the Jerusalemites to surrender:

---

352 This is comparable to events noted in B's account of Aššurbanipal's campaign against Teummān which relates that Ištar addressed Aššurbanipal directly (Bv_{47ff}) and through a message given to a seer in a dream (Bv_{50ff}).

353 The numbers in brackets denote the participant orientation functions excluding $18_{14\text{-}16}$.

354 The additional *reversals* are the transitions to וַיֹּאמֶר (2 Kgs.19_6) and וַיִּשְׁלַח (19_{20}). The *switches* are to וַיָּבֹא (19_1) and וַיַּעַל (19_{14}). The *srs*-function is present in the transition to וַיָּשָׁב (19_8).

1. Hezekiah is dependent on the Egyptians' support, which they are unable to provide (v.21),
2. Hezekiah is dependent on the Lord, whose altars he has abolished (v.22),
3. the Judean army is too weak to stand against the Assyrians (vv.23f), and
4. Sennacherib is sent by the Lord himself (v.25).

While the first two points concern internal participant relations, the last two refer to the main participant relation. With regard to the phraseology used it is noteworthy that in three of the four parts of Rabshakeh's speech בטח is prominent. Sennacherib's message to Hezekiah culminates in his claim to be sent by יהוה, which is the least expected of the four arguments. At precisely this point Rab-shakeh is interrupted by Hezekiah's officials.

After his refusal to continue his speech in Aramaic Rab-shakeh addresses the inhabitants of Jerusalem. While his first speech and the interruption had been introduced with a plain וַיֹּאמֶר (vv.19.26), the continuation of Rab-shakeh's speech is introduced by a cluster of verbs וַיַּעֲמֹד רַב־שָׁקֵה וַיִּקְרָא בְקוֹל־גָּדוֹל יְהוּדִית וַיְדַבֵּר וַיֹּאמֶר (v.28). This constitutes a further rise in the rhetorical level.

The second part of Rab-shakeh's speech, too, is well structured. Four negated exhortations, of which the first and the third are amplified by (כִּי) כֹּה אָמַר הַמֶּלֶךְ / מֶלֶךְ אשור (vv.29.31), introduce the different sections:

אַל־יַשִּׁיא לָכֶם
אַל־יַבְטַח אֶתְכֶם
אַל־תִּשְׁמְעוּ אֶל־חִזְקִיָּהוּ
אַל־תִּשְׁמְעוּ אֶל־חִזְקִיָּהוּ (vv.29.30.31.32)

While the first part states expressly that Hezekiah is unable to protect his people (18_{29}), this is not stated of the Lord who is referred to in the second section. אִכְלוּ and שְׁתוּ in the third section (v.31) remind of and contrast with v.27. The juxtaposition of life and death (וִחְיוּ וְלֹא תָמֻתוּ) in v.32 as the options left to the inhabitants of Jerusalem concludes the third section. The fourth section resumes the first two. In both passages נצל is prominent. Again it is stated that Hezekiah cannot save his people (v.32), but the last section goes beyond the second section in comparing the Lord to the gods of the conquered peoples (vv.33-36). Here the climax of the second part of Rab-shakeh's speech is found. In each of the two parts one root figured prominently, בטח in the first, נצל in the second.

With the description of the Jerusalemites' reaction in a parallelism the scene changes. The immediate confrontation is over and the narrative focusses on internal participant relations. Tension rises with the mention of Hezekiah as *agent* and the relation of his reaction to Sennacherib's message which is described more extensively than that of the people (19_1). The reference to Hezekiah going to the Temple and sending envoys to Isaiah constitutes a transition to a further participant. In Rab-shakeh's speech the final participant relation had been A*-B.[355] In a rhetorical question Sennacherib had claimed that the Lord could or would not save Jerusalem. Thus the conflict is intensified and tension rises further. This is even more the case with the Lord's announcement of Sennacherib's death (19_7). The scene switches again to Rab-shakeh and Sennacherib ($19_{8\text{-}9}$). On learning of Tirhakah's advance the Assyrian king sends another message to Hezekiah.[356] While the first message emphasized the relationship between Hezekiah and his subjects (A-A'), the second one focusses on the relationship between the Lord and Hezekiah (A*-A). Again we can note a rise of tension:

18_{29}: אַל־יַשִּׁיא לָכֶם חִזְקִיָּהוּ
19_{10}: אַל־יַשִּׁאֲךָ אֱלֹהֶיךָ.

The anonymity of Sennacherib's envoys sent to deliver his second message gives more prominence to the Assyrian king as the primary participant and thus corresponds to the intensification of the conflict recognizable between the contents

---

355 כִּי־יַצִּיל יהוה אֶת־יְרוּשָׁלִַם מִיָּדִי (v.35).

356 ... וַיָּשָׁב וַיִּשְׁלַח (v.9). 19_{9a} as fulfillment of the promise of v.7 is one of the basic arguments for the division of 2 Kgs.$18_{(13.)17ff}$ into different strands (cf. above, p.157, n.330). This view implies, that $19_{(36.)37}$ belongs to the same source as 19_7. There are, however, several difficulties with this opinion. The author of strand B_1 (18_{17}-$19_{9a.36f}$) remembered details of the campaign such as the siege of Lachish, the titles of the Assyrian officials, or the names of the Assyrian king and the Pharaoh as well as circumstances of Sennacherib's death; cf. Babylonian Chronicle $Iiii_{34\text{-}36}$ (cf. A.K.Grayson, *Assyrian and Babylonian Chronicles*, p.81) and Nabonidus' Babylon-stele $I_{35\text{-}40}$ (cf. St.Langdon, *Königsinschriften*, p.272 {Inschrift Nr.8}), and R.Borger's remarks in *TUAT* I/4, pp.391f). It does not seem plausible that he should have been wrong about the reason of Sennacherib's return to Assyria (cf. Chic.ii_{78}-iii_{16}). There is no reference to a battle against the Egyptians, Sennacherib's fear, Hezekiah's relief, or the emptiness of Sennacherib's boasts (cf. 18_4) in B_1.
A different interpretation of 2 Kgs.19_7 may be tentatively suggested here. Since Hezekiah's request repeatedly emphasizes the Lord's taking notice of Sennacherib's words (אוּלַי יִשְׁמַע יהוה אֱלֹהֶיךָ, אֲשֶׁר שָׁמַע יהוה אֱלֹהֶיךָ - 19_4) and the Lord's reply begins with אַל־תִּירָא מִפְּנֵי הַדְּבָרִים אֲשֶׁר שָׁמַעְתָּ (19_6) it cannot be ruled out that שָׁמַע שְׁמוּעָה (v.7) refers to Sennacherib having to take notice of the (fulfillment of the) Lord's announcements.

of the two messages. Hezekiah's reaction to Sennacherib is described more extensively than after Rab-shakeh's speech ($19_{14\text{-}19}$, cf. $19_{1\text{-}2}$). Now the focus is on *Hezekiah's* prayer rather than on *Isaiah's*,[357] another transition from a secondary to a primary participant. The Lord's answer to Hezekiah's prayer, too, is more extensive and on a higher rhetorical level than its counterpart, the reply to Isaiah's prayer. It contains comparisons, parallelisms and EEN-constructions. Then the narrative accelerates and the outcome of the conflict is related.

The structure of the Chronicler's version is much simpler than that of his *Vorlage*. Only one encounter between Assyrian envoys and the Jerusalemites is related.[358] After mentioning Sennacherib's invasion (2 Chr.32_1) he added references to Hezekiah's preparations for a siege (vv.2-6a) and a speech by the Judean king to encourage his people (vv.6b-9). This first part of the Chronicler's version, not paralleled in Sam.-Kgs., exhibits comparatively many terms, grammatical forms, and syntactical constructions common to the Chronicler's *Sondergut*. We can note לָרֹב, התחזק, שֶׁלַּח (v.5), קבץ, שָׂרֵי מִלְחָמוֹת (v.6), הָמוֹן (v.7), עזר (v.8).[359] This creates a linguistic unevenness between the two parts of the narrative. The building operations noted by the Chronicler as Hezekiah's preparations for a siege may well have been taken from a different source.[360] A speech of Hezekiah had been referred to but not quoted in the Kgs.-version ($18_{29\text{-}31}$).[361] By the upgrading of indirect to direct speech the account becomes more balanced. The Chronicler first relates a speech by the Judean king, then quotes the Assyrian king. Both speeches are directed towards the inhabitants of Jerusalem. The insertion together with the description of the Jerusalemites' reaction prevents the rise of tension. The Chronicler notes that they trusted Hezekiah and thus the

---

357 Cf.19_{1f}. It should not be ignored that 19_1,too, mentions Hezekiah going to the Temple.

358 Cf. also the Chronicler's omission of the Bath-shebah episode (2 Sam.11-12_{25}) from his account of David's Ammonite war.

359 Cf. S.R.Driver, *Introduction*, pp.535-540.

360 Cf. Is.22_{8ff}. References to building operations have also been added in other parts of the Chronicler's work (cf. 1 Chr.11_{8f}, 2 Chr.$8_{1\text{-}6}$ $11_{5\text{-}12}$ 14_{5f} 17_{12f} 26_{9f} 33_{14} and the discussion of these passages in P.Welten, *Geschichte und Geschichtsdarstellung*, pp.9-78). This indicates that these insertions are due to the Chronicler's personal preferences rather than to general developmental tendencies.

361 For the insertion of comparable speeches which G.v.Rad termed *levitische Predigt* ("levitical sermon") cf. also 1 Chr.$28_{2\text{-}10}$, 2 Chr.$25_{7\text{-}8}$ $15_{2\text{-}7}$ 19_{6f} $20_{15\text{-}17}$ 20_{20} $32_{7\text{-}8a}$ and von Rad's discussion in "Die levitische Predigt".

unsuccessfulness of Sennacherib's attempt to persuade the inhabitants of Jerusalem to surrender is anticipated. This is made explicit by the connection of the two passages with אַחַר זֶה (2 Chr.32_9). The outcome of the conflict is further hinted by adding to Sennacherib's comparison of the Lord to foreign gods who were not able to save thier peoples that the latter were only מַעֲשֵׂה יְדֵי הָאָדָם (32_{19}). The designations of אֱלֹהֵי יְרוּשָׁלַםִ and אֱלֹהֵי עַמֵּי הָאָרֶץ (32_{19}) are parallel. Since the latter were only "the work of men's hands", it was indicated that the fate of Jerusalem would be different from that of the foreign peoples conquered by the Assyrians.

The Chronicler's version of Sennacherib's message summarizes the Assyrian messages of the Kgs.-version.

עַל־מָה אַתֶּם בֹּטְחִים (2 Chr. 32_{10})	- cf. 2 Kgs.$18_{19\text{-}25.30}$ 19_{30}
הֲלֹא יְחִזְקִיָּהוּ מַסִּית אֶתְכֶם, אַל־יַסִּית אֶתְכֶם (2 Chr.$32_{11.15}$)	- cf. 2 Kgs.18_{32}
לָתֵת אֶתְכֶם לָמוּת (2 Chr.32_{11})	- cf. 2 Kgs.18_{32}
בְּרָעָב וּבְצָמָא (2 Chr.32_{11})	- cf. 2 Kgs.$18_{27.31}$
יהוה אֱלֹהֵינוּ יַצִּילֵנוּ (2 Chr.32_{11})	- cf. 2 Kgs.$18_{30.32}$
הֲלֹא־הוּא יְחִזְקִיָּהוּ הֵסִיר אֶת־בָּמֹתָיו . . . (2 Chr.32_{12})	- cf. 2 Kgs.18_{22}
הֲלֹא תֵדְעוּ מֶה עָשִׂיתִי אֲנִי וַאֲבוֹתַי . . . (2 Chr.32_{13})	- cf. 2 Kgs.$18_{33\text{-}35}$
כִּי יוּכַל אֱלֹהֵיכֶם לְהַצִּיל אֶתְכֶם מִיָּדִי (2 Chr.32_{14})	- cf. 2 Kgs.18_{35}
אַף כִּי אֱלֹהֵיכֶם לֹא־יַצִּילוּ אֶתְכֶם מִיָּדִי (2 Chr.32_{15})	- cf. 2 Kgs.18_{35}
אַל־יַשִּׁיא חִזְקִיָּהוּ אֶתְכֶם (2 Chr.32_{15})	- cf. 2 Kgs.18_{29}.

The Chronicler took up key words from the speeches in 'Kgs.' (בטח, נשא, סות, נצל), but did not retain them as *key words*. He thus omitted repetitions and reduced the rhetorical level.

Vv.16-20 are of special significance for an analysis of editorial techniques. The narrator with his mention of (a) further speech{es} by the Assyrian messengers (32_{16ff}) enters a different level of story telling. Not the events themselves but rather their significance is focussed on (לְחָרֵף ליהוה אֱלֹהֵי יִשְׂרָאֵל {v.17}, לְבַהֲלָם {v.18}, לְמַעַן יִלְכְּדוּ אֶת־הָעִיר {v.18}).[362] This is also apparent in the

---

[362] Cf. also 2 Chr.32_{19b} which was taken from Hezekiah's prayer (2 Kgs.19_{18b}) to the *main line* and בְּבֹשֶׁת פָּנִים (2 Chr.32_{21}). Comparable is further the Chronicler's replacement of
וַיֹּאמֶר . . . הֲתֵלֵךְ אִתִּי לְמִלְחָמָה רָמֹת גִּלְעָד by
וַיְסִיתֵהוּ לַעֲלוֹת אֶל רָמוֹת גִּלְעָד (1 Kgs.22_4 // 2 Chr.18_2). Cf. also 2 Chr.12_7 $28_{5.16}$ 32_{31}.
The difference between these two levels of narration parallels the difference between what J.L.Austin termed *locutionary*, *illocutionary*, and *perlocutionary acts* in the utterance of statements (*How to Do Things with Words*). While the Kgs.-version concentrated on the events themselves, which can be compared to the *locutionary aspect*,

Chronicler's omission of 2 Kgs.19_{35b}, where the Assyrians' surprise had been expressed by וְהִנֵּה. The order of narration in the Chronicler's version is thematic rather than chronological.[363] Having mentioned Sennacherib's letter(s) (v.17) he notes, that the Assyrian envoys spoke בְּקוֹל־גָּדוֹל יְהוּדִית (v.18).

The participant orientation pattern, too, was simplified:

2 Chr.32

v.1	בָּא	B(-A')	⇒ I						
	וַיָּבֹא	B-A'	⇒ I						
	וַיִּחַן	B-A'	⇒ I						
	וַיֹּאמֶר	B-A'	⇒ I						
v.2	וַיַּרְא	A-B	⇒ r						
v.3	וַיִּוָּעַץ	A-A'	⇒ I						
	וַיַּעְזְרוּהוּ	A-A'	⇒ I						
v.4	וַיִּקָּבְצוּ	A'	⇒ I						
	וַיִּסְתְּמוּ	A'	⇒ I						
				יָבוֹאוּ	B				
				וּמָצְאוּ	B				
v.5	וַיִּתְחַזַּק	A	⇒ I						
	וַיִּבֶן	A	⇒ I						
	וַיַּעַל	A	⇒ I						
	וַיְחַזֵּק	A	⇒ I						
	וַיַּעַשׂ	A	⇒ I						
v.6	וַיִּתֵּן	A-A'	⇒ I						
	וַיִּקְבְּצֵם	A-A'	⇒ I						
	וַיְדַבֵּר	A-A'	⇒ I						
v.7				חִזְקוּ					
				וְאִמְצוּ					
				אַל־תִּירְאוּ					
				וְאַל־תֵּחַתּוּ					
v.8	וַיִּסָּמְכוּ	A'	⇒ I						
v.9	שָׁלַח	B-B'-A'	⇒ r						
v.10				אָמַר	B-A'				
						בֹּטְחִים	A'		
						יֹשְׁבִים	A'		
v.11						מַסִּית	A-A'		
								יַצִּילֵנוּ	A*-A/A'
v.12						הֵסִיר	A-A*		
						וַיֹּאמֶר	A-A'		
								תִּשְׁתַּחֲווּ	A'-A*
								תַּקְטִירוּ	A'-A*

Chr. also emphasized their purpose (*illocutionary* aspect) or effects (*perlocutionary* aspects). This parallels in the Assyrian *annals* the redactorial tendency to concentrate on the emphasis on results rather than on the course of events.

363 Cf. also 2 Chr.$22_{7b.8}$ $28_{5.16\text{-}21}$ $32_{26.31}$.

v.13				תֵּדְעוּ	A'-B
				יָכְלוּ	C*-C'
v.14				יָכוֹל	C*-C'
				יוּכַל	A*-A'
v.15				אַל־יַשִּׁיא	A-A'
				וְאַל־יַסִּית	A-A'
				וְאַל־תַּאֲמִינוּ	A'-A
				לֹא יוּכַל	C*-C'
				לֹא־יַצִּילוּ	A*-A'
v.16	דִּבְּרוּ	B'-A*/A$^{(*')}$	⇒ I		
v.17	כָּתַב	B-A*	⇒ I		
			לֹא־יַצִּיל	A*-A'	
v.18	וַיִּקְרְאוּ	B'	⇒ I		
v.19	וַיְדַבְּרוּ	B'-A*	⇒ I		
v.20	וַיִּתְפַּלֵּל	A/A*'-A*	⇒ r		
	וַיִּזְעֲקוּ	A/A*'-A*	⇒ I		
v.21	וַיִּשְׁלַח	A*-A*'	⇒ I		
	וַיַּכְחֵד	A*'-B'	⇒ I		
	וַיָּשָׁב	B	⇒ r		
	וַיָּבֹא	B	⇒ I		
	הִפִּילֻהוּ	B'-B	⇒ I		
v.22	וַיּוֹשַׁע	A*-A-B/C	⇒ r		
	וַיָּנַח[364]	A*-A'-B/C	⇒ I		
v.23	מְבִיאִים	B/C-A*/A	⇒ r		
	וַיִּנַּשֵּׂא	B/C-A	⇒ I		

The participant orientation pattern indicates a greater emphasis on primary participants. Sennacherib's messengers remain unnamed,[365] Hezekiah's envoys are not even mentioned.[366] In the second part of his account the Chronicler does not

---

364 With LXX (*καὶ κατέπαυσεν αὐτούς* - וַיָּנַח לָהֶם) for MT וַיְנַהֲלֵם.

365 Cf. the Chronicler's הַמְּלָכִים אֲשֶׁר־בָּאוּ (1 Chr.19_9) for a list of Aramean kings (2 Sam.10_8). In his narration of the Babylonian embassy to Hezekiah (2 Kgs.20_{12-19} // 2 Chr.32_{31}) he replaced מְרֹאדַךְ בַּלְאֲדָן בֶּן־בַּלְאֲדָן מֶלֶךְ־בָּבֶל (2 Kgs.20_{12} {MT:...בראדך}) by שָׂרֵי בָבֶל. This parallels exactly the development of participant designations in Aššurbanipal's account of the rebellion of Egyptian vassal kings (see above, p.114, n.204).

366 Comparable is the omission from 1 Sam.31_7 (// 1 Chr.10_6) of the reference to Saul's armour-bearer. In other passages, however, the Chronicler retained mentions of the latter. Similarly the Chronicler mentions only Joab in his report of the execution of the census commanded by David (1 Chr.21_4), whereas the corresponding passage in Sam. had also mentioned army leaders (2 Sam.24_4). This created an inconsistency between David's command (לְכוּ ספרו {pl.!}, 1 Chr.21_2) and its fulfillment. In his version of Ahaziah's death the Chronicler has omitted, apart from the narration of Israelite affairs as the killings of Jezebel (2 Kgs.9_{30-37}) and Ahab's seventy sons (10_{1-14}), all references to Elisha or the latter's disciple (9_{1-6}). This passage deals with internal participant relations and has secondary participants as *main line agents*. The same is true for Jehu's

note the inhabitants of Jerusalem as *main line agents* (cf. 2 Kgs.18_{36}). Because of the omission of 2 Kgs.19_{35b} the same is true for the Assyrian army. Isaiah appears only once as *main line agent*, in a compound subject (2 Chr.32_{20}). Internal participant relations between B and B' are not mentioned on the *main line*.[367] The Chronicler's concentration on the main conflict can also be recognized in Hezekiah's designation as עַבְדּוֹ, with the pronominal suffix referring to יהוה (2 Chr.32_{16}),[368] describing Hezekiah's function in the conflict as that of a secondary participant for the Lord, and in the designation of the latter as אֱלֹהֵי יְרוּשָׁלָם (32_{19}). Correspondingly Sennacherib's letter, which in the Kgs.'-version was sent to Hezekiah (2 Kgs.$19_{10.14}$), according to the Chronicler was written לְחָרֵף ליהוה (2 Chr.32_{17}). In both versions the conflict had been resolved by the (angel of the) Lord's intervention.[369] The Chronicler has thus edited the narrative with its outcome in view.

We can also note a reduction of *reversals*. The participant orientation functions of the Chronicler's account are:

28 x I - 82.35 %
6 x r - 17.65 %

---

proclamation as king ($9_{11-14a.15b}$) and the dialogue between Joram and the watchman (9_{17-20}, with alternation between primary and secondary participants). Significant is the replacement of ... וְאָמַרְתָּ כֹּה־אָמַר יהוה מְשַׁחְתִּיךָ לְמֶלֶךְ אֶל־יִשְׂרָאֵל ... (2 Kgs.9_3) with ... ... אֲשֶׁר מְשָׁחוֹ יהוה (2 Chr.22_7). Cf. also the Chronicler's abbreviation of Kgs.' account of Hezekiah's illness and convalescence (2 Kgs.20_{1-11} // 2 Chr.32_{24}). The Chronicler mentions neither the prophet Isaiah, nor Hezekiah's servants, which had appeared as *main line agents* in Kgs. account. Consequently there are no internal participant relations in the Chronicler's version. Isaiah's announcements are represented in 2 Chr.32_{24} by וַיֹּאמֶר לוֹ with the Lord as grammatical subject. 2 Chr.32_{24} contains only one *reversal*.

A reverse alteration in 1 Chr.19_3 // 2 Sam.10_3 (בָּאוּ עֲבָדָיו > שָׁלַח דָּוִד אֶת־עֲבָדָיו) adapts the passage to the context (cf. 2 Sam.10_2 // 1 Chr.19_2). The additional references to Priests and Levites (cf. 1 Chr.15 16_{1-6} 23 24 26 27, 2 Chr.5_{12} 7_6 8_{14-15} 11_{13-14} 13_{9-10} 17_8 19_{8-11} 20_{19} $23_{2.4.6.7.8.18}$ 24_{5-6} 29-31 $34_{9.12.13.30}$ $35_{1-17.18}$) probably reflect the Chronicler's personal preferences rather than general tendencies of literary development.

367 Cf. the Chronicler's omission of 2 Sam.12_{27-30}.

368 This led to the juxtaposition in v.16 of עֲבָדָיו, with the suffix referring to Sennacherib, and עַבְדּוֹ, with the suffix referring to the Lord.

369 In the narration of Sennacherib's death the Chronicler uses the unusual expression הִפִּילֻהוּ בֶחָרֶב (2 Chr.32_{21}, cf. 2 Kgs.19_{37}: הִכֻּהוּ בַחֶרֶב), which alludes to the Lord's announcement in 2 Kgs.19_{6-7}. The latter passage had not been taken over by the Chronicler. This may indicate that the Chronicler presumed the knowledge of his *Vorlage* among his readers.

If we disregard the Chronicler's concluding remarks (2 Chr.$32_{22\text{-}23}$) the reduction of *reversals* is even greater (26 x I {86.67 %}, 4 x r {13.33 %}).

We can thus note that the structural differences between the accounts of Sennacherib's invasion of Judah as presented in Kgs. and Chr. parallel those between different versions of Sennacherib's and Aššurbanipal's campaign accounts.

C. The Microstructural Development of Assyrian Royal *Annals*

From our investigation of the development of the structure of Assyrian campaign accounts we received a partly negative answer to our question whether it is possible to establish the relative stage of development of Old Testament narratives. If we take the redactorial treatment of Assyrian campaign accounts as an empirical model, we may be able to suggest that a narrative with a certain discourse structure and participant orientation is in an *early stage* of literary development, but *late stages* cannot be identified with any certainty.

We shall thus proceed to investigate *minor* changes and analyze the effects of redactorial treatment to the grammatical texture of narratives. Again we need to emphasize that we can only *describe* the differences between versions, but not explain them. We can note alterations and their agreement or disagreement with more or less general tendencies of literary development. Since such tendencies can only be recognized from the alterations themselves they cannot provide explanations, but are only of statistical value.

We have already seen above that basically, if narratives were altered at all, they were abbreviated. The easiest way of abbreviation is, of course, that of plain omission. No replacement is given for the omitted text. We may distinguish two sorts of omitted material: Firstly, information that, apparently, was not thought to be important enough for retention and, secondly, information that was important, but already contained in the context or was regarded as being self-evident.[370]

---

[370] An interesting parallel may be seen in the results of D.J.Allerton's study of the formulation of sentences ("Deletion and proform reduction"). Allerton established the following hierarchy of treatment of information:

The different categories in which the alterations have been grouped cannot be strictly separated from each other. For example, the omission of a sentence may unify a passage and at the same time give more prominence to the later part of a series of actions. However, to avoid repetition we have generally noted alterations only once. There are other alterations for which no motivation is apparent or which are of too little significance to be considered here. It is further important to note that to all of the changes mentioned below contrasting examples may be adduced. Several, as for example the insertion of anticipatory remarks or A's additions of speeches, have already been mentioned above and these will not be repeated here. None of the general trends, which have become apparent in the present investigation, is universally valid and without exception. The redactor's personal preferences or the specific form or contents of some narratives may have prompted alterations against general tendencies. This has, of course, consequences for the application of our suggested empirical model to Old Testament narratives. Narratives, passages within narratives, sentences within passages may have been treated differently from their contexts.

Categories which have already been noted above, such as the emphasis on results or the tendency towards the unfication of the *main line*, will not be repeated here. For each of the major developmental tendencies one example from Sennacherib's annals and one from Aššurbanipal's annals will be given in the main text.

1. Omission

a) Omission of Main Clauses

(1) Omission of the First Part of a Series of Actions

We have already seen above that redactors often concentrated on results rather than on the sequence of events.[371] The omission of the first part of a series

---

'NEW' = Indefinite
'GIVEN' = Definite
'SUPER-GIVEN' = Proform
'HYPER-GIVEN' = Deleted (cf. p.236). Allerton related this to the general validity of a "law of least effort" (cf. p.213).

[371] Cf. above, pp.133f with n.274.

of actions is related to this. F's omission of Aššurbanipal's first Egyptain campaign is a drastic example. Further alterations related to this tendency are updates[372] and resolutions of the chronological order.[373] The tendency can also be observed on a smaller scale.

Example 1:

Bull 4 has omitted the report of the conquest of Lule's cities (Chic. $ii_{41\text{-}46}$) and mentions only the installation of a new king there.[374]

Example 2:

B, C, and F have omitted the contents of Gyges' dream (HT rev.16-18) with the mention Aššur's orders to Gyges and have only retained the narration of their fulfillment.[375]

(2) Omission of Sentences Without Relevance for the Main Course of Events

With the identification of omitted sentences as being of little importance for the main course of narration, there is, of course, the danger of circular reason-

---

372 Cf. above, p.91; p.92 with n.87; p.121, n.221; p.126, n.233; p.132 with n.268.

373 Cf. above, pp.86f; p.93; pp.121 with n.221; p.126; pp.135f with n.276; cf. also p.95, n.101.

374 Cf. also Bull 4's omissions of *alme* ("I surrounded") as the first of a series of successive verbs in Chic.ii_{72} and of *illikū rēṣīšun* ("these came to their aid") from Chic.-Tayl. (Chic. ii_{81}).

375 From HT's report of the Kirbit affair B and C omit that the inhabitants of Deru asked the Assyrian king for help and that Aššurbanipal dispatched his generals (rev.10-11). The description of the siege had already been omitted in HT (cf. above pp.133f, n.274). We can also note F's and A's omission of $Biii_{18\text{-}32}$ from the account of Aššurbanipal's campaign against Aḫšeri. The two latter editions have retained only the description of the destruction of the country and the taking of booty ($Fii_{26\text{-}31}$ // $Aii_{130\text{-}133}$). F and A have omitted the reference to the siege of Izertu and two other cities ($Bii_{47\text{-}49}$) and mention only the ravaging of the district ($Aiii_{2\text{-}3}$ // $Biii_{50\text{-}51}$). From B's report against Dunanu F and A have omitted B $vi_{21\text{-}22}$ which narrate that Aššurbanipal "covered Gambulu with his battle array like a storm". F and A only report the conquest and destruction of Dunanu's capital and the deportation of captives and booty (Fii_{77}-iii_5 // A $iii_{54\text{-}69}$).
A's insertion of a report of massacres among Uwaite''s subjects ($vii_{108\text{-}115}$), which contrasts with the omissions noted above adds details to the accounts of B (cf. $viii_{8\text{-}9}$) and VAT 5600+ (cf. $iv_{13\text{-}14}$). It may well be due to a different source which has not been preserved. For the addition of a stock-phrase cf. also $Aiii_{59f}$ // Fii_{80}.

ing. The very fact that these sentences were omitted shows that they were regarded as dispensible. However, the participant orientation patterns indicate main conflicts and sentences contributing to the narration of this main conflict can be distinguished from the remainder of the narrative. We can further note the omission of events that had no consequences in the further course of narration. Related to this also are omissions of negated sentences.

Example 3:

Rass. has omitted *ul innamir ašaršu* ("his {hiding-}place was not found") Bell, 1.10 which relates the unsuccessful pursuit of Merodach-baladan. The unsuccessfulness is expressed by a negated *main line* verb (*ul innamir*).[376]

Example 4:

A has omitted *ūšib ina kussîšu* ("he {sc. Indabigaš} ascended to the throne", $Fiii_{20}$ // $Bvii_{57b}$) after the mention of Tammaritu's dethronement (Aiv_{11} // $Bvii_{56\text{-}57a}$). This sentence was without immediate consequences for the main conflict (Aššurbanipal - Tammaritu).

(3) Omission of Descriptive Sentences

This category is related to the previous one. Here we note the omission of sentences with descriptive rather than narrative force. Formally these sentences are main clauses, but their function may be compared to that of adverbs or adjectives.

Example 5:

Bull 4 has omitted *narkabat šēpāya ina tikāte ušašši* ($Chic.i_{70}$), one of three sentences describing the difficulty of the terrain by narrating Sennacherib's actions:

---

376 We can further note Bull 4's omission of $Chic.i_{82}$ $iii_{6b\text{-}7}$.

qereb huršāni zaqrūti eqil namrāṣi ina sisê arkabma
narkabat šēpāya ina tikāte ušašši
ašru šupšuqu ina šēpāya rīmāniš attagiš

"in the midst of the high mountains, where the terrain was difficult, I rode on horseback,
I had my chariot carried on necks,
where the terrain was very difficult I clambered on foot like a wild ox" (Chic.i_{68-71}).[377]

Example 6:

HT obv.4 ([*epš*]*et maruštu ... ul ibbalkit ina libbīšu* - "he did not remember the harmful [de]ed ...") has no equivalent in the subsequent versions. This sentence does not denote a progress of events.[378]

b) Omission of Descriptive Sentence Constituents

We have already seen above that with progressive transmission the rhetorical level of several narratives was reduced. Sometimes, as e.g. in the case of E's account of the arrival of the Lydian messenger, whole passages with high rhetorical level were omitted in later versions. Redactors also omitted qualifiers from retained paragraphs and thus increased emphasis on the main line of narra-

---

377 We may also note the omission of Chic.i_{65}, referring to Aššur's encouragement of Sennacherib. The function of this sentence might parallel that of *ina emūq Aššur* ("in the might of Aššur", Chic.i_{35}), *ina tukulti Aššur* ("with the aid of Aššur", Chic.iii_{1}), *ina qibīt Aššur* ("on Aššur's command", Chic.v_{76}). The omission also reduces the number of *main line* participants by removing Aššur as grammatical subject from the *main line* of the account of Sennacherib's second campaign. Cf. also Bull 4's omission of Chic.ii_{15} (... *kīma imbari* ...- "... like fog ...") and of *urappiš mātī* ("I extended my land") from Chic.ii_{32}. The omission of *ušēme karmiš* ("I turned into wasteland") from Chic.i_{78} resolves the EEN-construction and leaves only the usual *appul aqqur* ("I destroyed, I devastated"). Thus the omission may also be regarded as an adaptation to common phraseology. The case is similar with the omission of *ditalliš ušēme* ("I reduced to ashes", Chic.i_{79-80}) by which a parallelism is resolved. Here, too, the more usual expression *ina girri aqmūma* ("I burned with fire") was preferred. (cf. Chic.ii_{19}, iv_{12}). Cf. also Bell.'s omission of *imqussu hattu* ("terror fell upon him"; BM 113203, 1.26).

378 It is also noteworthy that the *main line* verb is negated and that before and after this sentence Tarqu is the grammatical subject. Thus the omission also unifies the passage. Comparable are the omissions of *libbu ušarhissuma* ("I made {his} heart confident", HT obv.55), *ispunū abūbiš* ("they crushed {this city} like a flood"; HT obv.74), HT rev.7 (negated), and HT rev.18 by the later versions, of $Bvii_{47-48}$ (1.48 negated) by F (retained in A), and $Bii_{45.48-49}$ by F and A.

tion. They omitted adjectives,[379] appositions,[380] subordinate clauses,[381]

---

[379] Chic.-Tayl. has omitted *ṣeḫer rabi* ("small, great", Bell. l.22 // Chic.i_{22}). Bull 4 has omitted *zaqrūti* ("high"; Chic.i_{68} // Bull 4, l.9), *maḫra* ("former"; Chic.ii_{29} // Bull 4, l.16), *kabittu* ("heavy"; Chic.ii_{35} // Bull 4, l.17). F and A have omitted *zikra sinniš ṣeḫer u rabi* ("male, female, small, and great", Bvi_{37}). F (iii_9) has omitted *lā kēnu* ("disloyal") after the mention of Šamaš-šum-ukīn ($Bvii_8$) and has only retained *nak*[*ri* ("host[ile"). Thus the negated modifier was not taken over.
For insertions of adjectives cf. Bi_{76} (//Ai_{82}) // HT obv.17 (stock-phrase), Fi_{46} (//Aii_{36}) // Bii_{27} (//$Ciii_{55}$), Aii_{12} // HT obv.58.

[380] BM 113203, l.6 contains several appositions after the mention of Merodach-Baladan and a subordinate clause which refers back to one of the appositions. All these are omitted in the later versions. Cf. also Chic.-Tayl.'s omission of *nakri akṣi* ("hostile, stubborn") from Bell. l.20 (// Chic.i_{66}) and Bull 4's omissions of *āl bēlūtīya* ("my royal city") after the mention of Nineveh (Chic.iii_{47}), the name of the governor of Hararate (Chic.i_{55}), a list of booty items (Chic.$i_{55\text{-}56}$), *šūt rēšīya* ("my official") before *bēl paḫati* ("the governor", Chic.ii_6 and ii_{31}), and *kadrê bēlūtīya* ("presents for my lordship") after *mandattu* ("tribute", Chic.iii_{36}). Bull 4 has further replaced *bīt ṣēri kultārē mūšabīšunu* ("house of the steppe, tents, their dwellings", Chic.$i_{78\text{-}79}$) with *bīt ṣēri kultārēšunu* ("house of the steppe, their tents", l.11). From HT the later versions have omitted *ardu dāgil pānīya* ("servant, my subject") after the mention of Niku (obv.52), *āl šarrūtīšu ašar tukultīšu* ("his royal city, his strong point") after the mention of Memphis (obv. 20), *nīš ilāni* ("an oath of the gods") after *adê* ("vow", HT obv.54 // A ii_9; B, C, and F have omitted the complete passage), *šar Kūsi* ("king of Kūsi") after the mention of Tarqu (HT obv. 66, cf. Bii_7, $Ciii_{32}$, and Aii_{20}) and *mimma aqru* ("everything precious") from the list of booty items taken from Thebes (HT rev.1). HT (obv.50 // Aii_5) has omitted from Eiv_{10f} (BM 134481; cf. A.R.Millar, "Fragments", pl.20) *āl bēlūtīya* ("my royal city") after the mention of Nineveh. F and A have omitted *šar Elamti* ("king of Elam") after the mention of Tammaritu (Bvi_{58}). They have further omitted the names of conquered cities ($Biii_{34\text{-}36}$), appositions after the mention of the month of Ulūlu ($Bv_{77\text{-}78}$), the patronym after the mention of Dunanu (Bvi_{17}, cf. Fii_{74} and $Aiii_{52}$), and an apposition after the mention of Sapibel describing the city's geographical position (*ša qereb nārē* {"which is situated between rivers"}, Bvi_{24}; cf. Fii_{77}, $Aiii_{59}$). A has left out *ardīšu* ("his servant") after the mention of Indabigaš ($Fiii_{23}$) and *ḫišiḫti* ^d^*Aššur šar ilāni bēl gimri* ("the beloved one of Aššur, king of the gods, lord of the totality", Aii_{98} // HT rev.16). From HT's account of the Gyges affair the later versions have omitted *ālikūt maḫri* ("who preceded", HT rev.14). For additions of appositions cf. HT obv.25 // $Eiii_{13}$, HT obv.20 // $Eiii_3$, Bii_{36} (// Aii_{44}) HT rev.4, Aii_{58} // Bii_{55} (political relevance? Yaḫimilki was allowed to return to Tyre and may have succeeded Ba'alu as ruler there), Fii_{79} (//$Aiii_{58}$) // Bvi_{25}.

[381] From Bell. l.13 Rass. (// Chic.i_{42}) omitted *ša kīma mīrāni ṣahri qereb ekallīya irbu* ("Bēl-ibni, son of Rab-bāni, a scion of Babylon, who had grown up in my palace like a young dog"). Cf. also Rass.'s (// Chic.-Tayl. i_{58}) omission of *ša ultu ana nīrīya la kitnūšu* ("who from old had not submitted to my yoke" - negated!) from Bell. l.18, and Bull 4's omission of this clause from Chic.-Tayl. (Chic.i_{67}) and of *ša ina qitrub tāḫāzi umašširu* ("which he had left behind at the onset of battle") from Chic.-Tayl. (Chic.i_{26}). Cf., however, the addition of a subordinate clause in Chic.-Tayl. (Chic.iii_{19}). F has omitted from B's account of Tammaritu's escape to Assyria the remark that Tammaritu had spoken disrespectfully about the decapitation of Teummān

abbreviated construct chains[382] and circumlocutory expressions.[383] They often reduced the vividness of accounts. Thus in several cases we can note the omission of adverbs or adverbial phrases.[384] Since subordinate clauses are of descriptive

(Bvii$_{59-61}$). Cf. also the omissions of *la kanšu ana nīrīya* ("who had not submitted to my yoke", Bvi$_{20}$), *ša damiqti la ḫassu la iṣṣuru adē māmit ilāni rabûti* ("who was not mindful of the favour, did not keep the oath, the treaty of the great gods", Bvii$_{5-6}$), *ša nība la īšû* ("which had no number" = "countless", Bvi$_{35}$), *ša ela šâšu eqṣu* ("who was more stubborn than he", Bvii$_{45}$) by F and A. A has further left out [*ša ina mi*]*ṣir mātīšu ašbū* ("my troops [which] dwelt [in the terr]itory of his country", Bviii$_{6}$). IT has not retained the subordinate clauses after the mention of Lydia (Aii$_{95-96}$). From HT obv.61 the subsequent versions have omitted *ša* [*Kar-bēl*]*-matāte šumšu* ("the name of which is Kar-bēl-mātāte").
For additions of subordinate clauses cf. Bi$_{67}$ (// Cii$_{35}$, Ai$_{66f}$) // HT obv.14 Biii$_{3}$ // HT rev.21, Avii$_{88}$ // Bviii$_{1}$, and, perhaps, HT obv.52 (E's account mutilated).

382 Bull 4 replaced *ana nīr bēlūtīya* ("to the yoke of my lordship", Chic.ii$_{36}$) with *ana nīrīya* ("to my yoke"; Bull 4, 1.17). Cf. also Chic.ii$_{38}$ // Bull 4, 1.18; Chic.iii$_{16}$ // Bull 4, 1.27. From a list of rulers and cities in Chic.iii$_{32-34}$ Bull 4 has only retained the names of the cities (1.30). Comparable is the abbreviation of *ša ina šarrāni abbēya mamman lā išmû* ("which among the kings my fathers no one had heard", Chic.ii$_{34}$) to *ša šarrāni abbēya lā išmû* ("which the kings, my fathers had not heard"; Bull 4, 1.17). F has abbreviated *iṣbatū šēpē šarrūtīya* ("they seized my royal feet", Bvii$_{70}$) to *iṣbatū šēpēya* ("they seized my feet", Fiii$_{26}$) and omitted *mātīšu* ("of his land") after *nišē* ("people") from Bvi$_{37}$ (Fii$_{78}$, cf. also Bvi$_{27-35}$). A has omitted *amāt* ("word") before *lemuttim* ("of evil", HT obv.48 // Aii$_{1}$). B, followed by C and A, has abbreviated *miḫrit ummānātēya* ("before my troops"; HT obv.16 // Bi$_{74}$, Cii$_{74}$, Ai$_{80}$) to *ana maḫrīya* ("before me"). The alteration has also changed the reference from a secondary to a primary participant. Comparable is the omission of *ša Elamti* ("of Elam", Bvii$_{63}$) by Fiii$_{22}$ and Aiv$_{23}$.

383 Chic.i$_{30-35}$ // Bull 4, 1.6, Chic.iii$_{21-27}$ // Bull 4, 1.28 (cf. R.Borger, *Babylonisch-Assyrische Lesestücke*, p.76), BM 113203, 1.60 // Bell. 1.16, HT rev.4 // Bii$_{36}$, HT obv.69 // Bii$_{14}$, HT rev.20 // Aii$_{106}$.

384 Bull 4 has omitted *ina qitrub tāḫāzi* ("at the onset of battle", Chic.i$_{26}$), *arkīya* ("after me", Chic.ii$_{48}$), *nakriš* ("like an enemy", Chic.ii$_{77}$), *ina qabal tamḫāri* ("in the midst of the battle", Chic.iii$_{5}$), *ana ... epēš ardūti* ("to do servitude", Chic.iii$_{49}$). HT has omitted *arkānu* ("afterwards", Eii$_{27}$ // Ai$_{118}$). B, C, F and A have omitted *adi maḫrīya* ("to me", HT rev.19). F and A have omitted *ana dalāl ilūtīšun rabīti* ... ("to revere their great divinity", Bvii$_{66}$). The omission of the reference to the Assyrian officer from the same passage and Bvii$_{38}$ may be that of a secondary participant. F and A have further omitted (Bviii$_{57}$). C has omitted *eninna yâti* ("now to me", Bviii$_{57}$; cf.Cx$_{58}$). A has omitted *ina qereb tamḫāri baltussu* ("in the midst of the battle alive", HT rev.20; cf. Aii$_{106}$). IT has omitted *ana maḫrīya* ("to me", Aii$_{110}$).
Several of the added adverbial constructions are stock-phrases (cf. Bii$_{81}$ // Aii$_{74}$, Fiii$_{29}$ // Aiv$_{33}$ //Bvii$_{72}$, Biii$_{10}$ // HT rev.11, Avii$_{116}$ // Bviii$_{8}$, Aix$_{43}$ // Bviii$_{13}$), others clarify the narrative structure (Fiii$_{12}$ // Aiv$_{3}$ // Bvii$_{45}$), Aii$_{103}$ // HT rev.19f, Avii$_{117}$ // Bviii$_{9}$). Cf. also Aii$_{6}$ // Bii$_{6}$.

rather than narrative function their omission parallels that of descriptive main clauses as well as that of adverbs, adjectives, and appositions, all increasing the emphasis on the main line of narration. The effects of other alterations, as e.g. omissions from lists,[385] cannot be traced in the narrative structure. From some passages several qualifiers were omitted.[386]

2.. Contraction

A further means of abbreviating a *Vorlage* is that of contraction. While omitted material cannot be recovered in *late stages* of narratives without the existence of earlier *Vorlage* contracted passages are more likely to indicate the presence of a secondary edition. Thus the application of this technique by redactors may provide some criteria for the identification of *late stages*.

a) Subordination

A redactor combining material from two passages or sentences may co-ordinate or subordinate the retained text. An example of co-ordination, that of the accounts of Mugallu's, Iakinlu's, and Sandišarme's submissions has already been discussed above.[387] More often one passage or sentence was subordinated to another one.

Example 7:

---

385 Cf. BM 113203, ll.31-33 // Bell., l.8; Chic.i_{25} // Bell., l.7; Chic.ii_{13} // Bull 4, l.13; Chic.ii_{27} // Bull 4, l.15; Chic.ii_{73f} // Bull 4, ll.22-23; Chic.$iii_{8.11}$ // Bull 4, ll.25.26 (cf. Chic.ii_{74} // Bull 4, l.23); Bell. l.7 // Rass., (// Chic.-Tayl. i_{31}). HT has abbreviated the list of booty items from E's the account of the campaign against Kirbit (iv_{2f}): [*nišē*] *alpē ṣēnē* [*šall*]*assu kabittu išlulūni* ("people, cattle, sheep, his heavy spoil they carried off", restorations according to BM 134481 {cf. Millard, "Fragments", pl.20}) to *išlula nišēšu* ("he {? preceded by *ikšudû* - "they conquered" - and followed by *assuḫ* - "I uprooted"} carried off his people", HT rev.11). Cf. also the omission of Bvi_{31-33} by F and A.
For additions of or to lists cf. above, p.88, and Bii_{12} (// Aii_{23}) // HT obv.68, $Aii_{83-84.91-92}$ // $Ciii_{123-124}$, $iv_{1.3}$ (//$Bii_{83.88.90}$), $Aiii_{65}$ // Bvi_{35}, $Fiii_3$ (// $Aiii_{66}$) // Bvi_{35}.

386 Cf. Chic.i_{64} // Bull 4, l.9; Chic.ii_{47-49} // Bull 4, l.19; Chic.ii_{50-60} // Bull 4, l.20; Chic.ii_{67-68} // Bull 4, l.21; Chic.iii_{12-13} // Bull 4, l.26; HT obv. 5-8 // Ai_{57b-59} (//Bi_{56-59}, Cii_{22-26}); HT rev.16f // Aii_{98} // IT l.85; Bii_{86-87} // Fii_4; $Bvii_{7-8}$ // $Fiii_9$ // $Aiii_{137}$; $Bviii_{54-57}$ // $Cx_{47-49.58}$ // $Aviii_{60-62.64}$.

387 Cf. also Chic.-Tayl.'s combination of BM 113203, ll.58.62 in Chic.i_{57-60}.

BM 113203, l.26: ***u šū ēpiš lemnēti akāmu girrīya ana rūqēti ēmurma imqussu ḫattu gimir ellatīšu ēzibma ana Guzummani innabit***

"and that evil-doer saw the cloud of dust of my campaign from afar, terror fell upon him, he forsook all of his troops and fled to the land of Guzummanu".

BM 113203, l.34: ***urriḫma arkīšu ana Guzummani mundaḫṣīya ana qereb agamme u appārāte uma''irma 5 ūmē uba''ūšuma ašaršu ul innamir***

"I hurried after him to the land of Guzummanu (and) sent my warriors into the swamp and marshes; 5 days they searched for him, (but) his (hiding) place was not found".

Bell., l.6: ***ina qabal tamḫāri šuātu ēzib karāssu ēdiš ipparšidma ana Guzummani innabit qereb agamme u appārāte ērumma napištuš ēṭir*** (l.6).

"in the midst of that battle he forsook his camp, escaped alone to the land of Guzummanu and went into the swamp and marshes and saved his life".

Bull 4, l.4: ***šū ana šūzub napištīšu ēdiš ipparšidma***

"that one, to save his life he escaped alone".

Here we can note a combination of co-ordination and subordination. Bell. has placed side by side the narrations of Merodach-baladan's escape. It is apparent that the redactors have progressively reduced the number of *main line* verbs. This simplifies the discourse structure, because there are fewer verbs denoting progress of narration. In the two passages in BM 113203 five different grammatical subjects had been mentioned: Merodach-baladan, terror, Sennacherib, Sennacherib's soldiers, Merodach-baladan's hiding place. Bell. and Bull 4 have each replaced a main clause by an adverbial phrase and thus increased the ratio of modifiers per verb in the later versions. Both have reworded their *Vorlage*. The passages combined by Bell. related Merodach-baladan's fate. In BM 113203, l.26, he is mentioned as grammatical subject, in BM 113203, l.34 as grammatical object. Bell. harmonized the references to Merodach-baladan, who now dominates all *main line* verbs of this passage. The only phrase in BM 113203, l.26 which did not have Merodach-baladan as grammatical subject (*imqussu ḫattu* - "terror fell upon him") was omitted by Bell. The combination of the two passages from BM 113203 led to a resolution of the chronological order. Bell. also retained an equivalent of BM 113203, l.34. Thus the contraction could have been identified as being secondary. In Chic.-Tayl., however, the later passage is omitted. There only the verb-modifier ratio could have given slight, but not conclusive, indication of redactorial intervention. In Bull 4 all signs were removed. The case is different with Bell. l.5 which summarizes BM 113203, ll.5-25 and which was retained by both Chic.-Tayl. and Bull 4. Bell. l.5 contains only one *main line* verb, but several qualifiers:

> *ina rēš šarrūtīya ša Marduk-apla-iddina šar Karduniaš adi ummānāt Elamti ina tamerti Kiš aštakan taḫtâšu.*
>
> "at the beginning of my kingship I brought about the defeat of Merodach-baladan, king of Babylonia, and the armies of Elam in the plain of Kish".

There is no further sentence like this in Bell.'s account. Not the comparatively high number of qualifiers, but the unevenness within a narrative may thus be taken as a criterion for the identification of *late stages*. However, this identification does only affect the passage concerned, not the account as such. Indeed, in the retained portions of BM 113203's account Bell. has carried out only few noteworthy omissions.[388]

The different references to the deportation of the inhabitants of the people of the conquered district of Kirbit provide a good example from Aššurbanipal's campaign accounts:

Example 8:

> $Eiii_{32}$-iv_7: ... *ālāni imbariš iktumūma ... nišē ... išlulūni ... nišē āšibūti ālāni šunūti* ...[389]
>
> "... the cities they covered like fog, ... people ... they carried off, ... people living in these cities ...
>
> HT rev.12: *išlula nišēšu nišē ālāni šâtunu kišitti qātēya ...*
>
> "he[390] carried of his people, the people of these cities, captives of my hands"
>
> $Biii_{14}$: *[nišē] Kirbit mala ašlulu ...*
>
> "the people of Kirbit, as many as I had carried off".

Again we can witness progressive downgrading and subordination. HT has replaced ... *ālāni imbariš iktumūma* ("... like fog they covered the cities") with *kišitti qātēya* ("captives of my hands") and B has downgraded *išlula nišēšu* ("he carried off his people") to *mala ašlulu* ("as many as I had carried off").[391]

---

388 See above pp.85ff. For a further case cf. BM 113203, l.30 // Bell. l.8.

389 Cf. A.C.Piepkorn, *Historical Prism Inscriptions*, p.14, BM 128306 and BM 134481 (cf. A.R.Millard, "Fragments", pl.20), BM 134445 and BM 121018 (cf. R.Campbell Thompson, "A Selection", nos.20.21).

390 Cf. above, pp.121f, n.222.

391 Cf. also HT obv. 11-14 // B i_{66-70} (//C,A), HT obv. 69 // A ii 24, Bvi_{35-49} // $Fiii_2$ // $Aiii_{65}$, $Bvii_{3-46}$ // $Aiii_{136}$-iv_2, $Bvii_{93.94.97}$-$viii_1$ // A vii_{82-86}, HT obv.67 // Bii_{11} //

b) Replacement of Lists by Common Denominators

Related to the preceding category is the replacement of lists by common denominators.

Example 9:

Chic.i_{39ff}: *Urbi Aramu Kaldu ša qereb Uruk ... ušēṣâmma šallatiš amnu ina tayyartīya* ... (names) ... *Aramu lā kanšūti mitḫāriš akšud 208,000 nišē ... šallatu kabittu ašlula ana qereb Aššur*.

> "the Arabs, Arameans, Chaldeans, who were in Uruk ... I brought out (and) counted as booty. ... (names) ... Arameans who had not been submissive likewise I conquered. 208,000 people ... heavy spoil I carried off to Assyria."

Bull 4, 1.7: *ina tayyartīya Aramu ša šiddi Idiglat Puratti akšud ašlula šallašun*.[392]

> "on my return I conquered the Arameans who (lived along) the banks of Tigris (and) Euphrates, I carried off their spoil."

Example 10:

Bvi$_{27f}$: *aššassu mārēšu mārātēšu sekretīšu nārē nārātē*

> "his wife, his sons, his daughters, his concubines, male singers, female singers"

Aiii$_{61}$: *qinnūšu zēr bīt abīšu*

> "his family, the seed of the house of his father".[393]

Ciii$_{35}$ // A ii$_{22}$, Biv$_{74-78}$ // Fiii$_{61}$ // Aiii$_{37}$, Bvii$_{6}$ // Fiii$_{8}$, Bvii$_{45-46}$ Fiii$_{12}$ // Aiv$_{3-4}$, Cx$_{50-56}$ // Aviii$_{58}$, Ei$_{8-10}$ (cf. A.C.Piepkorn, *Historical Prism Inscriptions*, p.10) // Ai$_{54f}$, Biv$_{79-86}$ // Fii$_{68.70}$ // Aiii$_{45.48}$, E (BM 134445 iii$_{1}$) // HT rev.9, HT obv.21-22 // B i$_{84b-85a}$, HT obv.18 // Bi$_{77}$ (= Cii$_{77}$, Ai$_{82}$), IT 1.85 // Ai$_{104-106}$, Bvii$_{53}$ // Fiii$_{18}$ (cf. also A iv$_{10}$ // B$_{5}$), Eiv$_{5}$ (Cf. A.C.Piepkorn, *Historical Prism Inscriptions*, p.14, with the restoration of the mayor of Kirbit's name from BM 134481.) // B iii$_{12-13}$ // Civ$_{33-34}$, B vi$_{17-19}$ // Fii$_{53}$ // Aiii$_{27}$, Bii$_{65}$ // Hii$_{22}$.
For expansions cf. HT obv.48 // E (BM 128230 iii$_{6-7}$ {cf. A.R.Millard, "Fragments", pl.19}), Cii$_{121-122}$ // HT obv.41, Ciii$_{92}$ (//Fi$_{66}$, Aii$_{59}$) // Bii$_{56}$, Avii$_{86}$ // Bviii$_{1}$, Aix$_{52}$ // Bviii$_{21}$, Fiii$_{26}$ (//Aiv$_{25}$) // Bvii$_{70}$, Aix$_{53f}$ // Bviii$_{23}$, Aix$_{55}$ // Bviii$_{23}$, Cx$_{58}$ // Bviii$_{57}$, Aix$_{56}$ // Bviii$_{24}$.

392 Cf. also Bell., ll. 28-30 // Chic.-Tayl. ii$_{16ff}$ // Bull 4, 13-14, Chic.-Tayl. i$_{74-76}$ // Bull 4, 1.11, Chic.-Tayl. iii$_{45}$ // Rass., Chic.-Tayl. ii$_{62-63}$ // Bull 4 1.20, Chic.-Tayl. i$_{52}$ // Rass., Chic.-Tayl. ii$_{69-71}$ // Bull 4, 1.22.

393 Cf. also the A's replacement of the names of Egyptian vassal kings mentioned in HT obv.33 by *šarrāni annûti mala apqidu* ("these kings, as many as I had installed", i$_{118}$). The booty items listed in E's account of the campaign against Kirbit (Eiv$_{2f}$; cf. A.C.Piepkorn, *Historical Prism Inscriptions*, p.14) have been summarized to *šallassu* ("his spoil") by Biii$_{11}$ and Civ$_{32}$.

IV. Application of Results

We have already noted above that widespread literary-critical hypotheses applied to the study of Old Testament narratives were not supported by our study of the literary development of Assyrian campaign accounts. Since, however, these hypotheses purport to be derived from the texts themselves, only by an application of our new analogy to Biblical stories and a comparison with usual literary-critical methods can we reach further conclusions.

We shall thus examine the consequences of both the application of the empirical model proposed here and of common literary-critical methodology in an analysis of narratives from the Old Testament, 1 Kgs.22_{1-38} and 1 Kgs.20.[1] Of course, even if we succeed in establishing the superiority of one of the two methods against the other, this would not prove that *all* narratives were subjected to the same kind of editorial treatment. The purpose of the application of our results is rather to outline the consequences for the study of Old Testament narratives and to obtain a working hypothesis, the validity of which nevertheless has to be constantly examined. Since internal criteria for the identification of redactorial intervention are necessarily ambiguous such a working hypothesis is of crucial significance for the understanding of narratives in the Old Testament.

A. 1 Kgs.22_{1-38}

Scholarly opinion about the literary pre-history of the narrative in 1 Kgs.22 is not unanimous. While on one side the literary unity has been argued,[2] literary-critical analysis has led some scholars to the identification of different layers in the story.[3] Before we examine these attempts to reconstruct the literary

---

1 We shall concentrate on the literary aspects and disregard, as far as possible, the question of historicity. For a discussion of reasons adduced against the historicity of historical accuracy of 1 Kgs.22 cf. below, appendix IV.

2 Cf. e.g. J.Wellhausen, *Composition*, p.284; M.Noth, *Überlieferungsgeschichtliche Studien*, p.80; H.Cancik, *Grundzüge*, pp.198f.

3 W.Roth gives a brief review over the interpretations of 1 Kgs.22 by Wellhausen, Kittel, Greßmann, Noth, Montgomery, Würthwein, and Rofé (cf. "Story of the Prophet Micaiah"). He focusses, however, on the interpretations derived from literary-critical research rather than on the literary-critical work itself. Cf. also S.J.DeVries, *1 Kings*,

history we shall analyse the present form of the narrative with regard to the criteria applied in the above investigation of the transmission of Assyrian campaign accounts. The following table represents the participant orientation pattern of 1 Kgs.22_{1-38}.

v.1	וַיֵּשְׁבוּ	(C(')[4]-B(')[5])			
v.2	וַיְהִי	A[6]-B			
	וַיֵּרֶד	A-B	⇒ l		
v.3	וַיֹּאמֶר	B-B'	⇒ r		
				הַיְדַעְתֶּם	B'
				מַחְשִׁים	B/B'
v.4	וַיֹּאמֶר	B-A	⇒ l		
				הֲתֵלֵךְ	A-B-C
	וַיֹּאמֶר	A-B	⇒ r		
v.5	וַיֹּאמֶר	A-B	⇒ l		
				דְּרָשׁ־נָא	B-A*
v.6	וַיִּקְבֹּץ	B-B'[7]	⇒ r		
	וַיֹּאמֶר	B-B'	⇒ l		
				הַאֵלֵךְ	B-C
				אֶחְדָּל	B-C
	וַיֹּאמְרוּ	B'-B	⇒ l		
				עֲלֵה	B-C
				וְיִתֵּן	B*(-C)-B
v.7	וַיֹּאמֶר	A-B	⇒ r		
				וְנִדְרְשָׁה	A/B-A*'
v.8	וַיֹּאמֶר	B-A	⇒ r		
				שְׂנֵאתִיו	B-A*'
				לֹא־יִתְנַבֵּא	A*'-B
	וַיֹּאמֶר	A-B	⇒ r		
				אַל־יֹאמַר	B
v.9	וַיִּקְרָא	B-B'	⇒ r		
	וַיֹּאמֶר	B-B'	⇒ l		
				מַהֲרָה	B'
v.10	יֹשְׁבִים	B/A	⇒ l		
	מְלֻבָּשִׁים	B/A	⇒ l		
	מִתְנַבְּאִים	B'-B/A	⇒ l		
v.11	וַיַּעַשׂ	B'	⇒ l		
	וַיֹּאמֶר	B'-B	⇒ l		
				אָמַר	A*

---

p.270 ("seldom has a simple prophet story undergone so complex a process of editing and redaction, and seldom has a passage raised so wide a range of theological problems ...").

4 Aram.

5 Ahab.

6 Jehoshaphat.

7 Cf. נְבִאָיו (v.22) and נְבִיאֶיךָ (v.23) with the pronominal suffixes referring to Ahab.

						תְּנַגַּח	B-C		
v.12	נִבְּאִים	B'	⇒ I						
				עֲלֵה	B(-C)				
				וְהַצְלַח	B(-C)				
				וְנָתַן	A*(-C)-B				
v.13	דַּבֶּר	B'-A*'	⇒ I						
				יְהִי	A*'				
				וְדִבַּרְתָּ	A*'				
v.14	וַיֹּאמֶר	A*'-B'	⇒ r						
				אֲדַבֵּר	A*'				
v.15	וַיָּבוֹא	A*'-B	⇒ I						
	וַיֹּאמֶר	B-A*'	⇒ r						
				הֲנֵלֵךְ	A/B-C				
				נֶחְדָּל	A/B-C				
	וַיֹּאמֶר	A*'-B	⇒ r						
				עֲלֵה	B(-C)				
				וְהַצְלַח	B(-C)				
				וְנָתַן	A*(-C)-B				
v.16	וַיֹּאמֶר	B-A*'	⇒ r						
				מַשְׁבִּעֶךָ	B-A*'				
						לֹא־תְדַבֵּר	A*'-B		
v.17	וַיֹּאמֶר	A*'-B	⇒ r						
				רָאִיתִי	A*'-B'				
				ויֹּאמֶר	A*-A*'				
						יָשׁוּבוּ	B'		
v.18	וַיֹּאמֶר	B-A	⇒ r						
				אָמַרְתִּי	B-A				
						לוֹא־יִתְנַבֵּא	A*'-B		
v.19	וַיֹּאמֶר	A*'-B	⇒ r						
				שְׁמַע	B-A*				
						רָאִיתִי	A*'-A*		
v.20						וַיֹּאמֶר	A*		
								יְפַתֶּה	A*'-B
								וַיַּעַל	B
								וַיִּפֹּל	B
						וַיֹּאמֶר	A*'		
						אֹמֵר	A*'		
v.21						וַיֵּצֵא	A*'		
						וַיַּעֲמֹד	A*'		
						וַיֹּאמֶר	A*'-A*		
								אֲפַתֶּנּוּ	A*'(-B)
						וַיֹּאמֶר	A*-A*'		
v.22						וַיֹּאמֶר	A*'-A*		
								אֵצֵא	A*'
								וְהָיִיתִי	A*'
						וַיֹּאמֶר	A*		
								תְּפַתֶּה	A*'(-B)
								תוּכָל	A*'
								צֵא	A*'
								וַעֲשֵׂה	A*'

v.23				נָתַן	A*-A*'-B'				
				דִּבֶּר	A*'-B				
v.24	וַיִּגַּשׁ	B'-A*'	⇒ r						
	וַיַּכֶּה	B'-A*'	⇒ I						
	וַיֹּאמֶר	B'-A*'	⇒ I						
				עָבַר	A*'-B'				
v.25	וַיֹּמֶר	A*'-B'	⇒ r						
				רֹאֶה	B'				
v.26	וַיֹּאמֶר	B-B'	⇒ r						
				קַח	B'-A*'				
				וַהֲשִׁיבֵהוּ	B'-A*'				
v.27				וְאָמַרְתָּ	B'-B'				
						אָמַר	B		
								שִׂימוּ	B'-A*'
								וְהַאֲכִילֻהוּ	B'-A*'
v.28	וַיֹּאמֶר	A*'-B	⇒ r						
				לֹא־דִבֶּר	A*-A*'				
	וַיֹּאמֶר	A*'-B/B'	⇒ I						
				שִׁמְעוּ	B/B'				
v.29	וַיַּעַל	B/A	⇒ r						
v.30	וַיֹּאמֶר	B-A	⇒ I						
				הִתְחַפֵּשׂ	B[8]				
				וָבֹא	B				
				לְבַשׁ	A				
	וַיִּתְחַפֵּשׂ	B	⇒ I						
	וַיָּבוֹא	B	⇒ I						
v.31	צִוָּה	C-C'(-B)	⇒ sr						
				לֹא תִלָּחֲמוּ	C'-B				
v.32	וַיְהִי	(C'-A)	⇒ s						
	אָמְרוּ	C'	⇒ I						
	וַיָּסֻרוּ	C'-A	⇒ I						
	וַיִּזְעַק	A	⇒ r						
v.33	וַיְהִי	(C'-A)	⇒ r						
	וַיָּשׁוּבוּ	C'-A	⇒ I						
v.34	מָשַׁךְ	C'(-B)	⇒ s						
	וַיַּכֶּה	C'-B	⇒ I						
	וַיֹּאמֶר	B-B'	⇒ r						
				הֲפֹךְ	B'				
				וְהוֹצִיאֵנִי	B'-B				
v.35	וַתַּעֲלֶה								
	הָיָה מָעֳמָד	B	⇒ I						
	וַיָּמָת	B	⇒ I						
	וַיִּצֶק	(B)	⇒ I						
v.36	וַיַּעֲבֹר								
v.37	וַיָּמָת	B	⇒ I						
	וַיָּבוֹא	B	⇒ I						

8 Indirect speech? LXX, ***S***, ***T*** have 1st pers. sgl. That Ahab is the *agent* is evident from the context and from וְאַתָּה.

	וַיִּקְבְּרוּ	B'-B	⇒ I
v.38	וַיִּשְׁטֹף	B'	⇒ I
	וַיָּלֹקּוּ	X[9](-B)	⇒ r?
	רָחָצוּ	X[10](-B)	⇒ I

It is apparent that the participant orientation pattern is comparatively complex. There are two *switches* (3.64 %), thirty *identical* states (54.54 %), and almost as many *reversals* (22 x r, 1 x sr - 40% + 1.82%). The percentage of *reversals* is higher than in any of the Assyrian campaign accounts studied above. There are also many participants in the story. Apart from Ahab and Jehoshaphat, the narrative mentions four hundred prophets (vv.6,12f), Micaiah, son of Imlah (vv.6.13.15.24ff), a messenger sent by Ahab (vv.9.13) Zedekiah, son of Chenaanah (vv.11.24), the Lord (vv.13ff), the people of Israel (v.17), the heavenly court (vv.19f), a "lying spirit" (vv.21f), Amon, the governor of the city (v.26) and Joash, the king's son (v.26), king of Aram (v.32), thirty-two Aramean officers (v.31ff), an Aramean soldier (v.34), the driver of Ahab's chariot (v.34). Most of these are also mentioned on the *main line*.

The complexity of the participant relations is paralleled in the narrative structure. There are speeches with different levels of quotation and, apparently, little effort was made to unify the *main line*. Ahab's interruption of Micaiah's prophecy (v.18) could easily have been omitted by a redactor, which would have reduced the number of *reversals*, but evidently was not. The narrative is related on the locutionary[11] level and no anticipatory remarks are apparent. The narrator follows the course of events. This is recognizable in the separation of Ahab's dispatching of the messenger (v.9) and the mention of the latter's return (v.13) and, as was already noted, in Ahab's interruption of Micaiah's speech. No significant unevenness of the grammatical texture is apparent. The rhetorical level is comparatively high and there is a clear rise of tension in the story up to its resolution in the narration of Ahab's death (vv.34ff). Taking the development of Assyrian campaign accounts as point of departure, there is every indication that 1 Kgs.22_{1-38} is in an *early stage* of literary development. Various characteristics of the narrative have nevertheless led scholars to different conclusions.

---

9 הַכְּלָבִים.

10 הַזֹּנוֹת.

11 Cf. above, pp.167f, n.362.

1. E.Würthwein's Analysis

In a detailed study E.Würthwein distinguished several redactional layers and various minor additions in 1 Kgs.$22_{1\text{-}38}$.[12] He derived his identification of different strands by analyzing suspected inconsistencies and isolating self-sufficient passages. He suggested that the nucleus of the narrative was found in a campaign account, comprising vv.2b-4.29-37, into which a prophet story was incorporated. The prophet story itself is seen as the result of two redactions of a basic narrative. Würthwein identified vv.1.23.28b.35d.38a as minor additions by various redactors. It is important to note that his reconstruction only reckons with expansions, not abbreviations.

Würthwein assumed a first difficulty in the course of narration in the fact that Jehoshaphat's speech to Ahab is introduced twice, in v.4 and v.5, with וַיֹּאמֶר יְהוֹשָׁפָט אֶל־מֶלֶךְ יִשְׂרָאֵל in connection with the fact that Jehoshaphat asked Ahab to inquire the word of the Lord after he had already agreed to Ahab's suggestion. Furthermore, the consultation of the prophets remains without consequence in the further course of narration. However, the twofold introduction of Jehoshaphat's speech may be explained by the change in subject. Jehoshaphat agrees in principle to Ahab's suggestion, but would prefer to inquire the Lord's word first.[13] This

---

[12] Cf. *Die Bücher der Könige*, pp.255ff, "Zur Komposition von 1 Reg $22_{1\text{-}38}$".

[13] This would explain why, in contrast to 2 Kgs.3_{7}, אֶעֱלֶה is missing from Jehoshaphat's answer. Further cases of repeated speech introductions are found in Gen.$9_{1.8.12.17}$ $9_{25.26}$ $15_{2.3}$ $15_{5.7}$ $16_{9.10.11}$ ($17_{9.15}$) $20_{9.10}$ $24_{24.25}$ 27_{36} $37_{21.22}$ $41_{39.41}$ Ex.$3_{5.6}$ $3_{14.15}$ $4_{5.6}$ ($5_{4.5.6}$) $6_{1.2}$ ($7_{14.19}$ 7_{26}.8_{1} $16_{32.33}$) $33_{19.20.21}$ ($35_{1.4}$ Num.$24_{21.23}$) Dt.$9_{12.13}$ Jdg.$8_{23.24}$ $19_{12.13}$ 1 Sam.$17_{34.37}$ $23_{10.12}$ $26_{9.10}$ $26_{17.18}$ 2 Sam.($15_{3.4}$) $24_{22.23}$ (1 Kgs.$3_{23.24}$) 2 Kgs.$13_{17.18}$ Jer.$37_{17.18}$ (Ru.$3_{14.15}$ 2 Chr.$2_{10.11}$). Uncertain cases are given in brackets. The only case of repeated speech introduction in the Chronicler's *Vorlage*, as far as it is extant, the double introduction of Araunah's speech in 2 Sam.$24_{22.23}$, was resolved by the Chronicler (1 Chr.21_{23}). The only case of possible repeated speech introduction in the Chronicler's work is found in 2 Chr.2_{10f}: וַיֹּאמֶר חוּרָם מֶלֶךְ־צֹר בִּכְתָב וַיִּשְׁלַח אֶל־שְׁלֹמֹה ... וַיֹּאמֶר חוּרָם. The first part of Hiram's "speech" parallels 1 Kgs.5_{21}, which in Kgs. is not part of Hiram's letter but is given in 3rd pers. In Kgs. then follows the letter introduced separately. Thus 2 Chr.$2_{10.11}$ are not the result of a combination of sources. To be sure, in some cases the speech introductions have been ascribed to different sources (Gen.15_{2}: *J*, 15_{3}: *E*; Gen.16_{11}: *J*, $16_{9.10}$: redact. expansion; 24_{24}: *J*, 24_{25}: *E*; 7_{36a}: *J*, 27_{36b}: *E*; 37_{21}: *J* (רְאוּבֵן emended to יְהוּדָה), 37_{2}: *E*; $39_{39\text{-}40}$: *J*, 39_{41}: *E*; Ex.3_{5}: *J*, 3_{6}: *E*; 5_{4}: *J*, 5_{5}: *E*; 6_{1}: *J*, 6_{2}: *P*; 7_{14}: *J*, 7_{19}: *P*; 7_{26}: *J*, 8_{1}: *P*; (according to O.Eißfeldt, *Hexateuch-Synopse*), but there still

also removes the difficulty that Würthwein saw in the contents of Jehoshaphat's speech. Würthwein supposed that the narrative was written in Judah when the Judeans were Israelite vassals because of the negative view of Ahab, which also would explain why Jehoshaphat followed Ahab's order in spite of the danger involved. This, however, is mere speculation. One can, on the other hand, note that Ahab plays the leading rôle in the narrative and from the outset has the initiative. Thus it is quite conceivable that Jehoshaphat agreed in principle to Ahab's suggestion, but nevertheless preferred to inquire the word of the Lord. There is no real difficulty with the double speech introduction, but the explanation is rather to be found in the contents of Jehoshaphat's speech(es).

In Würthwein's analysis vv.2b-4.29-37 were isolated as a self-sufficient unit. He argued that vv.29ff do not refer back to the prophet story. A back reference may, however, be found in v.36, אִישׁ אֶל־עִירוֹ וְאִישׁ אֶל־אַרְצוֹ resuming אִישׁ־לְבֵיתוֹ of v.17. This does not, of course, reduce the self-sufficiency of vv.2b-4.29-37, but it is questionable whether self-sufficiency alone provides sufficient reason for assuming redactionist expansions.[14] It is always possible to isolate different scenes from a narrative, to ascribe them to different redactors, and to assign all linkages to attempts to harmonize the various sources. In principle no complex

---

remain enough cases to question the certainty of the division into sources in 1 Kgs.$22_{4.5}$. We thus conclude that the repeated speech introduction should, at least in this case, be regarded as a literary device rather than an indicator for redactions. It is, of course, possible that 1 Kgs.22_4 was adapted to 2 Kgs.3_7.
Interesting cases of double speech introductions are found in the Neo-Assyrian version of the Gilgameš-epic in Gilgameš's replies to Siduri and Uršanabi (the parallel passage in Gilgameš's reply to Utnapištim is not extant). Gilgameš first tells what happened to Enkidu and then addresses Siduri, resp. Uršanabi, resp. Utnapištim. While in the OB version of Gilgameš' reply to Siduri report and address are part of the same speech (in the OB version the preserved portions of the report of Gilgameš' encounter with Sursunabu / Uršanabi differ greatly from those of his encounter with Siduri; the report of Gilgameš's encounter with Utnapištim is not preserved), the Neo-Assyrian version has separate speech introductions for the direct addresses (Xii_{15} iii_{32} [v_{22}]) although Gilgameš is already speaking. Since the purpose of the reference to the Gilgameš epic is not to positively support a line of redaction-critical reasoning, but rather to argue against the *necessity* of a certain interpretation of literary features, it is permitted, even though as an empirical model the Akkadian epics had to be rejected. In this case it suffices to point out what *may* have happened! Thus another possible explanation for the twofold introduction of Jehoshaphat's speech would be, that the author/redactor intended to contrast the two parts of the speech.

14 Würthwein concedes this (cf. "Zur Komposition von 1 Reg 22_{1-38}", p.246).

narrative would be exempt from this approach. Yet to deny the possibility of complex narratives as works of authors rather than redactors is methodologically not justified. Nevertheless, the possibility that this passage might constitute a later expanded story nucleus may be conceded.

Würthwein's suggestion that the prophet story should itself have undergone two redactions before its insertion into the narrative is not convincing. If Würthwein's reconstruction was right, the prophet story in its original version would have to have existed independently. But, as shall be argued below, it is only understandable in connection with the campaign account. It is also improbable that the result of two further redactions should lead to a story that by coincidence could be inserted in a campaign narrative which did not have to be altered at all. There remains, however, the possibility that the original version of the prophet story as analyzed by Würthwein was included in the campaign account and that it was subjected to two redactions after it had become part of the account. Although this does not agree with Würthwein's analysis, we shall nevertheless follow up this possibility. Würthwein's reconstruction is attractive. It results in a story nucleus that is simple and coherent, although with a somewhat abrupt beginning. Jehoshaphat is mentioned as the grammatical subject of the first main clause although the story is mainly about the king of Israel.

The prophet story is regarded as the result of a basic narrative and two subsequent redactions. The various strands are thought to constitute a discussion of the problematic relationship between prophets of salvation and prophets of doom. In the first strand the confrontation between the two kinds of prophets is related. The second strand introduces Zedekiah ben Kenaanah and thus characterizes the behaviour of the prophets of salvation. The third strand discusses the prophets of salvation's claim to possess the spirit and reaches the conclusion that the spirit they have is a lying spirit. It is very doubtful whether this reconstruction can be deduced from the text. It rather seems to have been presupposed and thus determined the results of Würthwein's investigation. One would expect the reflections of later opinions to supplant earlier ones. Why should such a discussion have been necessary, if it was already apparent that Micaiah was the true and the four hundred were false prophets? It also seems strange that such a controversy should have been expressed in a *narrative*. Furthermore, as H.Seebaß[15] has pointed out, Ahab's attempt to disguise himself, but not Jehoshaphat receives its motivation from Micaiah's prophecy.

The basic version of the prophet story added to the campaign narrative is thought to be present in vv.5-9.13-18.26-28a. These passages do not constitute a self-sufficient story. V.5 would be a very abrupt beginning of a story mentioning both Jehoshaphat and the king of Israel. Jehoshaphat would not have been introduced as king of Judah. No reason is stated in this passage why anyone should seek the Lord's word. The prophet story would end with Micaiah being thrown into prison. For a prophet story this is not a satisfying conclusion. The narrator may be expected to relate which prophecy was fulfilled. No reason is given why this passage should have been added. Ahab's death could already have been regarded as the fulfillment of a prophecy (cf. 1 Kgs.21_{19}). To make this explicit the addition of vv.35d.38, regarded by Würthwein as later expansions, would have been sufficient, presupposing, of course, that 21_{19} was known to the redactor. The addition of a reference to four hundred prophets whose prophecy was evidently wrong is even less likely. The redactor would have added the reference to further participants, thus making the plot more complex. He would also have added reference to a prophecy that was not fulfilled. One could, however, argue that it was the prophecy of the four hundred prophets that was heeded by the two kings and thus it was thought necessary to include the reference to the false prophets. Such an insertion would, however, contrast with the general trends apparent in the transmission of Assyrian campaign accounts. That the twofold introduction of Jehoshaphat's speech is the result of redactorial activity is not very likely. It would have quite been conceivable if two independent sources had been interwoven, but this is evidently not the case with the campaign narrative and the prophet story. In v.13 the relative clause after וְהַמַּלְאָךְ would not have been necessary if the passage had followed immediately after v.9. V.28a refers back to v.19 to Micaiah's own statement and not to 16b which is part of Ahab's speech.

v.28: וַיֹּאמֶר מִיכָיְהוּ אִם־שׁוֹב תָּשׁוּב בְּשָׁלוֹם לֹא־דִבֶּר יְהוָה בִּי

v.19: וַיֹּאמֶר לָכֵן שְׁמַע דְּבַר־יְהוָה ...

---

15 Cf. "Micha ben Jimla", p.115.

v.16: וַיֹּאמֶר אֵלָיו הַמֶּלֶךְ עַד־כַּמֶּה פְעָמִים אֲנִי מַשְׁבִּעֶךָ אֲשֶׁר לֹא־תְדַבֵּר אֵלַי רַק־אֱמֶת בְּשֵׁם יְהוָה׃
According to Würthwein's analysis, however, v.19 had not yet been added. It is, of course, possible, that this portion was inserted. The redactor would have added a reference to a further protagonist, Micaiah ben Imlah, and even to a secondary participant, the סָרִיס. Since the prophet story had no independent existence it is strange that the name of the prophet of the Lord is mentioned, but not the name of the Israelite king. With H.Seebaß,[16] who refers to O.Thenius, it needs to be emphasized that there is nothing unusual in the fact that prophets were consulted in face of a war. Thus there is no break between v.4 and v.5 - neither in form nor in contents.

The second strand comprises vv.10-12.24-25. Würthwein followed Schwally[17] in his analysis of this passage. Schwally saw a difficulty in v.10. He regarded v.10 not as an introduction of that episode but rather to the preceding one and thus, in his opinion, it is given too late. The presence of such a "late" introduction in Jer.$36_{21.22}$, may be taken as indication that this feature of the narrative should be regarded as a literary technique rather than as a sign of redactorial activity.[18] A further difficulty is seen between vv.6-7 and v.12. Schwally argued that v.12 was written as if the author did not know vv.6-7. Therefore he regarded v.12 as a parallel rather than as a continuation of vv.6-7. וְכָל־הַנְּבִאִים in v.12, however, clearly refers back to the earlier mention of the prophets. The repetition is used to express the connection between Zedekiah and the four hundred prophets and for intensifying the description of the conflict between Micaiah and the false prophets. It further served to show more clearly the parallelism between Micaiah's first answer and the false prophets' message. Micaiah's first answer to Ahab (v.15) resembles v.12 more closely than v.6:

v.6: עֲלֵה וְיִתֵּן אֲדֹנָי בְּיַד הַמֶּלֶךְ
v.12: עֲלֵה רָמֹת גִּלְעָד וְהַצְלַח וְנָתַן יהוה בְּיַד הַמֶּלֶךְ
v.15: עֲלֵה וְהַצְלַח וְנָתַן יהוה בְּיַד הַמֶּלֶךְ.[19]

---

16 "Micha ben Jimla", p.116, n.21.

17 "Zur Quellenkritik", pp.159-161.

18 Cf. also (1 Sam.25_3) 2 Sam.13_{18} 13_{32} 15_{10} 16_{23} $19_{1.5}$ (19_{33}).

19 The missing of רָמֹת גִּלְעָד in v.15 is due to the fact that it was mentioned in the king's question preceding Micaiah's answer, whereas it had not been mentioned in the passage preceding v.12.

That Zedekiah was one of the four hundred is not stated in the text and thus an explicit back reference to the prophecy of the four hundred is not to be expected. Therefore its absence cannot be used to support any theory.[20] Zedekiah is introduced as Micaiah's opponent. Still the problem remains to be solved, that v.28a refers back to v.19, but according to Würthwein's analysis v.19 had not been added at this stage. Furthermore, for the insertion v.10 no motivation is apparent. Zedekiah's reaction to strike Micaiah is better understandable if Micaiah has accused him of speaking with a lying spirit. The prophecy of the four hundred would have been sufficient reason for Ahab's and Jehoshaphat's going to war in spite of Micaiah's message. Micaiah's threat towards Zedekiah (v.25) is without consequence in the narrative, as noted above. No reason is given why it should have been added and why a redactor should not have added a remark on the fate of Zedekiah.

The third strand consists of vv.19-22. In the isolation of this passage Würthwein followed P.Volz[21] in referring to different conceptions of רוּחַ in vv.20-22 and v.24.[22] רוּחַ in vv.19-22 is supposed to be even more personalized than in v.24. The usage of רוּחַ in v.24 is, however, compatible with the mention of a person,[23] whereas this is different in vv.22a.23. If thus a difference is seen, it should be set between vv.19-21.22b.24 and vv.22a.23. v.22 provides a link between both usages of רוּחַ. The distinction therefore is to be regarded as artificial. Volz further argued that according to v.24 the reason for the false prophecy is that the רוּחַ יהוה has left, whereas according to vv.19-22 the reason is the presence of a רוּחַ שֶׁקֶר. However, these statements do not exclude each other. F.Schwally further drew attention to the fact that רוּחַ, albeit a femininum, is construed here with masc. verbs, which he linked to a development of the imagery of later times. To retain the established link between v.18 and v.24 he was, however, forced to delete רוּחַ from v.24. This is methodologically not justified. Whether his

---

[20] *Contra* F.Schwally, "Zur Quellenkritik", p.161, E.Würthwein, "Zur Komposition von 1 Reg 22_{1-38}", p.251.

[21] *Geist Gottes*, p.20.

[22] P.Volz (*Geist Gottes*, p.20) regards v.23 as a secondary linkage between vv.19-22 and v.24. There the concept of רוּחַ is regarded as less personalized; cf. also H.Schweizer, "Literarkritischer Versuch", p.7, n.12.

[23] The verbal form is masc.! As for the usage of עבר מֵאֵת with רוּחַ there is no fundamental structural difference between אֵי־זֶה עָבַר רוּחַ־יהוה מֵאִתִּי and וַנַּעֲבֹר מֵאֵת אַחֵינוּ (Dt.2_8).

evolutionary view of the development of רוּחַ-conceptions is correct or not does not concern us here. It is important that vv.19-23 and v.24 agree in their grammatical usage of רוּחַ. Würthwein further regarded the linkage between v.18 and v.19 as bad. The connection between v.18 (לוֹא־יִתְנַבֵּא עָלַי טוֹב כִּי אִם־רָע) and the prophecy of vv.19ff is found in v.23 (וַיהוה דִּבֶּר עָלֶיךָ רָעָה), which was regarded by Würthwein as a redactorial expansion. The latter is, however, without foundation. Zedekiah's reply with its reference to the רוּחַ יהוה speaking through Micaiah presupposes the presence of Micaiah's second prophecy. Only Micaiah's second prophecy contains the prophet's express claim to speak the word of the Lord (v.19:לָכֵן שְׁמַע דְּבַר־יהוה). A further difficulty, according to Würthwein, is found between v.17 and vv.24-25. The first passage implies a disaster only for Ahab, whereas the second passage, according to Würthwein, implies a greater catastrophe. It is, however, not stated anywhere in the narrative that both judgments would be carried out through the same event. The reference of בַּיּוֹם הַהוּא (v.25) is not clear. Possibly it refers back to Micaiah's prophecy, possibly to the day of Zedekiah's fear. The threat against Zedekiah only states that Zedekiah will hide himself on "that day". Thus the difficulty is, or at least may be, artificial. F.L.Hossfeld and I.Meyer[24] have adduced the following reasons for vv.19-23 being secondary:

- at the beginning of v.19 the speaker is not mentioned by name,
- only in this passage Ahab is mentioned by name,
- vv.8 and 18 have רָע, v.23 has רָעָה,
- only in vv.19-23 the prophets are termed Ahab's prophets,
- in vv.19-23 Micaiah's message is not given in a metaphor,
- v.24 cannot refer to vv.19-23, because Zedekiah would have misunderstood Micaiah.
- the narrative parallels Is.6_{1-8}.

They also referred to the similarity between 1 Kgs.22 and Is.6_{1-8}.

Each passage within the narrative necessarily has its own peculiarities. Thus it is not enough to point out these peculiarities, it needs to be shown that these features demand the assumption of redactorial activity. Of the features adduced by Hossfeld and Meyer only the difference between רָע and רָעָה and the missing mention of the speaker at the beginning of v.19 may be regarded as

---

24 Cf. *Prophet gegen Prophet*, p.32f.

redaction-critically significant. While the latter may be due to the fact that in v.19 Micaiah resumes the speech which had been interrupted, the former feature clearly does not point to different sources. The word-pair טוֹב / רַע, רָע is shorter and more common than טוֹבָה / רָעָה. Co-occurrences of רָע, רַע and רָעָה are not unusual.[25] As for the supposed parallelism with Is.$6_{1\text{-}8}$, this may be due to an author just as well as to a redactor.

If Würthwein's reconstruction is correct, the redactor, who incorporated the third strand into the narrative, would have added a second prophecy by Micaiah, necessitated by the addition of the first redactor. For the addition of Micaiah's second prophecy, however, no reason is apparent. If a redactor had added vv.19-22 it would have been more natural to insert it *before* v.18 and thus reduce the number of changes of the grammatical subjects and have both prophecies of Micaiah in one passage, especially since Micaiah's prophecy ends with וַיהוה דִּבֶּר עָלֶיךָ רָעָה (v.23) and Ahab complains לוֹא יִתְנַבֵּא עָלַי טוֹב כִּי אִם־רָע (v.18). However, we are not able to assess what redactors might have preferred, we can only examine whether the assumption of a redaction is required by the narrative in its present state or not, or at least if the assumption of a redaction makes sense or not. Any hypothetical literary development of a given text could be explained with the assumption of a sufficient number of redactions. The explanation with the smallest number of supposed redactions should be preferred. Thus it seems easier to assume the literary unity of at least the prophet story than to assume the sequence of these developmental stages. The prophet story would have to have be inserted in its supposed first stage of development and it seems strange that subsequent redactions should have affected only the prophet story and not the campaign narrative. Furthermore, there are internal inconsistencies if the material thought to have been added in redactions is omitted from the story in its present form.

---

25 Cf. Gen.6_{5} $44_{29.34}$, Num.$11_{10.15}$, 1 Sam.$29_{6.7}$, 2 Sam. $13_{16.22}$*, 1 Kgs.$21_{20.21.25.29}$, 2 Kgs. ($8_{12.18}$) $21_{2.6.9.12.15.16.20}$, Is.$3_{9.11}$, Jer. ($6_{19.29}$) $7_{6.12.24}$ $11_{8.12.14.15.17}$* ($12_{4.14}$) $15_{11.21}$ $16_{10.12}$ ($18_{8.10.11.12.20}$) ($23_{10.11.12.14.17.22}$)* $32_{23.30.32.42}$ $39_{12.16}$* $40_{2.4}$ $42_{6^{*}.10.17}$, Mi.$2_{1.3}$ 3_{2}*(ק"י)$_{.11}$*, Ps.$34_{14^{*}.15^{*}.17^{*}.20^{*}.22^{*}}$ $41_{6.8}$ $52_{3^{*}.5^{*}}$ $94_{13.23}$ $140_{2.3}$, Job $2_{3.7.10.11}$, (Pr.$6_{14.18}$ $11_{15.19.21.27}$, $13_{17.19.21}$ $14_{22.32}$ $15_{26.28}$ $16_{4.6}$ $17_{11.13}$ $24_{16.20}$ $26_{23.26}$ $28_{5.14.22}$, Ko.$2_{17.21}$ $8_{6.9.12}$); passages containing the word-pair טוֹב / רַע, רָע are marked with asterisk.

By the insertion of the prophet story and subsequent redactions the story is thought to have expanded and become more complex. To the main line of events side lines would have been added, which contrasts with the developmental tendencies recognized in our analysis of the transmission of Assyrian royal campaign accounts.

2. H.Seebaß' Analysis

H.Seebaß[26] in his literary analysis of 1 Kgs.22 reached conclusions similar to those of E.Würthwein. The advantage of his reconstruction is, that it reckons with greater units of text and thus makes the imagined redactions simpler. Seebaß regards as the story nucleus vv.1-9.13-19a.26-38. The campaign account and a basic prophet story are regarded as a unity. A redactorial expansion is seen in vv.19b-23. Seebaß thus sets paragraph divisions differently from Würthwein (13-18.19-22.23). He follows Würthwein in regarding the references to Zedekiah in vv.10-12.24-25 as secondary. V.19a is regarded as belonging to the story nucleus and referring back to Micaiah's first prophecy. Thus he is forced to read לֹא כֵן with the LXX (οὐχ οὕτως) for לָכֵן of the MT (v.19). Seebaß' reconstruction differs from that of Würthwein in that the former regards vv.19b-23 as being added earlier than vv.10-12.24.25. In principle, however, both approaches are similar and thus to be rejected for the same reasons.

3. H.Schweizer's Analysis

A different reconstruction of the literary development of the narrative of Ahab's war against the Arameans was suggested by H.Schweizer.[27] Schweizer reached the conclusion that the present version of the narrative is the result of the combination a basic narrative with one major redaction and a few minor expansions. The basic narrative consists of vv.3.6.9.15-16.19-28a.29*.34-35.

---

26 Cf. "Micha ben Jimla".
27 Cf. "Literarkritischer Versuch".

The redactorial treatment as reconstructed by Schweizer was not consistent. In vv.1-9 the redactor mainly took material from 2 Kgs.3[28] whereas in vv.10ff he felt free to present his own material. Schweizer discovered a difficulty between v.6 and vv.4-5.[29] While the latter passage mentions both kings, Ahab's question in v.6 only uses the singular. He further saw a tension between v.6 and v.10, and between vv.11-12 and v.15. In v.15 the king's question has the plural whereas Micaiah's answer has the singular. Like F.Schwally H.Schweizer ignored the fact that Micaiah's answer in v.15 constitutes a repetition of the false prophets' message.[30] Thus the difference in number may not be used for literary critical purposes. The plural form in Ahab's question in v.15 probably refers back to that in v.7 (וְנִדְרְשָׁה).[31] The supposed difficulty with the "late introduction" in v.10 has already been discussed above.[32] The "late" mention of Zedekiah is due to the same reason as the repeated reference to the prophets and the introduction of the scene in v.10, it leads to an increase of tension. The mentions of the two prophetic

---

28 Schweizer's argument for a literary dependency of 1 Kgs.$22_{4b.7}$ on 2 Kgs.$3_{7.11}$ (cf. *Elischa in den Kriegen*, pp.32ff) is not convincing. Schweizer argued that a redactor having to omit אֶל־מוֹאָב from 2 Kgs.3_7 added רָמֹת גִּלְעָד at the end of the sentence which resulted in "bad Hebrew". The Chronicler therefore omitted לַמִּלְחָמָה from 2 Kgs.3_7. It seems strange that a Hebrew editor should not have realized that he created a sentence in "bad Hebrew". It would have been easier for an editor to replace one adverbial phrase with another of the same kind. Schweizer further argued that the comparisons in 1 Kgs.22_{4b} lack a verb for reference. He failed to notice that in 2 Kgs.3_7 כָּמוֹנִי כָמוֹךָ cannot refer back to אֶעֱלֶה but rather constitutes an independent sentence. Furthermore, in 1 Kgs.22_4 אֶעֱלֶה (referring to Ahab only) would have been out of place, since it was Jehoshaphat who asked for a consultation of prophets. Schweizer also claimed that by the omission of אֶת־יהוה from 2 Kgs.3_{11} the editor of 1 Kgs.22_7 would have obscured the meaning of the sentence, since it was not clear who was inquired. This, too, has to be refuted since a) נָבִיא לַיהוה occurs in the first part of the sentence in both versions (1 Kgs.22_7, 2 Kgs.3_{11}), and b) in 1 Kgs.22_5 Jehoshaphat asks דְּרָשׁ־נָא ... אֶת־דְּבַר יהוה and thus in v.7 (וְנִדְרְשָׁה מֵאוֹתוֹ ...) the supplement was not necessary. Since literary dependency could not be demonstrated two other possible explanations for the similarities seem more probable: they could be due to the use of a fixed formula (thus I.Lande, quoted by Schweizer, *Elischa in den Kriegen*, p.34, n.39) or to a common author of both narratives (thus O.Thenius, *Könige*, pp.273-4).

29 Cf. "Literarkritischer Versuch", p.6.

30 Cf. above, p.191.

31 *Contra* Schweizer, who regarded Ahab and Micaiah as the reference of the plural in v.15. It should be noted that the LXX and T^f have sgl. in v.15.

32 Cf. above, p.191.

opponents are close to each other. Thus the supposed difficulties are artificial and cannot be used for the identification of hypothetical sources.

Schweizer further regarded the continuation of v.18 by לָכֵן[33] (v.19) as problematic. The only reason given by him is that such a continuation would be "makaber sadistisch".[34] Since the personal taste of the literary critic must not determine his methodology no conclusions may be drawn from this. Schweizer also regards Micaiah's two prophecies as so different in content and phraseology that it cannot be made probable that they belong together. Again, Schweizer's conclusions depend on his presuppositions. To render this argument valid it needs to be demonstrated - not merely stated - that the differences in vocabulary between the two prophecies were not due to the differences in meaning and that they are incompatible with the assumption of a single narrator. The differences between the Chronicler's *Sondergut* and the material taken over from 'Sam.-Kgs.' are in any case far greater than those between the two prophecies.

A further inconsistency is seen between v.31 and vv.34-35.[35] Vv.34-35 relate an extensive battle which, according to Schweizer, contrasts with v.31. This verse, however, does not contain an order to prevent fighting against the Israelite and Judean army, but rather to concentrate on trying to kill the Israelite king. The inconsistency apparent to Schweizer is to be regarded as artificial. The narration of the order of the Syrian king increases tension because it increases the probability that Ahab's plot could be successful in spite of Micaiah's prophecy. That Micaiah as נָבִיא לַיהוה was the true prophet is presumed throughout the narrative. Thus the confrontation of prophetic message and the king's attempt to escape the judgment is increased. Schweizer also regarded the twofold mention of Ahab's death and the double time statement in vv.35-36 as indications of redactorial intervention and concluded that the story originally ended with v.35a.[36] However, בָּעֶרֶב (v.35) and כְּבֹא הַשֶּׁמֶשׁ (v.36) differ in meaning.[37] Unless a convincing explanation can be given, why a second time denotation should have been

33 The reading of pc mss, לֹא כֵן, creates an internal inconsistency with v.23. Thus the MT is to be preferred.

34 "Literarkritischer Versuch", pp.7f.

35 Cf. "Literarkritischer Versuch", p.8.

36 The different mentions of Ahab's death will be briefly discussed below.

37 Cf. Jos.8_{29}, $10_{26.27}$.

inserted, the presence of the two expressions should not be related to redactorial intervention, but rather explained from a narrative point of view.

Schweizer also discovered difficulties between vv.12a and (8.)10b. In 10b נבא is used in the Hithpa'el, whereas in v.12 it is found in the Niph'al. This, however, is not unusual.[38] Schweizer further saw a tension between v.10 and v.15. While v.10 mentions the king of Israel and the king of Judah, v.15 relates that Micaiah came to the Israelite king - Jehoshaphat is not mentioned. This, however, can be explained by the fact that it was Ahab who had sent for Micaiah and that it is only the Israelite king who addresses the prophet. It is the confrontation between Ahab and the prophet of the Lord, that is of importance for the further course of events. Thus, again, the inconsistency is to be regarded as artificial. Therefore, the narrative features referred to by Schweizer are better explained as literary techniques than as indications of redactorial intervention.

The insufficiency of Schweizer's analysis becomes even clearer when the supposed development of the narrative is investigated. The basic narrative according to Schweizer is to be found in vv.3.6.9.15-16.19-28a.29*.34-35. There are various inconsistencies in this hypothetical story nucleus. Schweizer himself recognizes that the call for the prophet Micaiah is unmotivated.[39] Further unmotivated features of the narrative are the Israelite king's adjuration of Micaiah to tell the truth, after Micaiah had almost verbatim (v.12 is not part of the basic narrative) repeated the message of the four hundred prophets. Only the second prophecy of Micaiah is part of the story nucleus. This part of Micaiah's message explains the message of the false prophets. Without Micaiah's first prophecy the second prophecy would refer to Micaiah's first answer to the king. One further would expect the four hundred prophets to figure more prominently in the text since they are addressed by the only prophecy given in the story nucleus. Schweizer's reconstruction of the original narrative mentions them only in v.6. The reconstruction of the basic narrative contains too many inconsistencies and difficulties to be convincing. Zedekiah's reply to Micaiah includes אֵי־זֶה עָבַר

---

38 Further co-occurrences of Niph'al and Hithpa'el of נבא are found in 1 Sam.10_{11} (ni), 1 Sam.$10_{5.6.10.13}$ (hith); 1 Sam.19_{20} (ni), 1 Sam. $19_{20.21(2x).23.24}$ (hith); Jer.14_{14} (ni), Jer.14_{14} (hith); Jer.23_{16} (ni), Jer.23_{13} (hith); Jer.26_{20} (ni), Jer.26_{20} (hith); Jer.29_{31} (ni), Jer.$29_{26.27}$ (hith); Ez.13_{17} (ni), Ez.13_{17} (hith); Ez.37_{7} (ni), Ez.37_{10} (hith).

39 Cf. "Literarkritischer Versuch", p.11.

רוּחַ־יהוה מֵאִתִּי (v.24). This, especially the reference to עבר, is better understandable if a prophecy of Zedekiah preceded that of Micaiah. Furthermore, the king injured by an Israelite soldier (the Arameans are mentioned only in v.35) orders his charioteer to take him away from the camp[40] (v.34) but nevertheless continues to fight.[41] Micaiah would not be expressly mentioned as grammatical subject until v.25 if v.15 followed upon v.9. Especially for וַיָּבוֹא in v.15 one would expect a grammatical subject to be mentioned. Apart from the internal inconsistencies and difficulties created by the assumption of a basic story nucleus, the formal development would sharply contrast with the developmental tendencies apparent in the transmission of the empirical model suggested above. Again the redactor's ability to insert a substantial amount of text without having to alter or omit even a single word of his main *Vorlage* is astonishing. It would have been much easier to rewrite the whole narrative. Schweizer does not give any reason why the text should have been expanded. His reconstruction has a very simple participant orientation pattern. The redactor would have added a time statement (v.1) and an introductory remark introducing another participant, the king of Judah, and mentioning his presence at the Ahab's court (v.2). A redactor emphasizing the parallelism to the story narrated in 2 Kgs.3 could have taken over 2 Kgs.3_{7a}, but apparently he did not. He added a conversation between Ahab and Jehoshaphat (vv.4-5). While in the basic narrative it was Ahab who asked the four hundred prophets, in the expanded narrative this happens on Jehoshaphat's initiative (v.5). No reason is apparent why v.5 should have been inserted. The redactor would further have added vv.7-8, the second part of Jehoshaphat's and Ahab's conversation. While in the story nucleus it was Ahab, who called for Micaiah, in the expanded story this happens on Jehoshaphat's initiative. Again, no reason is apparent for such an alteration. The redactor further would have added vv.10-11. It has already been pointed out above, that the presence of v.10 does not require the assumption of redactorial intervention and that עבר in Zedekiah's reply to Micaiah's second prophecy (v.11) presupposes a preceding prophecy by Zedekiah.

---

40 Schweizer prefers the MT (מִן־הַמַּחֲנֶה, v.34) as *lectio difficilior* to the reading of the LXX (ἐκ τοῦ πολέμου - מִן־הַמִּלְחָמָה).

41 The implications of הֲפֹךְ יָדְךָ and כִּי will be discussed below in connection with H.Weippert's reconstruction of the literary history of 1 Kgs.22.

If a redactor added references to Jehoshaphat, which according to Schweizer's reconstruction was the case, it seems strange that in v.11 he should use the sgl. (תְּנַגַּח) and not the plural. The redactor further added vv.13-14, the conversation between Micaiah and the messenger sent by Ahab. This conversation is not necessary for the further course of narration. The redactor would have added a mention of a secondary participant as grammatical subject. In the story nucleus the messenger did not occur on the *main line*. The redactor further would have added vv.17a,18. Assuming that אֲדֹנִים (v.17b) refers to both kings, Schweizer treats v.17b as a further redactorial expansion. However, it is more natural to treat the grammatical plural as a notional singular here and to regard the expression as a parallel to רֹעֶה.[42] Micaiah addresses Ahab, not Jehoshaphat. Even to Ahab's question, containing a 1st pers.pl.[43] reference, the prophet replies with 2nd pers.sgl. (v.15).[44] There is thus no break between v.17a and v.17b. It has already been mentioned above that this prophecy is necessary for understanding the further course of narration and thus should be regarded as part of the original story. An insertion of vv.32f would only have diverted attention from the main course of events towards the resolution of the conflict. Ahab's attempt to escape judgement was not successful. The references to internal participant relations between the king of the Arameans and his subjects were not necessitated by the redactor's hypothetical *Vorlage*. Unless a convincing reason can be adduced why a redactor should have inserted these verses they should be regarded as part of the *original* narrative. We have also pointed out that there is no break between vv.35 and 36. The time statements in v.35 and v.36 are not synonymous but complementary.[45]

Furthermore, it is difficult to see, why v.37 should not have been present in the original form of the story, since Micaiah claimed that Ahab would not return in peace and Ahab claimed that he would. This conflict would have remained unresolved, if Schweizer's reconstruction was right and vv.35b and 38 belong together. It is possible to argue that both passages are secondary, but then it would not have been necessary to separate them into two parts. It would have

---

42 Cf. e.g. Is.19_4, Mal.1_6.

43 The sgl. forms in the LXX can be explained as adaptations to vv.6 and 15b.

44 Cf. also v.20.

45 Cf. above, p.197.

been easier for a redactor to add both remarks at the end of the narrative. Since there is no compelling reason that the two remarks should be regarded as redactorial insertions. It seems better to regard them as belonging to the *original* story. Thus as the only possible part of Schweizer's discussion remains that a redactor adapted 1 Kgs.22 to 2 Kgs.3 by the addition of vv.4b.4cd.7abc.

4. O.H.Steck's Analysis

A variation of Schweizer's approach was presented by O.H.Steck[46]. The main differences are:

v.11	Schweizer: strand B	Steck: strand A
vv.13-14	Schweizer: strand B	Steck: strand A
v.15[47]	Schweizer: strand A	Steck: strand B
v.16	Schweizer: strand A*	Steck: strand B
v.17	Schweizer: strand A	Steck: strand B
vv.19-23	Schweizer: strand A	Steck: strand B
vv.36[48]-37	Schweizer: strand B	Steck: strand A

The cardinal point of Steck's analysis is found in the observation that there are two separate layers of tradition in vv.24-28 and vv.19-23. In his view vv.24-28 do not presuppose vv.19-23. Steck conceived the following differences in the two strands:

- in v.24 Zedekiah only refers to himself, not to the other prophets
- according to v.24 the רוּחַ יהוה has left Zedekiah, whereas according to vv.19-23 Zedekiah still has the spirit, though a רוּחַ שֶׁקֶר
- v.25 announces judgment for Zedekiah, while according to vv.19-23 he acts according to the Lord's order.
- according to vv.24-28 Zedekiah's prophecy is false, because he does not have the spirit whereas according to vv.19-23 it is false because he does have the spirit (רוּחַ שֶׁקֶר).

From these observations Steck unfolded his analysis which led him to the conclusion that a basic narrative consisting of vv.3.6.11.9.13-15aα.17.24-28a.29*. 34-35abα.36*-37 was supplemented by vv.2b.4.5.7-8.10.12.15*.16.18-23.29*.30-33.36*.[49] Steck's reconstruction differs from Schweizer's in that the former

---

46 Cf. "Bewahrheitungen".

47 + minor addition.

48 + minor addition.

49 Steck regards vv.1-2a.35bβ.38 as linkages to the context (cf. "Bewahrheitungen", p.92).

regards v.11 as part of the original narrative and thus the introduction of Zedekiah is not as abrupt as in Schweizer's reconstruction. From the observation that Jehoshaphat is not mentioned in some passages (vv.3.6.11.17.24-28.34-37), where Steck had expected him to be mentioned, Steck deduced that the Judean king did not participate in the original story. However, in v.3 a mention of Jehoshaphat is not necessarily to be expected, since Ahab asks Jehoshaphat separately in v.4. The prophets' reply in v.6 is given in sgl. (עֲלֵה) since it was Ahab, who had asked them. Since the story took place at Ahab's court and Ahab is the initiator of the campaign,[50] the fact that "only" Ahab is asking the prophets is not surprising. Ahab's leading rôle in the undertaking also explains why vv.11.17.24-28.34-37 lack mentions of the Judean king (cf. v.20!).

Keeping v.11 as part of the original narrative, Steck altered the succession of verses found in the MT of 1 Kgs.22 and placed v.11 before v.9. This led to an immediate succession of order and fulfillment. Steck argued that the present position of v.9 is due to the fact that the redactor created a second scene at the gate. But it is difficult to see why he should not have been able to retain v.11 after v.6 or why vv.10.12 would have been added at all. Thus there is no reason for an alteration of the order v.11 - v.9. to the present one. Furthermore, there is the problem of the relative clause after the mention of the messenger in v.13, which is not necessary if v.13 immediately followed upon v.9. Steck, however, did not regard Micaiah's first answer (v.15aßb) as part of the original story. An addition of a first answer which did not reflect Micaiah's true opinion[51] would contrast

---

50 Ahab did not ask Jehoshaphat ... הֲנֵלֵךְ but rather הֲתֵלֵךְ אִתִּי; cf. also v.31, where only the Israelite king is mentioned as main target of the Aramean's agression.

51 Evidence for the ironic character of Micaiah's first answer may be seen in the fact that Micaiah repeats the false prophets' message of v.12 and refers to the king with (בְּיַד) הַמֶּלֶךְ whereas in his second prophecy he uses 2nd pers. (נְבִיאֶךָ, עָלֶיךָ; v.23). Ahab did not believe it was Micaiah's true opinion, as is shown by v.16! For בְּיַד הַמֶּלֶךְ in v.12 the LXX has *εἰς χεῖρας σου καὶ τὸν βασιλέα Συρίας*. O.Thenius, *Bücher der Könige*, p.255, took this as a reflection of the original text (בְּיָדֶיךָ גַּם הַמֶּלֶךְ אֲרָם {better: מֶלֶךְ אֲרָם}; possible is also יָדְךָ, cf. vv.6.15 {A} and a *Vorlage* without גַּם {cf.v.13}) which having become illegible was corrected towards v.6. Micaiah learned from the messenger only the content of the first prophecy of the four hundred. It is, of course possible that the text of the second prophecy was adapted, but not to the four hundred's first prophecy, but rather to Micaiah's answer (v.15) and/or the parallel text in Chr. A lacks *Συρίας* whereas the other mss. lack *και*. It is difficult, if not impossible, to decide which reading is original. The reading of the LXX contains the difficulty that the

with the developmental tendencies recognized in the first part of the present work. While Schweizer had regarded Micaiah's second prophecy (vv.19-23) as original, Steck argued that Micaiah's first prophecy (v.17) belongs to the story nucleus. In this respect Steck's reconstruction is inferior to Schweizer's, since Zedekiah's reaction suits Micaiah's second prophecy better than his first, because the second prophecy is directed against the false prophets. Furthermore, the splitting of v.15 makes the redactorial process imagined for 1 Kgs.22 more complex and thus the analysis less plausible. Steck draws attention to the fact that Micaiah is introduced with patronym in both v.8 and v.9. Since both mentions occur in direct speech towards different people (v.8 to Jehoshaphat, v.9 to the messenger) the patronym is necessary in both instances and its presence may not be used for literary critical analysis. Jehoshaphat did not know Micaiah, and the messenger had to know exactly whom to fetch. If v.8 and v.9 were not speech but narration and one of the two verses had been added by a redactor, the latter would, presumably, not have used the patronym. This could only have a certain probability if two independent sources had been combined, which evidently is not the case in Steck's reconstruction of the literary development of 1 Kgs.22_{1-38}.

Steck regarded the succession of events narrated in vv.13-18 as complicated. But Micaiah's first answer is clearly ironic[52] and thus there is no reason to assume that he changed his message. Steck's distinction of Micaiah's speaking evil (יִתְנַבֵּא עָלַי ... רָע; v.18) from the Lord ordering disaster (וַיהוה דִּבֶּר עָלֶיךָ רָעָה) is artificial. Micaiah is only secondary participant for the Lord (נבא) and רָע as well as רָעָה refer to the consequences of the message for Ahab. Thus the difficulty

---

phraseology would differ from v.6 (יָדֶיךָ / יַד הַמֶּלֶךְ) without apparent reason. Then we would expect Micaiah's answer to be adapted to the prophecy of the four hundred rather than vice versa. On the other hand the development of MT's reading is more easily explained than that of the LXX; in 1 Kgs.22 the LXX generally gives a literal translation. The different readings may be due to scribal error, since יַד הַמֶּלֶךְ and יָדֶיךָ מֶלֶךְ (which may have constituted the Vorlage of A only differ in one letter /sound. *Συρίας* may have been taken from v.11 *Συρίαν* (cf. also $20_{13.42}$). Since the correctness of the LXX's reading has not been demonstrated yet, we base our investigation on the MT. That the text of Kgs. was adapted to Chr. does not seem likely. Thus the alteration of the text of Kgs. would have to have taken place before the Chronicler's work, but nevertheless the LXX had a text with the correct reading. It seems easier to assume that the MT has the correct text.

52 Cf. above, pp.202f, n.51.

referred to by Steck is to be regarded as artificial. Steck further took up the argument that according to vv.30-33 only the Israelite king is the target of the Arameans' attack and not his army.[53] It has already been argued above that this view is not tenable.

We shall now examine the redactional process that follows from Steck's analysis. In Steck's story nucleus difficulties are found in the course of narration:

- v.3 would be a sudden beginning for a narrative
- the calling of Micaiah (v.9) is unmotivated[54]
- in the reference to the messenger in v.13 the subordinate clause is redundant, the exhortation to Micaiah is not necessary, since it implies that Micaiah's prophecy of doom was expected, then the calling of the prophet is even less motivated.
- Zedekiah's reaction (v.24) is not motivated.

The redactorial process as suggested by Steck's analysis, too, contains difficulties. Steck[55] regarded it as the main purpose of Strand "B" to supplement strand "A". "B" added references to Jehoshaphat and linked the consultations of the prophets to requests by the Judean king (vv.5.7f). "B" also introduced a second scene in which Zedekiah appeared. "B" further added a speech of Micaiah before and after the original one. Especially, the addition of Micaiah's first reply would be completely unmotivated. The addition of vv.4-5, an order the fulfillment of which is already reported, would contrast with the tendencies established above. The same is true for the addition of vv.7-8. We have already discussed the hypothetical addition of v.10 above. By the introduction of a new scene the plot would have become more complex. The addition of v.12, too, seems unmotivated, since the information had already been supplied in v.6. This has, however, the advantage against Schweizer's reconstruction that the form of Micaiah's answer in v.15 is explained. It would nevertheless have been easier to retain the phraseology of v.6. Unless the difficulties in both the reconstructed basic layer and the proposed redactorial treatment can be adequately explained Steck's analysis cannot be regarded as convincing. It is not sufficient to identify separate layers in a narrative; the redactorial process, too, has to be made probable.

---

53 Thus also Josephus, *Antiquities* VIII,15,5 (H.Clementz' edition, vol.I, p.541), who adds that with the exception of the Israelite king nobody was killed during the battle.

54 Especially the presence of מַהֲרָה is noteworthy.

55 Cf. "Bewahrheitungen", p.93.

5. H.Weippert's Analysis

In a recent essay[56] H.Weippert developed H.Schweizer's and O.H.Steck's analyses further. She started with the observation that the various participants are mentioned with different types of reference.[57] The Israelite king participating in the story is seventeen times mentioned as "king of Israel", twelve times as "the king"[58], and only once as Ahab[59] (+ twice in a "redactorial end note"). Both mentions of his opponent in war are as "king of Aram". Jehoshaphat, however, is mentioned three times as "Jehoshaphat, king of Judah" and ten times as "Jehoshaphat" only. Micaiah is mentioned once as "prophet of the Lord", seven times as "Micaiah", and twice as "Micaiah son of Imlah".[60] Zedekiah is mentioned twice as "Zedekiah" and twice as "Zedekiah son of Kenaanah". Further participants are "Amon the ruler of the city" and "Jehoash the king's son"[61] and many more, not mentioned by name. The designations for the two kings as given

---

56 "Ahab el campeador?".

57 Already been noted by E.Würthwein, "Zur Komposition von 1 Reg 22_{1-38}", pp.247-248.

58 Some of these cases have to be disregarded because the designations occur in direct speech (הַמֶּלֶךְ in vv.6.8.12.13.15.27, מֶלֶךְ יִשְׂרָאֵל in vv.31.32). הַמֶּלֶךְ outside direct speech is found in vv.15.16.35.37. Especially the passage in vv.13-17 is remarkable:
וְהַמַּלְאָךְ אֲשֶׁר־הָלַךְ לִקְרֹא מִיכָיְהוּ דִּבֶּר אֵלָיו לֵאמֹר הִנֵּה־נָא דִּבְרֵי הַנְּבִיאִים פֶּה־אֶחָד טוֹב אֶל־הַמֶּלֶךְ
יְהִי־נָא דְבָרְךָ כִּדְבַר אַחַד מֵהֶם וְדִבַּרְתָּ טּוֹב׃ וַיֹּאמֶר מִיכָיְהוּ חַי־יְהוָה כִּי אֶת־אֲשֶׁר יֹאמַר יְהוָה אֵלַי
אֹתוֹ אֲדַבֵּר׃ וַיָּבוֹא אֶל־הַמֶּלֶךְ וַיֹּאמֶר הַמֶּלֶךְ אֵלָיו מִיכָיְהוּ הֲנֵלֵךְ אֶל־רָמֹת גִּלְעָד לַמִּלְחָמָה אִם־נֶחְדָּל
וַיֹּאמֶר אֵלָיו עֲלֵה וְהַצְלַח וְנָתַן יְהוָה בְּיַד הַמֶּלֶךְ׃ וַיֹּאמֶר אֵלָיו הַמֶּלֶךְ עַד־כַּמֶּה פְעָמִים אֲנִי מַשְׁבִּעֶךָ
אֲשֶׁר לֹא־תְדַבֵּר אֵלַי רַק־אֱמֶת בְּשֵׁם יְהוָה׃ וַיֹּאמֶר רָאִיתִי אֶת־כָּל־יִשְׂרָאֵל נְפֹצִים אֶל־הֶהָרִים כַּצֹּאן
אֲשֶׁר אֵין־לָהֶם רֹעֶה וַיֹּאמֶר יְהוָה לֹא־אֲדֹנִים לָאֵלֶּה יָשׁוּבוּ אִישׁ־לְבֵיתוֹ בְּשָׁלוֹם׃
Here the reference to Ahab by הַמֶּלֶךְ seems to prepare for the prophecy in which he is referred to with רֹעֶה and אֲדֹנִים. The other passage using הַמֶּלֶךְ outside direct speech (vv.35.37) narrates Ahab's death with v.36 referring back to v.17 (אֶל־עִירוֹ, אֶל־אַרְצוֹ / לְבֵיתוֹ). הַמֶּלֶךְ may also have been used in the narrative sections to clarify the contrast between the prophecy of the four hundred and the later events. The four hundred stated that הַמֶּלֶךְ would be successful, but הַמֶּלֶךְ died. Thus to a certain extent the designations for Ahab seem to have served literary purposes and thus should not be taken as traces of redactorial activity. That Ahab is mentioned by name in v.20 is due to the fact that he was enticed not because he was king of Israel but because he was *Ahab*.

59 V.20 (direct speech).

60 Weippert adds one mention as "zur Jahwebefragung geeigneter Mann" but this cannot properly be called a mention of Micaiah. In v.8 Micaiah is mentioned in direct speech.

61 Weippert adds the mention of Ahaziah in 1 Kgs.22_{40}, but this verse is not part of the narrative proper.

by the narrative portions[62] of MT and LXX are as follows:

v.2			יְהוֹשָׁפָט מֶלֶךְ־יְהוּדָה	*Ιωσαφατ βασιλεὺς* Ιουδα
	מֶלֶךְ יִשְׂרָאֵל[63]	*βασιλέα* Ισραηλ		
v.3	מֶלֶךְ־יִשְׂרָאֵל	*βασιλεὺς* Ισραηλ		
v.4	-	*βασιλεὺς* Ισραηλ		
			יְהוֹשָׁפָט	*Ιωσαφατ*
			יְהוֹשָׁפָט	*Ιωσαφατ*
	מֶלֶךְ יִשְׂרָאֵל	-[64]		
v.5			יְהוֹשָׁפָט	*Ιωσαφατ βασιλεὺς* Ιουδα
	מֶלֶךְ יִשְׂרָאֵל	*βασιλέα* Ισραηλ		
v.6	מֶלֶךְ יִשְׂרָאֵל	*ὁ βασιλεὺς* Ισραηλ		
	-	*ὁ βασιλεύς*[65]		
v.7			יְהוֹשָׁפָט	*Ιωσαφατ*
	-	*βασιλέα* Ισραηλ		
v.8	מֶלֶךְ־יִשְׂרָאֵל	*ὁ βασιλεὺς* Ισραηλ		
			יְהוֹשָׁפָט	*Ιωσαφατ*
			יְהוֹשָׁפָט	*Ιωσαφατ βασιλεὺς* Ιουδα
v.9	מֶלֶךְ יִסְרָאֵל	*ὁ βασιλεὺς* Ισραηλ		
v.10	מֶלֶךְ יִשְׂרָאֵל	*ὁ βασιλεὺς* Ισραηλ[66]		
			יְהוֹשָׁפָט מֶלֶךְ־יְהוּדָה	*Ιωσαφατ βασιλεὺς* Ιουδα
v.15	הַמֶּלֶךְ	*τὸν βασιλέα*		
	הַמֶּלֶךְ	*ὁ βασιλεύς*		
v.16	הַמֶּלֶךְ	*ὁ βασιλεύς*		
v.18	מֶלֶךְ־יִשְׂרָאֵל	*βασιλεὺς* Ισραηλ		
			יְהוֹשָׁפָט	*Ιωσαφατ βασιλέα* Ιουδα
v.26	מֶלֶךְ יִשְׂרָאֵל	*ὁ βασιλεὺς* Ισραηλ		
v.29	מֶלֶךְ־יִשְׂרָאֵל	*βασιλεὺς* Ισραηλ		
			יְהוֹשָׁפָט מֶלֶךְ־יְהוּדָה	*Ιωσαφατ βασιλέα* Ιουδα
v.30	מֶלֶךְ יִשְׂרָאֵל	*ὁ βασιλεὺς* Ισραηλ		
			יְהוֹשָׁפָט	*Ιωσαφατ βασιλέα* Ιουδα
v.32			יְהוֹשָׁפָט	*Ιωσαφατ βασιλέα* Ιουδα
			יְהוֹשָׁפָט	*Ιωσαφατ*
v.33	מֶלֶךְ יִשְׂרָאֵל	*βασιλεὺς* Ισραηλ		
v.34	מֶלֶךְ יִשְׂרָאֵל	*τὸν βασιλέα* Ισραηλ		
	-	-[67]		
v.35	הַמֶּלֶךְ	*ὁ βασιλεύς*		
v.37	הַמֶּלֶךְ	*ὁ βασιλεύς*		
	הַמֶּלֶךְ	*τὸν βασιλέα*[68]		

62 The mentions within speeches have been disregarded here, since e.g. the form of an address of a king may not have been open to the narrator's choice.

63 LXX^{L} adds Αχααβ.

64 LXX^{O}: + ※ *πρὸς βασιλέα* Ισραηλ.

65 LXX^{L}: + Ισραηλ.

66 LXX^{L}: + Αχααβ.

67 LXX^{L}: + *ὁ βασιλεύς*.

68 LXX^{L}: + Αχααβ.

From the fact that the Israelite king in MT's version of the story is not mentioned by name in 29 cases (including mentions within speeches) Weippert concluded that his name was secondarily introduced. She disregarded the additional mentions of the name by the LXX. While it is apparent that the LXX adapted mentions of Jehoshaphat to those of the Israelite king, it cannot be ruled out completely that the LXX in its mentions of Ahab was dependent on a Hebrew text and thus could represent a version closer to the original than MT.[69] In the investigation above it became apparent that later versions tended to concentrate on *functions* of events or participants rather than proper names.[70] Thus, e.g. in the Chronicler's version of Ahaz's call for help (2 Chr.28_{16}) Tiglathpileser is referred to as "king of Assyria" and not, as in 2 Kgs.16_{7}, mentioned by name. The same is true for the mention of the Aramean king in 2 Chr.$24_{23\text{-}24}$. Again the corresponding passage in 2 Kgs.$12_{18\text{-}19}$ had the name. Thus it cannot be ruled out that during the transmission of the narrative mentions of the Israelite king's name were replaced by those of his title.

In the Old Testament narratives about Ahab there is a striking inconsistency of referring to the Israelite king. While chs.18 and 21 almost exclusively use the proper name this is different in chs.20 and 22. Designations for the Israelite king in the narrative portions of ch.20 (LXX: ch.21) are:

v.2	אַחְאָב מֶלֶךְ־יִשְׂרָאֵל	Αχααβ βασιλέα Ισραηλ
v.4	מֶלֶךְ־ישׂראל	ὁ βασιλεὺς Ισραηλ
v.7	מֶלֶךְ־יִשְׂרָאֵל	ὁ βασιλεὺς Ισραηλ
v.11	מֶלֶךְ־יִשְׂרָאֵל	ὁ βασιλεὺς Ισραηλ
v.13	אַחְאָב מֶלֶךְ־יִשְׂרָאֵל	τῷ βασιλεῖ Ισραηλ
v.14	אַחְאָב	Αχααβ
	-	Αχααβ
v.15	-	Αχααβ
v.21	מֶלֶךְ יִשְׂרָאֵל	βασιλεὺς Ισραηλ
v.22	מֶלֶךְ יִשְׂרָאֵל	βασιλέα Ισραηλ
v.28	מֶלֶךְ יִשְׂרָאֵל	τῷ βασιλεῖ Ισραηλ
v.32	מֶלֶךְ יִשְׂרָאֵל	τῷ βασιλεῖ Ισραηλ
v.38	לַמֶּלֶךְ	τῷ βασιλεῖ Ισραηλ
v.39	הַמֶּלֶךְ	ὁ βασιλεύς
	הַמֶּלֶךְ	τὸν βασιλέα
v.40	מֶלֶךְ־יִשְׂרָאֵל	ὁ βασιλεὺς Ισραηλ

69 S.J.DeVries, *1 Kings*, pp.261f, regards the additional mentions of Ahab's name in the LXX as "explicative" and thus secondary.

70 Cf. above, pp.90f, pp.167f with n.362, p.170.

v.41	מֶלֶךְ יִשְׂרָאֵל	ὁ βασιλεὺς Ισραηλ
v.43	מֶלֶךְ־יִשְׂרָאֵל	ὁ βασιλεὺς Ισραηλ

Here the prophet / man of God mentioned in the narrative remains anonymous, but the name of the Aramean king is given. Again it may be argued that in ch.20, too, the mentions of Ahab are secondary.[71] But then the question has to be answered why the narrative was thought to be dealing with Ahab, since there is no other connection between Benhadad and Ahab reported in the OT. There is a very interesting parallel in 2 Kgs.3 narrating a war of Joram and Jehoshaphat against Moab. The designations for the two kings are:

v.4	לְמֶלֶךְ־יִשְׂרָאֵל	τῷ βασιλεῖ Ισραηλ		
v.5	בְּמֶלֶךְ יִשְׂרָאֵל	ἐν βασιλεῖ Ισραηλ		
v.6	הַמֶּלֶךְ יְהוֹרָם	ὁ βασιλεὺς Ιωραμ		
v.7			יְהוֹשָׁפָט מֶלֶךְ־יְהוּדָה	Ιωσαφατ βασιλέα Ιουδα
v.9	מֶלֶךְ יִשְׂרָאֵל	ὁ βασιλεὺς Ισραηλ		
			מֶלֶךְ־יְהוּדָה	ὁ βασιλεύς Ιουδα
v.10	מֶלֶךְ יִשְׂרָאֵל	ὁ βασιλεὺς Ισραηλ		
v.11			יְהוֹשָׁפָט	Ιωσαφατ
	מֶלֶךְ־יִשְׂרָאֵל	βασιλέως Ισραηλ		
v.12			יְהוֹשָׁפָט	Ιωσαφατ
	מֶלֶךְ יִשְׂרָאֵל	βασιλεὺς Ισραηλ		
			יְהוֹשָׁפָט[72]	Ιωσαφατ βασιλεὺς Ιουδα
v.13	מֶלֶךְ יִשְׂרָאֵל	βασιλέα Ισραηλ		
	מֶלֶךְ יִשְׂרָאֵל	ὁ βασιλεὺς Ισραηλ		

Joram is introduced with יְהוֹרָם בֶּן־אַחְאָב מָלַךְ עַל־יִשְׂרָאֵל (v.1) and then referred to by מֶלֶךְ יִשְׂרָאֵל (vv.4.5.9.10.11.12.13{2x}) and only once by הַמֶּלֶךְ יְהוֹרָם (v.6).[73] The Judean king, however, is mentioned four times as יְהוֹשָׁפָט

---

71 Thus S.J.DeVries, *1 Kings*, p.247, who regards the mentions of "Ahab" in v.2 and v.14 as later additions and prefers for v.13 the reading of the LXX lacking an equivalent for "Ahab". The LXX, however, has additional mentions of Αχααβ in vv.14.15. It is methodologically unjustified to regard in both the MT in v.13 and the LXX in (ch.21) vv.14.15 the longer text without further reasons as "explicative" (cf. DeVries, *1 Kings*, p.244). Cf. also the David-Goliath story (1 Sam.17) where Goliath is usually called הַפְּלִשְׁתִּי and only twice mentioned by name or Rab-shakeh's speech to the Jerusalemites (2 Kgs.$18_{19-25.29-35}$) mentioning Hezekiah by name and referring to the Assyrian king as הַמֶּלֶךְ הַגָּדוֹל מֶלֶךְ אַשּׁוּר (cf. M.Cogan and H.Tadmor, *II Kings*, pp.230f).

72 2 mss + מֶלֶךְ יְהוּדָה.

73 The two narratives are similar in that in both instances the Israelite king asks to join him against a foreign king, who acted wrongfully. The parallelism extends to phraseology:

1 Kgs.22_4: הֲתֵלֵךְ אִתִּי לַמִּלְחָמָה רָמֹת גִּלְעָד וַיֹּאמֶר ... כָּמוֹנִי כָמוֹךָ כְּעַמִּי כְעַמֶּךָ כְּסוּסַי כְּסוּסֶיךָ

2 Kgs.3_7: הֲתֵלֵךְ אִתִּי אֶל־מוֹאָב לַמִּלְחָמָה וַיֹּאמֶר אֶעֱלֶה כָּמוֹנִי כָמוֹךָ כְּעַמִּי כְעַמֶּךָ כְּסוּסַי כְּסוּסֶיךָ

(מֶלֶךְ־יְהוּדָה) and only once as מֶלֶךְ־יְהוּדָה. Both narratives have to be treated in the same way. If the designations for the king in 1 Kgs.22 are regarded as an indication that the story originally dealt with a different Israelite king then the same has to be assumed for 2 Kgs.3. There however, the chronological position of the narrative is clearer. There is a reference to Ahab's death in v.5 which seems to imply that the Israelite king mentioned in the narrative is Ahab's successor. It is interesting to note that in the first reference to Ahab, in v.4, again מֶלֶךְ־יִשְׂרָאֵל is employed, and only in the second mention in v.5 his name is given. But our concern is not with whether the story in 1 Kgs.22 was originally about Ahab but rather whether the picture of its evolution as it is drawn with the application of common literary-critical methods and presuppositions agrees with the empirical model suggested above. It is, of course, in principle not impossible that the story was originally not told about a specific king or a king not identical with Ahab. If the protagonist of the story was secondarily identified with Ahab, it nevertheless remains a striking fact that the redactor did make this clearer. The only mention of the king's name within the story proper is found in Micaiah's prophecy and not, where it would have been more expected, used by the narrator in a narrative portion.[74]

That there is no need to explain the references to the Israelite king in 1 Kgs.22 as secondary insertions is further underlined by the fact that in several Babylonian Chronicles the mentions of the protagonists are comparable to those of 1 Kgs.22.[75] A first example is provided by Chronicle 3's report of Nabopolassar's 12th year:[76]

In both instances the Judean king requests the consultation of a "prophet of the Lord:
1 Kgs.22_7: וַיֹּאמֶר יְהוֹשָׁפָט הַאֵין פֹּה נָבִיא לַיהוה עוֹד וְנִדְרְשָׁה מֵאוֹתוֹ
2 Kgs.3_{11}: וַיֹּאמֶר יְהוֹשָׁפָט הַאֵין פֹּה נָבִיא לַיהוה וְנִדְרְשָׁה אֶת־יהוה מֵאוֹתוֹ.
The remainders of the narratives, however, differ completely from each other.

74 If the story was written down in the northern kingdom it might not have been necessary to mention Ahab by name. H.Seebaß has proposed that the Israelite king was not mentioned by name because by this the typical characteristics of an era, which was marked by the alliance with Judah, were meant to be captured (cf. "Micha ben Jimla", p.116).

75 Text and designations of the Chronicles are taken from A.K.Grayson, *Assyrian and Babylonian Chronicles*.

76 BM 21901 (96-4-9,6); cf. A.K.Grayson, *Assyrian and Babylonian Chronicles*, pp.90-96.

24 *M[U] XII ina Abi Madayya ana muḫḫi Ninua kī x x x* [...]
25 *[x (x)x iḫīšamma Tarbiṣu ālu ša pīḫāt Ninua i[ṣṣ]abtū x*[...]
26 *[Id]iqlat irdīma ina muḫḫi Baltil ittadi ṣāltu ana libbi āli* ⌜*īpuš*⌝*m[a...]*
27 *[x]x ittaqar dabdâ nišē rabâti lemniš iltakan ḫubussu iḫtabat šil[lassu ištalal]*
28 *[šar A]kkadî u [ummā]nīšu ša ana rēṣūt Madayya illikū ṣāltu ul ikšudū āl[u] x* [...]
29 *[šar Akkad]î [u(?)]U[maki]štar ina muḫḫi āli aḫāmeš ittamrū ṭūbtu u sulummû itti aḫāmeš iškunū*
30 *[...Umaki]štar u ummānīšu ana mātīšu itūr šar Akkadî u ummānīšu ana mātīšu itūrū*

24 "12th ye[ar]: In the month Ab the Medes, when [...] against Nineveh
25 they hurried, Tarbiṣu, a city in the district of Nineveh, they captured [...]
26 they went along the [Ti]gris, set up (their camp) against Baltil, fought against the city [...]
27 they destroyed; they inflicted a terrible defeat upon a great people, they took their spoil, [carried off their] boo[ty]
28 [the king of A]kkad and his army, who had gone to the aid of the Medes, did not reach battle. The ci[ty ...]
29 [the king of Akkad] and C[yax]ares met one another because of the city. They established (a treaty of) reconciliation and peace and with one another.
30 [... Cyaxa]res and his army returned to his country, the king of Akkad and his army returned to his country".

Here we can note that in l.29 two kings are mentioned in grammatical co-ordination.[77] Cyaxares, king of the Medes, is mentioned by name only (as e.g. in l.30), without any apposition - not even introduced as king of the Medes, whereas Nabopolassar is generally referred to as *šar Akkadî* ("king of Akkad") without express mention of his name. Indeed, his name is mentioned only once, at the beginning of the tablet in l.1, dealing with his tenth regnal year; he otherwise is only referred to as "king of Akkad" (ll.6.8.10.11.16[78].18.19.20.21.28[79].29[80].30. 31.[32].38.38[81].40[82].46.47.49.53[83].56.58.59.63.64.[84]65[85].68.70.75.76). Contrarily, apart from Cyaxares (ll.29.30.40.47), also Sin-šarra-iškun (l.44), Aššur-uballiṭ (ll.[49.60].61.66) are mentioned by name. Strikingly l.30 exhibits another feature which is also found 1 Kgs.22: while in the first part of the line the com-

77 Cf. also l.40: *[š]ar Akkadî* [x] x [...*Um]akištar x x x-a-ni ušēbirma* ("[the k]ing of Akkad [... Cy]axares brought across") followed by *illikūma* ("they marched", l.41).
78 Only *šàr Akkadî*^{ki} preserved.
79 Only *A]kkadî* preserved.
80 Only *[šàr Akkad]î*⌜$^{ki(?)}$⌝ preserved.
81 Only *šàr Akk[adî*^{ki} preserved.
82 Only *[š]àr Akkadî*^{k}[^{i} preserved.
83 Only *šà]r Akkadî*^{ki} preserved.
84 Only *šàr [Akkadî]*^{ki} preserved.
85 Only *[šàr] Akkadî*[^{ki}] preserved.

pound subject is construed with a verb in the sgl., in the second part of the line a very similar grammatical subject is construed with a verb in the pl.[86]

The case is similar in Chronicle 4.[87] There, again, Nabopolassar is mentioned only in the first line and thereafter referred to as "king of Akkad" (ll.1.4.5.8.12.17.18.18.23.27), while his son Nebuchadnezzar is mentioned by name (ll.6.9.27), though in the first and final mentions with appositions.[88] In the preserved portion of Chronicle 5[89], which includes the first line of the tablet, we find another parallel to 1 Kgs.22. Just as Ahab in the Biblical account, Nabopolassar's name is not stated in his first mention in obv.1 (*šar Akkadî*), but only later (obv.9). His son Nebuchadnezzar is introduced as *Nabû-kudurrī-uṣur māršu rabû* [*mār*] *šarri ša bīt redûtu* ("Nebuchadnezzar, his eldest son, the crown prince", obv.1) and thereafter mentioned by name only (obv.8.9.10.12.15) until his accession is reported (obv.15). Then he is referred to as *šar Akkadî* in obv.21, rev.3.5. 8.9.11.14.16.18.21.25 and once as *šarru* ("the king"), which further parallels mentions of Ahab in 1 Kgs.22 (הַמֶּלֶךְ in vv.15.16.35.37). In Chronicle 5, rev.2 a certain *Nabû-šuma-*⌜*lišir*⌝ is mentioned in a passage where the Babylonian king is only referred to as "king of Akkad". Chronicle 7[90] is not well preserved.[91] It, therefore, does not permit firm conclusions. The extant mentions of the Babylonian king are: *šarru* ($i_{3(?).7.14}$, $ii_{5.[5.]10.18.19.23.[23.]}$, iii_{23}), *Nabû-nā'id* (iii $_{15.16}$). Because of the tablet's bad state of preservation it is not possible to argue with any certainty that the first mention of Nabonidus did not include his name, but in the light of the previous example it would be quite conceivable. Further participants are: *Nabû-bēl-dān aḫu* [... ("Nabu Bel-dan, brother [...", i_{15f}), *Kuraš šar Anšan* ("Cyrus, king of Anšan", ii_1) / *Kuraš* ($ii_{2.3}$, $iii_{12.15.18.19[.24]}$) / *Kuraš šar Parsu* ("Cyrus, king of Parsu", ii_{15}), *Ištumegu* (ii_2), ⌜*Ug*⌝*baru* ($iii_{15.22}$) / *Gubaru* (iii_{20}), *Kambuzia māru sa K*[*uraš*] ("Cambyses, son of C[yrus]", iii_{24}). Thus again we have an unbalanced pattern of participant mentions. If, therefore, it is argued

---

86 Cf. 1 Kgs.22_{10}: יֹשְׁבִים (pl.) and 1 Kgs.22_{19}: וַיַּעַל (sgl.).
87 BM 22047 (96-4-9,152); cf. A.K.Grayson, *Assyrian and Babylonian Chronicles*, pp.97-98.
88 Cf. also l.8, where he is referred to as *mār šarri* ("son of the king").
89 BM 21946 (96-4-9).
90 BM 35382 (Sp II 964).
91 Cf. A.K.Grayson, *Assyrian and Babylonian Chronicles*, p.104: "Besides some surface breaks the bottom and most of the left-hand side of the tablet is missing."

that the mentions of the Israelite king's name in 1 Kgs.22 are secondary, the same has to be held for the mentions of the Babylonian kings in the Babylonian Chronicles referred to above. There is, however, no indication at all for the latter.[92]

Weippert followed E.Würthwein in arguing that the twofold introduction of Jehoshaphat's speech(es) in vv.4.5 indicates two different sources / redactions.[93] Further features of the narrative in 1 Kgs.22, to which H.Weippert drew attention are that the death of the Israelite king is reported three times (vv.35.37.40)[94], that after Jehoshaphat's cry (v.32) nothing else is reported about him,[95] that it is not related what happened to Micaiah who had been thrown into prison,[96] and that the threat against Zedekiah has no consequences in the narratives. The last of the three mentions of Ahab's death is not part of the narrative

---

92 The parallels in the Babylonian Chronicles may suggest that the narrative in 1 Kgs.22 was recorded in the northern kingdom where the name of הַמֶּלֶךְ was self-evident. This contrasts with the view that the criticism of the Israelite king implies that the narrative was written down in Judah (cf. H.-C.Schmitt, *Elisa*, p.45).

93 Cf. above, pp.187f.

94 וַיִּשְׁכַּב אַחְאָב עִם־אֲבֹתָיו in v.40 is regarded as implying a peaceful death (probably first adduced by G.Hölscher, "Das Buch der Könige", p.185; taken up by H.Weippert {"Ahab el campeador?", p.464}, S.J.DeVries {*1 Kings*, p.97}, C.F.Whitley {"Deuteronomic Presentation", p.148} and others), claiming that the formula is not applied anywhere in the Old Testament to a violent death of a king. In 2 Kgs.14_{22} we find, however, the clause אַחֲרֵי שְׁכַב־הַמֶּלֶךְ עִם־אֲבֹתָיו, referring to the death of Amaziah, who is expressly stated to have been assassinated. DeVries notes this clause but regards it as a gloss. Even if this should be the case, it nevertheless shows that a violent death is compatible with its description as שׁכב. B.Alfrink, "L'expression שָׁכַב עִם אֲבוֹתָיו", p.109, interprets הַמֶּלֶךְ in 2 Kgs.14_{22} as referring to the king of Edom, but neither Edom nor its king are mentioned in this passage, only Elath. It therefore seems more probable that הַמֶּלֶךְ refers to Azariah's father Amaziah, who is mentioned in 1 Kgs.14_{21}. Thus the remark in 1 Kgs.22_{40} cannot be used for arguing that the story in 1 Kgs.22 originally dealt with a different Israelite king. As further indication of Ahab's peaceful death 1 Kgs.9_{26} is quoted, but that passage applies only to Ahab's *house*, not to Ahab himself. H.Seebaß, "Zu 1 Reg XXII 35-38" suggested, that the formula could be used, because the king did not die during the battle but later from his loss of blood (cf. H.Seebaß' reconstruction of the original text below, p.213, n.98). Anyway it remains to be shown that, even if presupposed that one or both of the two short remarks imply a peaceful death their historical reliability is greater than that of the narrative in 1 Kgs.22.

95 Cf. however אִישׁ אֶל־אַרְצוֹ in v.36 (cf. below, p.215 with n.102). Unless a reason can be given, why the final redactor did not relate Jehoshaphat's fate, Weippert's stages of development necessarily contain the same inconsistencies as she claims MT has.

96 Cf. E.Würthwein, "Zur Komposition von 1 Reg 22_{1-38}", pp.246-247.

proper but in an end note[97] and thus should not be counted. As for the second mention of the king's death, the LXX has it as a continuation of the direct speech from v.36 (MT: וַיָּמָת הַמֶּלֶךְ, LXX: ὅτι τέθνηκεν ὁ βασιλεύς {כִּי מֵת הַמֶּלֶךְ}, וַיָּבוֹא is represented by ἦλθον {וַיָּבֹאוּ}).[98] It is, therefore, no certain case either. וַיָּמָת can also be understood as Pluperfect, which would reduce the significance of the second mention of the king's death. The repetition of the mention of the king's death by an author seems more probable than that a redactor should have added a reference to it if one was already present. As for the other features of the narrative, the absence of narrations of the fates of Jehoshaphat and Micaiah and the unfulfilled threat against Zedekiah, these could be explained by omission, whether by the author or a later redactor cannot be decided. This, however, is not taken into consideration by H.Weippert. On the contrary, her reconstruction was based on the assumption of a continuous growth from a nucleus to the present version.

H.Weippert regards vv.3a-c.11a-d.29a*[99].34a-35c as the narrative nucleus:

[3]וַיֹּאמֶר מֶלֶךְ־יִשְׂרָאֵל אֶל־עֲבָדָיו הַיְדַעְתֶּם כִּי־לָנוּ רָמֹת גִּלְעָד וַאֲנַחְנוּ מַחְשִׁים מִקַּחַת אֹתָהּ מִיַּד מֶלֶךְ אֲרָם׃
[11]וַיַּעַשׂ לוֹ צִדְקִיָּה בֶן־כְּנַעֲנָה קַרְנֵי בַרְזֶל וַיֹּאמֶר כֹּה־אָמַר יהוה בְּאֵלֶּה תְּנַגַּח אֶת־אֲרָם עַד־כַּלֹּתָם׃
[29]וַיַּעַל מֶלֶךְ־יִשְׂרָאֵל רָמֹת גִּלְעָד׃
[34]וְאִישׁ מָשַׁךְ בַּקֶּשֶׁת לְתֻמּוֹ וַיַּכֶּה אֶת־מֶלֶךְ יִשְׂרָאֵל בֵּין הַדְּבָקִים וּבֵין הַשִּׁרְיָן וַיֹּאמֶר לְרַכָּבוֹ הֲפֹךְ יָדְךָ
וְהוֹצִיאֵנִי מִן־הַמַּחֲנֶה כִּי הָחֳלֵיתִי׃ [35]וַתַּעֲלֶה הַמִּלְחָמָה בַּיּוֹם הַהוּא וְהַמֶּלֶךְ הָיָה מָעֳמָד בַּמֶּרְכָּבָה נֹכַח
אֲרָם וַיָּמָת בָּעָרֶב.

While it remains to be made plausible why such a story should be transmitted in the first place, the main concern of the present part of the investigation

---

97 For another case where (because of particular circumstances) the death of a king has been reported in a narrative and in the end note cf. 2 Kgs.$14_{19.22}$, cf. also 1 Sam.$31_{4.5.6.7.8}$ 1 Kgs.$15_{27.28}$.

98 H.Seebaß has advanced a different explanation of the twofold mention of Ahab's death (cf. "Zu 1 Reg XXII 35-38"). He regards the MT of v.37 as correct but prefers his reconstruction of the *Vorlage* of the LXX in v.35. There MT reads: וַיָּמָת בָּעֶרֶב וַיִּצֶק דַּם־הַמַּכָּה אֶל־חֵיק הָרָכֶב. The LXX has: *ἀπο πρωὶ ἕως ἑσπέρας καὶ ἀπέχυννε τὸ αἷμα ἐκ τῆς πληγῆς εἰς τὸν κόλπον τοῦ ἅρματος*. Seebaß suggests that the LXX has preserved in this passage translations of variant readings which arose through scribal error: וַיָּמָת בָּעֶרֶב / מִבֹּקֶר עַד עֶרֶב (2 Chr.18_{34} has עַד הָעֶרֶב). The omission / addition of עד could be explained as Haplo- / Dittography. There remain וימת ב and מבקר. מ and ב are found in both phrases and ד/ר ק/ת ו/ר are similar in the Aramaic cursive script of the 4th and 3rd centuries. Seebaß regards מִבֹּקֶר עַד עֶרֶב as the original reading, since וַיָּמָת would have been mentioned too early in the narrative. וַיָּבוֹא שֹׁמְרוֹן with Ahab as grammatical subject would then contrast with Ahab's order עַד בֹּאִי בְשָׁלוֹם ... (v.27) and agree with Micaiah's confirmation of his prophecy ... אִם־שׁוֹב תָּשׁוּב בְּשָׁלוֹם (v.28).

99 וִיהוֹשָׁפָט is regarded as secondary addition.

is to examine whether the supposed expansion of this story agrees with the developmental tendencies recognized from the transmission of the empirical model proposed above. There are, however, serious inconsistencies in this supposed story nucleus. According to Weippert the Israelite king is injured before the battle by one of his own soldiers[100] but nevertheless he orders to take him out of his camp into battle. מַחֲנֶה, however, does not necessarily designate a stationary camp, but can also mean "army".[101] From Ahab's order to his charioteer it is clear that the narrator did not refer to the Israelite camp. הֲפֹךְ יָדְךָ implies a *return* and the injury is given as reason (כִּי) for the order. The Israelite king wants to return *because* and not *although* he is injured. If Weippert's reconstruction was right, both phrases would have to be regarded as later additions. Another difficulty with her proposed story nucleus is found in the fact that Zedekiah's prophecy was not fulfilled. Thus it is not superior to the Massoretic version where the fulfillment of Micaiah's threat against Zedekiah was not reported. H.Weippert claims that Zedekiah's prophecy *was* fulfilled in the story nucleus, but there is no hint of an Israelite victory. On the contrary, the king died. It is surprising that far-reaching alterations could have been applied to a narrative and nevertheless the wording of the original narrative have been completely preserved to allow its reconstruction. Furthermore, there would be no preparation for the situation of battle in v.35 if Weippert's analysis was correct. In the reconstructed nucleus Zedekiah would not be introduced as a prophet in v.11. If, however, v.11 is read after v.10 this becomes clear from the context, since Zedekiah may have been regarded as one of כָּל־הַנְּבִיאִים.

In the second stage, according to Weippert's reconstruction, the narrative was set into context with other stories about wars between Israel and Aram and expanded by vv.1ab.2a.36a-37c:

1 וַיֵּשְׁבוּ שָׁלֹשׁ שָׁנִים אֵין מִלְחָמָה בֵּין אֲרָם וּבֵין יִשְׂרָאֵל׃ 2 וַיְהִי בַּשָּׁנָה הַשְּׁלִישִׁית

36 וַיַּעֲבֹר הָרִנָּה בַּמַּחֲנֶה כְּבֹא הַשֶּׁמֶשׁ לֵאמֹר אִישׁ אֶל־עִירוֹ וְאִישׁ אֶל־אַרְצוֹ׃ 37 וַיָּמָת הַמֶּלֶךְ וַיָּבוֹא שֹׁמְרוֹן וַיִּקְבְּרוּ אֶת־הַמֶּלֶךְ בְּשֹׁמְרוֹן׃

While the insertion of a transition passage is conceivable it is not clear

---

100 "Das ist die Art und Weise, wie die Sage ihre Helden sterben läßt" (cf. "Ahab el campeador?", p.461).

101 Cf. e.g. Jdg.4_{16}.

why vv.36-37 should have been added. According to Weippert, the king's heroic death did not fit into the concept. The victory had to be turned into defeat. However, unless the presence of such a specific concept is demonstrated her explanation is not convincing. Any assumption of deliberate alteration could be justified by a reference to "not fitting into the concept of the redactor". Since in 1 Kgs.20 Ahab's victory against Benhadad is related, there is no reason why in this narrative the Israelite king should have to be defeated. Anyway the addition of vv.36-37 states neither victory or defeat expressly. This can only be deduced from the mention of the Israelite king's death which was already present in the first of Weippert's stages of development. In this second stage direct speech with an impersonal grammatical subject was added. A second time denotation being synonymous with the first one would have been added, too. However, the direct speech with אִישׁ אֶל־אַרְצוֹ only makes sense if the Judean king participates in the story.[102]

The next stage of the literary development as reconstructed by H.Weippert was marked by the insertion of the narrative, expanded by vv.35d.38a-40b, into the Ahab history. The added material is:

35 וַיִּצֶק דַּם־הַמַּכָּה אֶל־חֵיק הָרָכֶב׃

38 וַיִּשְׁטֹף אֶת־הָרֶכֶב עַל בְּרֵכַת שֹׁמְרוֹן וַיָּלֹקּוּ הַכְּלָבִים אֶת־דָּמוֹ וְהַזֹּנוֹת רָחָצוּ כִּדְבַר יהוה אֲשֶׁר דִּבֵּר׃
39 וְיֶתֶר דִּבְרֵי אַחְאָב וְכָל־אֲשֶׁר עָשָׂה וּבֵית הַשֵּׁן אֲשֶׁר בָּנָה וְכָל־הֶעָרִים אֲשֶׁר בָּנָה הֲלוֹא־הֵם כְּתוּבִים
עַל־סֵפֶר דִּבְרֵי הַיָּמִים לְמַלְכֵי יִשְׂרָאֵל׃ 40 וַיִּשְׁכַּב אַחְאָב עִם־אֲבֹתָיו וַיִּמְלֹךְ אֲחַזְיָהוּ בְנוֹ תַּחְתָּיו׃

It is, of course, possible that after the story was thought to deal with Ahab, the narration of Ahab's death was adapted to the prophecy (1 Kgs.21_{19}). One would, however, expect that as few alterations as possible were carried out and thus the passage describing the fulfillment left in one piece. It is also possible that v.35d, which has no equivalent in the prophecy, was added later to prepare for v.38. It seems strange that although the story was inserted into the Ahab narrative the name of the Israelite king should not have been mentioned. If the story so far, as part of the Ahab history, did not have to mention Ahab's name, why should this be necessary for the work of an author? The addition of v.40b without v.40a is improbable since the mention of an enthronement usually is given after

---

102 That אִישׁ אֶל־אַרְצוֹ implies the participation of both Israel and Judah was already noted by O.Thenius, *Bücher der Könige*, p.261.

that of the predecessor's death.[103] Again it would be possible to argue that v.40b was added first and then v.38, but even then it remains to be shown why the death succession sequence should have been interrupted. After the further addition of vv.39a and 40a the story comprised vv.1a-2a.3a-c.11a-d.29a*.34a-35c.39a.40a.b. This is regarded as the result of a basic narrative that had undergone two redactions, the first one having turned a victory into a defeat and the second ascribing the story to Ahab.

According to Weippert the final redaction led to a "Jehoshaphat recension" (addition of 2b.4a-10b.12a-28c.29a*.30a-33c) which is the narrative in its present form. The editor introduced a number of new participants: Jehoshaphat, king of Judah, four hundred prophets of Baal, the prophet Micaiah son of Imlah and a messenger. Also mentioned are Amon, governor of the city, and the Israelite king's son Joash. According to Weippert's own calculation the redactor added to the basic narrative (18 sentences) and the redactional expansions (9 + 7 sentences) further material to a total of 129 sentences. Again it is surprising to find that all the previous editions are preserved in their original wording in the final edition. It would have been much easier for the final redactor to rewrite the complete narrative, especially since passages like v.3 are of no importance for the "Jehoshaphat recension". It is also surprising that even the final redactor did not regard it as necessary to mention the Israelite king's name apart from v.20. The story would have developed from a simple nucleus with only few *primary participants* to a complex narrative with *primary* and *secondary participants* and remained thus. Weippert's reconstruction implies that the first version was written down, a redactor obtained either the original or a very faithful copy and changed the basic thrust of the narrative. A second redactor obtained either the original or a very faithful copy of the first redactor's work, and identified the Israelite king with Ahab. He did not know the very first version or agreed with the first redactor's treatment. In any case, he did not regard it as necessary to change the wording. Then a third redactor obtained either the original or a very faithful copy of the second redactor's work. He did not know the very first version or the first redactor's version

[103] Cf. 2 Sam.10_{1} 1 Kgs.11_{43} $14_{20.31}$ $15_{8.24.28}$ $16_{6.10.22.28}$ 22_{51} 2 Kgs.1_{17} $8_{15.24}$ 10_{35} 12_{22} $13_{9.24}$ $14_{16.29}$ $15_{7.10.14.22.25.30.38}$ 16_{20} 19_{37} 20_{21} $21_{18.26}$ 24_{6}. Exceptions are found in synchronistic remarks (1 Kgs.{12_{17}} 15_{25} 16_{29} 22_{25} 2 Kgs.3_{1} 15_{13}).

or, at least, he agreed with the second redactor's treatment of the first redactor's treatment of the original. He, too, did not regard is as necessary to change the wording, but rather tried to express his viewpoint by additions only. All subsequent potential redactors obtained the original or faithful copies of the third redactor's work. They did not know the very first version or the two first redactions or they agreed with all redactorial treatments of the narrative known to them and did not regard it as necessary to change the wording of the final one. Thus we either have to assume very extensive redactorial activity and by chance we have just this one of many different versions that were created of the story nucleus, or, we have to assume that each new version completely replaced its predecessor and had some kind of authoritative status. It is not sufficient to isolate different layers in a narrative; the analysis of the redactorial process involved is more important!

6. S.J.DeVries' Analysis

So far we have discussed attempts to reconstruct the development of 1 Kgs.22 proposing a story nucleus which was supplemented in subsequent redactions. S.J.DeVries suggested that 1 Kgs.22 is the result of a combination of two independent sources by a redactor.[104] He began his analysis by demonstrating the compositeness of the narrative in 1 Kgs.22. In addition to features already discussed above[105] DeVries drew attention to the following supposed inconsistencies: Ahab's suggestion in v.30 (לְבַשׁ בְּגָדֶיךָ) is regarded as being inconsistent with v.10 (מְלֻבָּשִׁים בְּגָדִים). וְכָל־הַנְּבִיאִים מִתְנַבְּאִים is claimed to be redundant after v.6 and to be inconsistent with the wording of v.12 (וְכָל־הַנְּבִאִים נִבְּאִים). The king summons a סָרִיס, but a מַלְאָךְ returns. DeVries further argued that לָכֵן (v.19) originally had to

[104] Cf. *Prophet Against Prophet*, pp.25-51; *1 Kings*, pp.265-266.

[105] The singular address in vss.10-12.15 (in v.15 S.J.DeVries, *1 Kings*, p.261, regards the sgl. {LXX, *T*^{f}} as original) in contrast with the co-ordination of the two kings at the beginning of v.10, Micaiah's different replies, scene change in v.10, double speech introduction in vv.4b.5, double introduction of Micaiah in vv.8.9. With regard to the incongruence of sgl. - pl. between v.10 and v.12 it may be added to our discussion above that Zedekiah's message, too, is given in the sgl. If thus v.10 and v.12b belong to different sources, the same must be true for v.10 and v.11. Thus DeVries' reconstruction is inconsistent. It has already been pointed out above that in v.15 the reading of the LXX can be explained as adaptation to v.6, and thus the MT has a superior text.

be preceded by something spoken by Micaiah. He also drew attention to the incongruence between דְּבָרֶיךָ[106] (pl.) and כִּדְבַר אַחַד מֵהֶם (sgl.) in v.13. In his opinion the plural points to Micaiah's different prophecies and therefore could only stem from a redactor's hand. DeVries further noted that the change of grammatical subject at the beginning of v.19 is not marked as such. He also argued that the two occurrences in 1 Kgs.22 of בַּיּוֹם הַהוּא referring to the future in v.25 and to the past in v.35 indicate two separate sources. DeVries adduced Dt.$31_{16\text{-}22}$ and 1 Sam.$3_{1\text{-}21}$ as the only other passages where the expression is used for future and past.

Various objections may be raised against the source-critical significance of the phenomena referred to. The סָרִיס mentioned in v.9 was not termed a מַלְאָךְ, because at this point he was no messenger. Other passages show the same development of designations.[107] The presence of לָכֵן in v.19 does not imply that it originally constituted a continuation of a speech of the prophet. Firstly, the text is uncertain[108] and, secondly, לָכֵן can be used to begin a speech.[109] It is true that וְכָל־הַנְּבִיאִים מִתְנַבְּאִים לִפְנֵיהֶם (v.10) does not present new information. The assumption, however, that in the original version of a given narrative every sentence must provide new information is not justifiable and thus it does not matter for literary critical purposes whether the sentence is redundant or not. The question may be asked why a redactor should have inserted a redundant sentence. DeVries does not explain where the inconsistency between v.10 and v.12b is to be found, possibly in the use of the pl. in לִפְנֵיהֶם in v.10 and the address in the sgl. in v.12b or between מִתְנַבְּאִים and נִבְּאִים. In either case, as we have seen above, the assumption of different strands is not necessary. As for the supposed incongruence of דְּבָרֶיךָ with דבר אַחַד מֵהֶם, it is noteworthy that the ק״, supported by mlt mss, ***S***, ***T***, ***V*** and the parallel passage in Chr., has the sgl. דְּבָרְךָ. But even if the כ״ has the original reading, it seems inconceivable that the messenger could

---

106 ק״: דְּבָרְךָ.

107 וַיִּקְחוּ שְׁנֵי רֶכֶב סוּסִים וַיִּשְׁלַח הַמֶּלֶךְ (2 Kgs.6_{32}), וַיִּשְׁלַח אִישׁ מִלְּפָנָיו בְּטֶרֶם יָבֹא הַמַּלְאָךְ אֵלָיו קַח רַכָּב וּשְׁלַח לִקְרָאתָם ... וַיֵּלֶךְ רֹכֵב (2 Kgs.$7_{14\text{-}15}$), אַחֲרֵי מַחֲנֵה־אֲרָם ... וַיָּשָׁבוּ הַמַּלְאָכִים הַסּוּס לִקְרָאתוֹ ... בָּא־הַמַּלְאָךְ עַד־הֵם (2 Kgs.$9_{17\text{-}18}$); cf. also הַמַּלְאָכִים in Josh.$6_{17\text{-}25}$ who had been mentioned as הָאֲנָשִׁים in ch.2.

108 LXX: *οὐχ οὕτως*.

109 Cf. Gen.4_{15} (LXX, σ', θ': *οὐχ οὕτως*), 30_{15}, Jdg.8_7 11_8 1 Sam.$28_{2(2x)}$.

have asked Micaiah to foretell a victory in several prophecies when only because Micaiah did exactly as he was told by the messenger further prophecies were demanded. דְּבָרֶיךָ would then be easier understood as "words" rather than "oracles". As for the different references of בַּיּוֹם הַהוּא, it is difficult to see why this should be incompatible with single authorship or redactorship. Furthermore, in all three passages adduced by DeVries the expression referring to the future occurs in direct speech while the expression referring to the past occurs in narrative. Thus the supposed inconsistency may be regarded as artificial. There remains the change of grammatical subject at the beginning of v.19. The LXX has an additional Μιχαιας, but no reason for an omission of מִכָיְהוּ is apparent. Thus we have to leave this question open. The assumption that v.19 was inserted by an editor does not solve the problem, since an editor, too, could have inserted a mention of the speaker. DeVries' claim that the story as it stands in 1 Kgs.22 has no meaningful sequence is subjective and need not be discussed here.

Although DeVries' attempt to demonstrate the compositeness was not found to be convincing, we shall continue to examine the implications of his reconstruction of the literary history of 1 Kgs.22_{1-38}. DeVries assumed that 1 Kgs.22_{4b} being dependent on 2 Kgs.3_7[110], which he regarded as "late Jehuite polemic",[111] is a late addition. Further redactorial expansions are וַיֹּאמֶר at the beginning of v.19, וְיַעַל וְיִפֹּל בְּרָמֹת גִּלְעָד in v.20, v.12a, and v.13. The remaining text was split into sources. Like E.Würthwein, DeVries isolated the different scenes and combined them into two sources. Those parts of the text which would have disturbed the unity of the hypothetical sources were ascribed to a redactor. The two sources isolated are: 1 Kgs.$22_{2b-4a.4bß-9.15-18.26-37}$ and 1 Kgs.$22_{10-12a.14.19^*.20a\alpha.20b-25}$.[112]

---

[110] Cf. the discussion of the relationship of 1 Kgs.22_{4b} - 2 Kgs.3_7 and 1 Kgs.22_7 - 2 Kgs.3_{11} above, p.296, n.28; pp.208f, n.73.

[111] Cf. *Prophet Against Prophet*, p.28.

[112] Vv.1-2a.35bß.38 were regarded as minor redactorial remarks. That vv.1-2 are secondary has also been argued by J.Morgenstern, "Chronological Data of the Dynasty of Omri" on the grounds that Jehoshaphat appears to have travelled to Samaria without his army, but is ready to go to war with his army when being asked by Ahab. Morgenstern dates a first campaign against the Arameans in 870 B.C. and then interprets 1 Kgs.22_{1-2} as having originally mentioned a journey of Jehoshaphat to celebrate (cf. 2 Chr.18_{1-2}) betrothal or marriage of Jehoram, Jehoshaphat's son, with Athaliah in 867 B.C. There is, however, not enough evidence to support Morgenstern's proposal.

Although narrative A does indeed constitute an internally consistent account, narrative B contains some difficulties. The narrative has no proper beginning. The reader / listener is not told why the prophets were consulted and וְכָל־הַנְּבִיאִים has no reference in narrative B.[113] In narrative B Micaiah is introduced without patronym. DeVries deduced from this that at the time narrative B was written Micaiah had become a legendary figure like Elijah and Elisha.[114] This assumption is without any foundation, but it is necessary for DeVries' reconstruction. It is easier to regard the mention of Micaiah in v.14 not as the first mention of the prophet and to question the validity of DeVries' reconstruction. V.14 with its emphasis on grammatical object (אֶת־אֲשֶׁר ... אֹתוֹ ...) seems unmotivated in narrative B, whereas, if the literary unity of 1 Kgs.$22_{1\text{-}38}$ is presupposed, it suits the messenger's attempt to influence Micaiah's message. DeVries' redactor would have had before him two narratives about the prophet Micaiah, son of Imlah. In each the king of Israel is about to campaign against the Arameans and in each Micaiah's message is opposed. DeVries does not adduce any reason why a redactor should have combined the two accounts. He could have simply left them in their original forms. Fortunately the two accounts were in such a form that it was possible to combine them without having to alter them. The redactor only had to add a few sentences. He added v.4bα and thus converted Ahab's speech into Jehoshaphat's. In 2 Kgs.3_7 it is Jehoshaphat who utters the same sentences. It seems strange that in 2 Kgs.3 they form Jehoshaphat's reply, whereas in 1 Kgs.22 they are part of Ahab's question. The redactor would also have added וַיֹּאמֶר at the beginning of v.19. It seems more probable that a redactor would have added מִכָיְהוּ, too, as the LXX did. No reason is apparent why Micaiah's speech consisting of vv.14.19 should have been split up by a redactor. V.14 could have been inserted before v.17. The addition of vv.12b-13 by the redactor with the introduction of a secondary participant would not have been necessary. The redactor would have added a speech (v.12b) which was phrased after Micaiah's speech in v.15, rather than adapting Micaiah's speech to that of the four hundred prophets, which would seem more probable since the narrator's / redactor's point was that

---

[113] Such a reference is, of course, not necessary (cf. v.6) but DeVries' reconstruction would be more convincing with it.

[114] Cf. *Prophet Against Prophet*, p.40.

Micaiah repeated the false prophets' message. The redactor would also have inserted רָמֹת גִּלְעָד, since the place was not mentioned immediately before his insertion in v.12. This contrasts with other instances of lack of attention for which, if DeVries' reconstruction is correct, the redactor was responsible. This, of course, is only valid if the MT of v.12 is correct. If the LXX has preserved the original reading the insertion does not make sense at all, since there is no hint in the narrative that it was Ahab's intention to capture the king of the Arameans. The redactor further would have added וְיַעַל וְיִפֹּל בְּרָמֹת גִּלְעָד to v.20. If this sentence is missing, no object for enticing Ahab is mentioned. There is no hint that this sentence should be secondary. In narrative B it is not clear whether the spirit is successful in enticing Ahab or not.

We thus conclude that DeVries' reconstruction is not superior to the ones discussed above. Two accounts about a certain prophet existed in such a form that they could be combined without major alterations. Just these two accounts were combined by a redactor. This requires more and more difficult assumptions than the presupposition of the literary unity of 1 Kgs.$22_{1\text{-}38}$ which, therefore, is to be preferred.

B. 1 Kgs.20

Another narrative which may be considered is found in 1 Kgs.20. Like 1 Kgs.$22_{1\text{-}38}$ the narrative may be compared to *early stages* of Assyrian campaign accounts. The discourse structure is complex, there are many participants on the *main line*, many *reversals*, secondary participants figure prominently and there are extensive references to internal participant relations. The story is related on the locutionary level[115] and appears to follow the chronological order. The rhetorical level is high and speeches contain different levels of quotations. Yet, various scholars have isolated various scenes and ascribed them to different authors or redactors.

[115] Cf. above, p.167f, n.362. A possible exception is v.33.

1. J.Wellhausen's Analysis

J.Wellhausen separated passages dealing with king and prophet from the rest of the narrative and regarded the former as secondary. In his opinion vv.13.14.22.28 were inserted to form a *vaticinium ex eventu.*[116] Similarly vv.35-43 are regarded as being dependent on 22_{1ff} and, as indicated by the agreement between 20_{43} and 21_4, presupposing ch.21 between chs.20 and 22.[117] However, the parallelism of וַיֵּלֶךְ מֶלֶךְ־יִשְׂרָאֵל עַל־בֵּיתוֹ סַר וְזָעֵף (20_{43}) and וַיָּבֹא אַחְאָב אֶל־בֵּיתוֹ סַר וְזָעֵף (21_4) does not necessitate the assumption of dependency of one passage on the other. Even though סַר וְזָעֵף occurs only in these two passages, the similarity in wording may be due to a common author/redactor. It may have been a fixed expression. Even if we regard a dependency as the most likely explanation, it remains to be shown that 20_{43} is dependent on 21_4 and not *vice versa*. And even if 20_{43} should be dependent on 21_4, it is difficult to see why this could not have been the case with ch.21 preceding ch.20. The designation of the purpose of a passage as to form a *vaticinium ex eventu* does not affect the literary unity of a narrative in which this passage is found. Thus Wellhausen's reconstruction remains inconclusive.

Wellhausen's analysis was developed by I.Benzinger[118], who adduced further reasons for regarding 1 Kgs.20 as a composite narrative. The passages mentioning prophet(s) are taken as being "non-essential" for the course of narration.[119] Benzinger further discovered internal difficulties, since according to v.12 the Arameans attacked first whereas in v.14 the prophet encourages Ahab to attack. He also referred to 1 Kgs.22 where the relationship between prophet and king is completely different. Benzinger suggested that the narrative was expanded because a reader of the story took offence at the fact that only Ahab's failures were regarded as divine ordinance but not his victories.

---

116 Cf. *Composition*, p.284.

117 "vv.35-43 beziehen sich gerade so auf 22,1ss wie 20,22 auf 20,23ss, vgl. v.13.14.28. Aber sie sind erst später eingesetzt, da sie wie 20,43 mit 21,4 zeigt, das 21. Kap. zwischen dem 20. und dem 22. voraussetzen". (cf. *Composition*, p.283).

118 Cf. *Bücher der Könige*, pp.116-122.

119 Cf. *Könige*, p.119.

Benzinger followed Wellhausen in separating vv.35-43 from the preceding mentions of the prophet. He drew attention to similarities with 1 Kgs.13. There is similar phraseology (בדבר יהוה in 20_{35} and $13_{1.2.5.9.17.18.32}$), in both narratives absolute obedience is demanded, and the prophet is punished by being killed by a lion; the prophet is not identical that of vv.13.14.22.28. While old sources are thought to deal with נְבִיאִים only, 1 Kgs.$20_{35\text{-}43}$ mention בְּנֵי הַנְּבִיאִים. This led him to assume a late date for 1 Kgs.$20_{35\text{-}43}$.[120]

Benzinger employed all three basic techniques for the source-critical analysis of Old Testament narratives: the search for internal difficulties, the comparison with the "usual" way of narration, and the isolation of self-sufficient units. If the passages mentioning the prophet are not necessary for the course of narration the same has to be said for vv.7-8 (the elder's council) and vv.23-26 (the Arameans' council). Narratives generally do not only consist of "necessary" passages. The fact that a passage appears to be non-essential does not imply that it is secondary. The similarity of 1 Kgs.$20_{35\text{-}43}$ to 1 Kgs.13 is indeed striking. But it remains doubtful whether the points of parallelism are specific enough to postulate dependency of one narrative on the other. בִּדְבַר יהוה also occurs in 1 Sam.3_{21}[121] Jer.8_9 Ps.33_6 2 Chr.30_{12}[122]. בְּנֵי הַנְּבִיאִים are mentioned in 2 Kgs.$2_{3.5.7.15}$ $4_{1.38(2x)}$ 5_{22} 6_1 9_1. Their mention in 1 Kgs.20 is thus not unusual. Further details will be discussed below.[123]

A further expansion of Wellhausen's analysis had already been presented by F.Schwally.[124] In his opinion, vv.15-20, too, suffered redactorial treatment. The mentions of נַעֲרֵי שָׂרֵי הַמְּדִינוֹת are to be regarded as secondary, because of the occurrence of מְדִינָה, an Aramaic word which otherwise occurs only in "late" texts. However, even if its presence is taken as an indication of a late date, this does not necessarily imply that the passage is later than its context. The whole narrative may be late. As will be argued below, however, the occurrence of מְדִינָה is compatible with a comparatively early date of 1 Kgs.20.[125]

---

120 Cf. *Bücher der Könige*, pp.121f.
121 mlt Mss 'כד' י; cf. ***T***^edd, ***V***; > LXX.
122 Pc. mss ***S***, ***T*** 'כד.
123 For the supposed internal contradiction as to who attacked first cf. below, pp.227f. For the relationship between 1 Kgs.$20_{35\text{-}43}$ and 1 Kgs.13 cf. below, pp.225f.
124 Cf. "Zur Quellenkritik", pp.158-159.
125 See below, pp.226f, n.133.

2. H.-C.Schmitt's Analysis

H.-C.Schmitt[126] listed the following difficulties which led him to the assumption of different layers of tradition in 1 Kgs.20:

- the Israelites' advance and their victory over the Arameans are reported in both, v.19f and v.21
- according to v.12 the Arameans attacked first, according to v.14 Ahab attacked first[127]
- in vv.1-12.21/31.32 the title "king of Israel"[128] is used while v.13-20 speak of "Ahab"
- vv.22.23 mention the "king of Aram" whereas vv.1.5.8.19 / 26.30.32.33 refer to him as "Benhadad"
- passages speaking of a battle in the מִישׁוֹר (v.23) or עֲמָקִים (v.28) are suspicious, for the environment of Aphek is not substantially different from that of Samaria
- in vv.1-34 prophets are mentioned only within redactorial expansions; it is therefore likely that vv.35-43, too, are comparatively late.

He thus reached the conclusion that 1 Kgs.20 is to be regarded as the result of three redactions of a basic layer. The latter consists of two narratives, vv.1-12.21 and vv.26f.29-34. The redactorial layers were seen in vv.13-20[129].22-25.28.35-43. Schmitt then proceeded to argue that the added material consists of three separate strands. Indications for this were seen in the different designations for participants and the different relationship between king and prophet. If Schmitt's reconstruction of the literary development of 1 Kgs.$20_{1\text{-}43}$ is correct, two narratives relating conflicts between Israel and Arameans were expanded by prophet stories and combined. First the second story was expanded by vv.22-25.28 and accordingly (?) the first story was expanded by vv.13-20. Finally a third prophet narrative (vv.35-43) was added. Schmitt regarded vv.22-25.28 as

---

[126] Cf.*Elisa*, pp.46-48.

[127] Already noted by J.Wellhausen, *Composition*, p.284. Cf. also I.Benziger, *Bücher der Könige*, p.119.

[128] "Ahab" in v.2 is regarded as redactorial insertion.

[129] Parts of this passage had already been ascribed to a redactor by F.Schwally, "Zur Quellenkritik", pp.157-159, who regarded Ahab's question in v.14 as "absurd". The mentions of the נַעֲרֵי שָׂרֵי הַמְּדִינוֹת in 15a.17a.19 were also regarded as secondary, since מְדִינָה is not Hebrew but Aramaic. Schwally further argued that v.19 is not necessary, since it had already been stated before that army and the "servants of the governors of the districts" had gone out of the city. V.30 was seen as "legendary" and discordant with the rest of the narrative, since Israel could have entered Aphek once the wall had fallen.

part of the extensive redaction adding references to prophets to which also 1 Kgs.22, 2 Kgs.3_{4ff}, and 2 Kgs.6_{24ff} were subjected.[130] With regard to the fundamental differences in the functions of the prophets between 1 Kgs.20 and 22, he argued that the redactor was forced to retain the positive picture of Ahab presented in 1 Kgs.20 and could not mention the prophet's name because he did not know any prophet with such a positive outlook towards the Omride dynasty. However, according to Schmitt's reconstruction the first redactor expanded not the whole basic layer but rather only vv.26f.29-34. There we do not find so positive a picture of Ahab that could not have been altered. Speculations as to whom or what hypothetical redactors might have known cannot render Schmitt's reconstruction more convincing. The differences between the prophetic functions in chs.20 and 22 may rather be taken as evidence against such an extensive redaction.

The various designations for the participating kings will be discussed below. Schmitt's argument for separating the different redactorial expansions from each other would mean that a redactor could or at least would only have used one designation for each of the participants. Consequently, the basic layer would have to be split up further with the result that almost every verse would constitute a separate strand. Schmitt's claim therefore has to be rejected. As for the different references to the prophet(s), Schmitt's line of argument is even less convincing. The prophets are mentioned as נָבִיא אֶחָד (v.13), הַנָּבִיא (v.22), and אִישׁ הָאֱלֹהִים (v.28). נָבִיא אֶחָד and הַנָּבִיא are the expected forms of first and second reference to a participant and אִישׁ הָאֱלֹהִים is used as a synonym.[131]

Schmitt further argued that vv.35-43 are "very late". Indications for this were seen in dependencies on various other Old Testament texts. The motif of punishment through a lion is thought to be taken from 1 Kgs.13, the expression

[130] References to prophets are thought to have been added in order to explain events during campaigns as fulfillment of prophecies; cf. H.-C.Schmitt, *Elisa*, p.49.

[131] Cf. 1 Sam.9_{9-10}: לְפָנִים בְּיִשְׂרָאֵל כֹּה־אָמַר הָאִישׁ בְּלֶכְתּוֹ לִדְרוֹשׁ אֱלֹהִים לְכוּ וְנֵלְכָה עַד־הָרֹאֶה כִּי לַנָּבִיא הַיּוֹם יִקָּרֵא לְפָנִים הָרֹאֶה׃ וַיֹּאמֶר שָׁאוּל לְנַעֲרוֹ טוֹב דְּבָרְךָ לְכָה נֵלֵכָה וַיֵּלְכוּ אֶל־הָעִיר אֲשֶׁר־שָׁם אִישׁ הָאֱלֹהִים׃, 1 Kgs.13_{18}: ... וַיֹּאמֶר לוֹ גַּם־אֲנִי נָבִיא כָּמוֹךָ (the addressed prophet is called אִישׁ הָאֱלֹהִים throughout the narrative), 2 Kgs.$5_{8.14,15}$: וַיְהִי כִּשְׁמֹעַ אֱלִישָׁע אִישׁ־הָאֱלֹהִים כִּי־קָרַע מֶלֶךְ־יִשְׂרָאֵל אֶת־בְּגָדָיו וַיִּשְׁלַח אֶל־הַמֶּלֶךְ לֵאמֹר לָמָּה קָרַעְתָּ בְּגָדֶיךָ יָבֹא־נָא אֵלַי וְיֵדַע כִּי יֵשׁ נָבִיא בְּיִשְׂרָאֵל׃... וַיֵּרֶד וַיִּטְבֹּל בַּיַּרְדֵּן שֶׁבַע פְּעָמִים כִּדְבַר אִישׁ הָאֱלֹהִים וַיָּשָׁב בְּשָׂרוֹ כִּבְשַׂר נַעַר קָטֹן וַיִּטְהָר׃ וַיָּשָׁב אֶל־אִישׁ הָאֱלֹהִים הוּא וְכָל־מַחֲנֵהוּ וַיָּבֹא וַיַּעֲמֹד לְפָנָיו וַיֹּאמֶר הִנֵּה־נָא יָדַעְתִּי כִּי אֵין אֱלֹהִים בְּכָל־הָאָרֶץ כִּי אִם־בְּיִשְׂרָאֵל וְעַתָּה קַח־נָא בְרָכָה מֵאֵת עַבְדֶּךָ׃.

עַל־בֵּיתוֹ סַר וְזָעֵף from 1 Kgs.21_4, and אִישׁ אֶחָד מִבְּנֵי אֱלֹהִים from Elisha-narratives (1 Kgs.4_1, 9_1). From this Schmitt deduced that the passage in 1 Kgs.$20_{35\text{-}43}$ presupposes the books of Kings in roughly their present extent. This line of argument assumes that all of the possible sources available to or narratives influencing the author / redactor of 1 Kgs.$20_{35\text{-}43}$ are extant in the Old Testament. This assumption is not justified and thus Schmitt's argument cannot be regarded as convincing. Furthermore, even if a literary dependency is assumed, it remains to be shown that 1 Kgs.20 is dependent on the other narratives and not vice versa.

There are several difficulties with Schmitt's reconstruction of the literary development of 1 Kgs.20. Firstly, it is not quite true that v.21 simply is a doublet of v.19f. V.21 rather constitutes a summarizing remark at the end of a narrative, which is shown by the resumption of אֶת־הַסּוּס וְאֶת־הָרֶכֶב from v.1 (וְסוּס וָרֶכֶב). This explains וַיֵּצֵא at the beginning of v.21. Furthermore, v.19f have the נַעֲרֵי שָׂרֵי הַמְּדִינוֹת and the people of Israel as grammatical subject whereas in v.20 it is the king of Israel. If vv.13-20 are ascribed to a "late" redactor the basic layer would not have mentioned Benhadad's fate. Since the latter figures prominently in vv.1-12[132] and the other Aramean kings are only mentioned in vv.1 and 12 in the basic layer, this would be unexpected. וַיִּלָּחֶם בָּהּ (v.1) has only Benhadad as grammatical subject and he issues the command to attack (v.12). Thus v.19f have to be part of the basic layer. Then, however, at least vv.15-18, too, must be regarded as part of the earliest version of the narrative.[133]

---

[132] Cf. especially v.7 where emphasis is placed on his personality.

[133] The mentions of מְדִינָה in vv.(14.)15.17.19 cannot be used as evidence for the compositeness of 1 Kgs.$20_{1\text{-}21}$ (*contra* F.Schwally, see above, p.224, n.129). A word used by a redactor could just as well have been used by an author. That מְדִינָה otherwise occurs only in "late" texts (Ez.19_8; Ko.2_8 5_7; Est.$1_{1.3.16.22}$ $2_{3.18}$ $3_{8.12.13.14}$ $4_{3.11}$ $8_{5.9.11.12.13.17}$ $9_{2.3.4.12.16.20.28.30}$, Da.8_2 11_{24}; Esr.2_1; Neh.1_3 7_6 11_3 (Hebrew passages) / Da.$2_{48.49}$ $3_{1.2.3.12.30}$; Esr.5_8 6_2 7_{16} (Aramaic passages) might only be used for dating the narrative as a whole. It is an interesting fact that this word occurs in a passage narrating an Israelite war against the Arameans. One might conjecture that the מְדִינוֹת were part of the Aramean rather than of an imagined Israelite administrative system. This would suit the fact that Benhadad was able to proceed as far as Samaria into Israelite territory, while after the defeat he was checked already at Aphek (cf. below, appendix IV, p.294 with n.13). The people of Israel and the נַעֲרֵי שָׂרֵי הַמְּדִינוֹת are carefully distinguished from each other.
Schmitt further argued that the presence of the word פֶּחָה in v.24, which is supposed to occur elsewhere only in exilic/post-exilic or undatable texts indicates a late date of that passage (vv.22-25.28). פֶּחָה is commonly regarded as an Akkadian loan word derived

Schmitt's next argument for the compositeness of 1 Kgs.20 rests on his interpretation of שׂים in v.12: וַיֹּאמֶר אֶל־עֲבָדָיו שִׂימוּ וַיָּשִׂימוּ עַל־הָעִיר. The LXX reads for this passage *καὶ εἶπεν τοῖς παισὶν αὐτοῦ Οἰκοδομήσατε χάρακα· καὶ ἔθεντο χάρακα ἐπὶ τὴν πόλιν*. The LXX has *χάραξ* to translate the following

---

from bēl pīḫāti/paḫāti. However, taken on its own this does not imply a "late" date. As a common Assyrian administrative term it is likely to have been widely known in the eighth and seventh centuries B.C. at least. This is also indicated by the probable occurrence of the term on a stele errected by Barrakīb for his father Panammu(wa), son of BRṢR, king of Jaʾudi (=Samʾal). The stele was found 1888 near Zinjirli and is dated by H.Donner and W.Röllig (*Inschriften* II, p.223) to the second part of the 8th ct. (between 733/32 and 727). The passage reads:
מלך.אשור.ר[...][12]אשור.פחי.ואחי.יאדי.וחנאה.מראה.מלך. אשור.על.מלכי.כבר.ברש [..ורץ].
Donner and Röllig regard פחי (and אחי, a defective form of איחי) as stat. cstr. pl. being construed with יאדי. The syntactical parallelism of אחי and פחי seems to indicate that the *governors* are not to be regarded as Assyrian officials but rather as officials of Jaʾudi. B.Landsberger (quoted by J.J.Koopmans, *Aramäische Chrestomathie* 1, p.74) has advanced an alternative explanation of l.12. He regards פחי and אחי as being derived from חיא with פ as conjunction ("and he lived and Jaʾudi lived / and he made Jaʾudi live"). The grammatical subject of this sentence would be Panammu(wa), which is indicated by the introduction of a new grammatical subject with מראה. J.C.L.Gibson, *Textbook* 2, p.84 follows Landsberger and refers to the fact that in Hebrew the pl. of פחה is פחות or פחוות - fem. The arrangement of topics on the stele would, however, favour the former explanation. The context would necessitate to translate חיא with "living/being well". The well-being of Jaʾudi is mentioned on the stele already in ll.9-10 whereas from l.10 onwards the relationship of Panammu(wa) with the Assyrian king and other kings is described. Furthermore, in l.17 איחה is followed by the apposition מלכו. This would parallel the co-occurrence of אחי and פחי in l.12. Cf. also l.3 where it is narrated that 70 איחי אבה were killed - the grammatical subject of the sentence may not have been preserved. The last grammatical subject mentioned is Hadad in l.2. איח further occurs in an inscription by Panammu(wa), son of QRL {cf. H.Donner and W.Röllig, *Inschriften* I, pp.38f, no.214} ll.24.27.28.30.31. Of these especially ll.28-30 seem to indicate that איח may imply some official function. Thus Donner and Röllig's interpretation is preferred here. According to S.A.Kaufman (*Akkadian Influences*, p.82) H.L.Ginsberg showed that the reading of פחה in the passage noted above is incorrect. Kaufmann refers to "Aramaic Studies Today", p.236, n.35. There, however, Ginsberg only *states* that פחי ואחי means "so he lived and Yʾdy lived" and discards the possibility of "and (he) let Yʾdy live" by referring to the causative prefix הin ll.4.8. פחה further occurs in a letter to Pharaoh Necho dated from the end of the seventh or the beginning of the sixth century B.C. (H.Donner and W.Röllig, *Inschriften* I, p.51, no.266, l.9).

A different explanation for the presence of פֶּחָה was advanced by I.Benzinger (*Bücher der Könige*, p.120): "Man kann vielleicht vermuten, dass ein aufmerksamer Leser, der die 32 שָׂרִים in 22_{31} schon vorfand, diese mit den 32 Königen so combinierte, dass er annahm, die Könige seien durch שָׂרִים ersetzt worden. Für שָׂרִים wäre dann später der übliche Titel פַּחוֹת eingesetzt worden." Since, however, in 1 Kgs.22_{31} שָׂרִים was evidently retained, Benziger suggestion is not convincing.

words כַּר (Ez.21_{27}), מֻצָּב (Is.29_{3}), מָצוֹד (Ec.9_{14}), מָצוֹר (Dt.20_{19}), and סֹלְלָה (Is.37_{33} Jer.$40(33)_{4}$ Ez.4_{2} 26_{8}).[134] Of these passages Ez.21_{27} is of special interest since here שׂים and an equivalent of *χάραξ* co-occur (לָשׂוּם כָּרִים עַל־שְׁעָרִים).[135] Thus it may be suggested that (אֶת־)כָּרִים was accidentally dropped from MT. While this is, of course, possible[136], it is not likely that the same word should have been accidentally omitted twice in the same verse. It seems more plausible that the LXX has supplemented an elliptic formula. In any case, the actual meaning of Benhadad's order is not clear. Even if כָּרִים is to be supplemented, the beginning of a siege by the Arameans does not constitute a contradiction to v.14.[137]

Schmitt also refers to the designations for the various participants to support his identification of various strands in 1 Kgs.20.

v.1	וּבֶן־הֲדַד מֶלֶךְ־אֲרָם	*υἱὸς* Αδερ[138]		
v.2			אַחְאָב מֶלֶךְ־יִשְׂרָאֵל	Αχαβ *βασιλέα* Ισραηλ
v.3	(בֶּן־הֲדַד	*υἱὸς* Αδερ)[139]		
v.4			מֶלֶךְ־יִשְׂרָאֵל	*ὁ βασιλεὺς* Ισραηλ
	(אֲדֹנִי הַמֶּלֶךְ	*κύριε βασιλεῦ*)		
v.5	(בֶּן־הֲדַד	*υἱὸς* Αδερ)		
v.7			מֶלֶךְ־יִשְׂרָאֵל	*ὁ βασιλεὺς* Ισραηλ
v.9	בֶּן־הֲדַד	*υἱοῦ* Αδερ		
	(לַדֹנִי הַמֶּלֶךְ)	-		
v.10	בֶּן־הֲדַד	*υἱὸς* Αδερ		
v.11			מֶלֶךְ־יִשְׂרָאֵל	*ὁ βασιλεὺς* Ισραηλ
v.13			אַחְאָב מֶלֶךְ־יִשְׂרָאֵל	*τῷ βασιλεῖ* Ισραηλ[140]
v.14			אַחְאָב	Αχααβ
			-	Αχααβ

---

[134] In Is.31_{9} the MT, וְסַלְעוֹ מִמָּגוֹר יַעֲבוֹר וְחַתּוּ מִנֵּס שָׂרָיו נְאֻם־יְהוָה אֲשֶׁר־אוּר לוֹ בְּצִיּוֹן וְתַנּוּר לוֹ בִּירוּשָׁלָםִ:, is represented by the LXX as *πέτρᾳ γὰρ περιλημφθήσονται ὡς χάρακι καὶ ἡττηθήσονται, ὁ δέ φεύγων ἁλώσεται. Τάδε λέγει κύριος Μακάριος ὅς ἔχει εν Σιων σπέρμα καὶ οἰκείους ἐν* Ιερουσαλημ.

[135] Cf. also Mi.4_{14}: מָצוֹר שָׂם עָלֵינוּ; LXX: *συνοχὴν ἔταξεν ἐφ᾽ ἡμᾶς*.

[136] The omission may be ascribed to Homoioteleuton:
שׂימו את כרימ וישׂימו את כרימ על העיר. If, for the first omission ימו is accepted as basis for the Homoioteleuton another ו would have to have been inserted before ישׂימו. The same is true for a possible omission of מֻצָּבִים (pl. not in the Old Testament) or מְצוֹרִים.

[137] For שׂים with the meaning of arranging an army for battle C.F.Keil, *Bücher der Könige*, pp.218f, refers to 1 Sam.11_{11} and Job 1_{17}. Then the phrase would not imply the actual attack.

[138] LXX^{L} (b,c_2), LXX^{O}: + *βασιλεὺς Συρίας*.

[139] Mentions in direct speech are given in brackets.

[140] B, LXX^{L}(bc_2e_2): text; rell.: *τῷ* Αχααβ (*τῷ*) *βασιλεῖ*.

v.15	-	-[141]		
v.16	-	-[142]		
	בֶּן־הֲדַד	υἱὸς Αδερ		
v.17	בֶּן־הֲדַד	-		
	לוֹ	τῷ βασιλεῖ Συρίας[143]		
v.18	-	-[144]		
v.20	בֶּן־הֲדַד מֶלֶךְ אֲרָם	υἱὸς Αδερ βασιλεὺς Συρίας		
v.21			מֶלֶךְ יִשְׂרָאֵל	βασιλεὺς Ισραηλ[145]
v.22			מֶלֶךְ יִשְׂרָאֵל	βασιλέα Ισραηλ
	(מֶלֶךְ אֲרָם	υἱὸς Αδερ βασιλεὺς Συρίας)		
v.23	מֶלֶךְ־אֲרָם	βασιλέως Συρίας		
v.26	בֶּן־הֲדַד	υἱὸς Αδερ		
v.28			מֶלֶךְ יִשְׂרָאֵל	βασιλεῖ Ισραηλ
v.30	בֶּן־הֲדַד	υἱὸς Αδερ		
v.31			(מֶלֶךְ יִשְׂרָאֵל	βασιλέα Ισραηλ)[146]
v.32			מֶלֶךְ יִשְׂרָאֵל	τῷ βασιλεῖ Ισραηλ
			-	-[147]
	(בֶּן־הֲדַד	υἱὸς Αδερ)		
v.33	(בֶּן־הֲדַד	υἱὸς Αδερ)		
	(בֶּן־הֲדַד	υἱὸς Αδερ)		
v.34	-	-[148]		
			-	-[149]
v.38			לַמֶּלֶךְ	βασιλεῖ Ισραηλ
v.39			הַמֶּלֶךְ	ὁ βασιλεὺς Ισραηλ
			הַמֶּלֶךְ	τὸν βασιλέα
v.40			מֶלֶךְ־יִשְׂרָאֵל	ὁ βασιλεὺς Ισραηλ
v.41			מֶלֶךְ יִשְׂרָאֵל	ὁ βασιλεὺς Ισραηλ
v.43			מֶלֶךְ־יִשְׂרָאֵל	ὁ βασιλεὺς Ισραηλ

An analysis of the designations employed for the Israelite king in 1 Kgs.20 does not confirm Schmitt's conclusions. In the supposed basic layer the latter is referred to by the narrator as מֶלֶךְ־יִשְׂרָאֵל (vv.4.7.11.21.31.32) and אַחְאָב מֶלֶךְ־יִשְׂרָאֵל (v.2). In the supposed redactorial expansions he is referred to as אַחְאָב מֶלֶךְ־יִשְׂרָאֵל (v.13), אַחְאָב (v.13.14), מֶלֶךְ־יִשְׂרָאֵל (vv.22.28.41.43), and הַמֶּלֶךְ (vv.38.39.40). Two of the four designations used for the Israelite king occur in

---

141 LXX^{L}: + καὶ (ὁ) βασιλεὺς Εζερ μετ' αὐτοῦ.
142 LXX^{L}: + ὁ βασιλεύς Εζερ μετ' αὐτῶν (e_2: -τῷ, b: -τοῦ).
143 ... וַיִּשְׁלַח בֶּן־הֲדַד וַיַּגִּידוּ לוֹ is represented in the LXX by καὶ ἀποστέλλουσιν καί ἀπαγγέλλουσιν τῷ βασιλεῖ Συρίας ... . The table above is thus somewhat misleading. LXX^{O} agrees with the MT: ἀπέστειλεν υἱὸς Αδερ καὶ ἀνήγγελαν αὐτῷ.
144 LXX^{L}: + ὁ βασιλεύς (Συρίας).
145 B: βασιλεὺς Ισραηλ; A: βασιλεὺς Συρίας.
146 For מֶלֶךְ יִשְׂרָאֵל resp. מַלְכֵי בֵּית יִשְׂרָאֵל מַלְכֵי חֶסֶד (v.31) N reads βασιλευς ... .
147 Z: + Αχααβ.
148 LXX^{L}, Z: + βασιλεὺς Συρίας.
149 LXX^{L}, Z: + Αχααβ.

both the basic layer and the redactorial expansions. הַמֶּלֶךְ is used only in vv.35-43. In the preceding passages two kings were mentioned and thus הַמֶּלֶךְ would have been ambiguous. In vv.35-43 only the Israelite king is mentioned. אַחְאָב is used but once by the narrator[150] and thus there is no clear-cut distinction of layers with regard to participant designations. With regard to the titles used for the Aramean king the result is the same. In vv.1-12.21 / 26f.29-34, the basic layer, the Aramean king is called by the narrator בֶּן־הֲדַד (vv.9.10.26.30). He is called בֶּן־הֲדַד מֶלֶךְ־אֲרָם in v.1. In the supposed redactorial expansions the narrator refers to him as בֶּן־הֲדַד (vv.16.17) בֶּן־הֲדַד מֶלֶךְ־אֲרָם (v.20), and מֶלֶךְ־אֲרָם (v.23). We thus note that two of the three designations employed occur in both the basic layer and the redactorial expansions. The single occurrence of the third designation, used only in v.23, is not enough evidence for an identification of different strata.[151] The case is slightly different for the designations employed by the Greek versions. There we find that in the supposed basic layer the LXX only uses *υἱὸς* Αδερ (vv.1[152].9.10.26. 30). With one exception (v.9) even in direct speech only this designation is employed (vv.3.32.33). The supposed redactorial expansions use various designations: *υἱὸς* Αδερ (vv.16), *βασιλεὺς* Συρίας (vv.17.23), and in v.20 and the prophetic speech in v.22 *υἱὸς* Αδερ *βασιλεὺς* Συρίας.[153] But there is still no clear-cut difference in designations for the Aramean king, since *υἱὸς* Αδερ is employed in both strands. We thus conclude that the designations for the various participants do not constitute valid criteria for the establishment of redactional layers. One would have to argue that any given redactor only used one designation, a claim without any evidence to support it.

Schmitt then proceeded to argue that the passages mentioning מִישׁוֹר (v.23) or עֲמָקִים (v.28) are secondary ("suspicious"). If the story presupposes that the geographical environment of Aphek is fundamentally difficult from that of

150 Twice according to the LXX.

151 The reference to the Aramean king in v.23 as מֶלֶךְ־אֲרָם may well be due to the preceding prophetic speech where the same designation is used rather than to a later redactor. Since in the prophetic speech the narrator does not have free choice of the designation used for the Aramean king, no literary-critical conclusions regarding different layers of tradition may be drawn therefrom.

152 Adapted by LXX^L and LXX^O to the Hebrew בֶּן־הֲדַד מֶלֶךְ־אֲרָם.

153 It is interesting to note that LXX^L and LXX^O, in spite of their tendency to adapt the Greek text to the Hebrew, differ from the MT here (מֶלֶךְ־אֲרָם).

Samaria and that is not the case, this could be used to question the accuracy of the narrative but not its integrity. A mistake could be made by a narrator just as well as by a redactor. But, accepting the correctness of the identification of Aphek with ʿEn-Gev[154] and of Schmitt's impression of its geographical situation, the narrative does not state that the Arameans aimed to fight against the Israelites there. The actual meaning of מִישׁוֹר in this passage is not certain. While the term usually describes the tableland of northern Moab,[155] in 1 Kgs.20 it might refer to the Golan[156] or the valley of Jezreel,[157] or it may not describe a specific region at all but just refer to general tactics. In any case, it cannot be used to identify sources.

Schmitt's final argument, that vv.35-43 are to be regarded as secondary, because the other passages mentioning prophets have been shown to be inserted by later redactors, is not justified. Nothing in the passage itself forces us to regard it as secondary.

The source- and redaction-critical analyses of the the 1 Kgs.$22_{1\text{-}38}$ and 1 Kgs.20 discussed above which concentrated on internal evidence were not able to reduce the number of inconsistencies and necessary assumptions. Thus we conclude that our working hypothesis derived from the suggested empirical model according to which 1 Kgs.$22_{1\text{-}38}$ and 1 Kgs.20 should be regarded as representing narratives in their *early stages* of literary development still remains valid.

V. Conclusions

In the methodological considerations above it was argued that both internal and external evidence have to be taken into consideration. In any literary-critical investigation some presuppositions have to be made which cannot be derived from the narrative investigated. These should, as far as possible, be based on external evidence. The latter is further needed as a corrective for the choice of

---

154 Cf. below, appendix IV, p.294, n.8
155 Cf. Y.Aharoni, *Land of the Bible*, p.39.
156 Thus L.Koehler and W.Baumgartner, *Lexikon*, 3rd ed., p.547.
157 Thus W.Gesenius - F.Buhl, *Handwörterbuch*[17], p.60, who also regard Aphek as having been situated there.

literary phenomena regarded as source-critically significant. The variety of reconstructions of the literary pre-history of 1 Kgs.20 and 1 Kgs.22_{1-38} discussed above illustrates the need for a further refinement of literary-critical methodology and for continuous examination of the presuppositions on which it is based. Especially the fact that not only the identification of sources and redactional layers have to be made probable but also the process of redaction appears to have been neglected. External evidence may further influence the the source- and redaction-critical interpretation of the considered text features. The presence of the latter could, in principle, be due to a certain mode of narration and thus be ascribed to the *original* or to redactorial intervention by addition, omission or alteration. None of these possibilities may *a priori* be excluded.

It was argued that the *late* stage of a valid empirical model with regard to its relationship to redactorial trends, has to be comparable to the Old Testament narrative(s) in question. Only general developmental trends may be referred to, because it is not sufficient to demonstrate what *may* have happened, but rather what may be *expected* to have happened. The four Akkadian epics considered did not meet the requirements of an adequate empirical model, because their *late stages* and the present form of Old Testament narratives exhibit fundamental structural differences. The usefulness of the Chronicler's work is, for several reasons outlined above, only a very limited one. An analysis of the Chronicler's treatment of his *Vorlage* may be of illustrative, even confirmative, but taken on its own not of demonstrative value.

The Assyrian campaign accounts, on the other side, fulfilled the conditions set to a valid analogy. Our investigation of the transmission of the latter basically confirmed A.T.E.Olmstead's generalizing view of a progressive abbreviation.[158] It is, however, important to note that it oversimplifies the matter.

---

[158] "The procedure of the Assyrian scribe is regularly the same. As soon as the king had won his first important victory, the first edition of the annals was issued. With the next great victory, a new edition was made out. For the part covered by the earlier edition, an abbreviated form of this was incorporated" (*Assyrian Historiography*, p.8). Abbreviations of Greek and Latin literature, the *'επιτομαί*, provide interesting parallels to the treatment of Assyrian annals. I.Opelt ("Epitome", cols. 968-972) mentions omissions of speeches, interpretative remarks, repetitions, contractions, but also some additions (cf. also 2 Makk.2_{19-26} for an epitomizer's description of his aims). It is important to note that some epitomes were accomplished by the same authors as their

We have seen that in several cases manuscripts written at a later date nevertheless provide an earlier text version.[159] Furthermore, there are additions and expansions as well as omissions and abbreviations. The latter are more numerous in number but the existence of the former should not be ignored. It reminds us that the application of any analogy necessarily implies some inaccuracy. An empirical model can only give a broad picture. Any narrative within a collection, any passage within a narrative, any sentence within a passage may have been treated differently from its context and general developmental trends. Yet analogies are necessary and provide us with an important touchstone for literary-critical methodology. The Old Testament is unique, indeed, but it remains to be demonstrated that its uniqueness implied unique modes of transmission. Unless this can be done it is necessary to include empirical models in source- or redaction-critical considerations. The parallelism between the Chronicler's treatment of his *Vorlage* and the literary development of Assyrian campaign accounts confirms this.

In our analysis of the development of Assyrian campaign accounts we were able to establish the following indications of narratives in their *early stages*:

- a complex discourse structure
    - the presence of several peaks
    - relation of sidelines to the main course of events
    - several scenes
- a complex participant orientation pattern
    - high ratio of *reversals*
    - many participants
    - secondary participant as *main line agents*
    - co-occurrence of primary and secondary participants as *agents* in comparable situations
    - main participant relation mentioned in the *supportive material* rather than on the *main line*
- a simple time organization
    - chronological order of narration
    - relation of sequence of events rather than concentration on results
- a high rhetorical level
    - comparatively extensive use of rhetorical devices

---

more extensive *Vorlagen* (cf. M.Galdi, *L'epitome*, pp.257ff, I.Opelt, "Epitome," cols.957f). Jerome expressly described the Biblical Books of Chronicles as epitomes of the Books of Kings (ep.53,8,18; quoted in I.Opelt, "Epitome", col. 946).

[159] Cf. e.g. Chic.-Tayl. as compared to Bull 4 or ed.A's version of Aššurbanipal's Egyptian campaigns as compared to eds.B,C, and F.

- descriptive sentences and phrases
- enumerations as compared to common denominators.

We have found far fewer signs of secondary versions:

- emphasis on the significance of the events rather than on the events themselves (illocutionary / perlocutionary aspects)[160]
- linguistic heterogeneity

It is in the nature of things that there are more indications for *early stages* of narratives. The work of an author can in various respects not be strictly separated from that of a redactor. Thus, for example, already in the earliest version of a story the narrator may decide to present the events in thematic rather than chronological order or emphasize significance of events rather than merely relate them. From the narrative alone we cannot decide whether such "redactions" took place in the narrator's mind before he actually told his story or were carried out by subsequent editors. This implies that the narrative features associated with *early versions* do not *have* to be present there. Narratives may be *episodic* already in their earliest extant version.[161]

All this has important consequences for source criticism. The assumption of universal progressive expansion or growth of Old Testament narratives with all its implications,[162] if it cannot be supported by further evidence, should be abandoned. This constitutes a serious obstacle for source criticism. If narratives were abbreviated and text omitted, earlier stages of development are lost and cannot be recovered.

A second result of our investigation applies to our understanding of supposed doublets and type scenes.[163] We have seen above in the investigation of the transmission of accounts of Iakinlu's, Mugallu's Sandišarme's and Ba'alu's submissions that stories exhibiting similar features were further assimilated to each

---

160 If the speeches added by ed.A are not taken from early sources, but rather express the redactor's ideology, they may be noted here. This provides an interesting parallel to the Chronicler's insertion of prophetic speeches (cf. above, pp.117f, n.212) and a comparison between them may yield further insights into the Chronicler's work and the redactions of Assyrian campaign accounts.

161 Cf. e.g. the Bīt-Imbi episode in ed. $Cx_{65a\text{-}k}$ (cf. above, p.151, n.311).

162 This concerns primarily the establishment of developmental stages of narratives, (cf. e.g. H.Gunkel's statement: "je knapper eine Sage ist, desto wahrscheinlicher ist es daß sie in alter Form erhalten ist", {*Die Urgeschichte und die Patriarchen*, p.26} and above, pp.2f, n.7 and pp.6f, n.11).

163 Cf. D.Irvin, *Mythyrion*.

other. With the application of common literary-critical methodology the three brief accounts in ed.A may have been identified as triplets, referring to the same incident. The same is true for B's accounts of Aššurbanipal's two Egyptian campaigns. However, since earlier versions are extant, we can demonstrate that the development was different; the accounts were assimilated, not dissimilated. The narratives' distinct features are not secondary but present in the earliest extant version. This presents a further difficulty for source criticism. Originally distinct features may have been omitted or altered and are thus not recoverable. We have further seen that the development of Assyrian campaign accounts with the trends recognized above, e.g. those of progressive abbreviation, the concentration on references to primary participants or on results,[164] may have led to inconsistent narratives; updates may have created anachronisms. It is, however, important to note that the general course of narration was not affected. This implies that the presence of inconsistencies and anachronisms does not automatically render a narrative untrustworthy.

The results of our investigation also affect the validity of the criteria for the identification of *Sagen* as opposed to historical literature in the Old Testament. We can note that most of the "epic laws of popular poetry" ("Epische Gesetze der Volksdichtung") proposed by A.Olrik[165] can be recognized in the Assyrian campaign accounts or can be explained by general tendencies of literary development in the latter. The most important of Olrik's laws are:

- "eingangsgesetz und gesetz des abschlusses",[166]
- "gesetz der wiederholung",[167]
- "gesetz der dreizahl",[168]
- "gesetz der szenischen zweiheit",[169]
- "gesetz des gegensatzes".[170]

---

164 Cf. above, pp.106f, n.142, p.121f, n.222, and pp.122f with n.224.

165 "Epische Gesetze". Olrik's suggestions were taken up be H.Gunkel in the 3rd ed. of his commentary on Genesis (p.LI, n.1); cf. also C.Westermann, *Genesis* 2, pp.33ff.

166 The narrative relates a conflict and its resolution.

167 Comparable situations are related in similar or identical wording.

168 The number "three" is of special significance. No more than three participants appear in a scene.

169 The narrative relates the confrontation between two protagonists.

170 Popular poetry tends to polarize, e.g. between good and evil.

Since secondary versions tend to concentrate on the main conflict, the characteristics of the first, third, and fifth of these "laws" may be explained by redactional treatment. The second law, that of repetition, does not apply to Assyrian campaign accounts, but rather to the epics considered above. It is important to note that it does not apply to Old Testament narratives either. Linguistic research suggests that the third "law" with its maximum of three participants is probably valid for any narrative literature.[171] For the present purpose it suffices to note that it applies to Assyrian campaign accounts. It is easily recognizable in episodic accounts and, since the number of participants is generally reduced during the process of transmission, also in secondary versions of complex accounts.

The present investigation has mainly yielded negative results, arguing against the validity of common source- and redaction-critical hypotheses. Literary-critical research plays an important rôle in the study of the Old Testament. Since its results are inseparably bound to its presuppositions, continuous re-examination of the latter is thus crucial. The preliminary nature of a methodology based on hypotheses including those suggested by the present investigation should thus be emphasized and undergo continuous re-examination.

The present investigation suggests an empirical model for the transmission of Old Testament narratives that implies a view of their literary development which differs markedly from that of common literary-critical methodology. It cannot answer all the questions raised and it does not claim to be able to. The search for empirical models - and this should include other literary genres - and the discussion of their applicability have to continue. The literary-critical methods and basic assumptions need further refinement to become less dependent on the source- and redaction-critic's presuppositions and expectations and to avoid criticism like that put forward by A.Ungnad.[172] Until further evidence is adduced, the analogy taken from the redactorial treatment of Assyrian Royal annals can, however, provide us with a valuable working hypothesis and a general conception of how Old Testament narratives may be expected to have been edited.

---

[171] Cf. J.E.Grimes, *Thread of Discourse*, p.269: "Four participants operating at once has not been found yet."

[172] Cf. above, pp.7ff, n.12.

Appendix I - The Chronicler's *Vorlage*

Table 1: Text Types

		$Sam._{MT}$	$Sam._{LXX}$	4QSamª	$Chr._{MT}$	$Chr._{LXX}$
1	1 Sam.31_3 // 1 Chr.10_3	אֶל	*ἐπί*	[1]על	עַל	*ἐπί*
2	1 Sam.31_4 // 1 Chr.10_4	לְ	*πρός*	[2]אל	אֶל	*τῷ*
3	2 Sam.5_3 // 1 Chr.11_3	-	-	[3]-	כִּדְבַר יהוה בְּיַד שְׁמוּאֵל	*κατὰ τὸν* *λόγον κυρίου* *διὰ χειρὸς* *Σαμουηλ.*
4	2 Sam.$5_{4b\text{-}5}$ // 1 Chr.11_3[5]	+	+	[4]-	-	-
5	2 Sam.5_6 // 1 Chr.11_5	כִּי אִם	*ὅτι*	[6]כי	-	-
6	2 Sam.5_8 // 1 Chr.11_5	וְיִגַּע בַּצִּנּוֹר וְאֶת־הַפִּסְחִים וְאֶת־הַעִוְרִים שְׂנֻאוּ נֶפֶשׁ דָּוִד עַל־כֵּן יֹאמְרוּ עִוֵּר וּפִסֵּחַ לֹא יָבוֹא אֶל־הַבָּיִת	*ἁπτέσθω ἐν* *παραξιφίδι καὶ* *τοὺς χωλοὺς καὶ* *τοὺς τυφλοὺς* *καὶ τοὺς* *μισοῦντας* *τὴν ψυχὴν* *Δαυιδ· διὰ τοῦτο* *ἐροῦσιν Τυφλοὶ* *καὶ χωλοὶ οὐκ* *εἰσελεύσονται* *εἰς οἶκον κυρίου*	[7]יגע ... [8]שנאה	-	-
7	2 Sam.5_8 //	-	-	-[9]	בָּרִאשׁוֹנָה	*ἐν πρώτοις*

---

1 Cf. E.C.Ulrich, *Qumran Text*, p.80.
2 Cf. E.C.Ulrich, *Qumran Text*, p.80.
3 Cf. E.C.Ulrich, *Qumran Text*, pp.60.188.
4 Cf. E.C.Ulrich, *Qumran Text*, p.60.
5 Cf. however, 1 Chr.29_{27}.
6 Cf. E.C.Ulrich, *Qumran Text*, pp.66.128.
7 Cf. E.C.Ulrich, *Qumran Text*, pp.83.129.
8 Cf. E.C.Ulrich, *Qumran Text*, p.136.
9 Cf. E.C.Ulrich, *Qumran Text*, p.189.

	1 Chr.11$_{6}$				יִהְיֶה לְרֹאשׁ וּלְשָׂר וַיַּעַל בָּרִאשׁוֹנָה יוֹאָב בֶּן־ צְרוּיָה וַיְהִי לְרֹאשׁ[10]	*καὶ ἔσται εἰς* *ἄρχοντα καὶ* *εἰς* *στρατηγόν·* *καὶ ἀνέβη ἐπ'* *αὐτὴν ἐν* *πρώτοις Ιωαβ* *υἱὸς Σαρουια* *καὶ ἐγένετο* *εἰς ἄρχοντα*
8	2 Sam.5$_{9}$ // 1 Chr.11$_{8}$	וַיִּבֶן דָּוִד סָבִיב	*καὶ ᾠκοδόμησεν* *τὴν πόλιν κύκλῳ*	ויבנה עיר[11]	וַיִּבֶן הָעִיר מִסָּבִיב[12]	*καὶ* *ᾠκοδόμησεν* *τὴν πόλιν* *κύκλῳ*
9	2 Sam.5$_{10}$ // 1 Chr.11$_{9}$	וַיהוה צְבָאוֹת	*κύριος* *παντοκράτωρ*[14]	יהוה[13]	וַיהוה צְבָאוֹת	*κύριος* *παντοκράτωρ*
10	2 Sam.5$_{11}$ // 1 Chr.14$_{1}$	וְחָרָשֵׁי עֵץ וְחָרָשֵׁי אֶבֶן קִיר[16] וַיִּבְנוּ	*καὶ τέκτονας* *ξύλων καὶ* *τέκτονας λίθων,* *καὶ ᾠκοδόμησαν*[17]	חרשי קיר [וי]בנו[15]	וְחָרָשֵׁי קִיר וְחָרָשֵׁי עֵצִים לִבְנוֹת	*καὶ* *οἰκοδόμους* *τοίχων καὶ* *τέκτονας* *ξύλων τοῦ* *οἰκοδομῆσαι*
11	2 Sam.5$_{13}$ // 1 Chr.14$_{3}$	פִּלַגְשִׁים וְנָשִׁים	*γυναῖκας καὶ* *παλλακὰς*[18]	פיל[ג]שים ו[19]	נָשִׁים	*γυναῖκας*
12	2 Sam.5$_{13}$ // 1 Chr.14$_{3}$	וַיִּוָּלְדוּ עוֹד לְדָוִד	*καὶ ἐγένοντο* *τῷ Δαυιδ ἔτι*	לדויד עוד[20]	וַיּוֹלֶד דָּוִיד עוֹד	*καὶ* *ἐτέχθησαν* *Δαυιδ ἔτι*

---

10 The reading could be expected in Samuel, too. There, however, Joab is already mentioned as leader. Flavius Josephus mentions David's offer (*Antiquities*, VII,3,1 {H.Clementz' edition, vol.1, p.402).

11 Cf. E.C.Ulrich, *Qumran Text*, 70.

12 The reading may have been prompted by the preceding עִיר דָּוִיד (11$_{7}$); cf. M.Rehm, *Textkritische Untersuchungen*, p.63.

13 Cf. E.C.Ulrich, *Qumran Text*, p.66.

14 LXX^{O}: + *ὁ θεός ὁ*.

15 Cf. E.C.Ulrich, *Qumran Text*, p.99

16 חָרָשֵׁי אֶבֶן קִיר may be a combination of חָרָשֵׁי אֶבֶן, represented by Sam.$_{LXX}$, and חָרָשֵׁי קִיר, represented by Chr.$_{MT}$ and 4QSam^{a}; cf. M.Rehm, *Textkritische Untersuchungen*, p.123.

17 LXX^{O}: *λίθων τοίχου*, LXX^{L}: *τοίχου* (*λίθων*).

18 LXX^{O}:*παλλακὰς καὶ γυναῖκας*.

19 Cf. E.C.Ulrich, *Qumran Text*, p.192.

20 Cf. E.C.Ulrich, *Qumran Text*, p.83.

13	2 Sam.6_2 // 1 Chr.13_6[22]	וְכָל־הָעָם אֲשֶׁר אִתּוֹ	*καὶ πᾶς ὁ λαὸς ὁ μετ' αὐτοῦ*	אתו[21]]	וְכָל־יִשְׂרָאֵל	*πᾶς* Ισραηλ
14	2 Sam.6_2 // 1 Chr.13_6	מִבַּעֲלֵי יְהוּדָה	*ἀπὸ τῶν ἀρχόντων* Ιουδα	בעלה / היא קרי[ת][23]	בַּעֲלָתָה אֶל־ קִרְיַת יְעָרִים אֲשֶׁר לִיהוּדָה	*ἀνέβη εἰς πόλιν Δαυιδ, ἣ ἦν τοῦ* Ιουδα
15	2 Sam.6_2 // 1 Chr.13_6	אֵת אֲרוֹן הָאֱלֹהִים אֲשֶׁר־נִקְרָא שֵׁם שֵׁם יְהוָה צְבָאוֹת יֹשֵׁב הַכְּרֻבִים עָלָיו	*τὴν κιβωτὸν τοῦ θεοῦ, ἐφ' ἣν ἐπεκλήθη τὸ ὄνομα κυρίου τῶν δυνάμεων καθημένου ἐπὶ τῶν χερουβιν ἐπ' αὐτῆς*	as in Sam., however with שם only once and without יהוה צבאות[24]	אֲרוֹן הָאֱלֹהִים יהוה יוֹשֵׁב הַכְּרוּבִים אֲשֶׁר נִקְרָא שֵׁם	*τὴν κιβωτὸν τοῦ θεοῦ κυρίου καθημένου ἐπὶ χερουβιν, οὗ ἐπεκλήθη ὄνομα αὐτοῦ.*
16	2 Sam.6_3 // 1 Chr.13_7	הָאֱלֹהִים	*κυρίου*	[יהו]ה[25]	הָאֱלֹהִים	*θεοῦ*
17	2 Sam.6_3 // 1 Chr.13_7	אֶת־הָעֲגָלָה חֲדָשָׁה	*τὴν ἅμαξαν*	א[ת] העגלה[26]	בָּעֲגָלָה	*τὴν ἅμαξαν*
18	2 Sam.6_4 // 1 Chr.13_7	וַיִּשָּׂאֻהוּ מִבֵּית אֲבִינָדָב אֲשֶׁר בַּגִּבְעָה עִם אֲרוֹן הָאֱלֹהִים וְאַחְיוֹ הֹלֵךְ לִפְנֵי הָאָרוֹן׃	*σὺν τῇ κιβωτῷ, καὶ οἱ ἀδελφοὶ αὐτοῦ ἐπορεύοντο ἔμπροσθεν τῆς κιβωτοῦ.*[28]	-[27]	-	-
19	2 Sam.6_5 // 1 Chr.13_8	וְכָל־בֵּית יִשְׂרָאֵל	*καὶ οἱ υἱοὶ* Ισραηλ	בני ישראל[29]	וְכָל־יִשְׂרָאֵל	*πᾶς* Ισραηλ
20	2 Sam.6_5 // 1 Chr.13_8	בְּכֹל עֲצֵי בְרוֹשִׁים	*ἐν ἰσχύι καὶ ἐν ᾠδαῖς*	עז] ו]בשירים[30]	בְּכָל־עֹז וּבְשִׁירִים	*ἐν πάσῃ δυνάμει*

---

21 Cf. E.C.Ulrich, *Qumran Text*, p.194.
22 Cf. also the table of correspondences in E.C.Ulrich, *Qumran Text*, pp.194-197.
23 Cf. E.C.Ulrich, *Qumran Text*, 194.
24 Cf. E.C.Ulrich, *Qumran Text*, p.194.
25 Cf. E.C.Ulrich, *Qumran Text*, p.194.
26 Cf. E.C.Ulrich, *Qumran Text*, p.195. חֲדָשָׁה (6_{3b}) - בַּגִּבְעָה (6_4) is missing in 4QSam[a] and LXX; Ulrich: "Dittography").
27 Cf. E.C.Ulrich, *Qumran Text*, p.195.
28 LXX[O]: + *καὶ ἦραν αὐτήν ἀπὸ οἴκου* 'Αμιναδαβ *(ὃς ἦν) ἐν (τῷ) ἐν βουνῷ.*
29 Cf. E.C.Ulrich, *Qumran Text*, p.195.
30 Cf. E.C.Ulrich, *Qumran Text*, p.195.

					καὶ ἐν ψαλτῳδοῖς[31]
21 2 Sam.6_6 // 1 Chr.13_9	נָכוֹן	Νωδαβ[32]	נו/ידן[33]	כִּידֹן	-[34]
22 2 Sam.6_6 // 1 Chr.13_9	אֶל־אֲרוֹן הָאֱלֹהִים וַיֹּאחֶז בּוֹ	τὴν χεῖρα αὐτοῦ ἐπὶ τὴν κιβωτὸν τοῦ θεοῦ κατασχεῖν αὐτὴν καὶ ἐκράτησεν αὐτήν	אל ארון ה[א]ל[הים][35]	אֶת־יָדוֹ לֶאֱחֹז אֶת־הָאָרוֹן	τὴν χεῖρα αὐτοῦ τοῦ κατασχεῖν τὴν κιβωτόν
23 2 Sam.6_7 // 1 Chr.13_{10}	שָׁם הָאֱלֹהִים	ἐκεῖ ὁ θεός	שם האלהי[ם][36]	-	ἐκεῖ
24 2 Sam.6_7 // 1 Chr.13_{10}	עַל־הַשַּׁל	-[37]	[על אשר שלח ידו] אל[38]	עַל אֲשֶׁר־ שָׁלַח יָדוֹ עַל־הָאָרוֹן	διὰ τὸ ἐκτεῖναι τὴν χεῖρα αὐτοῦ ἐπὶ τὴν κιβωτόν
25 2 Sam.6_7 // 1 Chr.13_{10}	עִם אֲרוֹן הָאֱלֹהִים	παρὰ τὴν κιβωτὸν τοῦ κυρίου ἐνώπιον τοῦ θεοῦ	ל[פני האל[ו]ה[ים][39]	לִפְנֵי אֱלֹהִים	ἀπέναντι τοῦ θεοῦ
26 2 Sam.6_9 // 1 Chr.13_{12}	וַיֹּאמֶר	λέγων	לאמר[40]	לֵאמֹר	λέγων
27 2 Sam.6_{13} // 1 Chr.15_{26}	שִׁשָּׁה צְעָדִים	(καὶ ἦσαν μετ' αὐτῶν ...) ἑπτὰ χοροί	[41]-	-	-
28 2 Sam.6_{13} // 1 Chr.15_{26}	שׁוֹר וּמְרִיא	μόσχος καὶ ἄρνα	שבעה פרים שבעה[ה	שִׁבְעָה־פָרִים וְשִׁבְעָה	ἑπτὰ μόσχους καὶ ἑπτὰ

31 LXX^{L}: ᾠδαῖς.

32 B. A: Ναχων, O^{-A}: Αχων, *L*: Ορνα τοῦ Ιεβουσαιου.

33 Cf. E.C.Ulrich, *Qumran Text*, p.195.

34 A: χειλων, b: χαιλων, e_2: χελων.

35 Cf. E.C.Ulrich, *Qumran Text*, p.195.

36 Cf. E.C.Ulrich, *Qumran Text*, p.195.

37 LXX^{OL}: + ἐπὶ τῇ προπέτειᾳ.

38 Cf. E.C.Ulrich, *Qumran Text*, p.195.

39 Cf. E.C.Ulrich, *Qumran Text*, p.196.

40 Cf. E.C.Ulrich, *Qumran Text*, p.196.

41 Cf. E.C.Ulrich, *Qumran Text*, p.196.

				אילים][42]	אֵילִם	*κριούς*
29	2 Sam.6_{14} // 1 Chr.15_{27}	-	-	10 words[43]	וְכָל־הַלְוִיִּם הַנֹּשְׂאִים אֶת־ הָאָרוֹן וְהַמְשֹׁרְרִים וּכְנַנְיָה הַשַּׂר הַמַּשָּׂא הַמְשֹׁרְרִים	*καὶ πάντες οἱ* Λευῖται *αἴροντες τὴν κιβωτὸν διαθήκης κυρίου καὶ οἱ ψαλτῳδοὶ καὶ* Χωνενιας *ὁ ἄρχων τῶν ᾠδῶν τῶν ᾀδόντων*
30	2 Sam.6_{14} // 1 Chr.15_{27}	וְדָוִד חָגוּר אֵפוֹד בָּד	*καὶ ὁ Δαυιδ ἐνδεδυκὼς στολὴν ἔξαλλον.*[45]	חגור[44]	וְעַל־דָּוִיד אֵפוֹד בָּד	*καὶ ἐπὶ Δαυιδ στολὴ βυσσίνη*
31	2 Sam.6_{15} // 1 Chr.15_{28}	וְדָוִד וְכָל־ בֵּית יִשְׂרָאֵל	*καὶ Δαυιδ καὶ πᾶς ὁ οἶκος* Ισραηλ	ודו[יד][46]	וְכָל־יִשְׂרָאֵל	*πᾶς* Ισραηλ
32	2 Sam.6_{17} // 1 Chr.16_{1}	וַיַּעַל דָּוִד עֹלוֹת לִפְנֵי יהוה	*καὶ ἀνήνεγκεν Δαυιδ ὁλοκαυτώματα ἐνώπιον κυρίου*	ויעל[47]	וַיַּקְרִיבוּ עֹלוֹת	*καὶ προσήνεγκαν ὁλοκαυτώ-ματα*
33	2 Sam.7_{23} // 1 Chr.17_{21}	וְלַעֲשׂוֹת לָכֶם הַגְּדוּלָּה	*τοῦ ποιῆσαι μεγαλωσύνην*	[לע]שות ג[דלה][48]	גְּדֻלּוֹת	*μέγα*
34	2 Sam.7_{23} // 1 Chr.17_{21}	וֵאלֹהָיו	*καὶ σκηνώματα*	ואהלים[49]	-	-
35	2 Sam.8_{1} // 1 Chr.18_{1}	אֶת־מֶתֶג הָאַמָּה	*τὴν ἀφωρισμένην*[50]	מתג האמה	אֶת־גַּת וּבְנֹתֶיהָ	*τὴν* Γεθ *καὶ τὰς κώμας αὐτῆς*

---

[42] Cf. E.C.Ulrich, *Qumran Text*, p.196.
[43] Cf. E.C.Ulrich, *Qumran Text*, p.196.
[44] Cf. E.C.Ulrich, *Qumran Text*, p.196.
[45] The *Vorlage* for *ἔξαλλον* may have been read by the LXX as בַּר (cf. M.Rehm, *Textkritische Untersuchungen*, p.53).
[46] Cf. E.C.Ulrich, *Qumran Text*, p.196.
[47] Cf. E.C.Ulrich, *Qumran Text*, p.197.
[48] Cf. E.C.Ulrich, *Qumran Text*, p.67.
[49] Cf. E.C.Ulrich, *Qumran Text*, p.71.
[50] Cf. E.C.Ulrich, *Qumran Text*, p.183.

36 2 Sam.8_2 // 1 Chr.18_2	וַתְּהִי	καὶ ἐγένετο	[51]וה[יות]	וַיִּהְיוּ	καὶ ἦσαν
37 2 Sam.8_4 // 1 Chr.18_4	אֶלֶף וּשְׁבַע־מֵאוֹת פָּרָשִׁים	χίλια[52] ἅρματα καὶ ἑπτὰ χιλιάδας ἱππέων	אלף ר[כב ושבע][53]	אֶלֶף רֶכֶב וְשִׁבְעַת אֲלָפִים פָּרָשִׁים	χίλια ἅρματα καὶ ἑπτὰ χιλιάδας ἵππων
38 2 Sam.8_6 // 1 Chr.18_6	לְדָוִד לַעֲבָדִים	(καὶ ἐγένετο ὁ Σύρος) τῷ Δαυιδ εἰς δούλους	[לדו]יד עבדים[54]	לְדָוִיד עֲבָדִים	καὶ ἦσαν τῷ Δαυιδ εἰς παῖδας
39 2 Sam.8_8 // 1 Chr.18_8	הַרְבֵּה	σφόδρα	רבה[55]	רַבָּה	σφόδρα
40 2 Sam.8_8 // 1 Chr.18_8	-	ἐν αὐτῷ ἐποίησεν Σαλωμων τὴν θάλασσαν τὴν χαλκῆν καὶ τοὺς στύλους καὶ τοὺς λουτῆρας καὶ πάντα τὰ σκεύη	[בה עשה שלמה את ים ...[56]	בָּהּ עָשָׂה שְׁלֹמֹה אֶת־יָם הַנְּחֹשֶׁת וְאֶת־הָעַמּוּדִים וְאֵת כְּלֵי הַנְּחֹשֶׁת	ἐξ αὐτοῦ ἐποίησεν Σαλωμων τὴν θάλασσαν τὴν χαλκῆν καὶ τοὺς στύλους καὶ τὰ σκεύη τὰ χαλκᾶ.
41 2 Sam.10_5 // 1 Chr.19_5	-	ὑπὲρ τῶν ἀνδρῶν	[57]על] האנשים	עַל־הָאֲנָשִׁים	περὶ τῶν ἀνδρῶν
42 2 Sam.10_5 // 1 Chr.19_5	שְׁבוּ בִירֵחוֹ	Καθίσατε ἐν Ιεριχω	שבו ירחו[58]	שְׁבוּ בִירֵחוֹ	καθίσατε ἐν Ιεριχω
43 2 Sam.10_6 // 1 Chr.19_6	-	-	אלף ככר כסף[59]	אֶלֶף כִּכַּר־כֶּסֶף	χίλια τάλαντα
44 2 Sam.10_6 //	וְאֶת־אֲרַם	-[60]	ומצוב]ה רכב	וּמִצּוֹבָה רֶכֶב	καὶ ἐκ Σωβα

51 Cf. E.C.Ulrich, *Qumran Text*, p.159f.
52 A: *ἑπτά*.
53 Cf. E.C.Ulrich, *Qumran Text*, p.56.
54 Cf. E.C.Ulrich, *Qumran Text*, p.159.
55 Cf. E.C.Ulrich, *Qumran Text*, pp.45-47.
56 Cf. E.C.Ulrich,, *Qumran Text*, pp.45-47.
57 Cf. E.C.Ulrich, *Qumran Text*, p.85.
58 Cf. E.C.Ulrich, *Qumran Text*, p.136.
59 Cf. E.C.Ulrich, *Qumran Text*, p.152.
60 LXX^{O}: *καὶ Ροωβ καὶ τὴν Συριαν Σουβα*, LXX^{L}: *καί Βαιθρααμ καὶ τὸν Συρον Σουβα*, M: *Βαιθροωβ καὶ τὸν Συριαν Σουβα*.

1 Chr.19_{6}	צוֹבָא		פרשים[61]	וּפָרָשִׁים	*ἅρματα καὶ ἱππεῖς*
45 2 Sam.10_{6} // 1 Chr.19_{7}	עֶשְׂרִים אֶלֶף רַגְלִי	*εἴκοσι χιλιάδας πεζῶν*	שנים שלשי]ם אלף רכב[63]	שְׁנַיִם וּשְׁלֹשִׁים אֶלֶף רֶכֶב	[62]*δύο καὶ τριάκοντα χιλιάδας ἁρμάτων*
46 2 Sam.10_{7} // 1 Chr.19_{7}	-	-	ובני] עמון נאספו מן ה[ערים[64]	וּבְנֵי עַמּוֹן נֶאֶסְפוּ מֵעָרֵיהֶם	*καὶ οἱ υἱοὶ Αμμων συνήχθησαν ἐκ τῶν πόλεων αὐτῶν*
47 2 Sam.24_{16} // 1 Chr.21_{15}	הָיָה	*ἦν*	עומד[65]	עֹמֵד	*ἑστώς*
48 2 Sam.24_{16} // 1 Chr.21_{15}	הָאֲוַרְנָה	*Ορνα*	א]רנה[66]	אָרְנָן	*Ορνα*
49 2 Sam.24_{16} // 1 Chr.21_{16}	-	-	וישא [דויד את עיביו ... בין] הארץ ובין [הש]מ[י]ם וחר[ב]ו שלופה בידו [נטויה על ירושלם ... הזקנים על פנ]יהם מתכ[סים ב]שקים[67]	וַיִּשָּׂא דָוִיד אֶת־עֵינָיו וַיַּרְא אֶת־ מַלְאַךְ יְהוָה עֹמֵד בֵּין הָאָרֶץ וּבֵין הַשָּׁמַיִם וְחַרְבּוֹ שְׁלוּפָה בְּיָדוֹ נְטוּיָה עַל־יְרוּשָׁלָםִ וַיִּפֹּל דָּוִיד וְהַזְּקֵנִים מְכֻסִּים בַּשַּׂקִּים עַל־פְּנֵיהֶם	*καὶ ἐπῆρεν Δαυιδ τοὺς ὀφθαλμοὺς αὐτοῦ καὶ εἶδεν τὸν ἄγγελον κυρίου ἑστῶτα ἀνὰ μέσον τῆς γῆς καὶ ἀνὰ μέσον τοῦ οὐρανοῦ, καὶ ἡ ῥομφαία αὐτοῦ ἐσπασμένη ἐν τῇ χειρὶ αὐτοῦ ἐκτεταμένη ἐπὶ Ιερουσαλημ·*

---

61 Cf. E.C.Ulrich, *Qumran Text*, p.152.
62 BS: + *ἁρμάτα καὶ ἱππεῖς* (cf. v.6).
63 Cf. E.C.Ulrich, *Qumran Text*, p.152.
64 Cf. E.C.Ulrich, *Qumran Text*, p.152.
65 Cf. E.C.Ulrich, *Qumran Text*, pp.156-159.
66 Cf. E.C.Ulrich, *Qumran Text*, pp.156-159.
67 Cf. E.C.Ulrich, *Qumran Text*, pp.91.156-159.

					καὶ ἔπεσεν Δαυιδ καὶ οἱ πρεσβύτεροι περιβεβλη- μένοι ἐν σάκκοις ἐπὶ πρόσωπον αὐτῶν.
50 2 Sam.24$_{17}$ // 1 Chr.21$_{17}$	יהוה	κύριον	יהוה[68]	הָאֱלֹהִים	θεόν
51 2 Sam.24$_{17}$ // 1 Chr.21$_{17}$	וְאָנֹכִי הֶעֱוֵיתִי	καὶ ἐγώ εἰμι ὁ ποιμὴν ἐκακοποίησα	[וא]נכי הרעה הרעתי[69]	הָהָרֵעַ הֲרֵעוֹתִי	κακοποιῶν ἐκακοποίησα
52 2 Sam.24$_{18}$ // 1 Chr.21$_{18}$	וַיֹּאמֶר לוֹ עֲלֵה הָקֵם	καὶ εἶπεν αὐτῷ ᾿Ανάβηθι καὶ στῆσον	ויאמר עלה[70]	לֵאמֹר לְדָוִיד כִּי יַעֲלֶה דָוִיד לְהָקִים	τοῦ εἰπεῖν πρὸς Δαυιδ ἵνα ἀναβῇ τοῦ στῆσαι
53 2 Sam.24$_{19f}$ // 1 Chr.21$_{19f}$	כַּאֲשֶׁר צִוָּה יהוה וַיַּשְׁקֵף אֲרַוְנָה	καθ' ὃν τρόπον ἐνετείλατο αὐτῷ κύριος. καὶ διέκυψεν Ορνα	[אכ]שר צוה יהוה וישקף[71]	אֲשֶׁר דִּבֶּר בְּשֵׁם יהוה וַיָּשָׁב אָרְנָן	ὃν ἐλάλησεν ἐν ὀνόματι κυρίου. καὶ ἐπέστρεψεν Ορνα
54 2 Sam.24$_{20}$ // 1 Chr.21$_{20}$	אֶת־הַמֶּלֶךְ וְאֶת־עֲבָדָיו עֹבְרִים עָלָיו וַיֵּצֵא אֲרַוְנָה וַיִּשְׁתַּחוּ לַמֶּלֶךְ אַפָּיו אָרְצָה׃	τὸν βασιλέα καὶ τοὺς παῖδας αὐτοῦ παρα- πορευομένους ἐπάνω αὐτοῦ, καὶ ἐξῆλθεν Ορνα καὶ προσεκύνησεν τῷ βασιλεῖ ἐπὶ πρόσωπον αὐτοῦ ἐπὶ τὴν γῆν.	את מלך ואת עבדיו עוברים עליו מתכסים] בשקים[72] וארנה דש חטים	אֶת־הַמַּלְאָךְ וְאַרְבַּעַת בָּנָיו עִמּוֹ מִתְחַבְּאִים וְאָרְנָן דָּשׁ חִטִּים	τὸν βασιλέα καὶ τέσσαρες υἱοὶ αὐτοῦ μετ' αὐτοῦ μεθαχαβιν· καὶ Ορνα ἦν ἀλοῶν πυρούς.

---

68 Cf. E.C.Ulrich, *Qumran Text*, pp.156-159.
69 Cf. E.C.Ulrich, *Qumran Text*, p.86.
70 Cf. E.C.Ulrich, *Qumran Text*, p.105.
71 Cf. E.C.Ulrich, *Qumran Text*, p.158.
72 Cf. no.49.

Table 2: References to *Sources*

	Sources in Chr.	Contents	Sources in Kgs.	Contents
David[73] (1 Chr. $29_{29\text{-}30}$)	דִּבְרֵי שְׁמוּאֵל הָרֹאֶה דִּבְרֵי נָתָן הַנָּבִיא דִּבְרֵי גָּד הַחֹזֶה	דִּבְרֵי דָּוִיד הַמֶּלֶךְ הָרִאשֹׁנִים וְהָאַחֲרֹנִים... עִם כָּל־מַלְכוּתוֹ וּגְבוּרָתוֹ וְהָעִתִּים אֲשֶׁר עָבְרוּ עָלָיו וְעַל־יִשְׂרָאֵל וְעַל כָּל־מַמְלְכוֹת הָאֲרָצוֹת		
Solomon (2 Chr.9_{29}, 1 Kgs.11_{41})	דִּבְרֵי נָתָן הַנָּבִיא נְבוּאַת אֲחִיָּה הַשִּׁילוֹנִי חֲזוֹת יֶעְדִּי הַחֹזֶה עַל־יָרָבְעָם בֶּן־נְבָט	שְׁאָר דִּבְרֵי שְׁלֹמֹה הָרִאשֹׁנִים וְהָאַחֲרוֹנִים	סֵפֶר דִּבְרֵי שְׁלֹמֹה	יֶתֶר דִּבְרֵי שְׁלֹמֹה וְכָל־ אֲשֶׁר עָשָׂה וְחָכְמָתוֹ
Rehoboam (2 Chr.12_{15}, 1 Kgs.14_{29})	דִּבְרֵי שְׁמַעְיָה הַנָּבִיא וְעִדּוֹ הַחֹזֶה	דִּבְרֵי רְחַבְעָם הָרִאשֹׁנִים וְהָאַחֲרוֹנִים	סֵפֶר דִּבְרֵי הַיָּמִים לְמַלְכֵי יְהוּדָה	יֶתֶר דִּבְרֵי רְחַבְעָם וְכָל־ אֲשֶׁר עָשָׂה
Abijah (2 Chr.13_{22}, 1 Kgs.15_{7})	מִדְרַשׁ הַנָּבִיא עִדּוֹ	יֶתֶר דִּבְרֵי אֲבִיָּה וּדְרָכָיו וּדְבָרָיו	סֵפֶר דִּבְרֵי הַיָּמִים לְמַלְכֵי יְהוּדָה	יֶתֶר דִּבְרֵי אֲבִיָּם וְכָל־ אֲשֶׁר עָשָׂה
Asa (2 Chr.16_{11}, 1 Kgs.15_{23})	סֵפֶר הַמְּלָכִים לִיהוּדָה וְיִשְׂרָאֵל	דִּבְרֵי אָסָא הָרִאשׁוֹנִים וְהָאַחֲרוֹנִים	סֵפֶר דִּבְרֵי הַיָּמִים לְמַלְכֵי יְהוּדָה	יֶתֶר כָּל־דִּבְרֵי־ אָסָא וְכָל־ גְּבוּרָתוֹ וְכָל־אֲשֶׁר עָשָׂה וְהֶעָרִים אֲשֶׁר בָּנָה
Jehoshaphat (2 Chr.20_{34}, 1 Kgs.22_{46})	דִּבְרֵי יֵהוּא בֶן־חֲנָנִי אֲשֶׁר הֹעֲלָה[74] עַל־סֵפֶר מַלְכֵי יִשְׂרָאֵל[75]	יֶתֶר דִּבְרֵי יְהוֹשָׁפָט הָרִאשֹׁנִים וְהָאַחֲרֹנִים	סֵפֶר דִּבְרֵי הַיָּמִים לְמַלְכֵי יְהוּדָה	וְיֶתֶר דִּבְרֵי יְהוֹשָׁפָט וּגְבוּרָתוֹ אֲשֶׁר־עָשָׂה וַאֲשֶׁר נִלְחָם
Jehoash (2 Chr.24_{27}, 2 Kgs.12_{20})	מִדְרַשׁ סֵפֶר הַמְּלָכִים	בָּנָיו וְרֹב הַמַּשָּׂא עָלָיו וִיסוֹד בֵּית הָאֱלֹהִים	סֵפֶר דִּבְרֵי הַיָּמִים לְמַלְכֵי יְהוּדָה	יֶתֶר דִּבְרֵי יוֹאָשׁ וְכָל־ אֲשֶׁר עָשָׂה

---

73 A further reference to sources for the account of David's reign possibly is the מִסְפַּר דִּבְרֵי־הַיָּמִים לַמֶּלֶךְ דָּוִיד (1 Chr.27_{24}; LXX: *ἐν βιβλίῳ λόγων τῶν ἡμερῶν τοῦ βασιλέως Δαυιδ*).

74 LXX: *κατέγραψεν*, Vulgate: *digessit*.

75 Cf. also 1 Chr.9_{1}.

Amaziah (2 Chr.25_{26}, 2 Kgs.14_{18})	סֵפֶר מַלְכֵי־ יְהוּדָה וְיִשְׂרָאֵל	יֶתֶר דִּבְרֵי אֲמַצְיָהוּ הָרִאשֹׁנִים וְהָאַחֲרוֹנִים	סֵפֶר דִּבְרֵי הַיָּמִים לְמַלְכֵי יְהוּדָה	יֶתֶר דִּבְרֵי אֲמַצְיָהוּ
Uzziah (2 Chr.26_{22}, 2 Kgs.15_{6})	כָּתַב יְשַׁעְיָהוּ בֶן־אָמוֹץ הַנָּבִיא	יֶתֶר דִּבְרֵי עֻזִּיָּהוּ הָרִאשֹׁנִים וְהָאַחֲרֹנִים	סֵפֶר דִּבְרֵי הַיָּמִים לְמַלְכֵי יְהוּדָה	יֶתֶר דִּבְרֵי עֲזַרְיָהוּ וְכָל־אֲשֶׁר עָשָׂה
Jotham[76] (2 Chr.27_{7}, 2 Kgs.15_{36})	סֵפֶר מַלְכֵי־ יִשְׂרָאֵל וִיהוּדָה	יֶתֶר דִּבְרֵי יוֹתָם וְכָל־מִלְחֲמֹתָיו וּדְרָכָיו	סֵפֶר דִּבְרֵי הַיָּמִים לְמַלְכֵי יְהוּדָה	יֶתֶר דִּבְרֵי יוֹתָם אֲשֶׁר עָשָׂה
Ahaz (2 Chr.28_{26}, 2 Kgs.16_{19})	סֵפֶר מַלְכֵי־ יְהוּדָה וְיִשְׂרָאֵל	יֶתֶר דְּבָרָיו וְכָל־דְּרָכָיו הָרִאשֹׁנִים וְהָאַחֲרוֹנִים	סֵפֶר דִּבְרֵי הַיָּמִים לְמַלְכֵי יְהוּדָה	יֶתֶר דִּבְרֵי אָחָז אֲשֶׁר עָשָׂה
Hezekiah (2 Chr.32_{32}, 2 Kgs.20_{20})	חֲזוֹן יְשַׁעְיָהוּ בֶן־אָמוֹץ הַנָּבִיא עַל־סֵפֶר מַלְכֵי־ יְהוּדָה וְיִשְׂרָאֵל	יֶתֶר דִּבְרֵי יְחִזְקִיָּהוּ וַחֲסָדָיו	סֵפֶר דִּבְרֵי הַיָּמִים לְמַלְכֵי יְהוּדָה	יֶתֶר דִּבְרֵי חִזְקִיָּהוּ וְכָל־גְּבוּרָתוֹ וַאֲשֶׁר עָשָׂה אֶת־הַבְּרֵכָה וְאֶת־הַתְּעָלָה וַיָּבֵא אֶת־ הַמַּיִם הָעִירָה
Manasseh (2 Chr.$33_{18.19}$, 2 Kgs.21_{17})	דִּבְרֵי מַלְכֵי יִשְׂרָאֵל[77]	יֶתֶר דִּבְרֵי מְנַשֶּׁה וּתְפִלָּתוֹ אֶל־אֱלֹהָיו וְדִבְרֵי הַחֹזִים הַמְדַבְּרִים אֵלָיו בְּשֵׁם יְהוָה אֱלֹהֵי יִשְׂרָאֵל	סֵפֶר דִּבְרֵי הַיָּמִים לְמַלְכֵי יְהוּדָה	יֶתֶר דִּבְרֵי מְנַשֶּׁה וְכָל־ אֲשֶׁר עָשָׂה וְחַטָּאתוֹ אֲשֶׁר חָטָא
	דִּבְרֵי חוֹזָי[78]	וּתְפִלָּתוֹ וְהֵעָתֶר־לוֹ וְכָל־חַטָּאתוֹ וּמַעְלוֹ וְהַמְּקֹמוֹת אֲשֶׁר בָּנָה בָהֶם בָּמוֹת וְהֶעֱמִיד		

76 A further reference to possible sources for the account on the reign of Jotham כֻּלָּם הִתְיַחְשׂוּ בִּימֵי יוֹתָם מֶלֶךְ־יְהוּדָה וּבִימֵי יָרָבְעָם מֶלֶךְ־יִשְׂרָאֵל (1 Chr.5_{17}; *πάντων ὁ καταλοχισμός ἐν ἐμέραις* Ιεροβοαμ *βασιλέως* Ισραηλ).

77 מַלְכֵי יִשְׂרָאֵל > LXX.

78 LXX: *τῶν λόγων τῶν ὁρώντων*.

		הָאֲשֵׁרִים וְהַפְּסִלִים לִפְנֵי הִכָּנְעוֹ		
Josiah (2 Chr. $35_{26\text{-}27}$, 2 Kgs.23_{28})	סֵפֶר מַלְכֵי־ יִשְׂרָאֵל וִיהוּדָה	יֶתֶר דִּבְרֵי יֹאשִׁיָּהוּ וַחֲסָדָיו כַּכָּתוּב בְּתוֹרַת יְהוָה: וּדְבָרָיו הָרִאשֹׁנִים וְהָאַחֲרֹנִים	סֵפֶר דִּבְרֵי הַיָּמִים לְמַלְכֵי יְהוּדָה	יֶתֶר דִּבְרֵי יֹאשִׁיָּהוּ וְכָל־ אֲשֶׁר עָשָׂה
Jehoiakim (2 Chr.36_8, 2 Kgs.24_5)	סֵפֶר מַלְכֵי יִשְׂרָאֵל וִיהוּדָה	יֶתֶר דִּבְרֵי יְהוֹיָקִים וְתֹעֲבֹתָיו אֲשֶׁר־עָשָׂה וְהַנִּמְצָא עָלָיו	סֵפֶר דִּבְרֵי הַיָּמִים לְמַלְכֵי יְהוּדָה	יֶתֶר דִּבְרֵי יְהוֹיָקִים וְכָל־ אֲשֶׁר עָשָׂה

For the reigns of Jehoram (cf. 2 Kgs.8_{23}), Ahaziah, Athaliah, Amon (2 Kgs.21_{25}), Jehoahaz, Jehoiachin, and Zedekiah the Chronicler has no literary reference.

Appendix II - Discourse Profiles

1. Aššurbanipal's Campaign against Aḫšeri

Discourse profile for B's account

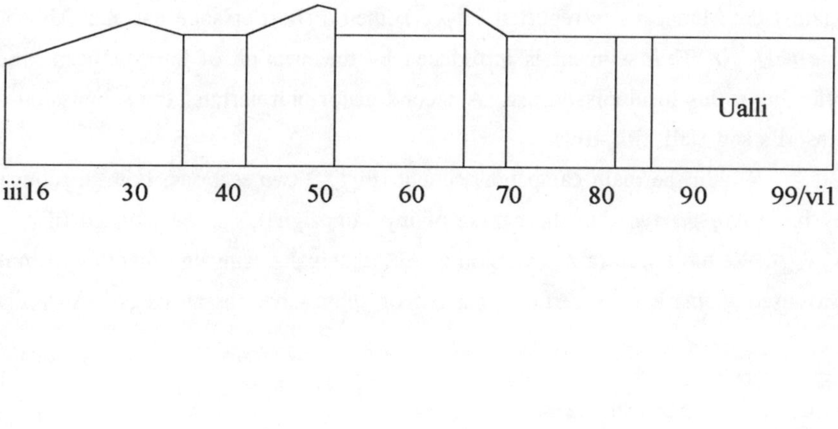

Discourse profile for B's account indicating alterations by F and A

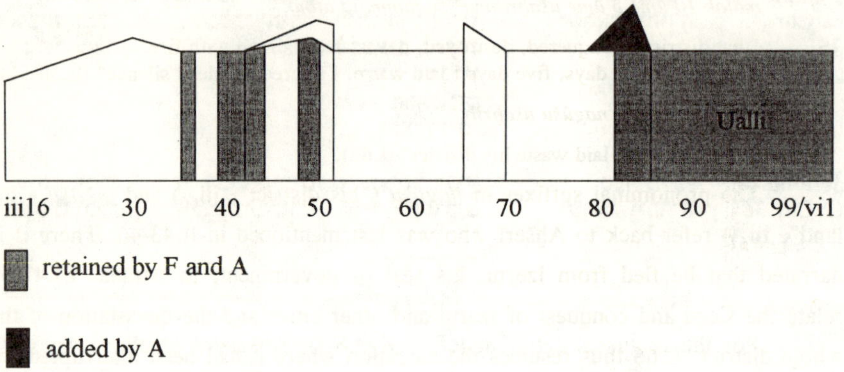

Comments:

The oldest of the major versions for Aššurbanipal's campaign against Aḫšeri is that of edition B. B begins the account with the campaign formula [*ina ḫanšê*] *girrīya eli Aḫšeri šar Mannayya lu allik* ("[in] my [fifth] campaign I marched against Aḫšeri, king of Mannayya", iii$_{16}$). The account is divided into various episodes. A first unit is framed by the mention of Aḫšeri as major enemy of Aššurbanipal (iii$_{16}$) and the narration of his death (iii$_{82-85}$). Within this larger section iii$_{16-69}$ narrate the campaign from the setting off of the Assyrian army to the safe return. After the account of the campaign proper a minor expedition against the Manneans is reported (iii$_{70-81}$), then a short episode narrates Aḫšeri's fate (iii$_{82-85}$). This segment is introduced by the mention of the Mannean king, referring to his insubmissiveness. A second major unit narrates the submission of Aḫšeri's son Ualli (iii$_{86}$-iv$_{2}$).

Within the main campaign account (iii$_{16-69}$) two sections, both introduced by *ina mētiq girrīya* ("in the course of my campaign"), can be isolated (iii$_{34-42}$, iii$_{52-65}$). We have seen in A's version of Aššurbanipal's campaign that this formula was used to mark an insertion of a list of submissive vassal kings.[1] A similar

1 Cf. above, p.126 with n.234.

function may be assumed in $iii_{34.51}$. We can further note a case of *resumptive repetition*[2] in ll.50-51 and l.66:

> *nagû šuātu akšud appul aqqur ina išāti aqmu*
> *mālak 10 ūmē 5 ūmē ušaḫribma*[3] *šaqummata atbuk*
>
> "that district I conquered, destroyed, devastated, burned with fire,
> a distance of 10 days, five days I laid waste, I poured out dead silence" (ll.50-51)
>
> *ina tīb tāḫāzīya nagûšu ušaḫrib*
>
> "by my attack I laid waste his district" (l.66).

The pronominal suffixes in *nagûšu* ("his district", iii_{66}) and *mātīšu* ("his land", iii_{67}) refer back to Aḫšeri who was last mentioned in ll.43-46. There it is narrated that he fled from Izertu, his seat of government, to Atrāna. Ll.47-51 relate the siege and conquest of Izertu and other cities and the devastation of the whole district. L.66 thus resumes the narration where it had been interrupted for the insertion.[4] It is not possible to determine when this insertion was made.[5] In our establishment of B's *discourse profile* we have concentrated on $iii_{16\text{-}33.43\text{-}51.66\text{-}69}$. Two further episodes ($iv_{3\text{-}8.9\text{-}17}$) were separated from the previous sections by a horizontal line in the inscription and are thus treated separately.

---

2 Cf. S.Talmon, "Synchroneity and Simultaneity". An example of resumptive repetition as a sign of redactorial insertion is provided by the insertion of $Cx_{50\text{-}56}$ where it is narrated that Yauta᾿ fled to Natnu, who offered him protection from the Assyrians. Thereafter C relates Natnu's submission to Aššurbanipal. The inserted passage is framed by resumptive repetition ($Cx_{45\text{-}48.57\text{-}59}$). A has transferred the account of Natnu's submission into the context of a campaign against Abiate᾿, Natnu's ally. Again the insertion was marked by resumptive repetition ($Aviii_{48.69}$). From F's account of Aššurbanipal's first campaign against Ummanaldasi (cf. $Fiii_{33\text{-}36}$), where $Fiii_{37f}$ is resumed by $Fiii_{70}$ is evident, that the presence of a resumptive repetition alone does not necessary imply that the framed section was inserted by a later redactor. If the text between these lines was secondarily incorporated the narrative in its earlier version would not have mentioned Ummanaldasi. Cf. also $Bvii_{57.77}$.

3 Thus K 1705, K 2732, eds. F and A. B erroneously has *ušaḫrirma*.

4 Similarly *alāk girrīya* ("the advance of my army", iii_{43}) refers back to *attallaka* ("I advanced", iii_{33}).

5 It should be noted that $Biii_{34\text{-}42}$ in its extant form is not a self-contained unit. *adi qereb Izertu* ("up to the city of Izertu", iii_{38}) receives its significance from the report of Izertu's conquest ($iii_{47\text{-}50}$). On the other hand in $Biii_{34\text{-}42}$ there are no pronominal references pointing outside the section (F and A have added *-šu*, "his", to *ālāni*, "cities", {$Biii_{37}$ // Fii_{26} // Aii_{130}}). It is only in iii_{44} that Izertu is described as *āl šarrūtīšu* ("his royal city"), in iii_{38} the city had been plainly mentioned. Since it might be expected that the significance of the city is mentioned at the earliest occurrence of its name, *adi qereb Izertu* may be seen as an adaptation of the inserted passage to the context.

As has been mentioned above, B begins the account with a campaign formula. The reason for Aššurbanipal's campaign (Aḫšeri's "sin") is given in subordinate clauses, *ša ana šarrāni abbēya lā kitnušu* ("who had not submitted to the kings, my fathers", l.19), *itappalu da[bab]āti* ("who had discussed intrigues" {?}, iii$_{19}$[6]). The *inciting event*, typically the arrival of a messenger or a request for help, is not mentioned. The first lines dealing with the campaign proper (ii$_{20ff}$) mention that the Assyrian army went off and set up camp.

The parallelism *ušmannu addina / aškuna karāšī*[7] ("the camp I built" / "I set up my camp") constitutes a rise of the surface structure level. The next lines mention that Aḫšeri learned of (*išmēma*) the Assyrian preparations for battle. Now both opponents have entered the scene and move towards each other - tension rises. The participant relation, which at the beginning of the account had been A-B, has changed to B-A. The description of Aḫšeri's advance is unusually extensive.[8] The supplements of *itbûni* ("they came") constitute an EEN-construction:

ina šāt mūši
ina[9] *šipir nikilti*
ana epēš tāḫāzi (*itbûni*)
ana mitḫuṣi ummānātēya

"during the night
stealthily
(they advanced) to give battle,
to fight my troops" (iii$_{25-27}$).

The whole passage is arranged as *overlay*:

ana	*epēš tāḫāzi*		*itbûni*
ana	*mitḫuṣṣi*	*ummānātēya*	
		ṣābē tāḫāzīya ittīšun imdaḫḫaṣū	
			iškunū abiktašun

6 Cf. BM 134441 (R.Campbell Thompson, "A Selection", p.104, no.25).

7 The actual text of Biii$_{21-22}$ is not certain. Piepkorn gives: "... *aškunu* [. . . . *k*]*a-ra-ši* . . . ("I set up [... the c]amp") and notes that the break is big enough to accommodate 11 signs. BM 134441 (cf. R.Campbell Thompson, "A Selection", p.104, no.25), l.19, however, has *aškuna karāši* with no break at all between the words. The text of BM 134441 is intelligible and constitutes a chiastic parallelism: *ušmannu addina / aškuna karāši*. There is thus no literary reason to assume that some words have been omitted.

8 For descriptions of the enemies' advance after having learned of the Assyrian advance cf. HT obv.5-8.16, Bi$_{57-62.66-67.73-74}$ iv$_{33-34}$ vii$_{9-29}$.

9 Not in BM 134477 (cf. R.Campbell Thompson, "A Selection", pp.103f, no.24).

"to give battle		they came
to fight		my troops
		the soldiers of my battle array fought with them.
		they accomplished their defeat" (iii_{26-29}).

The mention of the Assyrian victory is further amplified by a description of its extent (iii_{30}). The conflict is resolved and tension decreases, only to rise again with the mention of Aššurbanipal's advance. In the report of battle and victory 3rd p.pl. had been employed (participant relation A'-B'). Now the scope has switched back to the Assyrian king (iii_{31}). While the first confrontation appears to have taken place in Assyria,[10] Aššurbanipal then enters Mannean territory. The narration of this is intensified by *šaltiš* ("victoriously", l.33).

Again Aḫšeri learns of Aššurbanipal's advance (l.43),[11] but this time he leaves Izertu and escapes (ll.44-46). The report of the ravaging of the whole district (ll.47-50) is intensified by a description of the extent of the destruction (l.51), which parallels, and exceeds l.30:

mālak 3 bēri eqli šalmātīšunu umallû ṣēra rapša

"(over) an area of 3 double hours in length they filled the wide plain with their corpses" (iii_{30})

mālak 10 ūmē 5 ūmē ušaḫribma šaqummata atbuk

"a distance of 10 days, five days I laid waste, I poured out dead silence" (iii_{51}).

This section constitutes an EEN construction:

nagû šuātu	*akšud*
	appul
	akkur
	ina išāti aqmu
	mālak 10 ūmē 5 ūmē ušaḫribma šaqummata atbuk
"that district	I conquered,
	destroyed,
	devastated,
	burned with fire
	a distance of 10 days, five days I laid waste, I poured out dead silence" (iii_{50-51}).

While iii_{30} has the Assyrian army as agents, in the second passage Aššurbanipal himself is the grammatical subject. Thus in the narration the result

[10] Cf. iii_{21f}, restored after BM 134441 (cf. R.Campbell Thompson, "A Selection", p.104, no.25), ll.18f to *allikma qereb Dur-Aššur ušmannu addīma* ... ("I entered the city of Dur-Aššur, set up the camp ...").

[11] The wording exactly parallels l.23.

of the second confrontation contains the overall *peak* of B's account. The other sections do not exhibit substantial rise or decline of the rhetorical level.

2. Aššurbanipal's Campaign against Teummān (figure 3)

Discourse profile of B's account

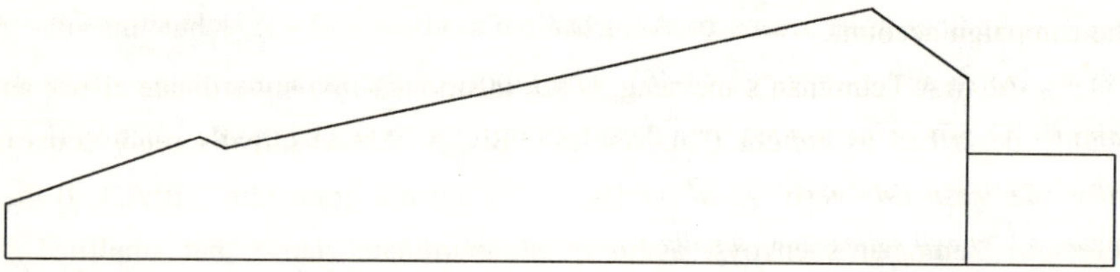

Comments:

Of the major editions the oldest extant report is provided by ed.B.[12] Because of the extensive use of direct speech, parallelisms and EEN constructions

[12] K 2652 (cf. M.Streck, *Assurbanipal* II, pp.189-195) may represent the text of one of B's *Vorlagen*. This inscription commemorates the dedication of a bow to Ištar and relates Aššurbanipal's prayer, Ištar's reply, and dream of a seer. The purpose of the inscription and the presence of *amšala* ("yesterday") in K 2652, obv.25 (B: *ina šāt mūši šuātu* - "during that night") point to a date not long after the event. K 2652 and ed.B differ greatly in their description of the campaign proper. In K 2652 only three lines (rev.11-13, l.10 probably corresponds to Bv_{75-76}) are devoted to the expedition. The text of K 2652 is not well preserved and, since it does not parallel ed. B, it cannot be restored with any certainty. According to K 2652 Teummān appears to have been killed by his subjects (rev.12: ...] *iddû pagar Teummān šar Elamti* [... - "...] they threw the body of Teummān, king of Elam [..."). B reports that Aššurbanipal decapitated the Elamite king (vi_1). In the preserved portions of K 2652 this is only referred to in rev.16: ...] *eli nikis qaqqadi Teummān šar Elam*[*ti*... ("...] concerning the severed head of Teummān, king of Elam [..."), which may refer back to the lost part of l.12. K 2652 with its reference to secondary participants appears to represent an older version compared to B (cf. also $Bvii_{60-61}$ // Aiv_{15}: *eli nikis qaqqadi Teummān ša*

the rhetorical level of B's account is comparatively high. The literary devices employed allow only a slow progress of narration. The narrative structure is complex and exibits two climaxes.

B begins its account with the campaign formula *ina sibê girrīya eli Teummān šar Elamti lu allik* ("in my seventh campaign I marched against Teummān, king of Elam", Biv_{87-88}). Teummān's relations with Assyria are described in a subordinate clause after the mention of his name. There it is stated that he had sent a messenger to Aššurbanipal demanding the extradition of the Urtaku's and Ummanaldaše's sons who had sought refuge in Assyria. The mention of Aššurbanipal's refusal clarifies the conflict the resolution of which is related in the campaign account.

At first Teummān's messengers are mentioned in a subordinate clause and plainly described as *rubêšu* ("his nobles", Biv_{94}). Aššurbanipal's reply contains only one *main line* verb: ... *ul aqbīšu* ("... I did not grant him", Biv_{96}). B then refers to Teummān's envoys, again in a subordinate clause, but amplified by *arḫišam* ("monthly") and this time Teummān's officers are mentioned by name and his messages are described as *mēreḫēte* ("insolences", Biv_{97-98}) . Correspondingly Aššurbanipal's reaction is related in a chiastic parallelism with two *main line* verbs: ... *ul amgur ul addinšu* ... ("... I did not permit, I did not give him ...", Bv_2). The repetitive structure delays the mention of the *inciting event* and thus increases tension.

Another parallelism, immediately following the previous one, has the adversaries in opposition and clarifies the conflict even further:

Teummān lemutta išteni'â
Sin išteni'šu itāt lemutti

"Teummān devised evil,
Sin devised for him portents of evil" (v_{3-5}).

It is noteworthy that this passage does not mention the Assyrian king. The conflict is still an indirect one.

---

ikkisu aḫurrû ummānātēya - "concerning the severed head of Teummān, which a common soldier of my army had cut off"). Since with regard to the date of K 2652 no final conclusion ca be reached, we have taken ed.B as our point of departure. The differences between K2652 and ed.B in the narration of Teummān's death provide an interesting parallel to 1 Sam.31_{9-10} // 1 Chr.10_{9-10}.

The narrative proceeds to describe astronomical phenomena (Bv_{5-10})[13], foreshadowing Teummān's accident (Bv_{10-12}).[14] The conflict seems to be resolved and tension decreases. However, in the next lines the reader/listener learns that Teummān nevertheless intends to attack (Bv_{14-15}). B then reports that Aššurbanipal received intelligence of the Elamite advance (Bv_{15-24}). The message and within the message Teummān's plan are quoted in direct speech and thus increase the rhetorical level.[15] Correspondingly the description of Aššurbanipal's emotional response, too, is unusually extensive. The Assyrian king prays to Ištar (Bv_{25-46}) and receives her reply (Bv_{46-49}), which is continued by a seer's dream (Bv_{49-67}). Aššurbanipal's prayer is artistically composed. There are several EEN-constructions built in. At first the order of the appositions after mention of Aššurbanipal's name follows Ehelolf's principle:

šar Aššur
binût qātīki
ša iḫšuḫūšu Aššur abu bānûki
ana ... imbu zikiršu

"king of Assyria,
creature of your hands,
whom Aššur, the father who begot you, desired,
whose name he called to ..." (Bv_{30-32}).

The supplements of *imbu zikiršu* ("whose name he called") are also arranged to an EEN-construction.

---

13 The reference of *inbu* ("fruit", Bv_9) is uncertain. It may either indicate the New Moon (thus W.von Soden, *Akkadisches Handwörterbuch* I, p.381) or the execution of Sin's plan.

14 The description of Teummān's illness is given in a triad:
šapatsu uktambilma
ēnu isḫirma
gabaṣu iššakin ina libbiša
"his lip was paralyzed,
the eye twisted,
a contraction was placed in its midst".
If with A 7962, P3, K 10621 we add *-šu* ("his") to *ēnu* ("eye"; cf. A.C.Piepkorn, *Historical Prism Inscriptions*, p.63, n.4) the passage would constitute an EEN-construction. A 7962 and K 2732 have *libbīšu* ("his heart") for *libbīša* ("its midst"; cf. A.C.Piepkorn, *Historical Prism Inscriptions*,p.63, n.7) thus altering the reference from *ēnu* to *Teummān* and increasing the parallelism.

15 For common descriptions of comparable events cf. e.g. HT obv. 9.24, B i_{63-64} ii_{17} $iv_{35-38.43-47}$.

ana udduš ešrēti
šullum parṣīšun
naṣār pirištīšun
šuṭūb libbīšun

"to renovate the sanctuaries,
perform their ordinances,
keep their secrets,
make glad their hearts" (Bv_{31-32}).

The next three lines lines contrast Aššurbanipal and Teummān:

anāku ašrīki ašteni'i allika ana palaḫ ilūtīki u šullum parṣīki
u šū Teummān šar Elamti lā mušāqir ilāni kuṣṣur kali ana mitḫuṣu ummānātēya

"I sought your place, I came to worship your divinity and to perform your ordinances and this Teummān, king of Elam, who does not esteem the gods, brought together all to fight my troops" (Bv_{33-36}).

The epithets of Ištar, apart from the first one, are also arranged according to their length:

(*bēlit bēltī*)
ilat qabli
bēlit tāḫāzi
mālikat ilāni

"(lady of ladies,)
goddess of war,
mistress of battle,
queen of the gods" (Bv_{37-38}).

The same is true for Aššurbanipal's description of Teummān's preparations for battle:

biltu [*lā ūbila*][16]
idkâ ummānšu
ikṣura tāḫāzi
uša''ala kakkēšu ana alāk Aššur

"he did not pay tribute
he mustered his army,
he assembled (for) battle,
he sharpened his weapons to march against Assyria" (Bv_{42-43})

---

16 The restoration of this line by A.C.Piepkorn is conjectural. If it is correct, then the first member would have one syllable more than the second. Only the last three members, all having *ana alāk Aššur* ("to march against Assyria") as supplement, would constitute an EEN construction. If the phrase can be reconstructed as *biltu ušabṭil* ("he withheld tribute"; cf. $Aiii_{24}$) the first and the second member of the construction would have the same number of syllables. It is, however, not reported that Teummān actually paid tribute.

and Ištar's advice and promise to the Assyrian king in the seer's dream:

akul akala
šiti kurunna
ningûta šukun
nu''id ilūtī

"eat food,
drink beer,
provide joyful music,
revere my divinity" (Bv_{65-66})

pānūka ul urraq
ul inarruṭa šēpēka
ul tašammaṭ lē'ûtka[17] *ina qabal tāḫāzi*

"your face shall not turn pale,
your feet shall not stumble,
your strength shall not fail in the midst of battle" (Bv_{69-70}).

The high rheorical level of *stage* and *inciting event* leads to an increase of tension at the beginning of the account of the campaign proper. The description of Aššurbanipal's mobilization of his forces, too, is more extensive than usual[18] and contains a chiastic parallelism.

...urḫu aṣbatma
ušteššera ḫarrānu

"... I took the road,
marched against" (Bv_{82-83}).

Overlay is used in the narration of Teummān's reaction:

	iṣbassu ḫattu	
Teummān	*iplaḫma*	*ana arkīšu itur*
		ērub qereb Šušan
	"terror siezed him	
Teummān	became afraid,	he turned back,
		he entered the city of Susa" (Bv_{58-86}).

The rise in the rhetorical level corresponds to the fact that the Assyrian king himself takes action, whereas in the previous section it had been the Assyrian gods.

Then B continues to describe Teummān's preparations for war and his advance. Teummān succeeded in seizing water-holes from the Assyrians. The

---

17 For *ul tašammaṭ lē'ûtka* von Soden, *Akkadisches Handwörterbuch* III, p.1155, reads *ul-ta-šam-maṭ zūtka* ("your sweat shall ?"). However, the parallelism with the preceding lines renders A.C.Piepkorn's reading more probable.

18 Cf. Bii_{18-19}; iv_{50} and the campaign introductions.

mention of the enemies' success against the Assyrians is unusual and leads to a rise in tension, since the resolution of the conflict is further delayed. Then very suddenly the Assyrian victory is reported. The change of situation is very abrupt and no emphasis is placed on the battle as such. B then continues with a description of the extent of the Elamite defeat, using a parallelism with a comparison, which marks a surface structure *peak* which in this passage corresponds to the *dénouement* of the notional structure:

ina pagrēšunu		*Ulaia askir*
ṣalmatešunu	*kīma baltāti ašāgi*	*umallâ tāmarti Šušan.*
"with their bodies		I blocked the river Ulaia,
their corpses	like thorns, thistles	filled the plain of Susa" (Bv$_{97-99}$).

The relation of Teummān's decapitation (Bvi$_{1-3}$) closes the circle to the beginning of the account. Further concluding remarks mention the submission of Elam (vi$_{4-5}$), the enthronement of Ummanigaš (ll.6-7) and Tammaritu (ll.8-9), and the taking and distribution of booty (ll.10-16).

Appendix III - Participant Orientation Patterns

1. Sennacherib's Second Campaign (Bell., ll.20-33, Chic.i$_{65}$-ii$_{36}$, Bull 4, ll.9-17)

			Bell.	Rass./Chic.-Tayl.	Bull 4
l.20	*utakkilannima* "he encouraged me"	A*[1]-A-(B)		+	-
	lu allik "I marched"	A-B	⇒I	I	+
	arkabma "I rode"	A-(B)	⇒I	I	I
l.21	*ušašši* "I had (my chariot) drawn"	A-(B)	⇒I	I	-
	attagiš "I went"	A-(B)	⇒I	I	I
l.22	*alme* "I surrounded"	A-B	⇒I	I	-
	akšud "I conquered"	A-B	⇒I	I	I

1 Grammatical subject: *Aššur*.

	ušēṣâmma	A-B	⇒ I	I	-
	"I brought out"				
	amnu	A-B	⇒ I	I	I[2]
	"I counted (as spoil)"				
1.23	*appul*	A-B	⇒ I	I	I
	"I destroyed"				
	aqqur	A-B	⇒ I	I	I
	"I devastated"				
	ušēme	A-B	⇒ I	I	-
	"I turned into wasteland"				
	aqmūma	A-B	⇒ I	I	I
	"I burned"				
	ušēme[3]	A-B	⇒ I	I	-
	"I reduced (to ashes)"				
1.24	*utīrma*	A-(B)	⇒ I	I	I
	"I turned round"				
	aṣbat	A-B	⇒ I	I	I
	"I made (that city a fortress)"				
	udannin	A-B	⇒ I	I	-
	"I strengthened"				
	ušēšib	A-B	⇒ I	I	I
	"I settled (conquered peoples therein)"				
1.25	*ušēridamma*	A-B	⇒ I	I	I
	"I brought down"				
	ušarme	A-B	⇒ I	I	I
	"I settled (them)"				
1.26	*amnūšunūti*	A-B	⇒ I	I	I
	"I counted them ⇒ I placed them"				
	ušēpišma	A-(B)	⇒ I	I	-
	"I had (a stela) made"				
	ušašṭirma	A-(B)	⇒ I	I	-
	"I had inscribed"				
	ulziz	A-(B)	⇒ I	I	-
	"I erected"				
1.27	*utīrma*	A-(B)	⇒ I	I	-
	"I turned (the front of my yoke)"				

---

2 *ašlula* ("I despoiled").

3 A.C.Piepkorn, *Historical Prism Inscriptions*, p.58: "*ú-še-lum* (for *mi*)"; R.Borger, *Babylonisch-Assyrische Lesestücke*, pp.72f does not list a difference between Bell. and

	aṣṣabat "I took (the road)"	A-(B)	⇒ I	I	I
	umašširma "he left"	B-(A)	⇒ r	r	r
	innabit "he fled"	B-(A)	⇒ I	I	I
1.28	*asḫup* "I overwhelmed"	A-B	⇒ r	r	r[4]
			-	-	I[5]
1.29	*appul* "I destroyed"	A-B	⇒ I	I	I
	aqqur "I devastated"	A-B	⇒ I	I	I
	aqmūma "I burned"	A-B	⇒ I	I	I
	akšiṭ "I cut down"	A-B	⇒ I	-	-
	atbuk "I poured out (dead silence)"	A-B	⇒ I	-	-
	ušālik (with *arbūta*) "I put to flight"	A-B	⇒ I	-	-
1.30	*ašlulam* "I carried off"	A-B	⇒ I	I	-
	ušālikšunūti (with *adi lā bašê*) "I brought them to nought"	A-B	⇒ I	I[6]	-
				I[7]	I[8]
1.31	*abtuqma* "I cut off (from his land)"	A-B	⇒ I	I	I
	uraddi "I added (to the territory of Assyria)"	A-B	⇒ I	I	-
	aṣbatma "I turned (*Elenzaš* into a royal city)"	A-B	⇒ I	I	I
	unakkirma "I changed (its former name)"	A-B	⇒ I	I	I
			-	I[9]	I

Chic.-Tayl. (*ušēme* - Chic.i_{80}).

4 *alme* ("I surrounded").

5 *akšud* ("I conquered")

6 *adi lā bašê ušālikšuma* ("I brought him to nought") referring to the enemies' king.

7 *uṣaḫḫir* ("I diminished").

8 *akšud* ("I conquered").

9 *ušēšib* ("I settled").

		-	I[10]	I
		-	I[11]	-
amḫur "I received"	A-B	(⇒ I)	(I)	(I)
ušaknissunūti "I subdued"	A-B	⇒ I	I	I

First section: 38 x I (95 %), 2 x r (5 %); second section: 2 (1) x I.

2. Sennacherib's Third Campaign, Part 1 (Chic.ii_{37-60}, Bull4, ll.17-20)[12]

			Rass.[13]	Chic.-Tayl	Bull 4
(ii_{37}	*lu allik* "I marched"	A-B		+	+)
ii_{39}	*isḫupūšu* "it overwhelmed him"	A*[14]-B	⇒ I	I	I
ii_{40}	*innabit* "he fled"	B-(A)	⇒ r	r	r
			-	I[15]	I
ii_{46}	*isḫupūšunūtima* "they overwhelmed them"	A*[16]-B'	⇒ r	r	-
	iknušū "they submitted"	B-A'	⇒ r	r	-
ii_{48}	*ušēšibma* "I enthroned"	A-B	⇒ r	r	r
ii_{49}	*ukīn* "I imposed"	A-B	⇒ I	I	-
ii_{60}	*iššûnimma* "they brought"	B-A	⇒ r	r	r[17]

10 *amnūma* ("I counted" ⇒ "handed over").
11 *urappiš* ("I extended {my land}").
12 Introductions of new participants divide Rass.'s account of Sennacherib's third campaign into four parts (//$ii_{38-60.60-72}$·ii_{73}-iii_{17} iii_{18-49}).
13 Line count according to parallel passages in Chic.
14 Grammatical subject: *pulḫi melammē bēlūtīya* ("the fear of the majesty of my lordship").
15 *šadâšu īmid* ("he fled to his mountain" = "he died").
16 Grammatical subject: *rašubbāt kakki Aššur bēlīya* ("the terrors of the weapon of Aššur, my lord").
17 *ūbilūni* ("they brought").

	iššiqū "they kissed"	B-A	⇒ I	I	-

3 x I (37.5 %), 5 x r (63.5 %)

3. Sennacherib's Third Campaign, Part 2 (Chic.ii_{60-72}, Bull 4, ll.20-22)

			Rass.	Chic.-Tayl	Bull 4
ii_{64}	*assuḫamma* "I tore away"	A-B'	⇒ (r)	(r)	(r)
	ūrâššu "I brought him"	A-B'	⇒ I	I	-
ii_{66}	*aškunma* "I installed (him)"	A-B'	⇒ I	I	I
	ēmissuma "I imposed on him"	A-B'	⇒ I	I	I[18]
ii_{68}	*išâṭ* "he bore (my yoke)"	B-A	⇒ r	r	-
ii_{72}	*alme* "I surrounded"	A-B'	⇒ r	r	-
	akšud "I conquered"	A-B'	⇒ I	I	I
	ašlula "I carried off"	A-B'	⇒ I	I	I

5 x I (71.43 %), 2 x r (28.57 %)

4. Sennacherib's Third Campaign, Part 3 (Chic.ii_{72}-iii_{17}, Bull 4, ll.22-27)

			Rass.	Chic.-Tayl.	Bull 4
ii_{78}	*iplaḫ*[19] "(their heart) became afraid"	B'-(A)	(⇒ r)	(r)	(r)
ii_{81}	*ikterūnimma* "they asked for help"	B'-C-(A)	⇒ s	s	s
	illikū "they came"	C/B'-A-(A)	⇒ r	r	-

18 *ukīn* ("I imposed").

19 Grammatical subject: *libbašun*.

iii$_1$	*uša''alū* "they sharpened (their weapons)"	C-C/B'	⇒ I	I	-
iii$_2$	*amdaḫiṣma* "I fought"	A-C/B'	⇒ r	r	r
	aštakan "I established (their defeat)"	A-C/B'	⇒ I	I	I
iii$_5$	*ikšuda*[20] "(my hands) captured"	A-C/B'	⇒ I	I	I[21]
iii$_7$	*alme* "I surrounded"	A-B'	⇒ s	s	-
	akšud "I conquered"	A-B'	⇒ I	I	-
	ašlula "I carried off"	A-B'	⇒ I	I	-
iii$_8$	*aqribma* "I drew near"	A-B'	⇒ I	I	s
iii$_9$	*adūkma* "I slew"	A-B'	⇒ I	I	I
iii$_{10}$	*ālul* "I hung (their bodies)"	A-B'	⇒ I	I	-
iii$_{11}$	*amnu* "I counted (as spoil)"	A-B'	⇒ I	I	I
iii$_{14}$	*aqbi* "I ordered"	A-B'	⇒ I	I	I
iii$_{15}$	*ušēṣâmma* "I brought out"	A-B'	⇒ I	I	I
iii$_{16}$	*ušēšibma* "I enthroned"	A-B'	⇒ I	I	I
iii$_{17}$	*ukīn* "I imposed"	A-B'	⇒ I	I	I

13 x I (76.46 %), 2 x s (11.77 %), 2 x r (11.77 %)

20 Grammatical subject: *qātāya*.

21 *aṣbat* ("I seized").

5. Sennacherib's Third Campaign, Part 4 (Chic.iii$_{18\text{-}49}$, Bull 4, ll.27-32)

			Rass.	Chic.-Tayl.	Bull 4
iii$_{23}$	*alme*	A-B'	(⇒ I)	(I)	(I)
	"I surrounded"				
	akšud	A-B'	⇒ I	I	I
	"I conquered"				
iii$_{27}$	*ušēṣâmma*	A-B'	⇒ I	I	I
	"I brought out"				
	amnu	A-B'	⇒ I	I	I
	"I counted (as spoil)"				
iii$_{29}$	*ēsiršu*	A-B	⇒ I	I	I
	"I shut in"				
	urakkisma	A-B	⇒ I	I	I
	"I built"				
iii$_{30}$	*utirra*	A-B'[22]	⇒ I	I	-
	"I turned (him) back"				
iii$_{31}$	*abtuqma*	A-B	⇒ I	I	I
	"I cut off (from his land)"				
iii$_{34}$	*addinma*	A-B	⇒ I	I	I
	"I gave"				
	uṣaḫḫir	A-B	⇒ I	I	I
	"I diminished"				
iii$_{36}$	*uraddima*	A-B	⇒ I	I	I
	"I added (to the former tribute)"				
iii$_{37}$	*ukīn*	A-B	⇒ I	I	I
	"I imposed"				
iii$_{38}$	*isḫupūšuma*	A-B[23]	⇒ I	I	I
	"it overwhelmed him"				
iii$_{41}$	*iršû*	B'-B-A	⇒ r	r	r
	(with *baṭlāti*) "they were useless"				
iii$_{48}$	*ušēbilamma*	B-B'-A	⇒ I	I	I
	"he sent"				
iii$_{49}$	*išpura*	B-B'-(A)	⇒ I	I	I
	"he sent"				

14 x I (93.33 %), 1 x r (6.67 %)

---

22 Grammatical object: *āṣê abul ālīšu* ("the one coming out of the city-gate").

23 Grammatical subject: *pulḫē melammē bēlūtīya* ("the terrible splendour of my lordship").

6. Aššurbanipal's Campaign against Kirbit

(Eiii$_{2}$-iv$_{9}$, HT rev.6-12, Biii$_{5-15}$, Civ$_{23-36}$)[24]

			E	HT	B/C[25]
			-	-	+[26]
	[. . .]			-	-
iii$_{2}$	[*taklūma*][27] "[they trusted]"	B'-(A)	⇒ I?	+	-
iii$_{3}$	*lā* [*pitluḫū*][28] "[they did] not [fear]"	B'-A*	⇒ I	I	-
iii$_{5}$	[. . .]			-	-
iii$_{7}$	*it*[	B'?-A'?	⇒ I?	-	-
[iii$_{8-9}$]				-	-
iii$_{10}$	*iḫ*[*tanabbatū*][29] "they pl[undered]"	B'?-A'	⇒ I?	I?[30]	r
iii$_{11}$	*ušaḫribū*[31] "they devastated"	B'?-A ?	⇒ I?	I?	-
iii$_{13}$	*ispunū* "they crushed"	B'?-A'?	⇒ I?	-	-
iii$_{15}$	*imḫurū'inni* "they approached me"	A'-A-B	⇒ r	r[32]	r
iii$_{16}$	*uṣallū* "they implored (my lordship)"	A'-A-B	⇒ I	I	-
iii$_{19}$	*uma''ir* "I sent"	A-A'-B	⇒ I	I	-

---

24 For the texts cf. BM 128306 (A.R.Millard, "Fragments of Historical Texts", pl.20) + BM 134445 (R.Campbell Thompson, "A Selection of Cuneiform Historical Texts", no.20).

25 For probable differences between B/C's *Vorlage* and HT cf. above, pp.98f.131.

26 *lu allik* ("I marched"; 4th campaign).

27 Cf. HT rev.7.

28 Cf. HT rev.7.

29 Cf. rev.9.

30 In HT rev.8 the mention of Tandayya marks the beginning of an *anacoluthon*. This may extend to l.9 (// Eiii$_{4-14}$) or only comprise no or only the first verb thereafter (*lā iknušu*/*ū* - "who / they had not submitted"), with the following verbs in 3rd p.pl.ind. rather than 3rd p.sgl.subj. The latter is supported by the readings of Biii$_{8}$//C, which insert *u nišē ašibūti Kirbit* ("and the people living in Kirbit") as express mention of the new grammatical subject.

31 Emended from *ušaḫrirū* according to HT rev.9.

32 *imdaḫarūnimma* ("they approached").

iii$_{20}$	*ēluma* "they went up"	A'-(B')	⇒ I	-	-
iii$_{21}$	*[i]lmū* "they [su]rrounded"	A'-B'	⇒ I	-	-
iii$_{23}$	*ikšudūma* "they conquered"	A'-B'	⇒ I	I	r[33]
	ispunū "they crushed"	A'-B'	⇒ I	-	-
iii$_{32}$	*iktumūma* "they covered (these cities like fog)"	A'-B'	⇒ I	-	-
iii$_{33}$	*isḫupū* "they overwhelmed"	A'-B'	⇒ I	-	-
iii$_{34}$	*idūkūma* "they killed"	A'-B	⇒ I	-	-
iv$_{1}$	*urassibū* "they slew"	A'-B'	⇒ I	-	-
iv$_{3}$	*išlulūni* "they carried off"	A'-B'	⇒ I	-	I[34]
iv$_{6}$	*iṣbatūni* "they seized"	A'-B	⇒ I	-	
	ublūni "they brought"	A'-B	⇒ I	-	I[35]
iv$_{7}$	*assuḫ* "I tore away"	A-B'	⇒ I	I	I
iv$_{8}$	*ušaṣbit* "I settled (them)"	A-B'	⇒ I	I	I
iv$_{9}$	*ušēšib* "I made dwell"	A-C	⇒ s	-	-

>21 x I (>91.30 %), 1 x r (<4.35 %), 1 x s (<4.35 %)

33 *akšud* ("I conquered") - A-B'.
34 *ašlula* ("I carried off") - A-B'.
35 *alqâ* ("I took") - A-B.

7. Aššurbanipal's Campaign against Aḫšeri

($Biii_{16}$-iv_{2}, Civ_{37-83}, Fii_{21-52}, Aii_{126}-iii_{26}, $Hiii_{2-9}$)[36]

			B	C	F	A	H
iii_{17}	*lu allik* "I marched"	A-B			+[37]	+[38]	
iii_{20}	*adki* "I mustered"	A-B	⇒ I		-	-	
	ušteššera (with *ḫarrānu*) "I took the road"	A-B	⇒ I		-	-	
iii_{21}	*allikma* "I marched"	A-B	⇒ I		-	-	
	addīma "I built (the camp)"	A-(B)	⇒ I		-	-	
	aškuna[39] "I set up (my camp)"	A-(B)	⇒ I	...]	-	-	
iii_{24}	*išmēma* "he heard"	B-A	⇒ r	[r]	-	-	
	u[ma]ʾʾera "he sent"	B-B'-A	⇒ I	I	-	-	
iii_{26}	*itbûni* "they advanced"	B'-A'	⇒ I	[I]	-	-	
iii_{28}	*imdaḫḫaṣū* "they fought"	A'-B'	⇒ r	[r]	-	-	
iii_{29}	*iškunū* "they accomplished (their defeat)"	A'-B'	⇒ I	I	-	-	
iii_{30}	*umallû* "they filled"	A'-B'	⇒ I	I[40]	-	-	
iii_{32}	*ērubma* "they entered"	A-B	⇒ I	[I]	I	I	
iii_{33}	*attallaka* "they marched"	A-(B)	⇒ I	[I]	I	I	

[*ina mētiq gir*]*rīya* ("[in the course of] my [cam]paign")

---

36 Cf. comments in appendix II.

37 *ušteššera ḫarrānu* ("I took the road").

38 *ušteššera ḫarrānu* ("I took the road").

39 Thus BM 134441 (cf. R.Campbell Thompson, "A Selection", p.104, no.25). A.C.Piepkorn, *Historical Prism Inscriptions*, p.50: *aškunu*.

40 *umalli* - A-B' ("I filled").

iii$_{38}$	*akšud*	A-B'	⇒ I	[I]	I	I
	"I conquered"					
iii$_{39}$	*appul*	A-B'	⇒ I	I	I	I
	"I destroyed"					
	aqqur	A-B'	⇒ I	[I]	I	I
	"I devastated"					
	aqmu	A-B'	⇒ I	I	I	I
	"I burned"					
iii$_{42}$	*ušēṣâmma*	A-B'	⇒ I	[…	I	I
	"I brought out"					
	amnu	A-B'	⇒ I		I	I
	"I counted (as spoil)"					
iii$_{43}$	*išmēma*	B-A	⇒ r		r	r
	"he heard"					
iii$_{44}$	*umaššir*	B-(A)	⇒ I		I	I
	"he left"					
iii$_{45}$	*innabit*	B-(A)	⇒ I		I	I
	"he fled"					
iii$_{46}$	*ēḫuz*	B-(A)	⇒ I	…]	I	I
	(with *marqītu*) "he took refuge"					
iii$_{47}$	*alme*	A-B'	⇒ r	r	-	-
	"I surrounded"					
iii$_{49}$	*ēsirma*	A-B'	⇒ I	I	-	-
	"I shut in"					
	usīq	A-B'	⇒ I	[I]	-	-
	"I hemmed in (their lives)"					
	ukarri	A-B'	⇒ I	[I]	-	-
	"I shortened (their lives)"					
iii$_{50}$	*akšud*	A-B'	⇒ I	[I]	r	r
	"I conquered"					
	appul	A-B'	⇒ I	I	-	-
	"I destroyed"					
	aqqur	A-B'	⇒ I	I	-	-
	"I devastated"					
	aqmu	A-B'	⇒ I	[I]	-	-
	"I burned"					
iii$_{51}$	*ušaḫribma*[41]	A-B'	⇒ I	[I]	I	I
	"they devastated"					

41 With K 1705, K2732 (ed. B) and eds. F and A (cf. A.C.Piepkorn, *Historical Prism*

	atbuk	A-B’	⇒ I	[I]	I	I
	"I poured out (dead silence)"					
iii$_{55}$	*akšud*	A-B’	⇒ I	[...	-	-
	"I conquered"					
	aqmu	A-B’	⇒ I		-	-
	"I burned"					
	ašlula	A-B’	⇒ I		-	-
	"I carried off"					
iii$_{56}$	*utīr*	A-B’	⇒ I		-	-
	"I annexed (to the territory of Assyria)"					
iii$_{61}$	*aspun*	A-B’	⇒ I		-	-
	"I crushed"					
	aqmu	A-B’	⇒ I		-	-
	"I burned"					
	adūk	A-B’	⇒ I		-	-
	"I killed"					
iii$_{62}$	*ašlula*	A-B’	⇒ I		-	-
	"I carried off"					
iii$_{64}$	*akšud*	A-B’	⇒ I		-	-
	"I conquered"					
	aspun	A-B’	⇒ I		-	-
	"I crushed"					
iii$_{65}$	*aqmu*	A-B’	⇒ I		-	-
	"I burned"					

ina tīb tāḫāzīya ("during the advance of my forces")

iii$_{66}$	*ušaḫrib*	A-B’	⇒ I		-	-
	"I devastated"					
iii$_{67}$	*uṣaḫḫir*	A-B’	⇒ I		-	-
	"I diminished"					
iii$_{69}$	*atūra*	A	⇒ I		-	-
	"I returned"					
iii$_{70}$	*akbusa*	A-(C)	(⇒ s)		-	-
	"I entered"					
iii$_{76}$	*akšud*	A-C	⇒ I		-	-
	"I conquered"					

Inscriptions, p.53, n.37-37.

iii$_{77}$	*assuḫ*	A-C	⇒ I		-	-	
	"I tore away"						
iii$_{79}$	*ašlula*	A-C	⇒ I		-	-	
	"I carried off"						
iii$_{80}$	*aṣbat*	A-C	⇒ I		-	-	
	(with *eššūti*) "I reorganized"						
iii$_{81}$	*utirra*	A-C	⇒ I		-	-	
	"I annexed (to the territory of Assyria)"						
iii$_{83}$	*imnûšu*	A*-B-B'/A*'[42]	(⇒ s/I)		(I)	(I[43])	
	"they delivered him"						
iii$_{84}$	*ušabšū*	B'(/A*')-B-(A)	⇒ r		r	I	
	(with *sīḫu elīšu*) "they rebelled against him"						
	iddû	B'(/A*')-B-(A)	⇒ I		I	I	
	"they threw (his body)"						
			-			I[44]	
			-			I[45]	
arkānu ("afterwards")							
iii$_{86}$	*ūšib*	B	(⇒ I)	...]	(I)	(r)	
	"seated himself (on the throne)"						
iii$_{89}$	*ēmurma*	B-A*	⇒ I	[I]	I	I	
	"he saw"						
	iknuša	B-A	⇒ I	[I]	I	I	...]
	"he submitted"						
iii$_{92}$	*iptâ*	B-(A)	⇒ I	I	I	I	I
	(with *upnāšu*) "he spread forth his hands"						
	uṣalla	B-A	⇒ I	I	I	I	I
	"he implored (my lordship)"						
iii$_{94}$	*išpurma*	B-A	⇒ I	[I]	I	I	I
	"he sent"						
	unaššiq	B-A	⇒ I	I	I	I	[I]
	"he kissed"						
iii$_{95}$	*aršīšuma*	A-B	⇒ r	[r]	r	r	-
	(with *rēmu*) "I took pity on him"						
iii$_{96}$	*umaʾʾirma*	A-A'-B	⇒ I	I	I	I	-
	"I sent"						

42 Aḫšeri's subjects function as secondary participants for Aššur and Ištar.
43 *tamnūšuma* ("she {sc. Ištar} counted {⇒delivered} him").
44 *indaššarū* - B'-B ("they dragged").
45 *ušamqitū* ("they slew") - B'-B(').

iii_{97}	*ušēbila* "he sent"	B-A	⇒ r	[r]	r	r	-
	iššûni "they brought"	B-A	⇒ I	[I]	I	I	I[46]
iv_{2}	*uraddima* "I added"	A-B	⇒ r	r	r	r	r
	ēmissu "I imposed on him"	A-B	⇒ I	[I]	I	I	I

[47]

---

iv_{6}	*akšud* "I conquered"	A-C		[...]	-	-	-
	ašlula "I carried off"	A-C	⇒ I	I	-	-	-
iv_{7}	*aṣbat* "I seized"	A-C	⇒ I	[I]	-	-	-
iv_{8}	*ubila* "I brought"	A-C	⇒ I	I	-	-	-
iv_{16}	*ikkisūnimma* "they cut off"	A'-C		[+]	-	-	-
iv_{17}	*ubilū* "they brought"	A'-C-A	⇒ I	[I]	-	-	-

[48]

---

8. Aššurbanipal's Campaign against Teummān (Biv_{87}-iv_{16}, $Fii_{53\text{-}73}$, $Aiii_{27\text{-}51}$)

			B	F	A
iv_{87}	*lu allik* "I marched"	A-B		+[49]	+[50]
iv_{96}	*ul aqbīšu* "I did not grant him"	A-B-A'	⇒ I	-	-
iv_{98}	*ištanappara* "he had been sending"	B-B'-A	⇒ r	-	-
iv_{99}	*uštarraḫ* "he boasted"	B-B'-(A)	⇒ I	-	-

---

46 *ušēbila* ("he brought") - B-A.
47 Ruling in ed.B.
48 Ruling in ed.B.
49 *išteššera ḫarrānu* ("I took the road").
50 *išteššera ḫarrānu* ("I took the road").

v_1	*atkil*	A-A*-(B)	⇒ r	-	-
	"I trusted"				
v_2	*ul amgur*	A-B	⇒ I	-	-
	"I did not permit"				
	ul addinšu	A-B	⇒ I	-	-
	"I did not give him"				
v_4	*išteni'â*	B-A	⇒ r	-	-
	"he planned"				
	išteni'šu	A^*_1[51]-B	⇒ r	-	-
	"he planned for him"				
v_6	*uštanīḫma*	A^*_1	⇒ I	-	-
	"he rested" ⇒ "he went into eclipse"				
	ēmuršuma	A^*_2[52]-A^*_1	⇒ I	-	-
	"he saw it"				
v_7	*uštanīḫ*	A^*_2-B	⇒ I	-	-
	"he rested" ⇒ "he set"				
v_9	*ukallimanni*	A^*_1-A-B	⇒ I	-	-
	"he showed me"				
v_{10}	*imḫuršuma*	A*[53]-B	⇒ I	-	-
	"it befell him"				
v_{11}	*uktambilma*	(A*)-B	⇒ I	-	-
	"it was paralyzed"				
	isḫirma	(A*)-B	⇒ I	-	-
	"it was twisted"				
v_{12}	*iššakin*	(A*)-B	⇒ I	-	-
	"it was placed"				
v_{14}	*ul ibāš*	B	⇒ r	-	-
	"he was not confounded				
	idkâ	B-B'-(A)	⇒ I	-	-
	"he mustered"				
v_{17}	*ašbāk*	A-A*	⇒ r	-	-
	"I was staying"				
v_{20}	*ušannûni*	A'-A	⇒ I	-	-
	"they told me"				
v_{26}	*amḫur*	A-A*	⇒ I	-	-
	"I took"				

---

[51] Grammatical subject: Sin.
[52] Grammatical subject: Šamaš.
[53] Grammatical subject: *miḫru* ("accident").

v_{27}	*aziz* "I stood"	A-A*	⇒ I	-	-
	akmis "I kneeled down"	A-A*	⇒ I	-	-
v_{28}	*ušappâ* "I asked"	A-A*	⇒ I	-	-
	illaka "(my tears) flowed"	A	⇒ I	-	-
v_{46}	*išmēma* "she heard"	A*-A	⇒ I	-	-
v_{47}	*iqbâ* "she said"	A*-A	⇒ I	-	-
v_{50}	*utūlma* "he lay down"	A*'	⇒ I	-	-
	inaṭṭal "he saw"	A*'	⇒ I	-	-
v_{51}	*igiltīma* "he woke up"	A*'	⇒ I	-	-
v_{52}	*ušannâ* "he told"	A*'-A	⇒ I	-	-
v_{80}	*adki* "I mustered"	A-A'-(B)	⇒ I	-	-
v_{82}	*aṣbatma* "I took (the road)"	A-B	⇒ I	-	-
	ušteššera (with *harrānu*) "I marched against"	A-B	⇒ I	-	-
v_{84}	*nadi* (with *madaktu*) "he had set up a camp"	B-(A)	⇒ r	-	-
v_{85}	*išmēma* "he heard"	B-A	⇒ I	-	-
	iṣbassu "(fear) seized him"	B[54]-(A)	⇒ I	-	-
v_{86}	*iplaḫma* "he became afraid"	B-A	⇒ I	-	-
	itūr "he turned (back)"	B-(A)	⇒ I	-	-

---

[54] Because of the parallelism with *iplaḫma* ("he became afraid") in the following line, Teummān has been regarded as notional subject.

	ērub "he entered"	B	⇒ I	-	-
v_{88}	*uzâ''iz* "he divided"	B-B'	⇒ I	-	-
v_{89}	*utirramma* "he sent"	B-B'	⇒ I	-	-
v_{90}	*ugdappiša* "he summoned (his allies)"	B-B'-A	⇒ I	-	-
v_{91}	*iškun* (with *ana* ...) "he made"	B-(A)	⇒ I	-	-
v_{92}	*iṣbat* "he seized"	B-A	⇒ I	-	-
v_{96}	*aškun* "I accomplished (his defeat)"	A-B	⇒ r	I[55]	I
v_{97}	*askir* "I blocked"	A-B	⇒ I	-	-
v_{99}	*umallâ* "I filled"	B'	⇒ r	-[56]	-
vi_{1}	*akkis* "I cut off"	A-B	⇒ r	-	+
vi_{5}	*isḫupšuma* "(the majesty of Aššur and Ištar) overcame it"	A*-B'	⇒ I	-	-
	iknušū "they submitted"	B'-A	⇒ r	-	
			-	I[57]	I
			-	I[58]	I
			-	I[59]	I
			-	I[60]	I
				I[61]	I
vi_{7}	*ušēšib* "I enthroned"	A-B	⇒ r	I[62]	I
vi_{9}	*aškun* (with *ana* ...) "I made"	A-B'	⇒ I	I	I

55 *aktum* ("I covered") - A-B'.
56 Cf. below n.59.
57 *adūk* ("I killed").
58 *uṣabbit* ("I seized").
59 *umalla* ("I filled").
60 *ušardi* ("I let flow").
61 *aṣrup* ("I dyed").
62 *ušēribšu* ("I brought him").

vi$_{15}$	*uṣâmma* "I brought out"	A-B'	⇒ I	-	-

42 x I (77.78 %), 12 x r (22.22 %)

9. Aššurbanipal's First Campaign against Ummanaldasi (Fii$_{33}$-iv$_{16}$, Aiv$_{110}$-v$_{62}$)

			F	A	
iii$_{35}$	*adki* "I mustered"	A-A'-B		+	
iii$_{36}$	*ušteššera* (with *ḫarrānu*) "I took the road"	A-B	⇒ I	I	
iii$_{37}$	*ūbil* "I brought"	A-A'-(B)	⇒ I	I	
iii$_{40}$	*išmû* "they heard"	B'-A	⇒ I	I	
iii$_{42}$	*isḫupšunūti* "it overwhelmed them"	A*[63]-B'	⇒ r	r	
iii$_{45}$	*imqutūma* "they hurried"	B'-A	⇒ r	r	
	iṣbatū "they seized"	B'-A	⇒ I	I	

ina mētiq girrīya ("in the course of my campain")

iii$_{48}$	*akšud* "I conquered"	A-B'	⇒ r	r	
iii$_{50}$	*anīr* "I killed"	A-B'	⇒ I	I	
iii$_{51}$	*akkis* "I cut off"	A-B'	⇒ I	I	
	apruʾ "I cut off"	A-B'	⇒ I	I	
iii$_{52}$	*alqâ* "I took"	A-B'	⇒ I	I	Bīt-Imbi episode
iii$_{56}$	*ušēṣâmma* "brought out"	A-B'	⇒ I	I	
	addīšuma "I threw him (into fetters)"	A-B'	⇒ I	I	

63 Grammatical subject: *puluḫti šarrūtīya* ("the terror of my kingship").

iii$_{57}$	*ūrâ*	A-B'	⇒ I	I[64]
	"I led (him to Assyria)"			
iii$_{61}$	*ušēṣâmma*	A-B'	⇒ I	I
	"I brought out"			
	amnu	A-B'	⇒ I	I
	"I counted (as spoil)"			
iii$_{63}$	*išmēma*	B-A	⇒ r	r
	"he heard"			
iii$_{64}$	*umašširma*	B-A	⇒ I	I
	"he left"			
iii$_{65}$	*innabitma*	B-A	⇒ I	I
	"he fled"			
	ēli	B-(A)	⇒ I	I
	"he went up (to his mountain)"			
iii$_{68}$	*išmēma*	B-A	⇒ I	I
	"he heard"			
iii$_{69}$	*umašširma*	B-(A)	⇒ I	I
	"he left"			
	iṣbat	B-A	⇒ I	I
	"he seized" ⇒ "he went to"			
iii$_{71}$	*ušērib*	A-B	⇒ r	r
	"I brought"			
	aškunšu	A-B	⇒ I	I
	"I installed him"			
iii$_{73}$	*imšīma*	B-A	⇒ r	r
	"he forgot"			
	išteni'â	B-A	⇒ I	I
	"he planned"			
				I[65]
iii$_{77}$	*ibrûma*	A*-B	⇒ r	r
	"they saw"			
	uba''û	A*-B	⇒ I	I
	(with *qātuššu*) "they called him to account"			
iii$_{78}$	*idkûniššuma*	A*-B	⇒ I	I
	"they pushed him (from his throne)"			

64 *ūrâšu* ("I led him").
65 *iqbi* ("he spoke") - B-[A].

	utirrūniššu	A*-B	⇒ I	I
	"they turned him away"			
	ušaknišūš	A*-B-A	⇒ I	I
	"they subdued him"			
iii$_{81}$	*ērubma*	A-(A)	⇒ I	-
	"I entered"			
	attalak	A-(B)	⇒ I	I
	"I marched"			

ina tayyartīya ("on my march back")

	utīr	A-B'	⇒ I	I
	"I turned (the front of my yoke to Assyria)"			
iv$_{11}$	*akšud*	A-B'	⇒ I	I
	"I conquered"			
iv$_{12}$	*appul*	A-B'	⇒ I	I
	"I destroyed"			
	aqqur	A-B'	⇒ I	I
	"I devastated"			
	aqmu	A-B'	⇒ I	I
	"I burned"			
iv$_{16}$	*ašlula*	A-B'	⇒ I	I
	"I carried off"			

10. Aššurbanipal's Second Campaign against Ummanaldasi (Fiv$_{17}$-vi$_{21}$, Av$_{63}$-vii$_{8}$)

			F	A
Fiv$_{19}$	*ušteššera*	A-B		+
	(with *ḫarrānu*) "I took the road"			
iv$_{23}$	*akšud*	A-B	⇒ I	I
	"I conquered"			
iv$_{24}$	*išmēma*	B-A	⇒ r	r
	"he heard"			
	isḫupšuma	A*[66]-B	⇒ I	I
	"it overwhelmed him"			
iv$_{25}$	*umašširma*	B-A	⇒ I	I
	"he left"			

66 Grammatical subject: *puluḫti Aššur u Ištar* ("the fear of Aššur and Ištar").

iv$_{26}$	*innabit*	B-A	⇒ I	I
	"he fled"			
iv$_{27}$	*ēbirma*	B	⇒ I	I
	"he crossed (the river Idide)"			
	iškun	B	⇒ I	I
	(with *ana* ...) "he made"			
iv$_{28}$	*[u]ktataṣṣar*	B-A	⇒ I	I
	"[he] assembled"			
iv$_{29}$	*akšud*	A-B'	⇒ r	r
	"I conquered"			
iv$_{30}$	*akšud*	A-B'	⇒ I	I
	"I conquered"			
iv$_{31}$	*akšud*	A-B'	⇒ I	I
	"I conquered"			
iv$_{32}$	*akšud*	A-B'	⇒ I	I
	"I conquered"			
iv$_{34}$	*akšud*	A-B'	⇒ I	I
	"I conquered"			
iv$_{35}$	*akšud*	A-B'	⇒ I	I
	"I conquered"			
iv$_{36}$	*akšud*	A-B'	⇒ I	I
	"I conquered"			
iv$_{37}$	*akšud*	A-B'	⇒ I	I
	"I conquered"			
iv$_{38}$	*akšud*	A-B'	⇒ I	I
	"I conquered"			
iv$_{39}$	*akšud*	A-B'	⇒ I	I
	"I conquered"			
iv$_{40}$	*akšud*	A-B'	⇒ I	I
	"I conquered"			
iv$_{41}$	*ardēma*	A-B	⇒ I	I
	"I marched"			
	allik	A-B	⇒ I	I
	"I went"			

ina mētiq girrīya ("in the course of my campaign")

iv$_{45}$	*akšud*	A-B'	⇒ I	I
	"I conquered"			
iv$_{46}$	*ul ūqi*	A-B'	⇒ I	-
	"I did not hesitate"			

	ul adgul	A-B’	⇒ I	-
	(with *pān* ...) "I did not wait"			
			-	I[67]
			-	I[68]
			-	I[69]
			-	I[70]
			-	I[71]
iv_{47}	*ēbir*	A-B’	⇒ I	I[72]
	"I crossed (the river Idide)"			
iv_{49}	*akšud*	A-B’	⇒ I	I
	"I conquered"			
iv_{50}	*appul*	A-B’	⇒ I	I
	"I destroyed"			
	aqqur	A-B’	⇒ I	I
	"I devastated"			
	aqmu	A-B’	⇒ I	I
	"I burned"			
iv_{51}	*utīr*	A-B’	⇒ I	I
	"I turned into (a heap of rubbish and a ruin)"			
iv_{52}	*adūk*	A-B’	⇒ I	I
	"I killed"			
	urassip	A-B’	⇒ I	I
	"I slew"			
iv_{54}	*innabitma*	B-A	⇒ r	r
	"he fled"			
iv_{55}	*iṣbata*	B-A	⇒ I	I
	"he seized ⇒ he went to (the mountain)"			
iv_{56}	*akšud*	A-B’	⇒ r	r
	"I conquered"			
iv_{58}	*akšud*	A-B’	⇒ I	I
	"I conquered"			
	appul	A-B’	⇒ I	I
	"I destroyed"			
	aqqur	A-B’	⇒ I	I
	"I devastated"			

---

67 *ēmurū* ("they saw") - A’.
68 *iplaḫū* ("they feared") - A’.
69 *ušabrīma* ("she {Ištar} showed") - A*-A’.
70 *iqbīšunūti* ("she told them").
71 *irḫuṣū* ("they trusted") - A-A*.
72 *ēbirū* ("they crossed") - A’.

iv$_{60}$	*aškun* (with *kamaršunu*) "I killed"	A-B'	⇒ I	I
iv$_{61}$	*ušabbir* "I broke"	A-B*	⇒ I	I
iv$_{62}$	*ušapšiḫ* "I appeased"	A-A*	⇒ s	I
iv$_{64}$	*ašlula* "I carried off"	A-B*/B'	⇒ s	I
			-	I[73]
iv$_{66}$	*attallak* "I marched"	A	⇒ I	I

ina tayyartīya ("on my march back")

iv$_{70}$	*a]kšud* "I] conquered"	A-B'	⇒ I	I
iv$_{71}$	*ēru]b* "I ente]red"	A-B'	⇒ I	I
	ūšib "I dwelt"	A-B'	⇒ I	I
iv$_{72}$	*[aptēma]* "[I opened]"	A-B'	⇒ I	I
v$_{2}$	*ušēṣâmma* "I brought out"	A-B'	⇒ I	I
	amnu "I counted (as spoil)"	A-B'	⇒ I	I
v$_{18}$	*ašlula* "I carried off"	A-B'	⇒ I	I
	ubbit "I destroyed"	A-B'	⇒ I	I
v$_{20}$	*ukappira* "I cut off"	A-B'	⇒ I	I
v$_{33}$	*ašlula* "I carried off"	A-B'	⇒ I	I
v$_{39}$	*alqâ* "I took"	A-B'	⇒ I	I
v$_{40}$	*adqâ* "I removed"	A-B'	⇒ I	I

---

73 *ērubma* ("I entered") - A.

v_{41}	*unassiḫa*	A-B'	⇒ I	I
	"I tore out"			
v_{42}	*ušalpit*	A-B'	⇒ I	I
	"I ravaged"			
v_{43}	*amnâ*	A-B'	⇒ I	I
	"I counted" ⇒ "I delivered (them)"			
v_{47}	*ērubū*	A'	⇒ I	I
	"they entered"			
v_{48}	*ēmurū*	A'	⇒ I	I
	"they saw"			
	iqmû	A'	⇒ I	I
	"they burned"			
v_{52}	*appul*	A-B'	⇒ I	I
	"I destroyed"			
	aqqur	A-B'	⇒ I	I
	"I devastated"			
	ukallim	A-B'	⇒ I	I
	"I let see" ⇒ "I exposed (their graves) to (the sun)"			
v_{53}	*alqâ*	A-B'	⇒ I	I
	"I took"			
v_{54}	*ēmid*	A-B'	⇒ I	I
	"I imposed"			
	uzammīšunūti	A-B'	⇒ I	I
	"I deprived them"			
v_{55}	*ušaḫrib*	A-B'	⇒ I	I
	"I devastated"			
	ušappiḫa	A-B'	⇒ I	I
	"I poured out"			
v_{65}	*ašlula*	A-B'	⇒ I	I
	"I carried off"			
v_{67}	*ēsipa*	A-B'	⇒ I	I[74]
	"I gathered"			
	alqâ	A-B'	⇒ I	I
	"I took"			
			-	I[75]
			-	I[76]

74 *ēriš* ("I demanded").
75 *aspun* ("I crushed") - A-B'.
76 *uzammâ* ("I deprived") - A-B' (cf. Fv_{71}).

v_{69}	*ušarbiṣa*	A-B'	⇒ I	I
	"I let (animals) lie down (there)"			
v_{71}	*uzammâ*	A-B'	⇒ I	I
	"I deprived"			
vi_{3}	*tušadgila*	A*[77]-A		+
	(with *pānū'a*) "she entrusted me"			
vi_{7}	*tukallim*	A*-A'		+[78]
	"she revealed"			
vi_{8}	*atmuḫ*	A-A*		+
	"I took (the hands of her great divinity)"			
vi_{9}	*taṣbata*	A*-A		+
	"she took (the road)"			
vi_{10}	*ušēribšima*	A-A*		+
	"I brought her"			
vi	*ušarmīš*	A-A*		+
	"I let her dwell"			
vi_{15}	[*ašruk*]	A-A*		+
	"[I gave]"			
	uraddi	A-A'		+
	"I added"			
vi_{21}	*uza''iz*	A-A'		+
	"I distributed"			

11. Aššurbanipal's campaign against Dunanu (Bvi_{17}-vii_{2}, Fii_{74}-iii_{5}, $Aiii_{52-69}$)

			B/C	F[79]	A
Bvi_{18}	*lu allik*	A-B		-	-
	"I marched"				
			-	I[80]	I

77 Grammatical subject: Nana.

78 *ukallimū* ("they revealed") - A'-A'.

79 The literary relationship between eds. F and A is difficult to discern. B agrees with A against F ($Aiii_{61}$//Bvi_{25}, $Aiii_{137}$//$Bvii_{8-9}$, Aiv_{5}//$Bvii_{48}$, Aiv_{10}//$Bvii_{53}$, Aiv_{14-15}//$Bvii_{60-61}$, Aiv_{40}//$Bvii_{70}$) and with F against A ($Fiii_{8-9}$//$Bvii_{8}$, $Fiii_{19}$//$Bvii_{57}$). The agreements of F and A against B necessitate the assumption of some kind of literary relationship between the two editions, either thy had an almost identical *Vorlage*, different from B, or A used both, B and F. If the former is true, in those cases where F and A disagree from each other and from B it is not possible to evaluate F's or A's redactorial treatment.

80 *eli … aškuna panīya* ("I turned towards …") - A-B.

vi$_{22}$	*aktum* "I covered"	A-B'[81]	⇒ I	-	-
vi$_{24}$	*akšud* "I conquered"	A-B'	⇒ I	I	I
			-	I[82]	I
			-	I[83]	I
vi$_{26}$	*ušēṣâ* "I brought out"	A-B	⇒ I	-	-
			-	I[84]	I
vi$_{28}$	*ušēṣâmma* "I brought out"	A-B'	⇒ I	-	-
	amnu "I counted (as spoil)"	A-B'	⇒ I	-	-
vi$_{30}$	*ušēṣâmma* "I brought out"	A-B'	⇒ I	-	-
	amnu "I counted (as spoil)"	A-B'	⇒ I	-	-
vi$_{32}$	[*ušēṣâ*]*mma*[85] "I brought out"	A-B'	⇒ I	-	-
	amnu "I counted (as spoil)"	A-B'	⇒ I	-	-
vi$_{34}$	*ušēṣâmma* "I brought out"	A-B'	⇒ I	-	-
	amnu "I counted (as spoil)"	A-B'	⇒ I	-	-
vi$_{36}$	*ušēṣâmma* "I brought out"	A-B'	⇒ I	I[86]	I
	amnu "I counted (as spoil)"	A-B'	⇒ I	-	-
vi$_{38}$	*ušēṣâmma* "I brought out"	A-B'	⇒ I	-	-

---

81 Since the target of Aššurbanipal's campaign in B is described with *eli Dunani mār Bēl-iqīša ana Gambuli* ("towards Dunanu, son of Bēl-iqīša, towards the land of Gambulu", Bvi$_{18}$), B and B' cannot be strictly separated as primary and secondary participants. We have nevertheless used both designations to destinguish between Dunanu and his subjects.

82 *ērub* ("I entered") - A-B'.

83 *utabbiḫ* ("I slaughtered") - A-B'.

84 *utammeḫa* ("I bound") - A-B/B'.

85 Restored according to prism D.

86 *ašlula* ("I carried off").

	amnu	A-B'	⇒ I	-	-
	"I counted (as spoil)"				
vi$_{41}$	*aṣbat*	A-C'	⇒ I(s)	-	-
	"I seized"				
vi$_{42}$	*akkis*	A-C'	⇒ I	-	-
	"I cut off"				
	arpis	A-C'	⇒ I	-	-
	"I slew"				
vi$_{43}$	*appul*	A-B'	⇒ I(s)	I	I
	"I destroyed"				
	aqqur	A-B'	⇒ I	I	I
	"I devastated"				
	ušḫarmiṭ	A-B'	⇒ I	I	I
	"I demolished"				
vi$_{44}$	*ušālik*	A-B'	⇒ I	-	-
	(with *adi lā bašê*) "I annihilated"				
vi$_{45}$	*ušaḫrib*	A-B'	⇒ I	-	-
	"I devastated"				
vi$_{46}$	*aprusa*	A-B'	⇒ I	-	-
	"I cut off"				
vi$_{48}$	*anīr*	A-B'	⇒ I	-	-
	"I killed"				
vi$_{49}$	*atūra*	A-B'	⇒ I	-	-
	"I returned"				
vi$_{51}$	*ālul*	A-C	⇒ s	-	-
	"I hung"				
vi$_{56}$	*ērubma*	A	⇒ I	-	-
	"I entered"				
vi$_{63}$	*ēmurūma*	C'-C	(⇒ r)	-	-
	"they saw"				
	iṣbassunūti	C'	⇒ I	-	-
	(with *šanê ṭēmi*) "they became insane"				
vi$_{64}$	*ibquma*	C'	⇒ I	-	-
	"he tore (his beard")"				
vi$_{65}$	*isḫula*	C'	⇒ I	-	-
	"he pierced (his abdomen)"				
vi$_{67}$	*umaḫḫira*	A-C	⇒ r	-	-
	"I brought"				

vi$_{70}$	*iṣbat* "he seized"	B[87]-B'-A	(⇒ sr)	-	-
vi$_{75}$	*ušēbil* "he sent"	B-B'-A	⇒ I	-	-
vi$_{82}$	*ūbilšunūti* "I brought them"	A-B	(⇒ r)	-	-
vi$_{86}$	*ašlup* "I tore out"	A-B'	(⇒ I)	-	-
	ašḫuṭa "I flayed"	A-B	⇒ I	-	-
vi$_{88}$	*iddûšuma* "they threw him"	A'-B	(⇒ I)	-	-
	itbuḫuš "they slaughtered him"	A'-B	⇒ I	-	-
vi$_{91}$	*anīr* "I killed"	A-B'	⇒ I	-	-
vi$_{92}$	*ušēbil* "I sent"	A-B'	⇒ I	-	-
vii$_{2}$	*ušaḫšila* "I had (his sons) crush (these bones)"	A-B'-B	⇒ I	-	-
			-	-	+[88]
vii$_{9}$	*išpura* "he sent"	B-C-A'	⇒ I	-	-
	ukkabasū "they tramped"	B/C-(A')	⇒ I	-	-
vii$_{20}$	*uma]"iršunūti*[89] "I s]ent them"	B-B'-A'	⇒ I	-	-
vii$_{21}$	*iškunšunūti* (with *ṭēmu*) "he gave them order"	B-B'-A	⇒ I	-	-
vii$_{22}$	*iqbi* "he spoke"	B-B'-A'	⇒ I	-	-
vii$_{28}$	*iṣbatūnimma* (with *urḫu*) "he took the road"	B'/C'-(A')	⇒ I	-	-

---

87 Ummanigaš, the *agent* of *iṣbat*, is mentioned as having been installed by the Assyrian king (Bvi$_{73}$) and thus may also be designated as A'.

88 A has inserted a passage about Šamaš-šum-ukīn's rebellion (Aiii$_{70-135}$).

89 Restored according to ed. C.

vii_{31}	*ēlûnimma*	A'-B'/C'	⇒ r	-	-
	"he went up"				
	iškunū	A'-B'/C'	⇒ I	-	-
	"they accomplished (the defeat)"				
vii_{34}	*ikkisūnimma*	A'-B'/C'	⇒ I	-	-
	"they cut off"				
vii_{35}	*ūbilūni*	A'-B'/C'	⇒ I	-	-
	"they brought"				
vii_{37}	*uma''ir*	A-B	⇒ I	-	-
	"I sent"				
vii_{38}	*iklāma*	B-A'	⇒ r	-	-
	"he restrained"				
vii_{39}	*lā utirra*	B-A	⇒ I	-	-
	"he did not return (an answer)"				
vii_{42}	*idīnūinni*	A*-B	⇒ r	-	-
	"they spoke (a just verdict against Ummanigaš) for me"				
vii_{43}	*ibbalkitma*	C-B	(⇒ srs)	(srs)	(srs)
	"he rebelled"				
vii_{44}	*urassip*	C-B	⇒ I	I	I
	"he slew"				
vii_{46}	*ūšib*	C	⇒ I	-[90]	-[91]
	"he seated himself (on the throne)"				
vii_{45}	*imḫur*	C-B	⇒ I	-	-
	"he received"				
vii_{48}	*ul išâl*	C-A	⇒ s	-	-
	"he did not inquire (after the well-being of my kingship)"				
vii_{50}	*illikamma*	C-B[92]	⇒ s	I	I
	"he marched"				
vii_{51}	*urriḫa*	C-A'	⇒ I	I	I
	"he hurried"				
vii_{54}	*ibbalkitūma*[93]	C'-C	⇒ r	I	I
	"they rebelled"				

---

90 Retained in a subordinate clause.

91 Retained in a subordinate clause.

92 From here onwards, B designates Šamaš-šum-ukīn.

93 *imḫurū* ("which they had received") and *išmû* ("which they had heard"; Bvii$_{53}$, [A*-A]) probably are subjunctives continuing *ša Aššur u Ištar usappû* ("which I had addressed to Aššur and Ištar"; Bvii$_{52}$).

vii$_{55}$	*urassibū* "they slew"	C'/C	⇒ I	I[94]	I
vii$_{57}$	*ūšib* "he seated himself (on the throne)"	C'	⇒ I	I	-
				I[95]	I
vii$_{65}$	*ipparšūnimma* "they fled" ⇒ "they hastened"	C'/C-A*	⇒ I	I[96]	I[97]
vii$_{70}$	*ipšilūnimma* "they crept"	C'/C-A*	⇒ I	I[98]	I[99]
					I[100]
					I[101]
	iṣbatū "they seized"	C'/C-A	⇒ I	-	I[102]
vii$_{71}$	*imnûma* "he delivered (himself to do my service)"	C-A	⇒ I	-	I
vii$_{72}$	*uṣalla* "he implored"	C-A	⇒ I	I	I
vii$_{74}$	*irībūni* "they gave (as replacement)"	A*-C	⇒ r	-	-
			-	I[103]	I
			-	I[104]	I
			-	-	r[105]
vii$_{76}$	*ulzissunūti* "I stationed them"	A-C/C'	⇒ I	-	I
			-	+[106]	+[107]
vii$_{78}$	*īdēma* "he recognized"	B-A	⇒ sr	-	-

---

94 *abiktašu iškun* ("he defeated him") - C'-C.
95 *innabtūnimma* ("they fled") - C-A. An equivalent of *innabtūnimma*, *ipparšidū* ("they escaped"), is already present in B, but there in a subordinate clause.
96 C'/C-C'.
97 C'/C-C'.
98 C'/C-C'.
99 C'/C-C'.
100 + *unaššiqma* ("he kissed") - C-A.
101 *ušēšir* ("he swept {the ground with his beard}") - C-A.
102 *iṣbatma* ("he seized") - C-A.
103 *izzizma* ("he stood") - C-A.
104 *idallala* ("he paid hommage") - C-A.
105 *rēmu aršīšuma* ("I took pity on him") - A-C.
106 C has inserted a description of a famine in Babylonia (Cviii$_{<115}$-ix$_{28}$).
107 A has added a description of a famine in Babylonia (Aiv$_{41-109}$). The contents parallel C's account, but the wording is different.

vii$_{88}$	*ušēṣâššunūti* "he released them"	B-A	⇒ I	-	-
vii$_{92}$	*ušēbila* "he sent"	B-A	⇒ I	-	-

12. Aššurbanipal's Campaigns against Arabs (Bvii$_{93}$-viii$_{63}$,[108] Cx$_{20-65}$, Avii$_{82-124}$ ix$_{42-64}$ vii$_{123-124}$ viii$_{42-47}$ viii$_{15-29}$ viii$_{52-64}$)[109]

			B	C	A
			-		+[110]
			-		I[111]
Bvii$_{95}$	*imḫurannima* "he approached me"	B[112]-A			-
	[uṣall]a "[he implor]ed"	B-A	⇒ I		-

---

[108] B's account can be divided into five parts, the beginnings of which are marked by introductions of new participants (vii$_{93}$-viii$_{22.23-31.32-38.39-50.51-63}$). All units are brief and no substantial rise or fall of tension is apparent. Only in the first and last sections passages are marked by a comparatively high rhetorical level. In the first section this is found in the unusual narration of the distribution of booty items in Assyria. Bviii$_{20-22}$ constitute an EEN-construction
aštammu ina nidni
sirāšû ina ḫabê
nukaribbu ina kīši imdanaḫarū [*ibi*]*lē u amēlūti*
"the landlady for a dish (cf. M.Weippert, "Kämpfe", p.46, n.31),
the brewer for a jug,
the gardener as wages received [cam]els and people (slaves)" .
This is set into contrast with the description of a famine among the Arabs (viii$_{25-27}$). A high rhetorical level is also found at the end of the fifth section. The final three lines concitute an EEN-construction:
anāku ḫadiš appaliss[*uma*]
pānīya damqūti elīšu aš[*kun*]
bilat mandattu šattišamma ukīn ṣīrušu
"I joyfully looked at [him],
I had good intentions for him,
a tribute of annual payments I imposed on him".

[109] An account of Aššurbanipal's campaigns against Arabs is also provided by VAT 5600+ (VAT 5600 + K 2802 + 3047 + 3049 + BM 98591). For the text cf. M.Weippert, "Kämpfe", pp.74-81. The inscription contains a letter by Aššurbanipal to the god Aššur. The literary relationship between B, VAT 5600+ and A is difficult to discern. VAT 5600+ first presents a historical introduction (I,3-12) which is found in neither of the other versions and then agrees with B against A in its order of narration and several readings (Bviii$_9$ // VAT 5600+ I.51 - Avii$_{118}$, Bviii$_{11}$ // VAT 5600+ I.53 - Avii$_{122}$, Bviii$_{24}$ // VAT 5600+ II,6 - Aix$_{55}$), but sometimes also agrees with A against B (I,50

vii_{97}	*ušazkirma* "I made him pronounce (the oath)"	A-B	⇒ r	-
vii_{98}	*utīrma* "I gave back"	A-B	⇒ I	-
	addinšu "I gave him"			-
vii_{99}	*iḫṭiamma* "he sinned"	B-A	⇒ r	-[113]
$viii_{1}$	*lā iṣṣurma* "he did not keep"	B-A	⇒ I	-[114]
	iṣlâ "he threw off"	B-A	⇒ I	-[115]
$viii_{2}$	*iprusma* "he restrained (his feet from inquiring after my well-being")"	B-A	⇒ I	r
$viii_{3}$	*iklâ* "he held back (his tribute)"	B-A	⇒ I	I
			-	s[116]
			-	s[117]
			-	I[118]

// $Avii_{117}$ - $Bviii_{9}$, VAT 5600+ I,55 // Aix_{43} - $Bviii_{13}$, VAT 5600+ I,38-44 // $Avii_{89-100}$). This, especially the presence of *ana Nabayate* ("to Nabatea") in VAT 5600+ II,23f (// $Avii_{124}$, cf. above, p.132, n.268), seems to indicate that VAT 5600+ was written later than B but earlier than A. In one passage, however, it is probable that A has preserved an earlier version compared to VAT 5600+ (cf. VAT 5600+ II,42 // $Aviii_{24}$). VAT 5600+ also agrees with C against B and A (VAT II,56-III,4 // Cx_{50-56}).

110 *adki* ("I mustered") - A-A'-B.

111 *ušteššera ḫarrānu* ("I took the road") - A-B.

112 *Yauta' mār Ḫazailu* ("Yauta', son of Ḫazailu). For a possible connection between the two forms of the name, Uwaite' and Yauta', cf. M.Weippert, "Kämpfe", p.40, n.6. Weippert's claims that the mention of the name without patronym refers to Uaite, son of Birdadda and that in $Aviii_{96}$-ix_{8} the campaign is directed against Uaite, son of Birdadda (cf. ix_{2}), whereas according to the corresponding passage in ed.B and VAT 5600+ the campaign was directed against Uaite, son of Hazael ("Kämpfe", p.49), are not justified. VAT 5600 II,56f refers to Uaite, son of Hazael (cf. ll.17.23). The supposed difference between Aix_{2} and the parallel passages in B and VAT 5600+ (M.Weippert, "Kämpfe", p.59) can, if we ignore the variations in the spelling of the name, be explained by haplography because of homoioteleuton or homoioarkton: "^{I}ua-a-te mār ^{I}ḫa-za-ilu mār aḫi abi ša ^{I}u-a-a-te-' mār ^{I}bir-^{d}dadda" (Aviii $_{1-2}$).

113 Subordinate clause.

114 Subordinate clause.

115 Subordinate clause.

116 *išmēma* ("he heard")- B-C.

117 *lā iṣṣura* ("he did not keep") - B-A.

118 *umašširannimma* ("he left") - B-A.

			-	s[119]
			-	I[120]
			-	I[121]
viii$_4$	*ušabalkitma* "he incited to rebellion"	B-B'-A	⇒ I	I[122]
viii$_5$	*iḫtanabbatū* "they plundered"	B'-A'	⇒ I	I
viii$_6$	*uma''era* "I sent"	A-A'-B	⇒ r	I
			-	I[123]
viii$_8$	*iškunū* "they accomplished (their defeat)"	A'-B'	⇒ I	I[124]
viii$_9$	*urassibū* "they slew"	A'-B'	⇒ I	I[125]
			-	r[126]
			-	I[127]
viii$_{11}$	*u[šā]ḫizū* "they set fire (to the tents)"	A'-B'	⇒ I	I
	ipqidū (with *ana išāti*) "they burned (them)"	A'-B'	⇒ I	I[128]
			-	r[129]
viii$_{13}$	*išlulūni* "they carried off"	A'-B'	⇒ I	-
viii$_{15}$	*umtanallū* "they filled"	A'-B'	⇒ I	-
viii$_{16}$	*uparris* "I distributed"	A-A'	⇒ I	-
	uza''iz "I divided"	A-A'	⇒ I	-
viii$_{19}$	*išammū* "they bought"	A'	⇒ I	

119 *iddinšunūti* ("he gave them") - B-B'-C.
120 *išpuramma* ("he sent") - B-B'-C.
121 *ištakan pīšu* ("he conspired") - B-C.
122 *ušamkirma* ("he incited to rebellion").
123 *adūk* ("I killed") - A-B'.
124 *aškun* ("I accomplished {his defeat}")- A-B'.
125 *urassip* ("I slew") - A-B'. M.Streck, *Assurbanipal*, p.66, n.c) notes the variant reading *urassibū* ("they slew").
126 *ipparšidma* ("he fled") - B-A*.
127 *innabit* ("he escaped") - B-(A).
128 *iqmû* ("they burned").
129 *innabit* ("he fled") - B-(A).

viii$_{21}$	*imdanaḫarū* "they received"	A'	⇒ I		-
viii$_{24}$	*ušamqit* "he slew"	A*-B/B'			-
viii$_{25}$	*iššakinma* "it took place"	A*'[130]	⇒ I		-
viii$_{26}$	*ēkulū* "they ate"	B'	⇒ r		-
viii$_{28}$	*išimūšu* "they brought (curses) upon them"	A*-B	⇒ r	. . .]	-
viii$_{31}$	*imḫuršuma* "it befell him"	B[131]	⇒ r	[+]	+
	innabit "he fled"	B-(A)	⇒ I	[I]	+[132]
viii$_{32}$	*ilikamma* "he came"	B[133]-A		+	-
viii$_{33}$	*unaššiq* "he kissed"	B-A	⇒ I	I	+[134]
	aškun "I established (a treaty with him)"	A-B	⇒ r	r	r[135]
viii$_{35}$	*aškunšu* "I installed him"	A-B	⇒ I	I	I
viii$_{38}$	*ukīn* "I imposed"	A-B	⇒ I	I	-
(viii$_{45}$	*iškunū*[136] "they accomplished (his defeat)"	A(')-B)		[+]	I[137]

---

[130] Grammatical subject: *sunqu* ("famine").

[131] Grammatical subject: *maruštu* ("evil").

[132] Subjunctive, as is indicated by its continuation with *isbatu* ("who seized"); cf. below, n.134.

[133] Grammatical subject: Abiate.

[134] Subjunctive: *iṣbatu* ("who seized").

[135] *ušazkiršuma* ("I made him swear").

[136] The Moabite king is mentioned as grammatical subject. Thus the verbal form may be a subjunctive. One would, however, expect an indicative. It is not possible to decide whether the form is subjunctive or indicative pl. or a scribal mistake.

[137] *aškun* ("I accomplished").

viii$_{48}$	*uṣabbit*	A'-B	(⇒ I)	-	r[138]
	"he seized(him)"				
viii$_{49}$	[*iddīma*][139]	A'-B	⇒ I	-	-
	"[he threw him] (into fetters)"				
viii$_{50}$	*ušēbila*	A'-B	⇒ I	-	I[140]
	"he sent"				
			-	+[141]	+
viii$_{53}$	*išmâ*	B[142]-A		+	+
	"he heard"				
			-	s[143]	-
			-	s[144]	-
			-	I[145]	-
viii$_{58}$	*išpu*[*ramma*[146]	B-B'-A	⇒ I	I	I[147]
	"he s[ent"				
	unaš]*šiq*[148]	B-A	⇒ I	I	-
	"he kis]sed"				
viii$_{60}$	*uṣṣanalla*	B-A	⇒ I	I	I[149]
	"he implored"				
viii$_{61}$	*apalliss*[*uma*[150]	A-B	⇒ r	r	-
	"I looked [at him"[151]				
viii$_{62}$	*aš*[*kun*	A-B	⇒ I	[I]	-
	(with *pānīya*) "I plan[ned"[152]				
viii$_{63}$	*ukīn*	A-B	⇒ I	[i]	-
	"I imposed"				

138 *iṣbatūnimma* ("they seized").
139 Restored after prism D.
140 *ūbilūni* ("they brought").
141 C reports the defeat of Adiya, queen of Arabia (Cx$_{39\text{-}44}$); cf. Bviii$_{11}$.
142 Natnu
143 *iqbīšuma* ("he spoke to him") - B-C.
144 *iplaḫma* ("he became afraid") - B-(A).
145 *iršâ naquttu* ("he came into trouble") - B.
146 Restored according to ed. D.
147 *issanqamma* ("he came")
148 Restored according to ed. D.
149 *iš'ala* ("he inquired {after the well-being of my kingship}").
150 Restored according to prism D.
151 Cf. above, p.287, n.108.
152 Cf. above, p.287, n.108.

Appendix IV - Ahab in 1 Kgs.22

The present study concentrates on literary, not on historical aspects of the transmission of narratives. However, if the investigated narrative claims to relate historical events, the two questions cannot be entirely separated from each other. While, of course, it may be doubted whether the former is true for 1 Kgs.22, the burden of proof rests on those who question the narrative's historicity or historical accuracy. The presence of "common motifs" or *Wandermotive*[1] alone does not provide sufficient evidence. This was admitted by A.Jepsen[2] who nevertheless argued from other reasons that 1 Kgs.22 constitutes a prophet legend to which various fairy tale motifs were added. Both matters, historical reliability and literary development, are inseparably bound to each other. If one assumes that 1 Kgs.22 is the result of various redactions, the historicity of the narrated events must be questioned. If on the other hand the historicity of the narrative is questioned this may have consequences for a literary-critical analysis.

For historical reasons it has been claimed that the Israelite king mentioned in the narrative in 1 Kgs.22 originally was not Ahab, but that 1 Kgs.22 rather constitutes a compilation from sources dealing with the alliances of Jehoshaphat with Joram and Joram with Ahaziah. C.F.Whitley[3] argued that the Biblical accounts draw a distorted picture of Ahab. Ahab's children bear Yahwistic names[4] and there is no evidence for altars being set up for Baal by Ahab outside Samaria. Ahab is said to appear throughout in the same narratives as Elijah and Elisha. Internal inconsistencies within this group of narratives are seen between 1 Kgs.$19_{15\text{-}16}$ and 2 Kgs.8_{13} 9_4. Whitley reached the conclusion that there is reason to suspect the accuracy of the documents under consideration. He argued that a ruler of Ahab's strength would not have submitted to a Syrian king as is narrated in 1 Kgs.20. In 1 Kgs.20_{13} the Israelite army is described as having consisted of 7,000 men, which Whitley thinks is too little compared with Ahab's army at Qar-

---

1 Cf. H.Weippert, "Ahab el campeador?".
2 Cf. "Israel und Damaskus," p.156, n.15.
3 Cf. "Deuteronomic Presentation".
4 This had already been noted by J.Wellhausen, *Prolegomena*, p.289.

qar (10,000). In his view a small Israelite army would better suit the time of Hazael's invasion during the reign of Jehoahaz, son of Jehu (2 Kgs.13_{1-9}). Benhadad's offer to return cities conquered by his father (1 Kgs.20_{34}) corresponds to Jehoash's victories over Benhadad, son of Hazael (2 Kgs.13_{25}). The presence of Syrian troops in Samaria (2 Kgs.6_{24f}) is thought to suit the reign of Ahab best. Whitley also discovered an inconsistency between the representations of Jehu and Hazael by the Deuteronomic writer and Assyrian documents. He reached the conclusion that wars against the Arameans ascribed by the Biblical writer to the dynasty of Omri rather belong to the later dynasty of Jehu.[5] Whitley also referred to 1 Kgs.22_{40} as evidence of Ahab's natural death and to parallels in phraseology in other narratives to explain how the narration of the killing of Ahab arose. In 2 Kgs.9_{14-15} it is narrated that Joram was killed by an arrow, just as it was related of Ahab in 1 Kgs.22_{34}. Both kings were killed as punishment for the killing of Naboth. Joram retires wounded from the battle and is killed by Jehu's arrow - Ahab is hit by an arrow and dies from the loss of blood. From this Whitley deduced that 1 Kgs.22 is a conglomerate of different strands.

However, the parallels drawn between the various Biblical accounts may be artificial; many differences between them could also be adduced. According to Whitley's own analysis the size of Ahab's army at Qarqar[6] included the Judean forces. Furthermore, the Old Testament reports an extensive famine in Israel during Ahab's reign (1 Kgs.18). Thus the size of Ahab's force mentioned in 1 Kgs. 20 is not surprising (2 Kgs.13_7 notes that after the Aramean invasion 10,000 soldiers and 10 chariots were left to Jehoahaz). The correspondence of Benhadad's offer to Jehoash's victory is indeed striking, since no war between Omri and Benhadad I. is reported. An explanation may be seen in 1 Kgs.15_{20} where it is reported that Benhadad took cities from Baasha. The second part of 1 Kgs.20_{34} would then refer to a different time, after the foundation of Samaria by Omri. The cities referred to in 2 Kgs.13_{25} as being conquered by the Arameans during the reign of Jehoahaz were probably *Galilean* cities,[7] since Jehu had lost all of Gilead to

---

5 Cf. "Deuteronomic Presentation", pp.147f.

6 According to Shalmaneser III's Monolith 10,000 men and 2,000 chariots (cf. F.E.Peiser, "Monolith-Inschrift", p.272).

7 Cf. C.F.Keil, *Bücher der Könige*, p.311.

Hazael, if the identification of Aphek (1 Kgs.$20_{26.30}$) with ‘En-Gev (with the ancient name being preserved at Fiq) at the eastern shore of the Sea of Galilee is correct.[8] The cities referred to in 1 Kgs.20_{34}, however were probably situated in *Gilead*. Thus the two passages should be regarded as referring to different incidents. J.M.Miller[9] assumed that the Israelite kings originally were anonymous in the stories of the Elisha Cycle. He followed Whitley in regarding the two battle accounts in 1 Kgs.20 as belonging to the three victories mentioned in 2 Kgs. 13_{25}. The third narrative is found in the "extremely composite account" of 1 Kgs. 22 (the LXX has these three accounts in immediate succession). Miller argued that Ahab died a peaceful death, referring to 1 Kgs.21_{27-29} and 22_{40}. While it is evident that 22_{40} does not exclude a violent death[10] the MT of 21_{29} speaks of the *house* of Ahab (בֵּיתוֹ) rather than of the king himself.[11] And it is the *house* of Ahab that is mentioned in 2 Kgs.9_{7-9} in Elisha's order to Jehu to carry out judgement (cf. also 2 Kgs.10_{30}).

Miller also argued that the Assyrian annals imply that Israel and Syria were allies rather than enemies during Ahab's last years. The Monolith Inscription of Shalmaneser III.[12] mentions Ahab and Hadadezer as members of a coalition in Shalmaneser's 6th year. This alone does not present enough evidence to exclude the possibility of a war between Israel and the Arameans. Miller further questioned the necessity of conquering Ramoth-gilead since 2 Kgs.10_{32-33} implies that Gilead was in Israelite hands. However, according to 1 Kgs.22_{3} Ahab wanted to capture a city not a region. In the same verse he states: "Do you know that Ramoth-gilead belongs to us and we keep quiet ...". And Ramoth-gilead is where the battle takes place (v.29). Thus in the narrative it is presupposed that Gilead is in Israelite hands.[13]

---

8 Cf. Y.Aharoni, *Land of the Bible*, p.335; J.M.Miller, "The Rest of the Acts of Jehoahaz", p.339, prefers S.Toltowsky's identification of Aphek with the present village of Faqqua situated on Mt. Gilboa.

9 Cf. "Elisha Cycle".

10 Cf. above, p.212, n.94.

11 The LXX (20_{29}) omits these words; A, LXX^{O} have ἐπὶ τὸν οἶκον αὐτοῦ. The omission by the LXX may be explained by the increased parallelism with the first part of the prophecy.

12 Cf. above, p.293, n.6.

13 Contrast 1 Kgs.20_{26} with the battle taking place at Aphek implying that Gilead was occupied by the Arameans; cf. also 1 Kgs.20_{34} mentioning the restoration of cities to

Miller, like Whitley, concluded that different stories were combined to produce the narrative in 1 Kgs.22, but unlike Whitley he only reckoned with two stories, one of them narrating the battle at Ramoth-gilead during which Joram was injured (2 Kgs.8_{28}), the other one dealing with Jehoahaz (2 Kgs.13). Both battles took place at the same location and thus the accounts could easily be confused. Then the battle accounts in 1 Kgs.20 and 22 were adapted to the stories of the Elisha cycles by replacing the kings' names with מֶלֶךְ יִשְׂרָאֵל and later subjected to a reverse treatment. The anonymous stories were ascribed to well known personalities. In a further redaction the stories in 1 Kgs.22 and 2 Kgs.3 were again revised to emphasize Jehoshaphat's piety. Miller further argued that the Moabite campaign narrated in 2 Kgs.3 could only take place during the reign of Jehoshaphat, since only after the latter's death did Edom have a king (2 Kgs.8_{20-22}) and in 2 Kgs.3_9 the "king of Edom" is mentioned. However, 2 Kgs.8_{20} states that Edom revolted from the Judean rule and set up a king of their own. It is not stated that previously there had not been a "king" of Edom. A governor over Edom may well have been mentioned as "king" but nevertheless have been subject to the king of Judah.

A.Jepsen[14] argued that an Israelite-Aramean war would not suit the historical picture (alliance at Qarqar) for Ahab's reign. He also drew attention to the fact that at the time of Jehu's assassination of Joram Ramoth-gilead was in Israelite hands. He further saw a difference between Ahab's relationship to the נְבִיאִים as depicted in 1 Kgs.22 and that of 1 Kgs.17-19 where Ahab is shown as the prophets' enemy. Jepsen also referred to 1 Kgs.20_{34} and argued that a defeat of Omri by the Arameans leading to a loss of Israelite cities and the establishment of bazaars by Arameans in Samaria would not suit Omri's reign. That Israel and Damascus fought as allies against Shalmaneser does, however, not *a priori* exclude the possibility of wars between them. If 1 Kgs.22_1 refers back to 1 Kgs.20, then a Syro-Ephraimite war would also have preceded the alliance, for it is not likely that both wars took place *after* Qarqar.[15] It is quite conceivable that

Israel.

14 Cf. "Israel und Damaskus".

15 Jehu paid tribute to Shalmaneser III in 841 B.C., the battle at Qarqar took place in 853 B.C., Jehu reigned for 6 years (1 Kgs.10_{36}), before him reigned Jehoram for 12 years (2 Kgs.3_1) and Ahaziah for 2 years (1 Kgs.22_{51}) - accession years counted.

Israel and Syria could have put their quarrels aside as long as the Assyrian threat lasted. The Israelite occupation of Ramoth-gilead at the time of Jehu's accession, too, does not imply historical inaccuracy in 1 Kgs.22. As was pointed out above, Gilead was probably in Israelite hands at the time of 1 Kgs.22, thus the border city could well have been captured by Jehoram. As for Ahab's relationship towards the נְבִיאִים, it was Jezebel, not Ahab, who had the prophets of the Lord killed (1 Kgs.$18_{4.13}$ 19_{2}) and Ahab's addresses to Elijah in 1 Kgs.18_{17} and 21_{20} parallel his statements about Miciah (1 Kgs.$22_{8.18}$).[16] According to Jepsen, however, 1 Kgs.20 originally did not refer to Ahab's reign.

Jepsen further argued that Ahab would not suit as a contemporary of Benhadad, but rather, as indicated by an Assyrian inscription[17] as a contemporary of Hadadezer who succeeded Benhadad and was assassinated by Hazael and thus 1 Kgs.22 is thought to have taken place in Jehu's dynasty, the king in question being Jehoash, whose father Jehoahaz was had been defeated by the Arameans (2 Kgs.10_{32}). However, according to 2 Kgs.$8_{7\text{-}15}$ Benhadad was killed and his throne usurped by Hazael, which is paralleled in the Assyrian records by the narration of the usurpation of Hadadezer's throne by Hazael and by a reference to Hadadezer's death.[18] Thus both records mention that the throne of the Aramean king contemporary to Ahab was usurped by somebody named Hazael. If Jepsen's suggestion is accepted two errors have to be assumed in the Biblical accounts for that period. The name of the Israelite king mentioned in 1 Kgs.22 originally was not Ahab, and it was not Benhadad, but Hadadezer who was killed by Hazael. It is, of course, theoretically possible, but very unlikely that both kings, Benhadad, son of Hazael and contemporary of Jehoash, and Hadadezer, were killed by somebody named Hazael. It is less difficult to assume that the Benhadad of the Biblical account and the Hadadezer of the Assyrian text are in fact the same person[19] This was suggested by W.F.Albright on the basis of his reconstruction of the so-called

---

16 Cf. also 1 Kgs.20_{13ff}.

17 Cf. E.Michel, "Assur-Texte", p.57.

18 *šadâšu emēdu* - "to go to his mountain" = "to disappear forever" (cf. E.Michel, "Assur-Texte", p.57 {l.25}).

19 For a possible parallel in Aššurbanipal's annals cf. above, p.288, n.112.

Melcarth-stele.[20] However, W.T.Pitard's new reading of the inscription indicates that the stele probably was not set up by any of the known kings of Damascus.[21]

We conclude that there is no cogent historical evidence that 1 Kgs.22 originally did not deal with Ahab.

20 Cf. "A Votive Stele".
21 Cf. *Ancient Damascus*, pp.137-144.

ABBREVIATIONS

AAA	Annals of Archaeology and Anthropology
AfO	Archiv für Orientforschung
AJA	American Journal of Archaeology
AJSL	American Journal for Semitic Languages and Literatures
AOAT	Alter Orient und Altes Testament
BASOR	Bulletin of the American Schools of Oriental Research
Bell.	Bellino Cylinder (cf. above, p.71)
Chic.-Tayl.	Chicago-Taylor Prisms (cf. above, p.72)
Chr.	Biblical book of Chronicles
Chr.$_{LXX}$	Septuagint version of Chr.
Chr.$_{MT}$	Massoretic Text of Chr.
HT	Haran-Tablets (cf. above, p.97, n.112)
HTR	Harvard Theological Review
IT	Ištar-Tablet (cf. above, pp.122f, n.224)
JAOS	Journal of the American Oriental Society
JBL	Journal of Biblical Literature
JCS	Journal of Cuneiform Studies
JL	Journal of Linguistics
JRAS	Journal of the Royal Asiatic Society
LA	Late Assyrian version (Atraḫasīs epic)
LV	Late Version (Etana epic)
LXX	Septuagint
LXX^{L}	(Proto-)Lucianic Recension of LXX
LXX^{O}	Origenic (Hexaplaric) Recension of LXX
MAV	Middle Assyrian Version (Etana epic)
MT	Massoretic Text
MVAG	Mitteilungen der Vorderasiatischen Gesellschaft
NA	Neo-Assyrian version (Gilgameš epic)
OB	Old Babylonian version (Anzu epic, Atraḫasīs epic, Gilgameš epic)
OB Me.	Fragment of the Gilgameš epic, published by B.Meissner (cf. above, p.50, n.71)
OB Mi.	Fragment of the Gilgameš epic, published by A.R.Millard (cf above, p.50, n.71)

OB Penn.	Pennsylvania Tablet (cf. above, p.44, n.56)
OLZ	Orientalistische Literaturzeitung
OV	Old Version (Etana epic)
RA	Revue d'Assyriologie et d'Archéologie Orientale
RB	Revue Biblique
Sam.-Kgs.	The Biblical books of Samuel and Kings
'Sam.-Kgs.'	The Chronicler's *Vorlage*, not identical with Sam.-Kgs.
Rass.	Rassam Cylinder (cf. above, pp.71f)
Sam.-Kgs.$_{LXX}$	The Septuagint version of Sam.-Kgs.
Sam.-Kgs.$_{MT}$	The Massoretic Text of Sam.-Kgs.
SB	Standard Babylonian version (Anzu epic)
SVT	Supplements to Vetus Testamentum
TUAT	Texte aus der Umwelt des Alten Testaments. Ed. O.Kaiser et al. Gütersloh, 1982-
TZ	Theologische Zeitschrift
VT	Vetus Testamentum
WO	Die Welt des Orients
ZA	Zeitschrift für Assyriologie
ZAW	Zeitschrift für die alttestamentliche Wissenschaft
4QSam^a	Fragments of the Samuel scroll from Qumran, cave 4

Abbreviations in text-critical remarks, if not listed above, follow *Biblia Hebraica Stuttgartensia*. Ed. K.Elliger and W.Rudolph. Stuttgart, 1976/7, and A.E.Brooke, N.McLean, H.St.J.Thackeray (eds.), *The Old Testament in Greek according to the Text of Codex Vaticanus, supplemented from other Uncial Manuscripts, with a critical Apparatus containing the Variants of the chief ancient Authorities for the Text of the Septuagint*. Cambridge, 1906ff.

BIBLIOGRAPHY

Aharoni, Y. *The Land of the Bible. A Historical Geography*. Trans. A.F.Rainey. Philadelphia, 1962.

Albright, W.F. "A Votive Stele Erected by Ben-Hadad I of Damascus to the God Melcarth." *BASOR* 87 (1942), 23-29.

Alfrink, B. "L'expression שָׁכַב עִם אֲבוֹתָיו." *Oudtestametische Studiën* 2 (1943), 106-18.

Allerton, D.J. "Deletion and Proform Reduction." *JL* 11 (1975), 183-237.

Alster, B. *Dumuzi's Dream. Aspects of Oral Poetry in a Sumerian Myth*. Mesopotamia 1. Copenhagen, 1972.

Alter, R. *The Art of Biblical Narrative*. New York, 1981.

Austin, J.L. *How to Do Things with Words*. Eds. J.O.Urmson and M.Sbisà. Cambridge MA, ^{2}1975.

Aynard, J.M. *Le prisme du Louvre AO 19.939*. Paris, 1957.

Barth, H. and Steck, O.H. *Exegese des Alten Testaments. Leitfaden der Methodik; ein Arbeitsbuch für Proseminare, Seminare und Vorlesungen*. Neukirchen-Vluyn, ^{9}1980.

Barthélemy, D. *Les devanciers d'Aquila. Première publication intégrale du texte des fragments du Dodecapropheton*. SVT 11. Leiden, 1963.

Barton, J. *Reading the Old Testament. Method in Biblical Study*. London, 1984.

Bauer, Th. *Das Inschriftenwerk Assurbanipals*. Assyriologische Bibliothek, N.F. II,2. Leipzig, 1933.

Becker, J. *1 Chronik*. Die Neue Echter Bibel. Kommentar zum Alten Testament mit der Einheitsübersetzung. Lfg.18. Würzburg, 1986.

Benzinger, I. *Die Bücher der Könige erklärt*. Ed. K.Marti. Kurzer Handkommentar zum Alten Testament 9. Freiburg i.B./ Leipzig / Tübingen, 1899.

Bertheau, E. *Die Bücher der Chronik erklärt*. Kurzgefasstes exegetisches Handbuch zum Alten Testament 15. Leipzig, 1873.

Biggs, R.D. "An Archaic Version of the Kesh Temple Hymn from Tell Abū Ṣalābīkh." *ZA* 61 (1971), 193-207.

Borger, R. *Die Inschriften Asarhaddons Königs von Assyrien*. AfO Beiheft 9. Graz, 1956.

-----. *Babylonisch-Assyrische Lesestücke*. Roma, ^{2}1979.

Borger, R. et al. *Rechts- und Wirtschaftsurkunden. Historisch-chronologische Texte*. TUAT I. Gütersloh, 1984.

Brinkman, J.A. "Merodach-Baladan II." *Studies Presented to A. Leo Oppenheim*. Eds. R.D.Biggs and J.A.Brinkman. Chicago, 1964, 6-53.

-----. *Prelude to Empire. Babylonian Society and Politics, 727-626 B.C.* Philadelphia, 1984.

Brunet, A.-M. "Le Chroniste et ses sources." *RB* 60 (1953), 481-508.

-----. "Le Chroniste et ses sources." *RB* 61 (1954), 349-86.

Campbell Thompson, R. *The Epic of Gilgamish*. Oxford, 1930.

-----. *The Prisms of Esarhaddon and Assurbanipal Found at Niniveh 1927-28*. London, 1931.

-----. "A Selection from the Cuneiform Historical Texts from Nineveh (1927-32)." *Iraq* 7 (1940), 85-131.

Campbell Thompson, R. and Mallowan, M.E.L. "The British Museum Excavation at Nineveh 1931-32." *AAA* 20 (1933), 71-186 (+pll.XXXV-CVI).

Cancik, H. *Grundzüge der hethitischen und alttestamentlichen Geschichtsschreibung*. Wiesbaden, 1976.

Childs, B.S. *Isaiah and the Assyrian Crisis*. Studies in Biblical Theology, Second Series 3. London, 1967.

Cogan, M. and Tadmor, H. "Gyges and Ashurbanipal. A Study in Literary Transmission." *Orientalia* 46 (1977), 65-85.

-----. "Asshurbanipal's Conquest of Babylon. The First Official Report - Prism K." *Orientalia* 50 (1981), 229-40.

-----. *II Kings*. The Anchor Bible 11. Garden City NY, 1988.

Cooper, J.S. "Gilgameš Dreams of Enkidu. The Evolution and Dilution of Narrative." *Essays on the Ancient Near East in Memory of Jacob Joel Finkelstein*. Ed. M. de Jong Ellis. Memoirs of the Connecticut Academy of Arts & Sciences 19. Hamden CN, 1977, 39-44.

-----. "Symmetry and Repetition in Akkadian Narrative." *JAOS* 79 (1977), 508-12.

-----. *The Return of Ninurta to Nippur. an-gim dím-ma*. Analecta Orientalia 52. Roma, 1978.

Cross, F.M. "The History of the Biblical Text in the Light of Discoveries in the Judean Desert." *HTR* 57 (1964), 281-94. Repr. in *Qumran and the History of the Biblical Text*. Eds. F.M.Cross and S.Talmon. Cambridge MA, 1975, 177-195.

Culley, R.C. "An Approach to the Problem of Oral Tradition." *VT* 13 (1963), 115-25.

DeVries, S.J. *Prophet Against Prophet. The Role of the Micaiah Narrative (1 Kings 22) in the Development of Early Prophetic Tradition*. Grand Rapids MI, 1978.

-----. *1 Kings*. Word Biblical Commentary 12. Waco TX, 1985.

Dijk, J. van. "Le dénouement de «Gilgameš au bois de cèdres» selon LB 2116." *Gilgameš et sa légende*, 69-81.

Dion, P.E. "Sennacherib's Expedition to Palestine." *Église et Théologie* 20 (1989), 5-25.

Donner, H. and Röllig, W. *Kanaanäische und aramäische Inschriften* I-II. Wiesbaden, 1971-1973.

Driver, S.R. *An Introduction to the Literature of the Old Testament*. International Theological Library. Edinburgh, ^{9}1913. Repr. 1920.

-----. "The Speeches in Chronicles." *The Expositor* 5 (1895), 241-56.

Ehelolf, H. *Ein Wortfolgeprinzip im Assyrisch-Babylonischen*. Leipziger Semitistische Studien 4,3. Leipzig, 1916. Repr. 1979.

Eißfeldt, O. *Hexateuch-Synopse*. Leipzig, 1922. Repr. Darmstadt, 1983.

-----. *Einleitung in das Alte Testament unter Einschluß der Apokryphen und Pseudepigraphen sowie der apokryphen- und pseudepigraphenartigen Qumrān-Schriften*. Tübingen, ^{4}1976.

Ellis, R. *Foundation Deposits in Ancient Mesopotamia*. New Haven / London, 1986.

Fales, F.M. "A Literary Code in Assyrian Royal Inscriptions." *Assyrian Royal Inscriptions. New Horizons in Literary, Ideological, and Historical Analysis*. Papers of a Symposium held in Cetona (Siena) June 26-28, 1980. Ed. F.M.Fales. Roma, 1981, 169-202.

Flavius Josephus, *Jüdische Altertümer*. Trans. H.Clementz. Bd.I. Wiesbaden, s.d.

Fokkelman, J.P. *Narrative Art and Poetry in the Books of Samuel. A full interpretation based on stylistic and structural analysis*. Vol.I. King David (II Sam 9-20 & 1 Kings 1-2. Assen, 1981.

-----. *Narrative Art and Poetry in the Books of Samuel. A full interpretation based on stylistic and structural analysis*. Vol II. The Crossing Fates (I Sam.13-31 & II Sam.1). Assen, 1986.

Freedman, R.D. *The Cuneiform Tablets in St.Louis*. Ph.D. Dissertation Columbia University. New York, 1975.

-----. *Assurbanipal's "Annals", Prism C.* (unpublished).

Frye, R.M. "The Synoptic Problems and Analogies in Other Literatures." *The Relationships Among the Gospels. An Interdisciplinary Dialogue*. Ed. W.O.Walker. San Antonio, 1978.

Galdi, M. *L'epitome nella litteratura latina*. Napoli, 1922.

Galling, K. *Die Bücher der Chronik, Esra, Nehemia übersetzt und erklärt*. Das Alte Testament Deutsch 12. Göttingen, 1954.

Gesenius, W. - Buhl, F. *Hebräisches und aramäisches Handwörterbuch über das Alte Testament*. Leipzig, ^{17}1915. Repr. Wiesbaden, 1962.

Gibson, J.C.L. *Textbook of Syrian Semitic Inscriptions* 2. Oxford, 1975.

Ginsberg, H.L. "Aramaic Studies Today." *JAOS* 62 (1942), 229-238.

Gilgameš et sa légende. Études recueilles par Paul Garelli à l'occasion de la VIIe Rencontre Assyriologique Internationale (Paris - 1985). Cahiers du Groupe François-Thureau-Dangin. Paris, 1960.

Gonçalves, F.J. *L'expédition de Sennachérib en Palestine dans la littérature hébraïque ancienne*. Publications de l'Institut Orientaliste de Louvain 34. Louvain-la-Neuve, 1986.

Grayson, A.K. *Assyrian and Babylonian Chronicles*. Texts From Cuneiform Sources 5. Locust Valley NY, 1975.

-----. "The Chronology of the Reign of Ashurbanipal." *ZA* 70 (1980), 227-45.

Grimes, J. E. *The Thread of Discourse*. Janua Linguorum Series Minor 207. Berlin / New York / Amsterdam, 1975.

Gunkel, H. *Genesis übersetzt und erklärt*. Göttingen, ^{3}1910. Repr. ^{9}1977.

-----. *Die Urgeschichte und die Patriarchen (Das erste Buch Mosis)*. Die Schriften des Alten Testaments I,1. Göttingen, 1911.

Hallo, W.W. and Moran, W.L. "The First Tablet of the SB Recension of the Anzu Myth." *JCS* 31 (1979), 65-115.

Hecker, K. *Untersuchungen zur akkadischen Epik*. AOAT Sonderreihe. Veröffentlichungen zur Kultur und Geschichte des Alten Orients. Kevelaer / Neukirchen-Vluyn, 1974.

Hölscher, G. "Das Buch der Könige, seine Quellen und seine Redaktion." ΕΥΧΑΡΙΣΤΗΡΙΟΝ. Studien zur Religion und Literatur des Alten und Neuen Testaments. Festschrift H.Gunkel. Ed. H.Schmidt. 1.Teil. Göttingen, 1923, 158-213

Honor, L.L. *Sennacherib's Invasion of Palestine. A Critical Source Study*. New York, 1966.

Hossfeld, F.L. and Meyer, I. *Prophet gegen Prophet. Eine Analyse der alttestamentlichen Texte zum Thema: wahre und falsche Propheten*. Biblische Beiträge 9. Fribourg, 1973

Hruška, B. *Der Mythenadler Anzu in Literatur und Vorstellung des Alten Mesopotamien*. Tudományegyetem Ókori Történeti Tanszékeinek Kiadványai 13. Budapest, 1975.

Hume, D. *Dialogues Concerning Natural Religion*. Ed. M.Bell. London, 1990.

Irvin, D. *Mytharion. The Comparison of Tales from the Old Testament and the Ancient Near East*. AOAT 32. Kevelaer, Neukirchen-Vluyn, 1978.

Jastrow, M., Jr. "Adam and Eve in Babylonian Literature." *AJSL* 15 (1899), 195-214.

Jastrow, M., Jr. and Clay, A.T. *An Old Babylonian Version of the Gilgamesh Epic on the Basis of Recently Discovered Texts*. New Haven / London, 1920.

Jepsen, A. "Israel und Damaskus." *AfO* 14 (1942), 153-72.

Johnstone, W. "Reactivating the Chronicles Analogy in Pentateuchal Studies with Special Reference to the Sinai Pericope in Exodus." *ZAW* 99 (1987), 16-37.

Kaufman, S.A. *The Akkadian Influences on Aramaic*. Assyriological Studies 19. Chicago, 1974.

Keil, C.F. *Biblischer Commentar über die nachexilischen Geschichtsbücher. Chronik, Esra, Nehemia und Esther*. Leipzig, 1870.

-----. *Die Bücher der Könige*. Biblischer Commentar. Leipzig, ^{2}1876. Repr. Gießen, 1988.

Kinnier Wilson, J.V. *The Legend of Etana. A New Edition*. Warminster, 1985.

Kitchen, K.A. *Ancient Orient and Old Testament*. London, 1966.

-----. *The Third Intermediate Period in Egypt* (1200 - 650 B.C.). London, 1973.

Klostermann, A. "Chronik, die Bücher der." *Realencyclopädie für protestantische Theologie und Kirche*. Ed. A.Hauck. Leipzig, 1898, 84-98

Knudsen, E.E. "Fragments of Historical Texts from Nimrud." *Iraq* 29 (1967), 49-69.

Koehler, L. and Baumgartner, W. *Hebräisches und aramäisches Lexikon zum Alten Testament*. 3rd ed. Leiden, 1967-.

König, E. *Einleitung in das Alte Testament mit Einschluss der Apokryphen und der Pseudepigraphen des Alten Testaments*. Bonn, 1893.

Koopmans, J.J. *Aramäische Chrestomathie. Ausgewählte Texte (Inschriften, Ostraka und Papyri)* 1 . Leiden, 1962.

Kramer, S.N. "The Death of Gilgamesh." *BASOR* 94 (1944), 2-12.

-----. "The Epic of Gilgameš and Its Sumerian Sources." *JAOS* 64 (1944), 7-23.83.

-----. "Gilgamesh and the Land of the Living." *JCS* 1 (1947), 3-46.

-----. "Gilgamesh and Agga [with comments by Thorkhild Jacobsen]." *AJA* 53 (1949), 1-18.

Kropat, A. "Die Syntax des Autors der Chronik verglichen mit der seiner Quellen. Ein Beitrag zur historischen Syntax des Hebräischen." *BZAW* 16. Gießen, 1909.

Kupper, J.R. "Les différentes versiones de l'épopée de Gilgameš." *Gilgameš et sa légende*, 97-102.

Lambert, W.G. "New Fragments of Babylonian Epics." *AfO* 27 (1980), 71-82.

-----. "*The Evolution of the Gilgamesh Epic*, by Jeffrey H. Tigay, Philadelphia: University of Pennsylvania, 1982. Pp. Xx+184. $30." Review Article. *JBL* 104 (1985), 115-16.

Lambert, W.G. and Millard, A.R. *Atra-ḫasīs. The Babylonian Story of the Flood*. Oxford, 1969.

Landsberger, B. "Einleitung in das Gilgameš-Epos." *Gilgameš et sa légende*, 31-36.

-----. "Zur vierten und siebenten Tafel des Gilgamesch-Epos." *RA* 62 (1968), 97-135.

Langdon, St. *Die neubabylonischen Königsinschriften*. Trans. R.Zehnpfund. Vorderasiatische Bibliothek 7. Leipzig, 1912.

-----. "The Sumerian Epic of Gilgamish." *JRAS* (1932), 911-42.

Læssøe, J. "On the Fragments of the Hammurabi Code." *JCS* 4 (1950), 173-87.

-----. "Literacy and Oral Tradition in Ancient Mesopotamia." *Studia Orientalia Ioanni Pedersen ... Dicata*. Copenhagen, 1953, 205-218.

Lemke, W.E. "The Synoptic Problem in the Chronicler's History." *HTR* 58 (1965), 349-63.

Levine, L.D. "Manuscripts, Texts and the Study of the Neo-Assyrian Royal Inscriptions." *Assyrian Royal Inscriptions. New Horizons in Literary, Ideological, and Historical Analysis*. Papers of a Symposium held in Cetona (Siena) June 26-28, 1980. Ed. F.M.Fales. Roma, 1981, 49-70.

-----. "The Second Campaign of Sennacherib." *JNES* 32 (1973), 312-17.

Liverani, M. "Critique of Variants and the Titulary of Sennacherib." *Assyrian Royal Inscriptions. New Horizons in Literary, Ideological, and Historical Analysis* Papers of a Symposium held in Cetona (Siena) June 26-28, 1980. Ed. F.M.Fales. Roma, 1981, 225-57.

Longacre, R.E. *The Grammar of Discourse*. New York, 1983.

-----. "Interpreting Biblical Stories." *Discourse and Literature*. Ed. T.A. van Dijk. Amsterdam, Philadelphia, 1985, 169-85.

-----. "A Spectrum and Profile Approach to Discourse Analysis." *Text* 1 (1981), 337-59.

Lord, A.B. *The Singer of Tales*. Harvard Studies in Comparative Literature 24. Cambridge MA, 1960.

Luckenbill, D.D. *The Annals of Sennacherib*. Chicago, 1924.

MacLaren, M. Jr. "On the Composition of Xenophon's Hellenica. Part I." *American Journal of Philology* 55 (1934), 121-39.

-----. "On the Composition of Xenophon's Hellenica. Part II." *American Journal of Philology* 55 (1934), 249-62.

Martin, W.J. "Tribut und Tributleistungen bei den Assyrern." Studia Orientalia Edidit Societas Orientalis Fennica VIII,1. Helsingforsieae, 1936, 1-50.

Matouš, L. "Les rapports entre la version sumérienne et la version akkadienne de L'épopée de Gilgameš." *Gilgameš et sa légende*, 83-94.

Meissner, B. "Ein Altbabylonisches Fragment des Gilgamosepos. Mit 4 Aetzungen und 2 Lichtdruck-Tafeln." *MVAG* 7 (1902), 1-15.

Merril, E.H. *Kingdom of Priests. A History of Old Testament Israel*. Grand Rapids MI, 1987.

Michel, E. "Die Assur-Texte Salmanassers III (858-824)." *WO* 1/I-III (1947-48), 5-20.57-71.205-222.

Millard, A.R. "Fragments of Historical Texts from Nineveh. Assurbanipal." *Iraq* 30 (1969), 98-111.

-----. "Gilgamesh X. A New Fragment." *Iraq* 26 (1964), 99-105.

Miller, J. M. "The Elisha Cycle and the Accounts of the Omride Wars." *JBL* 85 (1966), 441-54.

-----. "The Rest of the Acts of Jehoahaz (1 Kings 20 $22_{1\text{-}38}$)." *ZAW* 80 (1968), 337-42.

Moore, G. F. "Tatian's *Diatessaron* and the Analysis of the Pentateuch." *JBL* 9 (1890), 201-215. Repr. in *Empirical Models for Pentateuchal Criticism*. Ed. J.H.Tigay. Philadelphia, 1985, 243-256

Morgenstern, J. "Chronological Data of the Dynasty of Omri." *JBL* 59 (1940), 385-96.

Mowinckel, S. "Die vorderasiatischen Königs- und Fürsteninschriften. Eine stilistische Studie." ΕΥΧΑΡΙΣΤΗΡΙΟΝ. *Studien Zur Religion und Literatur Alten und Neuen Testaments*. Festschrift H.Gunkel. Ed. H.Schmidt. 2.Teil. Göttingen, 1923, 278-322.

Nassouhi, E. "Prisme d'Assurbanipal daté de sa trentième année, provenant du Temple de Gula a Babylone." *AfK* 2 (1924-25), 97-106.

Nielsen, E. *Oral Tradition. A Modern Problem in Old Testament Introduction*. London, 1954.

Noth, M. *Überlieferungsgeschichtliche Studien I. Die sammelnden und bearbeitenden Geschichtswerke im Alten Testament*. Schriften der Königsberger Gelehrten Gesellschaft. 18. Jahr. Geisteswissenschaftliche Klasse. Heft 2. Halle (Saale), 1943.

Nougayrol, J. "Ningirsu, vainqueur du Zû." *RA* 46 (1952), 87-97.

Oberhuber, K. "Gilgamesch." *Das Gilgamesch-Epos*. Ed. K.Oberhuber. Wege der Forschung 215. Darmstadt, 1977, 1-22.

Olmstead, A.T.E. *Assyrian Historiography. A Source Study*. The University of Missouri Studies. Social Science Series III,1. Columbia MO, 1916.

Olrik, A. "Epische Gesetze der Volksdichtung." *Zeitschrift für Deutsches Altertum und Deutsche Litteratur* 51, N.F. 39 (1909), 1-12.

Opelt, I. "Epitome." *Reallexikon für Antike und Christentum* 5. Ed. Th.Klauser. Stuttgart, 1962. 944-973.

Peiser, F.E. "Die Monolith-Inschrift III Rawl. 7.8." *Historische Texte des altassyrischen Reiches*. Keilinschriftliche Bibliothek. Sammlung von assyrischen und babylonischen Texten in Umschrift und Übersetzung 1. Ed. E.Schrader *et al*. Berlin, 1889. Repr. Amsterdam, 1970. 150-175.

Piepkorn, A.C. *Historical Prism Inscriptions of Ashurbanipal I*. The Oriental Institute of the University of Chicago Assyriological Studies 5. Chicago, 1933.

Pitard, W.T. *Ancient Damascus*. Winona Lake IN, 1987.

Polzin, R. *Late Biblical Hebrew. Toward a Typology of Biblical Hebrew Prose*. Harvard Semitic Monographs 12. Missoula MT, 1976.

Postgate, J.N. *Taxation and Conscription in the Assyrian Empire*. Studia Pohl. Series Maior 3. Rome, 1974.

Rad, G. von. "Die levitische Predigt in den Büchern der Chronik." *Festschrift Otto Procksch*. Leipzig, 1934, 113-24. Repr. in *Gesammelte Studien zum Alten Testament* 1. Theologische Bücherei 8. München, 1965, 248-261.

Rast, W.E. *Tradition History and the Old Testament*. Philadelphia, 1972.

Rehm, M. *Textkritische Untersuchungen zu den Parallelstellen der Samuel-Königsbücher und der Chronik*. Münster, 1937.

Ringgren, H. "Oral and Written Transmission in the Old Testament." *Studia Theologica* 3 (1949), 34-59.

Roth, W. "The Story of the Prophet Micaiah (1 Kings 22) in Historical-Critical Interpretation 1876-1976." *The Biblical Mosaic. Changing Perspectives*. Eds R.Polzin and E.Rothman. The Society of Biblical Literature Semeia Studies. Philadelphia PA / Chico CA, 1982, 105-37.

Rudolph, W. *Chronikbücher*. Handbuch zum Alten Testament I,21. Tübingen, 1955.

Saggs, H.W.F. "Additions to Anzu." *AfO* 33 (1986), 1-29.

Schmitt, H.-C. *Elisa. Traditionsgeschichtliche Untersuchungen zur vorklassischen nordisraelitischen Prophetie*. Gütersloh, 1972.

Schott, A. "Zu meiner Übersetzung des Gilgameš-epos." *ZA* 42 (1934), 92-134.

Schwally, F. "Zur Quellenkritik der historischen Bücher." *ZAW* 12 (1892), 153-61.

Schweizer, H. *Elischa in den Kriegen. Literaturwissenschaftliche Untersuchung von 2 Kön.3; 6,8-23; 6,24-7,20*. Studien zum Alten und Neuen Testament 37. München, 1974.

-----. "Literarkritischer Versuch zur Erzählung von Micha Ben Jimla (1 Kön 22)." *BZ* N.F. 23 (1979), 1-19.

Seebaß, H. "Micha Ben Jimla." *Kerygma und Dogma* 19 (1973), 109-24.

-----. "Zu 1 Reg XXII 35-38." *VT* 21 (1971), 380-83.

Smend, R. *Die Entstehung des Altes Testaments*. Stuttgart, Berlin, Köln, Mainz, ^{3}1984.

Soden, W. von. "Beiträge zum Verständnis des babylonischen Gilgameš-Epos." *ZA* 53 (1959), 209-235.

-----. *Akkadisches Handwörterbuch*. Wiesbaden, 1965-81

-----. "Kleinere Beiträge zu Text und Erklärung babylonischer Epen." *ZA* 58 (1967), 189-195.

Soden, W.von (ed.) *Das Gilgamesch-Epos, übersetzt und mit Anmerkungen versehen von Albert Schott*. Stuttgart, 1958. Repr. 1986.

Spalinger, A. "Assurbanipal and Egypt. A Source Study." *JAOS* 94 (1974), 316-28.

Stade, B. "Anmerkungen zu 2 Kö. 15-21." *ZAW* 6 (1886), 156-92.

Steck, O.H. "Bewahrheitungen des Prophetenworts. Überlieferungsgeschichtliche Skizze zu 1.Könige 22,1-18." *»Wenn nicht jetzt, wann dann?«. Festschrift Hans-Joachim Kraus*. Eds. H.G.Geyer *et. al.* Neukirchen-Vluyn, 1983, 87-96.

Stoebe, J. "Über die Grenzen der Literarkritik." *TZ* 18 (1962), 385-400.

Streck, M. *Assurbanipal und die letzten assyrischen Könige bis zum Untergang Ninivehs* 1-3. Vorderasiatische Bibliothek 7. Leipzig, 1916.

Tadmor, H. "The Three Last Decades of Assyria." *Proceedings of the 25th Congress of Orientalists, Moscow (August, 1960)*. Moscow, 1964, 241-42.

Talmon, S. "The Presentation of Synchroneity and Simultaneity in Biblical Narrative." *Scripta Hierosolymitana* 27 (1978), 9-26.

Thackeray, H.St.J. *The Septuagint and Jewish Worship*. Schweich Lectures 1920. London, 1921.

Thenius, O. *Die Bücher der Könige erklärt*. Kurzgefasstes exegetisches Handbuch zum Alten Testament 9. Leipzig, ^{2}1873.

Tigay, J.H. *Literary-Critical Studies in the Gilgamesh Epic. An Assyriological Contribution to Biblical Literary Criticism*. Yale University Ph.D. 1971.

-----. *The Evolution of the Gilgamesh Epic*. Philadelphia, 1982.

-----. "The Stylistic Criterion of Source Criticism in the Light of Ancient Near Eastern and Postbiblical Literature." *Empirical Models for Biblical Criticism*. Ed. J.H.Tigay. Philadelphia, 1985, 149-73.

Tigay, J.H. (ed.) *Empirical Models for Biblical Criticism*. Philadelphia, 1985.

Torrey, C.C. "The Chronicler as Editor and as Independent Narrator." *AJSL* 25 (1908/9), 157-73.180-207.

Tov, E. "Lucian and Proto-Lucian." *RB* 79 (1972), 101-113. Repr. in *Qumran and the History of the Biblical Text*. Eds. F.M.Cross and Sh.Talmon. Cambridge MA, 1975, 293-305.

Ulrich, E.C. Jr. *The Qumran Text of Samuel and Josephus*. Harvard Semitic Monographs 19. Missoula MT, 1978.

Ungnad, A. "Gilgamesch-Epos und Odyssee." *Das Gilgamesch-Epos*. Ed. K.Oberhuber. Wege der Forschung 215. Darmstadt, 1977, 104-137.

Vansina, J. *Oral Tradition as History*. London / Nairobi, 1985.

Vogelzang, M.E. "Kill Anzu! On a Point of Literary Evolution." *Keilschriftliche Literaturen. Ausgewählte Vorträge der XXXII Rencontre Assyriologique Internationale Münster, 8.-12.7.1985*. Eds. K.Hecker and W.Sommerfeld. Berlin, 1986, 61-70.

Volz, P. *Der Geist Gottes und die verwandten Erscheinungen im Alten Testament und im anschließenden Judentum*. Tübingen, 1910.

Weidner, E. "Die älteste Nachricht über das persische Königshaus, Kyros I., ein Zeitgenosse Assurbanaplis." *AfO* 7 (1931/32), 1-7.

Weippert, H. "Ahab el Campeador? Redaktionsgeschichtliche Untersuchungen zu 1 Kön 22." *Biblica* 69 (1988), 457-79.

Weippert, M. "Die Kämpfe des assyrischen Königs Assurbanipal gegen die Araber. Redaktionskritische Untersuchung des Berichts in Prisma A." *WO* 7 (1973-74), 39-85.

Wellhausen, J. *Die Composition des Hexateuchs und der historischen Bücher des Alten Testaments*. Berlin, ^{3}1899, repr. ^{4}1963.

-----. *Prolegomena zur Geschichte Israels*. Berlin und Leipzig, ^{6}1927, repr. 1981.

Welten, P. *Geschichte und Geschichtsdarstellung in den Chronikbüchern*. Wissenschaftliche Monographien zum Alten und Neuen Testament 42. Neukirchen-Vluyn, 1973.

Westermann, C. *Genesis. 2. Teilband. Gen.12-36*. Biblischer Kommentar Altes Testament I/2. Neukirchen-Vluyn, 1981.

Wette, W.M.L. de. *Kritischer Versuch über die Glaubwürdigkeit der Bücher der Chronik mit Hinsicht auf die Geschichte der mosaischen Bücher und Gesetzgebung*. Beiträge zur Einleitung in das Alte Testament. Halle, 1806 Repr. Hildesheim, New York, 1971.

Whitley, C.F. "The Deuteronomic Presentation of the House of Omri." *VT* 2 (1952), 137-52.

Willi, Th. *Die Chronik als Auslegung. Untersuchungen zur literarischen Gestalt der historischen Überlieferung Israels*. Forschungen zur Religion und Literatur des Alten und Neuen Testaments 106. Göttingen, 1972.

Williamson, H.G.M. *1 and 2 Chronicles*. The New Century Bible Commentary. Grand Rapids, Mich. / London, 1982.

Wise, M.R. and Lowe, I. "Permutation Groups in Discourse." *Georgetown University School of Languages and Linguistics Working Papers* 4 (1972), 12-34.

Wiseman, D.J. "Additional Neo-Babylonian Gilgamesh Fragments." *Gilgameš et sa légende*, 123-35.

Witzel, M. "Sumerische Rezension der Himmelsstier-Episode aus dem Gilgameschepos." *OLZ* 34 (1931), 402-09.

Würthwein, E. *Die Bücher der Könige. 1 Kön.17 - 2 Kön.25*. Das Alte Testament Deutsch 11/2. Göttingen, 1984.

-----. "Zur Komposition von 1 Reg 22_{1-38}." *Das ferne und das nahe Wort*. Festschrift Leonhard Rost. Ed. F.Maass. Berlin, 1967, 245-254.